CAMBRIDGE STUDIES IN EIGHTEENTH-CENTURY
ENGLISH LITERATURE AND THOUGHT 2

Women's Place in Pope's World

How was Alexander Pope's personal experience of women transformed into poetry, and how in turn did he and his writing figure in the lives of the women he wrote about? How characteristic of his age was Pope's attitude towards women? What exactly was the role in his life of individual women such as his mother, Patty Blount, and Lady Mary Wortley Montagu?

Valerie Rumbold's is the first full-length study of these important issues. Making use of previously little-known manuscripts, she focuses both on Pope's own life and art, and on early eighteenth-century assumptions about women and gender. She offers readings of some of the well-known poems in which women feature prominently, and follows Pope's response throughout his writings in general. His own alienation from the dominant culture (through religion, politics, and physical handicap), and his troubled fascination with certain kinds of women, make this subject complex and compelling, with wide implications. Dr Rumbold brings to light new information, and shows how the women with whom he dealt can themselves be seen as individuals with presence and dignity.

The growth in recent years of eighteenth-century literary studies has prompted the establishment of this new series of books devoted to the period. The series will accommodate monographs and critical studies on authors, works, genres and other aspects of literary culture from the later part of the seventeenth century to the end of the eighteenth.

Since academic engagement with this field has become an increasingly interdisciplinary enterprise, books will be especially encouraged which in some way stress the cultural context of the literature, or examine it in relation to contemporary art, music, philosophy, historiography, religion, politics, social affairs, and so on. New approaches to the established canon are being tested with increasing frequency, and the series will hope to provide a home for the best of these. The books we choose to publish will be thorough in their methods of literary, historical, or biographical investigation, and will open interesting perspectives on previously closed, or underexplored, or misrepresented areas of eighteenth-century writing and thought. They will reflect the work of both younger and established scholars on either side of the Atlantic and elsewhere.

Women's Place in Pope's World

VALERIE RUMBOLD

Lecturer in English
University College of North Wales
Bangor

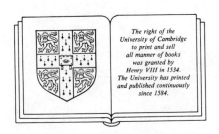

The right of the
University of Cambridge
to print and sell
all manner of books
was granted by
Henry VIII in 1534.
The University has printed
and published continuously
since 1584.

CAMBRIDGE UNIVERSITY PRESS

CAMBRIDGE

NEW YORK PORT CHESTER MELBOURNE SYDNEY

Published by the Press Syndicate of the University of Cambridge
The Pitt Building, Trumpington Street, Cambridge CB2 1RP
40 West 20th Street, New York, NY 10011, USA
10 Stamford Road, Oakleigh, Melbourne 3166, Australia

First published 1989

Printed in Great Britain at the University Press, Cambridge

British Library cataloguing in publication data

Rumbold, Valerie
Women's place in Pope's world. – (Cambridge
studies in eighteenth-century English
literature and thought; 2)
1. Poetry in English. Pope, Alexander, 1688–1744
Critical studies
I. Title
821'.5

Library of Congress cataloguing in publication data

Women's place in Pope's world / Valerie Rumbold.
p.   cm. – (Cambridge studies in eighteenth-century English
literature and thought: 2)
Bibliography.
Includes index.
ISBN 0–521–36308–X
1. Pope, Alexander, 1688–1744 – Characters – Women. 2. Pope,
Alexander, 1688–1744 – Relations with women. `3. Women and
literature – Great Britain – History – 18th century. 4. Poets,
English – 18th century – Biography. 5. Women – Great Britain –
Biography. 6. Women in literature. I. Title. II. Series.
PR3633.R84   1989
821'.5 – dc19   88–36645 CIP

ISBN 0 521 36308 X

To the memory of
Dorothy May Proctor
1928–1982

But grant, in Public Men sometimes are shown,
A Woman's seen in Private life alone:
Our bolder Talents in full light display'd,
Your Virtues open fairest in the shade.   *Characters of Women*

You knew his mother, and how good a woman she was.
                              Patty Blount to Spence in 1749

Contents

Contents

Plates

Preface

The aim of this study is to set Pope's writing to and about women in its cultural and personal context, and to ask how he and his writing figured in the lives of the women who appear in it. By relating his attitudes to prevailing assumptions about gender, and showing how in some respects he seeks to challenge or evade them, I hope to balance the sense of Pope as characteristic voice of the age with the more complicated presence of a man alienated from the dominant culture by religion, politics and physical handicap; and by writing in detail about the individual women who mattered to him – women often known to posterity only through the footnotes to his poetry – I hope also to reassert their dignity as people in their own right, who had their views of Pope just as he had his views of them.

This is especially important in respect of the women he most loved, his mother and Patty (christened Martha) Blount, women who make less of a figure in women's history than pioneers like Lady Mary Wortley Montagu precisely because they contented themselves with the 'shade' in which female personality seemed 'fairest' to contemporary taste. They, not the writers and thinkers who insisted on sharing the 'full light' with the 'bolder Talents' of men, represent the majority of gentlewomen in the period; and it would be wrong to ignore the traces, faint as they often are, of these conventional lives. Yet Pope's devotion to women who quietly accepted society's prescriptions was complicated by his attraction to those who, like Lady Mary, shared the verbal energy and public self-assurance that Patty was content to leave to men. Indeed, his troubled fascination with striking and assertive women is a recurring theme both in his poetry and in his personal life.

Rather than giving an exhaustive account of the few major poems in which Pope deliberately sets women in the spotlight, I have tried to trace the pattern of his response through his writing as a whole. Unfortunately, in order to bring the book within a reasonable compass, I have had to leave out some potentially rewarding topics: in particular, I have not considered the question of women as subject and audience in Pope's major translations; I have discussed only a few of the comments on his work by contemporary women readers; and I have not by any means exhausted the possibilities for detailed biography among the lesser-known women members of his circle.

It would have been impossible to write a book of this kind without the generosity of the owners of manuscripts in allowing me to quote from their archives. For material from the Stuart Papers I acknowledge the gracious permission of Her Majesty the Queen; for the correspondence of Charles and Mary Caesar I thank Mr and Mrs Charles Cottrell-Dormer, whose kind hospitality made my visit to Rousham one of the high points in my research; and for access to copies of the Blount archives I thank Mr J. J. Eyston, lineal descendant of Patty Blount's brother Michael. Without his generous permission to quote from the papers of his ancestors the book would lack its central core. I am also much indebted to Richard Williams, custodian of the Blount archives, for the patience and enthusiasm with which he has guided me through the collection and answered my numerous questions.

In writing this book I have wandered into several areas which are new to me, and I am grateful to all those who have given me the benefit of their expertise, both in discussing my work generally and in answering particular queries: I should especially like to thank Eveline Cruickshanks, Andrew Hanham, Frances Harris, Anthony Harvey, Ragnhild Hatton, Sheila Landi, Alex Lindsay, Julian Litten, Roger Lonsdale, Nathalie Rothenstein and Stephen Taylor. I have also been made vividly aware of how much I owe to past scholars, especially to Charles Wentworth Dilke, who began in the 1850s the task of sifting a hundred years' accumulation of dubious Popiana, and who, lacking even a reliable edition of Pope's letters, brought to the task a constructive scepticism that is none the less impressive for the passage of another hundred years. In this century, George Sherburn's edition of the *Correspondence* and James Osborn's of Spence's *Anecdotes*, together with the *Twickenham Edition* of the poems, have made thinking about Pope an altogether more practicable undertaking. Amongst scholars of the present I owe a particular debt to Maynard Mack, who gave me as I embarked on this project the incalculable benefit of his support and criticism, and who completed his bounty by publishing, at the best possible time for me, his long-awaited *Alexander Pope: A Life*, which, by clearing away so many untenable theories of chronology, motive and identity, saved me months of labour and my reader many lengthy footnotes. I am also grateful to Isobel Grundy for her thorough and stimulating reading of my drafts and for her many valuable suggestions. Peter Dixon too has kindly given my drafts the benefit of his meticulous attention. My greatest debt, however, is one that will be immediately recognised by readers of Howard Erskine-Hill's *The Social Milieu of Alexander Pope*: his faith in the importance of individual lives and in the feasibility of finding out about them has been a constant inspiration. I am grateful to all those who have read and criticised my work: the most valuable discussions are not always those that end in full agreement; and where I have persisted in error the responsibility is mine alone.

The writing of this book was made possible by a Research Fellowship at

Jesus College, Cambridge. To the Society I offer my heartfelt thanks for the many ways in which it has supported me. My husband, who has been the principal sufferer by my undertaking over the four difficult and disrupted years it has taken to complete, has nonetheless sustained me by his insistence on the importance of my work. Finally, the dedication remembers one who, though she did not live to see this book begun, would have been its most delighted reader.

Abbreviations

Corr.	*The Correspondence of Alexander Pope*, edited by George Sherburn, 5 vols. (Oxford, 1956)
DNB	*Dictionary of National Biography*, edited by Leslie Stephen and Sidney Lee, 63 vols. (London, 1885–1900)
EC	*The Works of Alexander Pope*, edited by Whitwell Elwin and William John Courthope, 10 vols. (London, 1871–86)
HW Corr.	*The Yale Edition of Horace Walpole's Correspondence*, edited by W. S. Lewis, 48 vols. (London, 1937–83)
Hervey	*Lord Hervey's Memoirs*, edited by Romney Sedgwick (London, 1952)
LM Essays	*Essays and Poems and Simplicity, a Comedy*, edited by R. Halsband and I. Grundy (Oxford, 1977)
LM Letters	*The Complete Letters of Lady Mary Wortley Montagu*, edited by Robert Halsband, 3 vols. (Oxford, 1965)
LM Life	Robert Halsband, *The Life of Lady Mary Wortley Montagu*, corrected edition (Oxford, 1961)
Lothian MSS	*Report on the Manuscripts of the Marquess of Lothian Preserved at Blickling Hall, Norfolk*, Historical Manuscripts Commission (London, 1905)
Prose Works	*The Prose Works of Alexander Pope*, edited by Norman Ault and Rosemary Cowler, 2 vols. (Oxford, 1936–86)
Spence	Joseph Spence, *Observations, Anecdotes and Characters of Books and Men*, edited by James M. Osborn, 2 vols. (Oxford, 1966)
Suffolk Corr.	*Letters to and from Henrietta, Countess of Suffolk and her Second Husband the Hon. George Berkeley*, edited by J. W. Croker, 2 vols. (London, 1824)
Swift Corr.	*The Correspondence of Jonathan Swift*, edited by Harold Williams, 5 vols. (revised edition, Oxford, 1965)
TE	*The Twickenham Edition of the Works of Alexander Pope*, 11 vols. (London, 1939–69)

1

Assumptions and ironies

1

Although the few celebrated poems in which Pope sets women in the limelight provide the natural focus for any attempt to understand his attitude to the sex, it is important to remember that the vast bulk of his output is concerned only tangentially with issues of gender. In effect, he can write at length about the human race as if it were entirely masculine. Furthermore, when his attention is not specifically drawn to some female friend or heroine, his casual references to women frequently relapse into dismissive commonplace.

This was a period in which women of the middle and upper classes learned to see themselves less as skilled housewives or assistants in the family business than as leisured companions.[1] Joseph Addison and Richard Steele, writing in *The Spectator*, repeatedly urged women towards the ideal of a sex 'created as it were for Ornament', 'formed to temper Mankind', and endowed with 'gentle Softness, tender Fear, and all those parts of Life, which distinguish her from the other Sex, with some Subordination to it, but such an Inferiority that makes her still more lovely'.[2] Yet if women's elegant leisure was the natural destiny of a sex created for men's delight, it was also, in line with motives less easily professed, a proud declaration of the wealth that allowed husbands and fathers to maintain wives and daughters in idleness, as conspicuous consumers of the luxury goods which so excited the commercial imagination of the age. The extravagance and frivolity with which contemporary moralists taxed women were in effect the occupational hazards of a role which it suited men to have them play; and against this background outright misogyny became less acceptable than the politely patronising attitude expressed in such characteristic expressions as 'the fair sex'.[3] Although Pope was to an extent insulated by the old-fashioned style of housekeeping which persisted in many

---

[1] For varying interpretations of this change, see Lawrence Stone, *The Family, Sex and Marriage in England 1500–1800* (London, 1977), pp. 199–201, 325–404; Ellen Pollak, *The Poetics of Sexual Myth: Gender and Ideology in the Verse of Swift and Pope* (Chicago, 1985), pp. 1–76; Laura Brown, 'The Defenceless Woman and the Development of English Tragedy', *Studies in English Literature*, 22 (1982), 429–43.

[2] *The Spectator*, edited by Donald F. Bond, 5 vols. (Oxford, 1965), I, 242, 433; II, 70.

[3] Katharine Rogers, *The Troublesome Helpmate: A History of Misogyny in Literature* (London, 1966), pp. 166–80.

Catholic families, this was nevertheless the ordinary view of women in the
wider culture for which he has often been cast as prime spokesman. Yet,
ironically, as far as contemporary definitions of gender were concerned, he
found himself in a peculiarly difficult situation.[4]

Religion, politics and illness combined to bar Pope from the full enjoyment
of the privileges reserved for men in his society. If, as he states in *Characters
of Women*, it is the distinction of woman to develop her personality to the full
only in private life, his disqualifications from public life brought him to a condition in that respect parallel to hers, despite his easy assumption that he
belongs to the busy world of men:

> But grant, in Public Men sometimes are shown,
> A Woman's seen in Private life alone:
> Our bolder Talents in full light display'd,
> Your Virtues open fairest in the shade.[5]

As a Roman Catholic Pope was excluded from the universities, from public
office, and from the inheritance or purchase of land, all three factors which
traditionally   distinguished   upper-class   males.[6]   Pope's   characteristic
eagerness to belittle the advantages he lacked should not blind us to the actual
importance of such deprivations: critics of his Homer translation were quick
to claim that he 'doth not understand *Greek* thoroughly, for he never was at
any University'; and when he attacked the sterility of university education he
was surely in part reassuring himself that he had missed nothing worth having.[7] Others might have frowned on an enthusiasm for the classics in which
translations encountered in childhood had played so large a part, but Pope
rather congratulated himself on having learned to read for the meaning, to
discern 'the greatness of Homer's beauties through all the rags that were flung
over him'.[8] Exclusion from public office, like exclusion from university,
helped to foster a derisive attitude which is at least partly defensive. The post
most appropriate to his talents would have been the laureateship; but the
impression given by the *Dunciad* is that the unobtainable distinction is beneath

---

[4] On the role of the Catholic mistress of the house, see Maynard Mack, *Alexander Pope: A Life*
(London, 1985), pp. 28–29. Old-fashioned housekeeping is a virtue for which Pope praises his
Catholic friends Elizabeth and John Caryll. (See Howard Erskine-Hill, *The Social Milieu of Alexander Pope: Lives, Example and the Poetic Response* (London, 1975), pp. 80–82.) The Blount Papers
include letters and recipes of Mary Eugenia Blount which emphasise the managerial role of
a Catholic housewife on a country estate in the generation after Pope (Blount Papers,
c. 65).

[5] *Epistles to Several Persons (Moral Essays)*, II.199 (*Epistle to a Lady: Of the Characters of Women*,
hereafter *Characters of Women*); *The Twickenham Edition of the Works of Alexander Pope*, 11 vols.
(London, 1939–69), III.ii, 66–67 (hereafter *TE*).

[6] For a summary of Catholic disabilities, see John M. Aden, *Pope's Once and Future Kings: Satire
and Politics in the Early Career* (Knoxville, 1978), pp. 3–20.

[7] J. V. Guerinot, *Pamphlet Attacks on Alexander Pope 1711–1744: A Descriptive Bibliography* (New
York, 1969), p. 40; Joseph Spence, *Observations, Anecdotes and Characters of Books and Men*, edited
by James M. Osborn, 2 vols. (Oxford, 1966), nos. 14–31.

[8] Spence, no. 29; for the influence of Cowley's versions of Latin verse, see *TE*, VI, 4–5.

contempt. As consolation for the impossibility of a paternal inheritance in land he turned to Horace and asserted the sufficiency of a rented home for a rational life of hospitality and decent frugality:

> . . . not happier . . .
> In Forest planted by a Father's hand,
> Than in five acres now of rented land.[9]

He ridiculed the conventional patriarchal motive in acquiring property:

> "Pity! to build, without a son or wife:
> "Why, you'll enjoy it only all your life".   (Satires, II.ii.163)

And he went on to detail with glee the pitfalls that beset fathers intent on transmitting estates to their posterity. Yet despite such disclaimers, his letters show that his lack of an heir was frequently in his thoughts, and in the end he compromised by leaving a newly purchased house to his old and dear friend Patty Blount, a choice of heir which enraged his half-sister by its denial of the claims of family.[10] Catholic disabilities cast their shadow even over this last tribute to the most enduring of his friendships: 'I must desire you to say nothing of what I tell you concerning my purchase of the House in town, which is done in another's name', he wrote to Hugh Bethel.[11]

In addition to his exclusion from public life as a Catholic, Pope shared the long eclipse of his Tory friends after 1714, exchanging the brief glamour of association with men in high office for systematic contempt for a court life identified with corruption.[12] His heroes are men denied office, set apart from the artificial supports to self-esteem implicit in the public life that is now as closed to them as it is to Pope. To the first Earl of Oxford, once Queen Anne's Treasurer, he writes:

> In vain to Desarts thy Retreat is made;
> The Muse attends thee to the silent Shade:
> 'Tis hers, the brave Man's latest Steps to trace,
> Re-judge his Acts, and dignify Disgrace.
> When Int'rest calls off all her sneaking Train,
> And all th'Obliged desert, and all the Vain;
> She waits, or to the Scaffold, or the Cell,
> When the last ling'ring Friend has bid farewell.[13]

---

[9] *Imitations of Horace*, Satires, II.ii.133, 135 (*TE*, IV, 65).

[10] No-one ever seems to have called Martha Blount 'Martha'; and I have therefore adopted the diminutive 'Patty' which was used by everyone who was on first-name terms with her. For the house Pope gave her, see chapter 9.5; for Pope's half-sister, Magdalen Rackett, see chapter 2.2.

[11] *The Correspondence of Alexander Pope*, edited by George Sherburn, 5 vols. (Oxford, 1956), IV, 509 (hereafter *Corr.*). For an account of Bethel, an old mutual friend of Pope and Patty, see *TE*, IV, 346–47.

[12] See for example the triumph of Vice which concludes *Epilogue to the Satires*, Dialogue I, lines 141–70 (*TE*, IV, 308–9).

[13] *Epistle to Robert Earl of Oxford*, line 27 (*TE*, VI, 239–40).

In this talk of 'Desarts' (not the most obvious term for a country house full
of admiring family and friends) we have an echo of the poetry of retirement
as it flourished among Royalists after the Civil War, when the implied alternative of a public life was no longer real.[14] Yet even defeated Royalists, once
they had compounded for their estates, were better off in many ways than
Pope.

In particular, Pope was to suffer chronic ill health from adolescence until
his death at the age of fifty-six: the privacy doubly forced on him as a Catholic
and a Tory was further limited by Potts' Disease, a tubercular infection of the
bone which progressively disabled him.[15] Because of this he could not
seriously think of emigrating as his friend Edward Blount did after the collapse of his scheme for procuring Catholic civil rights (although he soon
repented of the idea and came home).[16] Indeed, Pope's family could see no
point in his learning modern languages as it was obvious to them that he
would never be strong enough to travel, and envy of opportunities he would
have known how to use to the full plays its part in his satire of the English
fop on the Grand Tour: 'Europe he saw, and Europe saw him too'.[17] If
resettlement in a Catholic country was the most obvious escape from internal
exile, an alternative or supplementary compensation (also practised by Edward Blount) could be the cultivation of a satisfying family life in rural retirement (Corr., I, 425; II, 86). This was the path taken by Pope's friend John
Caryll, whom Pope delighted to praise as a patriarch and upholder of old-
fashioned social virtues. However, Caryll's preoccupation with the interests
of his relations sprang from a strong identification with family, supported by
a happy and fruitful marriage which Pope was prepared to praise but not to
imitate.[18] Less than five feet tall and deformed by curvature of the spine, he
was acutely conscious of being 'that little Alexander the women laugh at'; and
he declared, 'I have no way so good to please 'em, as by presenting 'em with
any thing rather than with my self' (Corr., I, 114; II, 290). This was no basis
for seeking a wife; and when Caryll offered to give his god-daughter Patty
Blount a dowry if that was all that stood between them, Pope made clear the
limits of their relationship: 'I have no tie to your God-daughter but a good
opinion, which has grown into a friendship with experience that she deserved
it' (III, 75).

Thus the interests and responsibilities of a husband and father were no
more available to him than the public reinforcements of masculine self-esteem

[14] Maren-Sofie Røstvig, *The Happy Man: Studies in the Metamorphoses of a Classical Ideal,
1600–1760*, 2 vols. (Oslo, 1954–58), I, 60–62.
[15] Marjorie Nicolson and G. S. Rousseau, *This Long Disease, my Life: Alexander Pope and the
Sciences* (Princeton, 1968), pp. 7–86.
[16] Eamon Duffy, ' "Englishmen in Vaine": Roman Catholic Allegiance to George I', *Studies in
Church History*, 18 (1982), 345–65 (pp. 347–62); Corr., I, 424–25; II, 176. (Edward Blount was
only remotely related to Patty.)
[17] Spence, nos. 26, 51; *Dunciad B*, IV.294 (*TE*, V, 373).
[18] Erskine-Hill, *Social Milieu*, pp. 72–82; Corr., I, 123.

denied by his religion and politics; and it is poignant that his image of his role
in his own family, after his father's death, places him as mother, with all the
gain in tenderness and eclipse of autonomy which maternity implies:

> Me, let the tender Office still engage
> To rock the Cradle of reposing Age.[19]

For many years he made strenuous efforts to live up to expectations of male
robustness: at the first onset of chronic illness in adolescence he went riding
regularly in the hope of preserving his health; as a young man he actively
sought the reputation of a rake; one hot day in 1735 he exhausted himself by
surrendering his coach to a woman with a broken arm and walking three miles
into Oxford; and in the next year he was dragged into the Thames when
Catherine Talbot missed her footing while he was helping her into a boat.[20]
All this was really beyond him; and he admitted as much when he wrote in
anticipation of a visit to the second Earl of Oxford's Cambridgeshire home
at Wimpole that 'while you used Manlyer Exercises' he would 'nod over a
Book in your Library' (*Corr.*, III, 53). As he declined with age into increasing
dependence, he confessed more readily his need for a quiet, regular, passive
existence (IV, 68, 147, 179, 419). He needed a nurse more than a valet; and
it was a female attendant who was able to reveal the detailed indignities
recorded in Johnson's *Life*:

Most of what can be told concerning his petty peculiarities was communicated by a
female domestick of the Earl of Oxford, who knew him, perhaps, after the middle of
life. He was then so weak as to stand in perpetual need of female attendance; extremely
sensible of cold, so that he wore a kind of fur doublet, under a shirt of very coarse
warm linen with fine sleeves. When he rose, he was invested in a bodice made of stiff
canvass, being scarcely able to hold himself erect till they were laced, and he then put
on a flannel waistcoat. One side was contracted. His legs were so slender, that he
enlarged their bulk with three pair of stockings, which were drawn on and off by the
maid; for he was not able to dress or undress himself, and neither went to bed nor rose
without help. His weakness made it very difficult for him to be clean . . . The indulgence and accommodation which his sickness required, had taught him all the
unpleasing and unsocial qualities of a valetudinary man. He expected that every thing
should give way to his ease or humour, as a child, whose Parents will not hear her cry,
has an unresisted dominion in the nursery.[21]

It is suggestive that this corseted, querulous figure makes Johnson think not
just of a spoilt child, but of a spoilt *female* child. Lord Bathurst had shown
similar intuition when he upbraided Pope for neglecting his health: 'Is it not
enough to have the headache four days in the week, and to be as sick as a

---

19 *An Epistle to Dr. Arbuthnot*, line 408 (*TE*, IV, 127).
20 Spence, nos. 69, 71; Norman Ault, *New Light on Pope, with some Additions to his Poetry hitherto
   Unknown* (London, 1949), pp. 301–307; *Corr.*, III, 493; *The Correspondence of Jonathan Swift*,
   edited by Harold Williams, 5 vols. (revised edition, Oxford, 1965), IV, 528 (hereafter *Swift
   Corr.*)
21 Samuel Johnson, *Lives of the English Poets*, edited by George Birkbeck Hill, 3 vols. (Oxford,
   1905), III, 197–8.

breeding woman the other three?'; and Pope himself exclaimed when his plans were curtailed by illness: 'Would to God I were like any other thing they call a Man!' (*Corr.*, III, 299; IV, 293). In effect, like 'a breeding woman', he had to plan his activities around the whims of his body. It cannot have been easy to accept that 'Manlyer Exercises' were not for him.

2

Pope's beautifully poised 'Ode to Solitude', allegedly first written at the age of twelve, and later carefully revised, is a fine example of a poem that generalises about the human condition from an essentially male viewpoint. It makes a good place to start an exploration of women's place in his work at large, for, despite its precocious origins, it concerns itself with an ideal that remained dear to him throughout his life:

> Happy the man, whose wish and care
> A few paternal acres bound,
> Content to breathe his native air,
>   In his own ground.

> Whose herds with milk, whose fields with bread,
> Whose flocks supply him with attire,
> Whose trees in summer yield him shade,
>   In winter fire.

> Blest! who can unconcern'dly find
> Hours, days, and years slide soft away,
> In health of body, peace of mind,
>   Quiet by day,

> Sound sleep by night: study and ease
> Together mix'd; sweet recreation,
> And innocence, which most does please,
>   With meditation.

> Thus let me live, unseen, unknown;
> Thus unlamented let me dye;
> Steal from the world, and not a stone
>   Tell where I lye.   (*TE*, VI, 3)

The first stanza alone raises two major issues which affected women's standing in the eighteenth century: education and inheritance.

Education is, ironically, the theme that the contemporary woman reader – Pope's mother, for example – would be most likely to miss. Not being schooled in the classics, she would probably not register the Horatian echo in the first line by which the poet places his poem in its tradition. To be deaf to such allusions is to experience eighteenth-century writing in a muted, often puzzling way; yet this, however mitigated by translations, was the condition of most of the period's female readers. There is, for example, the cautionary tale of young Mrs Pilkington, helping Swift to sort his letters from Pope:

'But, Sir', said I, 'here is a Latin Sentence writ in italics, which, I suppose, means something particular; will you be so kind as to explain it?' 'No', replied he, smiling; 'I will leave that for your husband to do'.[22]

The tag turned out to be embarrassingly indecent, so female curiosity was duly punished (Pilkington, p. 67). For educated men the classical languages were a symbol of their cultural superiority, marking their graduation from the female tutelage of the nursery to the male world of public life. When Fanny Burney's father expressed disapproval of Dr Johnson's offer to teach her Latin, their mutual friend Hester Thrale commented tartly, 'because then She would have been as wise as himself forsooth'.[23] She may have been remembering a Johnsonian remark that caused Boswell characteristic disquiet:

> Whether he meant merely to say a polite thing, or to give his opinion, I could not be sure; but he said men knew that women were an overmatch for them; and therefore they chose the weakest or most ignorant. If they did not think so, they never could be afraid of women knowing as much as themselves. I must have this more amply discussed with him.[24]

The second of the factors highlighted in the first stanza of the 'Ode' is, however, by far the more important, since the complex of customs and beliefs evoked by the phrase 'paternal acres' lies at the heart of long-established assumptions about women's role and function. The belief that property belongs by nature to men and that their sons are its natural heirs may have been immemorial, but it was nonetheless vividly present to the imagination of the age: Richardson brings Clarissa to her death through her brother's rage at seeing his 'natural' dependant made a proprietor in her own right, and Jane Austen uses the dispossession of women in favour of men as a trial of female character in *Pride and Prejudice*.[25] Pope himself was caught up in a similar situation when his old acquaintance Michael Blount, admittedly with the full sanction of custom, required his mother and sisters, including Pope's beloved Patty, to leave home on his marriage, and subsequently failed to pay regularly the allowances on which they were expected to maintain themselves. In this case Pope was fired by indignation and exerted himself over many years to obtain adequate support for Patty (see chapter 5.3).

An important though by no means universal rationalisation of the restric-

22 *Memoirs of Mrs Pilkington, 1712-1750, Written by Herself* (London, 1748-54; reprinted 1928), p. 62.
23 *Thraliana: The Diary of Mrs. Hester Lynch Thrale (later Mrs. Piozzi) 1776-1809*, edited by Katharine C. Balderston, 2nd edition, 2 vols. (Oxford, 1951), I, 502.
24 *Boswell's Journal of a Tour to the Hebrides with Samuel Johnson, LL.D.*, edited by Frederick A. Pottle and Charles H. Bennett (London, 1936), p. 118; cited by Mrs Thrale, *Thraliana*, I, 171-72.
25 Samuel Richardson, *Clarissa; or, the History of a Young Lady*, edited by Angus Ross (Harmondsworth, 1985), pp. 53-54, 56, 77-78; Jane Austen, *Pride and Prejudice*, edited by Frank W. Bradbrook and James Kinsley (Oxford, 1970), pp. 23, 54, 62.

tion of inheritance to males is expounded by Boswell, whose obsession with
the perpetuation of estates in the male line led him into a protracted disagreement with his father:

My father and I had a warm dispute at night on male and female succession. I argued
that a male alone could support a family, could represent his forefathers. That females,
in a feudal light, were only vehicles for carrying down men to posterity, and that a
man might as well entail his estate on his post-chaise, and put one into it who should
bear his name, as entail it upon his daughter and make her husband take his name
. . . I fell upon a most curious argument which diverted my own fancy so much that
it was with difficulty I could preserve my gravity when uttering it. 'If', said I, 'you
believe the Bible, you must allow male succession. Turn to the first chapter of Matthew: ''Abraham begat Isaac, Isaac begat Jacob'', &c. If you are not an infidel, if you
do not renounce Christianity, you must be for males'. Worthy man! he had patience
with me. I am quite firm in my opinion on this point. It will not do to say a grandson
by a daughter is as near as a grandson by a son. It leads into a nice disquisition in
natural philosophy. I say the stamen is derived from the *man*. The woman is only like
the ground where a tree is planted. A grandson by a daughter has no connection with
my original stock. A new race is begun by a father of another name. It is true a child
partakes of the constitution of his mother, gets some of his mother's blood in his veins.
But so does he as to his nurse, so does he as to the ox whose beef he eats. The most
of the particles of the human frame are changed in a few years' rotation. The stamen
only continues the same. Let females be well portioned. Let them enjoy liberally what
is naturally intended for them: dowries as virgins, a share of what their husbands have
while wives, jointures when widows . . . In every age some instances of folly have
occurred to humble the pride of human nature. Of these, the idea of female succession
is one of the most striking.[26]

Elsewhere he refers tellingly to 'the opinion of some distinguished naturalists':

Our species is transmitted through males only, the female being all along no more than
a *nidus*, or nurse, as Mother Earth is to plants of every sort; which notion seems to
be confirmed by that text of scripture, 'He was yet *in the loins of his* FATHER when
Melchisedeck met him' (Heb. vii. 10); and consequently, that a man's grandson by
a daughter, instead of being his *surest* descendent, as is vulgarly said, has, in reality,
no connection whatever with his blood.[27]

To the ancient world the female contribution to conception had been far from
obvious. In the *Eumenides* of Aeschylus, Apollo upholds Orestes' claim that he
is not kin to the mother he has murdered; and his reasoning is essentially the
same as that outlined by Boswell.[28] Aristotle, offering a theoretical account
of conception, likens the process to carpentry: the father is the carpenter, the
mother the wood, and the child the finished product; and this model is taken
up by Thomas Aquinas, who stresses its hierarchical implications:

---

[26] *Boswell in Search of a Wife 1766–1769*, edited by Frank Brady and Frederick A. Pottle (London, 1957), pp. 270–72.

[27] *Boswell's Life of Johnson*, edited by George Birkbeck Hill and revised by L. F. Powell, 6 vols.
(Oxford, 1934–50), II, 414.

[28] *Aeschylus*, with an English translation by Herbert Weir Smyth, Loeb Classical Library, 2 vols.
(London, 1957), II, 335.

The generative power in a female is imperfect in relation to that which is in a male. And so, just as in the arts, an inferior art disposes the matter while the superior art imposes a form, as said in the *Physics*, so female generative power prepares the matter while male active power fashions the matter which has been prepared.[29]

The pervasive metaphorical pattern insists that women are not originators. For Boswell woman is soil to the seed, for Aristotle and Aquinas she is the raw material to the craftsman, and behind both analogies we sense her affinity with primeval chaos awaiting the male word of God in creation. Indeed, both levels of this metaphor are brought together in Aquinas's account of the conception of Christ, in which he is at pains to establish the passivity which Mary shared with all women: 'either she effected something, which would make her the father of Christ, or she effected nothing' (LII, 55). Not suprisingly, researchers down to Boswell's time frequently assumed that the natural order must display this hierarchy – hence the hostile response of John Cook to William Harvey's equally erroneous but dissection-based claim that the mother, not the father, produced the preformed embryo:

As the Earth seems a Nidus for all Seeds of Vegetables, so the Ova of the Female serve for the like Use . . . to think otherwise would be making Woman the chief Person in the Creation, in as much as she is supposed to contain her Species, both materially and formally, in her self, and needs only a little of the Spirit of the Male Sperm to set those Animalcula in Motion; so that instead of God's giving Woman for a Help-mate to Man towards Procreation, he is thus made Woman's Help-mate; and so hath the least share in this Action; whereas by Nature he was designed the chief Agent in it, and that from his Loins should proceed all Mankind . . . which the Text of St. *Paul* well alludes to, when he says of *Levi*, that he was yet in the Loins of his father, when Melchisedeck met him.[30]

More in accord with the assumed order of things was the rival animalculist (homunculist) theory, which identified the preformed embryo in the male spermatozoa, a theory familiar to modern readers from the opening of Sterne's *Tristram Shandy*.[31] It was also familiar to Mrs Pope, who was shown 'some of the *semen masculinum* with animalcula in it' when her son took her to Mr Hatton's clock and microscope shop (*Corr.*, I, 465). Perhaps even for those few mothers who understood the implications of the supposed homunculus it was too academic a theory to impair their sense of relationship to their children; but if they needed a theory that would enable them to take the

---

[29] Aristotle, *Generation of Animals*, with an English translation by A. L. Peck, Loeb Classical Library (London, 1963), I.xxi–xxii; St Thomas Aquinas, *Summa Theologiae*, Latin text and English translation, 61 vols. (Blackfriars, Cambridge, 1963–76), LII, 55.

[30] John Cook is quoted in Louis A. Landa, 'The Shandean Homunculus: The Background of Sterne's "Little Gentleman" ', in *Restoration and Eighteenth-Century Essays in Honour of Alan Dugald McKillop*, edited by Carrol Camden (Chicago, 1963), pp. 49–68 (p. 57). For an account of the various theories see Joseph Needham, *A History of Embryology*, 2nd edition, revised with the assistance of Arthur Hughes (Cambridge, 1959), pp. 37–44, 205–11.

[31] Laurence Sterne, *The Life and Opinions of Tristram Shandy, Gentleman*, edited by Ian Campbell Ross (Oxford, 1983).

credit, or – perhaps more likely – the blame for the way their children turned
out, they could turn to the belief that offspring were also influenced by their
mothers' behaviour and disposition before birth and by their milk afterwards.
The latter notion provides grounds for maternal self-congratulation in the
verse epistle which Pope, or perhaps Swift, put into the mouth of Bounce,
Pope's Great Dane bitch:

> Before my Children set your Beef,
> Not one true *Bounce* will be a Thief;
> Not one without permission feed,
> (Though some of *J*—'s hungry Breed)
> But whatso'er the Father's Race,
> From me they suck a little Grace.[32]

Although the chimerical homunculus owed its 'discovery' to the new
technology of the microscope, its power lay in old-fashioned assumptions
about the structure of society – hence its appeal to the reactionary sentiments
of Boswell and the fictional Walter Shandy. From such a point of view the
order implicit in the social organisation of England before the Civil War was
still· valid:

So long as a person occupied an inferior status within a household – as a child, servant, apprentice, or even as a wife – and was subordinated to the head, his social
identity was altogether vicarious. The family was represented to the larger community
by its head – its patriarch, as it were – and thus those whom he commanded were
'subsumed' in his social life. Thus, the father-master of each family was both its link
with society as a whole and its authority, and his status was universally recognised.[33]

Despite radical attempts during the Civil War to form an understanding of
society on new foundations, this old-established order still underlay the
mainstream of political theory; and therefore debate about the nature of
parenthood had distinct political overtones.[34] This, rather than any zeal for
women's rights, is clearly the principal reason why John Locke, in his *Two
Treatises of Government* (composed before 1683, published in 1689), makes
claims favourable to the status of wives and mothers.[35] His context is Sir
Robert Filmer's *Patriarcha* (composed in the early 1640s, published in 1680),
a defence of Stuart absolutism on the grounds that God gave Adam a fatherly
power over his descendants which was absolute, and that all present kings
enjoy the same power either by inheritance or by usurpation.[36] Under the

[32] 'Bounce to Fop', line 49 (*TE*, VI, 368); for attribution see Pat Rogers, *Eighteenth Century Encounters: Studies in Literature and Society in the Age of Walpole* (Brighton, 1985), p. 36.
[33] Gordon J. Schochet, *Patriarchalism in Political Thought: The Authoritarian Family and Political
Speculation and Attitudes Especially in Seventeenth-Century England* (Oxford, 1975), pp. 65–66.
[34] For refusal of the patriarchal model, see Gerrard Winstanley, *The Law of Freedom and Other
Writings*, edited by Christopher Hill (Harmondsworth, 1973), pp. 77–78.
[35] John Locke, *Two Treatises of Government*, edited by Peter Laslett, 2nd edition (Cambridge,
1970), p. 51.
[36] Sir Robert Filmer, *Patriarcha and Other Political Works*, edited by Peter Laslett (Oxford,
1949).

pressure of the Exclusion Crisis Locke attempted to undermine the doctrine of Adam's sole authority by arguments as relevant to the domestic as to the political hierarchy: he showed that if Adam's authority rested on having begotten his children it could not logically have extended to Eve; he pointed out that Filmer's use of the commandment 'Honour thy father and thy mother' (Genesis 20:12) to support sole paternal power involved supressing the mother's right; and he cited numerous other Biblical texts in which the rights of mothers paralleled those of fathers (Locke, pp. 231, 201–4). Indeed, the assertion that mothers also have authority is useful by definition to advocates of contractual obligation, since the existence of natural rights not acknowledged by existing social arrangements suggests that those arrangements must be contractual rather than natural. Even Hobbes, who as a defender of absolutism might be expected to deny the authority of mothers, finds it convenient to attribute power over their children to mothers in the state of nature. In this scheme the father gains authority over the child only by the mother's consent to marriage, which places her and her belongings in his power.[37]

In the politics of the state, the revolution of 1688 constituted a blow to hereditary absolutism, yet in most families and in society at large the heirs of Adam, in whose supremacy Filmer's thinking had its roots, reigned relatively unshaken. Mary Astell, realising that political and social doctrines were out of step, takes a polemical delight in restating the orthodox connection:

Again, if absolute Sovereignty be not necessary in a State, how comes it to be so in a Family? Or if in a Family why not in a State; since no Reason can be alledged for the one that will not hold more strongly for the other? If the Authority of the Husband, so far as it extends, is sacred and inalienable, why not that of the Prince? The Domestick Sovereign is without Dispute elected; and the Stipulations and Contract are mutual; is it not then partial in Men to the last Degree, to contend for, and practise that Arbitrary Dominion in their Families, which they abhor and exclaim against in the State? For if Arbitrary Power is evil in it self, and an improper Method of Governing Rational and Free Agents, it ought not to be practis'd any where, nor is it less, but rather more mischievous in Families than in Kingdoms, by how much 100,000 Tyrants are worse than one.[38]

Yet, however illogical, patriarchy in the home was to endure long after its abandonment as a justification for absolutism in the state.

The remaining stanzas of the 'Ode' further reveal the importance of male privilege in Pope's conception of the Good Life. His Happy Man has the air of having stepped fresh from Filmer's world, endowed like Adam with a divinely given rapport with his environment:

---

[37] Thomas Hobbes, *Leviathan, or the Matter, Forme and Power of a Commonwealth Ecclesiasticall and Civil*, edited by Michael Oakeshott (Oxford, 1960), ch. 20, pp. 129–31.
[38] Mary Astell, *Some Reflections upon Marriage*, 5th edition (Dublin, 1730), p. 66.

Whose herds with milk, whose fields with bread,
Whose flocks supply him with attire,
Whose trees in summer yield him shade,
    In winter fire.

He does not simply possess his 'paternal acres' but relies on them to serve his
needs, without, as far as the rhetoric is concerned, any necessity for laborious
human mediation. Secure at the apex of the hierarchy that sustains him, he
rests in a vision of the fruitful earth in which work is at most a peripheral concern. Indeed, the way language works to suggest that the land is his willing
servant is reminiscent of Carole Fabricant's perception that landscape is in
effect seen as female in this period, requiring from the owner discipline and
protection in return for service and pleasure.[39] Sustained in this way, the
Happy Man lives as if the Fall had never happened.

Although men, if rich enough, could avoid the curse of work laid on Adam
after the Fall, women had for the most part to accept their curse in full:

Unto the woman he said, I will greatly multiply thy sorrow and thy conception: in sorrow thou shalt bring forth children; and thy desire shall be to thy husband, and he shall
rule over thee.   (Genesis 3:16)

After the dissolution of the monasteries this was the only career available to
well-born Englishwomen; and its consequences constitute the most obvious
impediment to those aspects of the Good Life that Pope's poem next
commends:

Blest! who can unconcern'dly find
Hours, days, and years slide soft away,
In health of body, peace of mind,
    Quiet by day,

Sound sleep by night: study and ease
Together mix'd; sweet recreation,
And innocence, which most does please,
    With meditation.

The careers of Alice Thornton and Hester Thrale show vividly the distance
between their sex and Pope's Happy Man.[40] Mrs Thornton bore nine
children between 1651 and 1668, of whom six died at birth or soon afterwards; and of the thirteen borne by Mrs Thrale between 1763 and 1781 only
four survived. Even when not actually incapacitated, these women were
absorbed in the constant distractions of life with small, often ailing children,
and only in widowhood did they enjoy anything approaching the quiet that
the Happy Man takes for granted. The best commentary is by Mrs Thrale

[39] Carole Fabricant, 'Binding and Dressing Nature's Loose Tresses: The Ideology of Augustan
Landscape Design', *Studies in Eighteenth-Century Culture*, 8 (1979), 109–135.
[40] *The Autobiography of Mrs. Alice Thornton*, edited by Charles Jackson, Surtees Society, 62
(Durham, 1873); Mary Hyde, *The Thrales of Streatham Park* (Cambridge, Mass., 1977).

herself, responding to criticism for not having recorded more of Dr Johnson's sayings:

Little do these wise Men know or feel, that the Crying of a young Child, or the Perverseness of an elder, or the Danger however trifling of any one – will soon drive out of a female Parent's head a Conversation concerning Wit, Science or Sentiment, however She may appear to be impressed with it at the moment: besides that to a *Mere de famille* doing something is more necessary & suitable than even hearing something; and if one is to listen all Even^g and write all Morning what one has heard; where will be the Time for tutoring, caressing, or what is still more useful, for having one's Children about one: I therefore charge all my Neglect to my young ones Account, and feel myself at this moment very miserable that I have at last, after being married fourteen Years and bringing eleven Children, leisure to write a *Thraliana* forsooth; – though the second Volume *does* begin with Mr Johnson.

(*Thraliana*, I, 158)

It is hardly surprising that the women Pope loved best had either completed their families or never had children at all.

Another factor which tended to set women apart from the calm of the Happy Man was the use of space in the home. Although Mrs Thornton and Mrs Thrale escaped the literal confinement to a shared sitting room deplored by Virginia Woolf, we still have the sense from their writings that their husbands were peripheral to life in the home, pursuing outside interests or retiring to privacy inside, while their wives stood at the centre, overseeing children and servants and entertaining all comers.[41] When Jane Austen, herself notoriously constrained by the publicity of the family sitting room, makes Mr Bennet rebut his wife with the zeugma 'first, that you will allow me the free use of my understanding on the present occasion; and secondly, of my room', she ironically affirms the link that Mr Bennet's wit denies (Austen, p. 101). Even in the Pope household the contrast between chaotic female community and calm male retirement could be sharply defined:

His Mother quite childish . . . fell out of her Chair, as she was fuggeling her clothes that did not sit easy under her, into the fire, upon the Fender, her head broke in Three places; Mrs *Racket* sitting working in the Window – Mr *Pope* never knew either, tho' in the house.[42]

The vignette easily takes on archetypal overtones: while the man whose activities give prestige to the household applies himself unhearing to his central concerns, his married sister sits with her sewing, keeping his mother company.

Yet finally, despite the 'Ode's' uncritical investment in the male privilege that alone can offer 'paternal acres' to be enjoyed in alternate 'study and ease', the genre in which Pope is working points him towards implica-

---

[41] Virginia Woolf, *A Room of One's Own*, 2nd edition (London, 1931), pp. 99–100.
[42] George Sherburn, 'New Anecdotes about Alexander Pope', *Notes and Queries*, 203 (1958), 343–49 (p. 348).

---

tions of retirement which he develops in ways ironically closer to the acceptable behaviour of women than of men. Although 'innocence, which most does please, / With meditation' is in full harmony with the programme of serious reading urged on women by *The Spectator*, it is in marked tension with much that Pope was to spend his life doing, especially when seen in the context of the desire to be 'unseen, unknown'; for however one part of him may yearn for retirement and simplicity, the author in him needs a place in the public eye (*The Spectator*, I, 152–59). Similarly, in his final refusal to pay tribute to his individuality ('not a stone / Tell where I lie') he suggests that to do otherwise would imply a moral taint, a scruple which is far closer to the contemporary reality of female than of male decorum. What the 'Ode to Solitude' does is to give Pope a space in which to indulge the choice of being as women have to be, secluded from the world in which men make names for themselves, for like all such retirement poems its ostensible purpose is to repudiate the world of business, power and status. Thus the 'Ode' takes its place in his life with the other contexts which he established for the ideal of self-effacing virtue: his retirement to Twickenham, his devotion to his aged mother, his repudiation of court favour, and his limitation of his own memorial to a brief note of his death on the stone on which he had commemorated the virtues of his parents.[43] Here, as if he had never been famous, he denies any identity beyond that of his parents' son, yet his officious literary executor William Warburton, incapable of honouring a sentiment so contrary to the public status of a great poet, imposed upon this simple monument a grandiose and tasteless claim:

> Who never flattered folks like you.
> Let Horace blush, and Virgil too.[44]

These were indeed Pope's words; but with the title he had given them, 'Epitaph For One who would not be buried in Westminster Abbey', they were carefully distanced from autobiography: their appearance on his tomb as a public claim to have surpassed the integrity of the great poets of antiquity would have horrified him. The contrast between the intended and the actual memorial points the irony of his relation to the world in which he was so anxious to distinguish himself; for despite the appeal of a pure, powerless self-abandonment, that world remained the necessary context for his poetry.

---

[43] For the significance of Pope's retreat to Twickenham see Maynard Mack, *The Garden and the City: Retirement and Politics in the Later Poetry of Pope* (London, 1969); for his care of his mother see chapter 2.3–4 below; for his instructions for the addition to his parents' monument, see his will, printed in *The Prose Works of Alexander Pope*, edited by Norman Ault and Rosemary Cowler, 2 vols. (Oxford, 1936–86), II, 506.

[44] For Warburton's impact on Pope and his circle, see chapter 9.1, 5; for the monument see *TE*, VI, 376.

3

In taking a wider view of the place of women in the poems not specifically concerned with gender it is convenient to begin with three ambitiously generalis-
ing works: the *Essay on Man*, the *Essay on Criticism* and *Of the Knowledge and
Characters of Men*.

In the *Essay on Man*, which seldom registers the existence of more than one
gender, God, the representative human being, 'the poor Indian' and the
representative child are all male; and Pope's propositions about human
nature are illustrated for the most part with examples from the public life of
men, notably from history and the professions (*TE*, III.i). The process is clear
in his enumeration of the 'happy frailties' proper to various sub-groups of the
species:

> Shame to the virgin, to the matron pride,
> Fear to the statesman, rashness to the chief,
> To kings presumption, and to crowds belief.
>
> (*Essay on Man*, II.242)

Since all a woman can do is marry or wait to marry, her doings naturally
require less coverage.

When in Epistle III Pope considers the origin of society, he begins with the
impulse to procreation in which women were supposed to find the significance
of their lives. His treatment of the mating of animals stresses mutuality: 'Each
sex desires alike'; and when the young are born 'the mothers nurse it and the
sires defend', a division of labour which he does not explicitly interpret as a
hierarchy (lines 119–26). Human couples are initially differentiated from the
animals by the longer association required by their offspring's prolonged
helplessness, from which distinctively human social feelings grow:

> And still new needs, new helps, new habits rise,
> That graft benevolence on charities.   (line 137)

As an account of marriage this is remarkably free from implications of subordination; but later, when Pope returns to the family to trace from it the origins
of government, women have simply disappeared, and 'father' and 'son' alone
represent the experience of family life (lines 211–34). As authority is now
vested in the father, the invisible mother must belong to the subordinate offspring caste, despite the inability of the myth to explain how she got there.
It is evident that the apparent equality of mother and father in the animal
kingdom can have no place in a myth of the human family which justifies the
basic hierarchy of society. Although Genesis does not figure in this non-
Biblical account of social and political origins, its justification of female subordination and the reflections of the doctrine in traditional social structure are
implicit in Pope's assumption that this is not an issue.

Whereas the *Essay on Man* looks to the first principles of human life, the

Essay on Criticism looks to a highly developed world of literary culture (*TE*, I, 239–326). It is a poem which fully bears out the envious words of Anne Finch, Countess of Winchilsea: 'Happy the race of men / Born to inform or to correct the pen.'[45] Although the summarising statement that 'Most men are born with some Taste, but spoil'd by false *Education*' may be understood of people in general, the use of terms like 'Taste' and 'Education' suggests that the real subject is men – and men of the upper classes at that. The poor are hardly less represented in this world than are women, who appear only as personifications, sexual chattels or examples of poor judgement. As personifications they uniformly extend their patronage to male achievers, as if female authority can be countenanced only symbolically: 'High on *Parnassus*' Top her Sons she [Greece] show'd' (line 94). Even for a personification, female gender entails the risk of sexual appropriation: once Criticism is personified as the Muse's handmaid, sexual harassment is inevitable: 'Who cou'd not win the Mistress, woo'd the Maid' (line 105). Metaphor too assumes a system in which women are chattels:

> A Muse by these is like a Mistress us'd,
> This hour she's *idoliz'd*, the next abus'd.   (line 432)

> What is this Wit which must our Cares employ?
> The *Owner's Wife*, that *other Men* enjoy.   (line 500)

Women also figure as silly, corruptible creatures: only fools 'value *Books*, as Women *Men*, for *Dress*' (line 305). In the reign of Charles II, which exposed them to libertine amusements, they showed by their easy corruptibility that the only female virtue is the virtue which has never known temptation:

> The Fair sate panting at a *Courtier's Play*,
> And not a Mask went *un-improv'd* away:
> The modest Fan was lifted up no more,
> And Virgins *smil'd* at what they *blush'd* before.   (line 540)

Political interference, in metaphor as in fact, goes hand in hand with sexual transgression as Pope condemns the age when 'Jilts ruled the State' (line 538).

Perhaps the most striking example of a poem which professes to consider the species but actually focuses on the male sex is *Of the Knowledge and Characters of Men*.[46] In this context, 'men' evidently means 'people', for Queen Caroline forms a quartet with three men, and of the six sketches which close the poem, two are of women; but the catalogues which define the diversity of the species are, in effect, relevant only to the sex which experiences the status of bishops, judges, chancellors, ministers or kings; the education of squires, tradesmen, soldiers, scriveners or churchmen; and the variety of mood produced by business, gambling, hunting and parliamentary debates.

[45] *The Poems of Anne Countess of Winchilsea*, edited by Myra Reynolds (Chicago, 1903), p. 100.
[46] Epistle I of the *Epistles to Several Persons (Moral Essays)*, addressed to Richard Temple, Viscount Cobham (*TE*, III.ii, 15–38: hereafter *Characters of Men*).

There is the usual tendency to regard women as accessories ('If Fortune or a Mistress frowns') and as fools ('What made . . . Europe a Woman, Child, or Dotard rule?', 'Women and Fools must like him or he dies'); while as phenomena they rank with the most perplexing objects of curiosity unveiled by the theory of the ruling passion: 'Priests, Princes, Women, no dissemblers here'.[47] It has often been assumed that *Characters of Women* was written as a pendant to *Characters of Men*, but the secondary status of the former is even more striking when it is realised that it was in all probability the first to be conceived: the option of leaving *Characters of Women* in first place and presenting *Characters of Men* as a pendant considering the male sex 'only as contradistinguished from the other' clearly does not exist for Pope.[48]

Various passages throughout Pope's poetry remind us that the systems which structured public life operated for the most part on the assumption that all full members of society were male: 'the whole Course of Modern Education . . . which confines Youth to the study of *Words* only' attacked in *Dunciad* IV, and the political system which it supports, are primarily the business of men, as is the world of commerce, and in the latter connection it is noteworthy that the only women shown as active financial agents are Phryne and Sappho (Sir Robert Walpole's mistress Maria Skerret, and her friend Lady Mary Wortley Montagu), whose usurpation of a male role merely confirms their disgrace as creatures of a corrupt court.[49] It is more surprising to find that when Pope turns to his own family, it is his father rather than his mother who emerges as an individual. Adapting Horace's autobiography to his own, he focuses on his father's moral worth, although Horace here makes no direct reference to his father:

> Besides, my Father taught me from a Lad,
> The better Art to know the good from bad
>
> . . .
>
> For Right Hereditary tax'd and fin'd,
> He stuck to Poverty with Peace of Mind.[50]

Yet there is no reason to think that his mother was a less loyal Catholic, or less impressive in her moral influence. Even in the *Epistle to Dr. Arbuthnot*, in which Pope recalls the praise which Horace bestows on his father, once we penetrate the aura of affectionate reverence which surrounds both parents, we find that the stress falls squarely on his father: all we learn of his mother's character is, 'that harmless Mother thought no Wife a Whore'.[51] Nothing

---

[47] *Characters of Men*, lines 55, 152, 183, 177.

[48] Miriam Leranbaum, *Alexander Pope's 'Opus Magnum' 1729–1744* (Oxford, 1977), pp. 64–65, 76–77, 79.

[49] *Dunciad* IV, note on 501 (*TE*, V, 391); *Epistle to Bathurst: Of the Use of Riches*, lines 121–24 (*TE*, III.ii, 101–2).

[50] *Imitations of Horace*, Epistles, II.ii.54, 64 (*TE*, IV, 169).

[51] Horace, *Satires, Epistles, Ars Poetica*, with an English translation by H. Rushton Fairclough, Loeb Classical Library (London, 1929), Satires I.vi.71–99; *To Arbuthnot*, line 384 (*TE*, IV, 126).

could be further from the truth than to suggest that this shows a lack of
interest in his mother, as the end of the poem amply demonstrates: the difference in emphasis is a sign of the general hiddenness of female identity in
a culture rich in precedents for exploring the qualities of men.

Complementary to the male-centredness of Pope's culture is the fact that
the women who do figure in it often do so as objects comparable to other
things that a man might wish to possess:

> And Curio, restless by the Fair-one's side,
> Sighs for an Otho, and neglects his bride.[52]

> And if we count among the Needs of life
> Another's Toil, why not another's Wife?[53]

> Think we all these are for himself? no more
> Than his fine Wife, alas! or finer Whore.[54]

> Why, if the Nights seem tedious – take a Wife.[55]

> For, mark th'advantage [of money]; just so many score
> Will gain a Wife with half as many more,
> Procure that beauty, make that beauty chaste,
> And then such Friends – as cannot fail to last.[56]

The moralist points the absurdity; but the stress falls squarely on male folly
rather than on any claim for women's autonomy. Similarly, there seems to
be no particular irony in Pope's rendering of Horace's 'amabilis hospes, /
Comes in uxorem' as 'fond of his Friend, and civil to his Wife', although the
line could easily be read out of context as a gibe at a complacent husband.[57]

Whatever the precise weighting of this strain in Pope's satire, it is obvious
that at least in casual references he has no difficulty in accepting the associated
doctrine that whether women succumb or chastely resist, their energies are
centred on sexual relationships with men. In his epigram 'To a Lady with
the Temple of Fame', which he inscribed in Patty's presentation copy, the
joke underlines this assumption.[58] The only females in the *Temple* itself are
the fickle goddesses Fame and Fortune; and women's absence is only to be
expected, since the nearest they come to fame is the good repute of preserving
their chastity:

> What's Fame with Men, by Custom of the Nation,
> Is call'd in Women only Reputation:

---

[52] *To Mr. Addison, Occasioned by his Dialogues on Medals*, line 43 (*TE*, VI, 204).
[53] *To Bathurst*, line 27 (*TE*, III.ii, 88).
[54] *Epistle to Burlington: Of the Use of Riches*, line 1 (*TE*, III.ii, 136).
[55] *Imitations of Horace*, Satires, II.i.16 (*TE*, IV, 5).
[56] *Imitations of Horace*, Epistles, I.vi.77 (*TE*, IV, 241–42).
[57] *Imitations of Horace*, Epistles, II.ii.189 (*TE*, IV, 179).
[58] *The Temple of Fame* (*TE*, II, 253–89); 'To a Lady with the Temple of Fame' (*TE*, VI, 127–28).

> About them both why keep we such a pother?
> Part you with one, and I'll renounce the other.

Like Pope's poem, *The Tatler*'s project for a table of fame had honoured only
men; and ironically the only female considered is the Roman Lucretia, whose
status as the heroic wife who, unable to avoid rape, expressed her refusal by
suicide confirms what Pope's joke suggests, that the whole drama of a
woman's life is contained within her relation to the other sex.[59] Yet Lucretia
more than anyone would be sensitive to the impropriety of publicity, so it is
only to be expected that Mr Bickerstaff should offer an implicit rebuke to the
woman who had proposed her: 'I did not think it proper to place her there,
because I knew she would not care for being in the Company of so many Men
without her Husband'.

Women's physical allure accounts for their sole representation in the summary of the glories of Rome which Pope admires in Addison's medals:

> In one short view subjected to your eye
> Gods, Emp'rors, Heroes, Sages, Beauties, lie.[60]

Helen of Troy understandably had a place in Horace's summary of the deeds
that have inspired great poetry; but in Pope's paraphrase of this passage the
discussion is moved to a higher and therefore an entirely masculine plane:

> Sages and Chiefs long since had birth
> E're Caesar was, or Newton nam'd,
> These rais'd new Empires o'er the Earth,
> And Those new Heav'ns and Systems fram'd.[61]

In a system that confines women within sexuality, chastity is necessarily
woman's characteristic virtue and lust her characteristic vice. Of chastity in
itself Pope has very little to say, except for the paradoxical praise of married
love: 'Chaste as cold Cynthia's virgin light, / Productive as the Sun'.[62]
Moon and sun are to become increasingly potent symbols in Pope's writing
about women; but the flimsiness of this enthusiasm for chilly fecundity helps
to explain why chastity figures less as a theme than as the assumption behind
satirical condemnation. As early as his adolescent imitation of Rochester's
'On Nothing' Pope was conscious that desire was simply inadmissible for
women when he praised silence as 'the only Honour of the wishing Dame'.[63]
The problem of chastity and the value set on it is also crucial to the 'Epilogue
to Jane Shore', written for the actress Anne Oldfield, herself notoriously a
kept woman, to be spoken at the conclusion of her portrayal of Jane Shore,
mistress to Edward IV.[64] Pope makes her begin in mock surprise that vir-

---

59 *The Tatler*, edited by Donald F. Bond, 3 vols. (Oxford, 1987), II, 34.
60 *To Mr Addison*, line 33 (*TE*, VI, 203).
61 *Imitations of Horace*, Odes, IV.ix.9 (*TE*, IV, 159).
62 'Two Choruses to the Tragedy of Brutus', II, line 23 (*TE*, VI, 153).
63 'On Silence', line 26 (*TE*, VI, 18).
64 *TE*, VI, 113–15; for a detailed account of Anne Oldfield, see *DNB*.

tuous ladies are prepared to applaud the representation of a whore; but then she reflects that it is only 'wicked custom' that makes them pretend a horror of unchastity that they are far from feeling. Moreover, despite the value set on it by custom, chastity cannot in her view be equated with virtue:

> The godly dame who fleshly failings damns,
> Scolds with her maid, or with her chaplain crams.   (line 21)

That there are more deadly sins than one comes very well from a woman who lives by disregard for that one, and it is fitting that she should conclude with an ironic reference to the conventional equation of virtue with chastity when she refers to the royal mistress as 'in all the rest so *impudently* good' (line 48; my italics). On the other hand, although Pope makes Mrs Oldfield suggest that women have vices and virtues to which chastity is completely irrelevant, the very fact that he presents her as so concerned to play down its value may confirm for the women in the audience that brazen it as she may, sexual continence is still properly the mainspring of their moral universe. A similar underlying morality is found in the irreverent satire 'A Roman Catholick Version of the First Psalm, For the Use of a Young Lady'; for here a text which recommends religion to men as a means of attaining prosperity is travestied as one which recommends chastity to women as a means of attaining sexual satisfaction, as if this means to a woman all that material and spiritual prosperity means to a man.[65] As in the words written for Mrs Oldfield, Pope plays with the recognition that society seems to preach a ludicrously narrowing morality to women; yet one effect of the self-consciously wicked pose is undoubtedly to focus women's attention on sexuality as their proper realm.

A similar libertine knowingness emerges in representations of girls torn between chastity and desire, which clearly has nature on its side:

> Th'advent'rous Lover is successful still,
> Who strives to please the Fair *against her Will*.[66]

> As some coy Nymph her Lover's warm Address
> Nor quite indulges, nor can quite repress.[67]

> While a kind Glance at her Pursuer flies,
> How much at variance are her Feet and Eyes![68]

Although in more soberly moralising contexts Pope may condemn the mature sensuality which enables fortune-hunters to 'win rich Widows by their Chine and Brawn' (it is not in any case nearly as flattering to the conqueror as the melting reluctance of the 'coy Nymph'), he is positively repelled by

---

[65] *TE*, VI, 164–66: the title is a malicious addition by the publisher Edmund Curll, for whose relations with Pope see *TE*, IV, 356–57.

[66] 'Prologue design'd for Mr. Durfy's Last Play', line 5 (*TE*, VI, 101).

[67] *Windsor Forest*, line 19 (*TE*, I, 150).

[68] *Pastorals*, 'Spring', line 59 (*TE*, I, 66).

women who can suppress their sexuality not through virtue, but, as he sees
it, through avarice:

> In Love's, in Nature's spite, the siege they hold,
> And scorn the Flesh, the Dev'l, and all but Gold.[69]

> Shall One whom Nature, Learning, Birth, conspir'd
> To form, not to admire, but be admir'd,
> Sigh, while his Chloe, blind to Wit and Worth,
> Weds the rich Dulness of some Son of earth?[70]

However powerful the ideal of chastity may have been for the female decorum
of the period, the libertine tradition of the Restoration wits remained a powerful influence for Pope, and the image of the girl whose chastity fights a losing
battle remained deeply attractive to him. In contrast with the vices of cold
calculation, seductibility at least proved that a girl's heart was in the right
place.

   This vein of feeling is closely allied to the familiar notion of women's softness, a major premise of Pope's *Characters of Women*. This is the characteristic
that enables women to be tender mistresses, mothers and general comforters,
but it also confirms their deficiency in the mental powers on which humanity
prides itself. Proper judgement depends on firmness: hence it is natural to
Pope to couple 'women and fools' to denote the unthinking part of mankind.
In his imitation of Horace's essay on the practicalities of extra-marital sex,
for example, Pope uses this phrase where Horace mentions only fools, after
which Pope launches into a satire on extremes in women's dress for which
there is no parallel in the original.[71] The phrase also appears in a revealing
context in *Characters of Men*, when Wharton's inconsistent behaviour is explained by his compulsion to win praise even from those whose praise is not
worth having:

> Born with whate'er could win it from the Wise,
> Women and fools must like him or he dies.

>   (line 182; *TE*, III.ii, 30)

In the *Dunciad* the degeneracy of the aristocracy is blamed in part on the silly
mother, who, with her addiction to fashionable frivolity, 'begg'd the blessing
of a Rake'; but Pope sounds bitterest in his reflections on the memorial poems
that women ask him to write:

> Each Mother asks it for her Booby Son,
> Each Widow asks it for the Best of Men,
> For him she weeps, and him she weds agen.[72]

---

[69] *Imitations of Horace*, Epistles I.i.131 (*TE*, IV, 289); *The Second Satire of Dr. John Donne*, line 23
   (*TE*, IV, 133).
[70] *Imitations of Horace*, Epistles, I.vi.40 (*TE*, IV, 239).
[71] *Imitations of Horace*, Sermones, I.ii.27–34 (*Sober Advice from Horace*) (*TE*, IV, 76–79).
[72] *Dunciad B*, IV.286 (*TE*, V, 372); *Epilogue to the Satires*, Dialogue II, line 107 (*TE*, IV, 319).

For such women all values are levelled in the corrupt flux of their bodily affections. Women are regularly associated with fluidity, men with firmness, and in Pope's view, the hack writers who flatter the royal family understand all too well the distinction between manly panegyrics ('Rend with tremendous Sound your ears asunder, / With Gun, Drum, Trumpet, Blunderbuss & Thunder') and mellifluous feminine vacuity:

> Then all your Muse's softer Art display,
> Let *Carolina* smooth the tuneful Lay,
> Lull with *Amelia*'s liquid Name the Nine,
> And sweetly flow through all the Royal Line.[73]

Pope's crowning example of female softness is the 'Harlot form' of Opera, who, with her insistence that music should be concerned less with meaning than with pretty noises, leads the attack on order in *Dunciad* IV.[74] This epitome of frivolity and dependence provides not so much a softening of the cares of state as a subversion of legislative duty:

> By singing Peers upheld on either hand,
> She tripp'd and laugh'd, too pretty much to stand.   (line 49)

Although the style of femininity that Pope so contemptuously associates with prostitution and cultural decline in this passage was brought into particular prominence by the contemporary aspiration to bring up daughters in genteel idleness, and by the role of moneyed women as consumers of the silks, china and tea that consolidated family status in polite society, it was also a logical development of a long physiological tradition. Hippocrates had declared that 'a woman's flesh is more spongelike and softer than a man's'; and Aristotle had used the criterion of temperature to account for the deficiencies he perceived in women, assuming that men must be hotter to account for their unique ability to 'cook' the dynamic semen to perfection:

Everything reaches its perfection sooner in females than in males – e.g., puberty, maturity, old age – because females are weaker and colder in their nature; and we should look upon the female state as being as it were a deformity, though one which occurs in the ordinary course of nature. While it [the female foetus] is within the mother, then it develops slowly on account of its coldness, since development is a sort of concoction, concoction is effected by heat, and if a thing is hotter its concoction is easy; when, however, it is free from the mother, on account of its weakness it quickly approaches its maturity and old age, since inferior things all reach their end more quickly.[75]

Not surprisingly, Aristotle found a general lack of robustness characteristic of female animals:

[73] *Imitations of Horace*, Satires, II.i.25, 29 (*TE*, IV, 7).

[74] *Dunciad B*, IV.45–70 (*TE*, V, 345–48).

[75] Ann Ellis Hanson, 'Hippocrates: Diseases of Women', *Signs*, 1 (Winter 1975), 567–84 (p. 572); Aristotle, *Generation of Animals*, I.xx (p. 103), IV.vi (pp. 459–61); and see Suzanne Said, *Women and Female in the Biological Treatises of Aristotle* (Odense, 1982).

Again, the female is less muscular and less compactly jointed, and more thin and delicate in the hair – that is, where hair is found; and, where there is no hair, less strongly furnished in some analogous substance. And the female is more knock-kneed, and the shin-bones are thinner; and the feet are more arched and hollow in such animals as are furnished with feet.[76]

Since the human race is nature's highest work, the natural distinction of sexes is there developed to its greatest extent:

The fact is, the nature of man [i.e. the species] is the most rounded off and complete, and consequently in man the qualities or capacities referred to are found in their perfection. Hence woman is more compassionate than man, more easily moved to tears, at the same time is more jealous, more querulous, more apt to scold and to strike. She is, furthermore, more prone to despondency and less hopeful than the man, more void of shame or self-respect, more false of speech, more deceptive, and of more retentive memory. She is also more wakeful, more shrinking, more difficult to rouse to action, and requires a smaller quantity of nutriment.   (IX.1.608b)

For European women the ancient consensus gained additional authority by its transmission through the New Testament in the doctrine of 'the weaker vessel'.[77] Thus, by the time Pope teased Patty Blount with the definition of her sex as 'matter too soft a lasting mark to bear', the complex of physiological, mental and moral assumptions which had accumulated around the polarisation of firm male and fluid female was generally accepted as part of the natural order.[78] It remained, however, an ambivalent distinction: despite Swift's vehemence in declaring that 'there is no Quality whereby Women endeavour to distinguish themselves from Men, for which they are not just so much the worse', he still felt the need to confirm that the dearest of his women friends had a proper softness as well as the less conventional qualities for which he respected her: 'With all the softness of temper that became a lady, she had the personal courage of a hero'.[79] For Pope too the myriad associations of the notion of women's softness were to provide grounds for responses ranging from utter loathing, through irritation, amusement and patronising compliment, to sympathy, admiration and devoted love.

[76] Aristotle, *Historia Animalium*, translated by D'Arcy Wentworth Thompson (*The Works of Aristotle*, edited by J. A. Smith and W. D. Ross, IV; Oxford, 1910), IV.11.538b.
[77] Antonia Fraser, *The Weaker Vessel: Woman's Lot in Seventeenth-Century England* (London, 1984), pp. 1–6.
[78] *Characters of Women*, line 3 (*TE*, III.ii, 46).
[79] Jonathan Swift, 'A Letter to a Young Lady, on her Marriage', *Irish Tracts and Sermons*, edited by Herbert Davis and Louis Landa (Oxford, 1968), p. 93; 'On the Death of Mrs. Johnson' (i.e. Esther Johnson, affectionately known as Stella), *Miscellaneous and Autobiographical Pieces, Fragments and Marginalia*, edited by Herbert Davis (Oxford, 1969), p. 229.

2

Women at home

1

For Pope his mother was woman at her best: 'Matrum Optima, Mulierum Amantissima' he called her on the obelisk which he erected in her memory.[1] The views through his intricately contrived garden converged on this monument, just as, we may suspect, all his dealings with the opposite sex hinged on an ideal created in her image.

Edith Pope was born in Yorkshire in 1643, the fourteenth of sixteen known children of William and Thomasine Turner, descendants of the York trading community who counted various holders of civic office among their family and friends.[2] By the time Edith met her husband her parents were dead and she had moved to London, probably to be with her eldest sister, Christiana, widow of the miniaturist Samuel Cooper. Other sisters seem to have belonged to the household, and it was probably the son of her married sister Alice Mawhood who introduced Edith to her future husband. Samuel Mawhood, who was to be of vital assistance to the Popes when he used his legal rights as a Protestant to take their Binfield home in trust for them, had been sent from his parents' home in Yorkshire to London as an apprentice draper, and he was close enough to his aunt Christiana to be made executor of her will. As Pope's father was also a draper, Mawhood was very likely his link with the Turner sisters (Rumbold, pp. 31–34).

The marriage between Edith and Alexander Pope senior gave grounds for joy and relief on both sides. Edith had been unmarried at least as late as 1684, by which time she was forty-one and probably resigned to the role of dependent spinster (p. 32). Her husband was three years younger and had been widowed in 1679. His son Alexander and daughter Magdalen had been farmed out to his married sister, wife of an Anglican clergyman, but in 1682 the son had died (Mack, *Life*, pp. 3, 21). Many men would have looked immediately for a second wife young enough to offer hope of another son; yet Alexander

[1] Mack, *Life*, p. 366; *Garden*, pp. 28–29, plates 11, 19, 21; Peter Martin, *Pursuing Innocent Pleasures: The Gardening World of Alexander Pope* (Hamden, Connecticut, 1984), pp. 59–60, plates 26, 31.
[2] Valerie Rumbold, 'Alexander Pope and the Religious Tradition of the Turners', *Recusant History*, 17 (1984), 17–37 (pp. 17–29); Mack, *Life*, pp. 3–4, 17–20.

24

waited at least five years before marrying Edith, then aged at least forty-one. Perhaps her success as wife and stepmother was predictable; but her other triumph was one that no one could have foreseen with any confidence: only a month from her forty-fifth birthday, she gave birth to a son (p. 4).

Edith's stepdaughter Magdalen later recalled a revealing incident from the early days of her father's second marriage:

Made his Wife soon after they were Married, send 2sh. after a Mantua maker, Mrs. Shepherd who had come to decay, because if She said She gave but 10 where others gave 12, She would injure the Woman's character with those that might not know it was on account of her having employ'd her of the first, before She raised her Price; if She said 12, She would tell a Lye.[3]

Not only did he respect truth to the extent of paying more than necessary (which many would have found a laughable weakness in a merchant), he also showed tact and compassion for someone economically vulnerable. From this and other testimony it is clear that he was an impressive character; yet he was far removed from any arbitrary and overbearing model of paternal authority; and the example of masculinity which he gave his son was well-attuned to a household of pious women whose only other male member was the priest (Mack, *Life*, pp. 48, 829). Pope stressed his father's integrity, a strength expressed not in bluster but in fortitude:

> that Father held it for a rule
> It was a Sin to call our Neighbour Fool
> . . .
> Stranger to Civil and Religious Rage,
> The good Man walk'd innoxious thro' his Age.
> No Courts he saw, no Suits would ever try,
> Nor dar'd an Oath, nor hazarded a Lye:
> Unlearn'd, he knew no Schoolman's subtle Art,
> No Language, but the Language of the Heart.
> By Nature honest, by Experience wise,
> Healthy by Temp'rance and by Exercise:
> His Life, tho' long, to sickness past unknown,
> His Death was instant, and without a groan.
> Oh grant me thus to live, and thus to die!
> Who sprung from Kings shall know less joy than I.[4]

> Besides, my Father taught me from a Lad,
> The better Art to know the good from bad
> . . .
> But knottier Points we knew not half so well,
> Depriv'd us soon of our Paternal Cell;
> And certain laws, by Suff'rers thought unjust,
> Deny'd all Posts of Profit or of Trust:

---

[3] Sherburn, 'New Anecdotes', p. 348.   [4] *To Arbuthnot*, lines 382, 394 (*TE*, IV, 125–27).

Hopes after Hopes of pious Papists fail'd,
While mighty WILLIAM's thundring arm prevail'd.
For Right Hereditary tax'd and fin'd,
He stuck to Poverty with Peace of Mind.[5]

Although Pope knew none of his uncles, he was well endowed with aunts, particularly on his mother's side, and as a child he was close to at least two of these.[6] Christiana, a wealthy and childless widow, was the effective head of his mother's family, her elder by a full twenty years. She was his godmother, and when she died, just before his fifth birthday, she left him 'my painted china dish with a silver foote and a dish to sett it in and after my sister Elizabeth Turner's decease I give him all my bookes pictures and Meddalls sett in gold or otherwise' (Rumbold, p. 33). This and other hints suggest that the Turner sisters provided an atmosphere in which interest in the arts was sure of encouragement: in particular, the terms of the bequest to Elizabeth, together with the fact that her death in 1710 was commemorated in Pope's list of 'Departed Relations and Friends', make it likely that she was the 'old aunt' who lived with the Popes and taught him to read.[7] Moreover, Christiana must have chosen him quite deliberately as the recipient of her books, pictures and medals, probably because he had already shown an interest in them, for she had several other nephews and nieces to be remembered, most of whom received only money. In addition she bequeathed her husband's apparatus for grinding colours to Edith, suggesting that she too had an interest in painting (Mack, *Life*, p. 19). At the very least the Turner circle could not fail to suggest to a child that painting and drawing were important. Christiana's husband had also been an exceptional lutenist; and it seems likely that music had been a feature of the Turner home in York; but if it persisted into the girls' adult lives it has left no trace. Music never attained for Pope the significance of the other arts, and there is no evidence that anyone in the household played the harpsichord that came as part of the furnishings of his house at Twickenham.[8]

Thus Pope's early life was enriched by a circle of cultured and affectionate elderly aunts. Their pictures, some of them perhaps by Cooper, remained with him until his own death.[9] In 1717 he wrote on his mother's behalf to one of his Protestant aunts to break the news of the death of one of the sisters. He had probably visited this branch of his family in York when he went there with Burlington in 1716 (*Corr.*, I, 370, 433–44). From the atmosphere of affec-

---

[5] *Imitations of Horace*, Epistles, II.ii.54 (*TE*, IV, 169).

[6] The one maternal uncle who may still have been alive had emigrated to Spain, and Pope's father had quarrelled with his only brother (Mack, *Life*, p. 21; Rumbold, p. 32).

[7] Spence, no. 14; *The Works of Alexander Pope*, edited by Whitwell Elwin and William John Courthope, 10 vols. (London, 1871–86), I, ix (hereafter EC).

[8] Rumbold, pp. 26, 29; Mack, *Life*, pp. 226–31; Morris R. Brownell, *Alexander Pope and the Arts of Georgian England* (Oxford, 1978), pp. 368–71.

[9] He left the portraits to Magdalen in his will (*Prose Works*, II, 507).

tion and mutual service amongst the sisters, who were formally divided by religion (six wise and six foolish virgins, a relation had said), Pope was learning a lesson he would value far above the accomplishments his aunts could teach:

> In Faith and Hope the world will disagree,
> But all Mankind's concern is Charity.[10]

Pope's recollection that he 'learnt to read of an old aunt' reminds us of a factor almost as important to the domestic atmosphere as its Catholic piety and the imbalance between the sexes; for it was the elderliness of most of its members that put the finishing touch to a culture which would have exasperated many small boys both then and now (Spence, no. 14). Pope was far from feeling this: the knack of getting on with his elders, so characteristic of his social life in early manhood, was learnt very young. When his Aunt Christiana died, just before his fifth birthday, she was seventy, more like a grandmother than an aunt. By then his mother was forty-nine, his father forty-seven, his nurse forty-five, and his Aunt Elizabeth fifty-seven. It is hardly surprising that even before the onset of illness when he was about twelve, we hear nothing of the enthusiasms which make indulgent relations in rowdier families remark that 'boys will be boys' (Mack, *Life*, pp. 153–55). There is one glimpse of him aged about three playing at filling a toy cart with stones, but there is no other record of his ever playing at anything that did not involve books or pen and paper (Spence, nos. 3–4). Even at school he is said to have retired to his sketching when the other boys played games, and in his own eyes the highlight of his brief school career was the production of his Homeric play, with the school gardener dragged in to represent in Ajax a remote ideal of manly strength (Mack, *Life*, pp. 49–51). The ideal was to become even more remote as the boy with no brothers or uncles to suggest rough games lapsed into chronic illness. As an adolescent he was quite apart from the mainstream of his contemporaries, and in his twenties he was aware of his oddity to the extent of trying to be, or at least to appear, a rake; but the strain of late hours and tavern company was beyond him (pp. 289–93).

The fact that he passed with hardly an interval from infancy to invalidism consolidated his relationship with that most immediate female presence of his infancy, his nurse Mary Beach. In effect he was as swaddled and dependent in his later years as a contemporary baby·(p. 14). She did not live to see him reduced to quite that state, nor, mercifully, could anyone at the time have suspected that she had in all probability infected him with the turberculosis of the bone which made him so unusually dependent (p. 153).

It is possible that Mary had previously nursed his half-sister and his dead half-brother, for his father's tax assessments during his first marriage show that a 'Mary' was his only resident employee at that time (pp. 813–16).

---

10 Rumbold, p. 29: *Essay on Man*, III.307 (*TE*, III.i, 125).

Nothing is known of any child of hers, or indeed, of any Mr Beach; but the
fact that she stayed with the Popes from 1688 until her death might suggest
that she was by then a childless widow, all the more likely to lavish affection
on her employer's family. As an 'Old Gentlewoman' she seems to have
occupied a position in some respects more like that of a relation than a servant, taking a full part in the family's social life (*Corr.*, II, 32). When Parnell
visited Binfield in 1714 Pope jested that she was so charmed with him that
'(for all I know) [she] would even marry Dennis [presumably Parnell's
servant] for your Sake because he is your man & loves his master'; and she
was evidently a favourite with the Harcourt family (*Corr.*, I, 225, 491; II,
115). Indeed it seems from a note sent by Simon Harcourt the younger that
one of her roles was to be companion to Edith: 'the charriot will be with you
to morrow about eleven in which you must remember to bring my friend
nurse' (I, 491). To judge by the account of Pope's father's death given by
Magdalen, Mary was Edith's habitual recourse at moments of crisis.[11] Yet
her principal function, as a friend recognised, was to care for Pope: 'I must
not forget Good Old Nurse; I hope the Country Air, Regular Hours, and the
Care of the Old Gentlewoman will Re-establish your Health' (*Corr.*, II, 32).

When Mary died in 1725 Pope commemorated her both publicly, on a plaque
outside Twickenham church, and privately, in his list of 'Departed Relations
and Friends'.[12] In this list, where although a servant she is one of only three
women among the 24 entries, it is her fidelity that is stressed, 'nutrix mea
fidelissima'. This is also the theme of the public tribute: 'Alex. Pope, whom
she nursed in his infancy and constantly attended for thirty-eight years in
gratitude to a faithful old servant, erected this stone.'[13] Two days after her
death he meditated on the relationship in a letter to Lord Oxford, who had
recently lost his new-born and only son. Pope begins simply enough, with a
tribute which anticipates the terms of his inscription; but he soon moves on
to a more problematic discussion of the sensibility which makes men like
Oxford and himself so vulnerable to such losses:

My poor old Nurse, who has lived in constant attendance & care of me, ever since I
was an Infant at her breast, dyed the other day. I think it a fine verse, that of your
friend Mr Prior.

                              – and by his side,
          A Good man's greatest loss, a faithful Servant, dy'd!

and I don't think one of my own an ill one, speaking of a Nurse,

          The tender Second to a Mother's cares.
                                                    Hom. Odyss. 7.

[11] Sherburn, 'New Anecdotes', p. 348.
[12] Mack, *Life*, pp. 823–24; EC, I, ix.
[13] An irreverent response is recorded in *Gentleman's Magazine*, 54 (1784), 895, somewhat im-
    plausibly attributed to Lady Mary Wortley Montagu: 'No wonder that he's so stout and so
    strong, / Since he lugg'd and he tugg'd at the bubby so long.'

Surely this Sort of Friend is not the least, and this sort of Relation, when continued thro life, Superior to most that we call so. She having been tryd, & found, kind & officious so long, thro so many accidents and needs of life, is surely Equal to a meer Natural Tye. Indeed tis Nature that makes us Love, but tis Experience that makes us Grateful: and I believe, to thinking minds, Gratitude presents as many Objects & Circumstances to render us melancholy, as even Hope itself (that great Painter of Ideas) can do. But in truth, both what good-naturd minds have experienced, & what they Expect to experience, fills them to the brimm: The better a man is, the more he expects & hopes from his Friend, his Child, his fellow creature; the more he reflects backward & aggrandizes every Good he has receivd; His own Capacity of being Good & kind & grateful, makes him think others have been, or would be so.

(Corr., II, 336–37)

Apparently grief, here filtered through Homeric recollection in a way that substantiates Mack's suggestion of Homer's influence on the young man's notions of family piety, is the penalty incurred by the 'Capacity of being Good & kind & grateful' (Mack, *Garden*, p. 29).

In this letter Pope reveals an important mechanism in all his most intense relationships. He always took pleasure in setting those he loved in the best light, however implausible it might seem to others, and refused to dwell on the complications and contradictions which might have forced him to judge them more harshly: perhaps the two most notable beneficiaries were the ill-assorted idols of his later years, Bolingbroke and Warburton, but in this meditation on his nurse the process is explicit, showing how he cultivated the affection and generosity he aspired to by expecting the best of her and seeing the best in her. This response to Mary Beach raises two recurring problems. First, Pope had a great deal to gain psychologically by idealising particular people. Secondly, the sheer energy of his feeling can be dazzling, making it harder to see much that is individual in those he idealised. If these factors make it difficult to assess Warburton and Bolingbroke, who at least had public lives outside their contacts with Pope, they make it even harder to know women whose only claim to fame is that he loved them.

2

It is an indication of Edith's capacity for love that despite the claims of her own baby she won her stepdaughter's lasting affection. By the time Pope was born Magdalen was at least ten; yet despite the inevitable tensions of a reconstituted family the children grew up on good terms with each other and with their parents (Mack, *Life*, pp. 4, 813–14). They did not, however, live for long under the same roof, for by 1694, when Pope was only six, Magdalen was married to Charles Rackett of Hammersmith, where the Popes appear to have been living at the time, and in 1695 her first child was born (pp. 402–3). She was still only about sixteen, and her child lived only six months, facts which may have something to do with the families' evident desire to

establish themselves within easy reach of each other. The process began with
Charles Rackett's purchase of Whitehill House in Binfield, which was
occupied by a tenant. Soon after the tenant had gone, in 1698, Rackett sold
the property to his father-in-law, and at about the same time he bought nearby
Hall Grove for his own family. Although Pope had perhaps not lived long
enough with his sister to know her intimately, especially in view of the ten-
year age gap, she was a frequent visitor throughout the Binfield years.

It is suggestive that from the beginning Pope's references to Magdalen in
his letters – she is never referred to in his poetry – show a tension between
family piety and basic disparity of temperament. One cause of friction was
the case of the Westons, a marital disagreement in which Pope sided with the
wife and the Racketts with the husband, prompting Pope to comment that
'they have not been my relations these two months – The consent of opinions
in our minds is certainly a nearer tie than can be contracted by all the blood
in our bodies' (Corr., I, 144). Yet even here there was no open breach: when
Pope was staying with the Racketts and Mr Weston was expected, he simply
left (I, 426, 428). Magdalen was obviously happy to visit her brother in 1718
and to carry copies of the Homer translation between him and his copyist; yet
in a letter to the copyist, her neighbour Thomas Dancastle, his humour,
though affectionate, suggests how different in outlook they were:

Here is good Mrs Rackett in a melancholy way for want of your good company: she
says Chiswick is a very lonely place in comparison of Hallgrove; where, &
whereabouts, there are kept above 20 Coaches, besides Stages on the Heath which are
without number. This very moment she is in great distress, the spout of her Tea-pot
being stoppd, & she in impatient expectation of that Due Benevolence it ought to
dispense for her Breakfast.   (I, 519)

This vein of mild satire, so typical, for example, of the depictions of
fashionable women in The Spectator, enables writers to express an amused and
half-reproving tenderness for their female relations, confirming both their
love for and their difference from them. In the case of Pope's feeling for
Magdalen, it was obviously crucial that she was literally confined within the
domestic sphere by her young family: in 1719, for example, Edith is asked
to come and comfort her on the death of a baby; and sympathy is probably
behind Pope's insistence later that year on a visit from his 'dear sister' (II,
4, 9). By the time Charles Rackett died in 1728 Magdalen had four children
destined to survive; and at least two had died in infancy. It is hardly surprising that she was closer to Edith, for whom the Rackett boys must have
had the charm of the grandchildren her son would never provide. Being a conscientious wife and the mother of small children was a double disqualification
for intimacy with a man devoted to occupations requiring leisure and a clear
head.

The crisis which made Magdalen dependent once and for all on her brother's concern occurred in 1723, when her husband and one of her sons were implicated in 'blacking', a form of poaching with strong if obscure political connotations which had recently been made a capital offence (Mack, *Life*, pp. 402–6). The Racketts' involvement may even connect them with Jacobite intrigue, and it has been suggested that Walpole suspended prosecution conditionally on Pope's agreeing not to write against the government. If this was the case, Pope paid a high price for his duty to his sister, but the suggestion has not been readily accepted, largely because the date seems too early for Walpole to have so strong an interest in silencing Pope. Yet even if the consequences of the blacking affair were less dramatic, there is a strong likelihood that they included financial difficulties for Magdalen, and indirectly for Pope; for after 1723 Charles Rackett is heard of no more, having in all probability fled the country, as his son Michael certainly did. When Charles died, apparently in 1728, his finances were in such disarray that Pope devoted a large proportion of his business correspondence for the rest of his life to keeping Magdalen and her sons afloat.

From 1729 he writes regularly to Magdalen and to his legal advisor William Fortescue about her problems, and it is hard not to sense that as well as being touched by the bad luck that dogs her Pope is slightly, perhaps unfairly, irritated.[14] She finds it difficult to get debts paid; she cannot find suitable employment for her sons (one qualified as a lawyer only to find the profession closed to Catholics at the last minute); she cannot realise her capital investment in Hall Grove as no one will buy; and when Pope gives her money she loses it by not properly understanding her own interests.[15] Several of his friends also became involved at his instigation; John Caryll tried to help one of Magdalen's sons, although, interestingly, he could not remember how she was related to Pope; Bethel offered assistance; and Ralph Allen lent Pope £150 to help another son, apparently the sum which Pope attempted to return in his will.[16] Although these nephews evoked his genuine concern (and one apparently gave him particular satisfaction by his virtuous indifference to wealth), the fact remains that Magdalen's problems were a considerable burden to him, one imposed by his conscientious assumption that as head of the family he must take responsibility for his sister because her husband was no longer there to do so (Spence, nos. 111, 357).

Yet Magdalen too could have found grounds for resentment had she looked for them: if her father had not remarried she and not Pope would have been his heir, and she would have been spared a role which became in some respects that of a walk-on extra in the drama of her brother's life. The strains in her position can be appreciated from the skeleton biography which Joseph

[14] For Fortescue, see *TE*, IV, 360.
[15] These topics are frequently cited: see particularly *Corr.*, II, 530; III, 6–7, 39, 91, 112, 149–50, 153, 223–24; IV, 21, 203.
[16] *Corr.*, III, 172–73; IV, 21; Spence, no. 360. For Ralph Allen, see Erskine-Hill, *Social Milieu*, pp. 204–40, and chapter 9.5 below.

Spence began to construct as his friendship with Pope developed in the late 1720s. He first recorded Magdalen's recollections in 1728, the year of her husband's death, when she told him how as a small child Pope had been attacked by a cow while playing under her supervision (Spence, no. 3). Whether or not she realised it, she was interesting less in herself than as a witness to her brother's life, a role which could conceivably become irksome; yet with her father and her husband dead she would have been lost without her brother's zeal in taking responsibility for her affairs.

Ten years later, in 1738, she furnished Spence with more anecdotes, most significantly the brief note that 'I never saw him laugh very heartily in all my life' (no. 10). When Spence read this to Patty Blount in 1749, after Pope's death, she contradicted it; and Spence explained this from his knowledge of Pope's relationships with the two women: 'Probably he was more gay or less according to his liking the company: Mrs. B's he always liked, and Mrs. R's never.' This is a very strong statement, especially from a man who enjoyed the reputation of being 'the sweetest tempered gentleman breathing'; and it helps to suggest how deeply rooted the habit of duty must have been in Pope to produce such commitment to Magdalen's welfare.[17] After his death, Magdalen recollected that he had a 'very bad opinion of women', although she went on to talk resentfully about the women he liked: it was evidently she who had felt slighted.[18]

Another of Magdalen's reminiscences to Spence shows that she was far from dazzled by her brother's celebrity: 'For you know, to speak plain to you, my brother has a maddish way with him' (no. 28). Spence glosses this, 'Little people mistook the excess of his genius for madness': although Magdalen prided herself on having her feet firmly on the ground, Spence saw in this the sign of her inferiority. There is certainly something between disapproval and naive astonishment in her reaction to Pope's early absorption in study:

I believe nobody ever studied so hard as my brother did in his youth. He did nothing but write and read.   (no. 27)

She was not, however, totally without interest in writing, for she recollected after his death that he had once, as a child, illustrated an indecent ballad she had composed with some of her friends, and when in 1742 she explained that he had been inhibited from erecting a memorial to his dog inscribed 'O rare Bounce' by the fear of being thought to parody the celebrated epitaph on Ben Jonson, she clearly understood what was at issue.[19] Yet it was not literature that held them together, and another remark from the same year reverts to

---

[17] For this assessment of Spence, see Christopher Pitt, quoted in George Sherburn, *The Early Career of Alexander Pope* (Oxford, 1934), p. 1.

[18] Sherburn, 'New Anecdotes', p. 348.

[19] Sherburn, 'New Anecdotes', p. 349; Spence, no. 267.

the essential ground of their relationship: ' 'Tis most certain that nobody ever
loved money so little as my brother' (no. 354). By now his generosity had
been her support for fifteen years, and she gives him full credit for it.

Yet in the long term it was this relationship and the expectations it
engendered that soured her feelings for her brother. If she had ever believed
his duty to his father's daughter to be his paramount concern, his will was
ample proof that she had deceived herself: although the Racketts were not
forgotten, the principal heir was Patty Blount (*Prose Works*, II, 507). Ironically,
their financial problems had run in parallel through Pope's correspondence
with Fortescue, often being discussed in the same letters. At some level
Magdalen must have known that Patty had the stronger hold over her
brother, but his final infringement of the claims of blood enraged her. Once,
when Pope was luxuriating in the thought of Teresa Blount's tenderness for
her sister Patty, then seriously ill, he had confessed (whether forgetfully or
ironically) that he 'never had a sister', implicitly lamenting an enviable area
of sensibility that fate had closed to him (*Corr.*, I, 264). In contrast, when he
told Patty in *Characters of Women* that fate had given her a poet, he was defining
a tie above the accident of birth, and it was this relationship that he chose to
honour in the disposal of his estate (line 292).

As well as family mementos, his will gave Magdalen £300, £100 each to two
of her sons, and converted a bond for £500 due from another into a gift. In
contrast, Patty received most of his furniture and belongings, £1,000, and the
interest on the residue of his estate. Only after her death were further
payments to be made to the Racketts, who were further incensed by the fact
that as Pope had agreed to buy the lease of a house for Patty before he died,
Patty expected the cost to be deducted from the estate from which they
ultimately stood to benefit (see chapter 9.6). Magdalen's first reaction was to
try to have the will set aside, but this came to nothing. Ironically, since both
she and Patty had an interest in the estate they had initially to negotiate over
its management: as in the more famous case of Bolingbroke and Warburton,
the will had the effect of forcing together one of the least compatible pairs in
the poet's circle.

Not surprisingly, Magdalen and her sons saw as little as possible of Patty
after Pope's death, and in 1762 George Arbuthnot (Dr Arbuthnot's son and
Patty's lawyer) remarked that 'I really do not know where any of them are,
or if living' (Blount Letters, I, 154). Yet during the three or four years by
which Magdalen survived her brother she continued to be approached as a
source of Popiana. One group of reminiscences which apparently dates from
this period was recorded by Jonathan Richardson the younger, a close friend
of the poet, and these remarks have a sharper edge than any she had made
during his lifetime.[20] According to her, for example, he failed to notice when

[20] Sherburn, 'New Anecdotes', pp. 348–49; for Jonathan Richardson the younger, son of the
painter, see William Kurtz Wimsatt, *The Portraits of Alexander Pope* (London, 1965), pp. 142–43.

his mother fell dramatically into the fire, although he was in the house; he
fussed over his mother to the point that she told Magdalen she wished he
would leave her alone; he spoke coarsely of Teresa Blount; and he let Patty,
'a great Romp, & by no means a Prude', dupe him into believing her a virtuous woman.

Although it is hardly endearing to find Magdalen casting doubt on the
quality of her brother's devotion to Edith or on the good faith of the woman
Magdalen insisted on believing his mistress (he 'made a Secret of his Commerce there to his Sister', she told Richardson), it is at least understandable
that she should seize the opportunity to rewrite received history. Her less than
adulatory tone reminds us that there are disadvantages in being sister to a
genius.

3

Although Pope's love for his mother is celebrated, she herself is hardly known.
Three drawings of her by Jonathan Richardson survive, one from her early
sixties, the others from her late eighties: they agree in the calmness and dignity
of her expression, and the earliest, with its somewhat hooded gaze and lips
set in a slight downward curve, gives a hint of the elegant self-assurance captured in Samuel Cooper's picture of her eldest sister, Christiana.[21] We can
only regret the absence of a comparable portrait of Edith.

Pope mentions his mother in only two poems. In the *Essay on Man* she is
the final example in a list designed to show that the virtuous, like everyone
else, live lives of unpredictable duration:

> Or why so long (in life if long can be)
> Lent Heav'n a parent to the poor and me?
> (IV.109; *TE*, III.i, 138)

This is a remarkably discreet allusion, although the circle of those who can
grasp it is widened by Pope's status as a public figure in his own time: Swift
testifies, for example, that 'the papers have been full' of the news of her death
(*Corr.*, III, 378). More explicit are the allusions to her in *To Arbuthnot*, which
make an interesting comparison with the much more direct portrayal of his
father. Horace had set a precedent for praising one's father, but there was no
such precedent for praise of a mother.[22] The very fact that Pope tries to
include both shows his awareness that the Horatian model is inadequate; yet
he still leaves us with a relatively vague impression of his mother:

[21] For the three drawings, see Wimsatt, pp. 150–51, 173–76. One is engraved as frontispiece to
EC, VIII; another survives as a copy reproduced in Mack, *Life*, plate 64; and a photograph
of the earliest is included in Wimsatt, example 10. For a reproduction of Cooper's portrait of
Christiana, see Daphne Foskett, *Samuel Cooper and his Contemporaries* (London, 1974), p. 3,
no. 2.

[22] Horace, *Satires, Epistles and Ars Poetica*, Satires, I.iv.105–29; vi.71–99.

>   that Father held it for a rule
>   It was a Sin to call our Neighbour Fool,
>   That harmless Mother thought no Wife a Whore.
>
> (line 382; TE, IV, 125)

Quite apart from the typical distribution of the lines between the sexes, Edith makes less of an impression because her virtues are expressed negatively: she does no harm and refrains from slanderous speculations. Although negative praise is also important in defining her husband, he is commended for positive virtues as well, both in this poem and in *The Second Epistle of the Second Book of Horace*, where Pope (this time without a direct hint from Horace) focuses on his moral teaching and his response to Catholic disabilities, both arguably themes equally relevant to his mother.[23] As *To Arbuthnot* progresses, information accumulates around her without touching her individuality: Pope explains in a note that the 'part' of the family's 'noble Blood' that was 'shed in Honour's Cause' is a reference to her brothers who died in the Civil War, and she is once more glanced at in negative commendation when he commends his father for not 'marrying Discord in a Noble Wife' (lines 381, 388, 393). Even the famous lines on Edith's last illness are not so much about her as about her son watching her:

>   Me, let the tender Office long engage
>   To rock the Cradle of reposing Age,
>   With lenient Arts extend a Mother's breath,
>   Make Languor smile, and smooth the Bed of Death,
>   Explore the Thought, explain the asking Eye,
>   And keep a while one Parent from the Sky!
>
> (line 408)

The first extant version of this passage, described in 1731 as 'a few Lines I sent t'other Day from her Bed-side to a particular Friend' reveals something of the fear of loss that lies behind his contemplation:

>   Me long, ah long! may these soft Cares engage;
>   To rock the Cradle of reposing Age,
>   With lenient Arts prolong a Parent's Breath,
>   Make Languour smile, and Smooth the Bed of Death.
>   Me, when the Cares my better Years have shown
>   Another's Age, shall hasten on my own;
>   Shall some kind Hand, like B***'s or thine,
>   Lead gently down, and favour the Decline?
>   In Wants, in Sickness, shall a *Friend* be nigh,
>   Explore my *Thought*, and watch my asking *Eye*?
>
> (Corr., III, 226)

The final line, which is obviously modelled on his observation of Edith in her last days, is, in the preliminary fragment, part of Pope's worry about himself:

---

[23] *Imitations of Horace*, Epistles, II.ii.53–67 (*TE*, IV, 169).

he remembers that there will be no child to care for him, when, partly owing
to the strain of nursing her, he is reduced to the same condition. It is a natural
reflection, and it takes its rise from his love for her and his long dependence
on her; but bringing her into imaginative focus is not its primary aim. It is
arguable that any more vivid evocation of his mother's life in verse would
have seemed to him less a tribute than an impropriety.

Edith hardly appears in the correspondence before 1717, when with the
sudden death of her husband she was plunged into a combination of depression and illness which was to persist and worsen during her fifteen years of
widowhood. Even before this Pope had felt that her 'infirmities' made it
dangerous for her to travel, and the asthma which troubled her in later life
was evidently of long standing, to judge by Magdalen's report of her father's
dying words: he 'told Mrs *Pope*, he had a touch of Her disorder, Shortness
of Breath'.[24] Pope also believed that he had inherited his headaches from
her.[25] Unlike her husband, whose life 'to sickness passed unknown', she
existed in a state of debility in which every attack of illness seemed likely to
prove fatal (*To Arbuthnot*, line 403). Yet she had considerable underlying
toughness, for time after time she recovered, even surviving a fall into the fire
as late as October 1730, so that by the following March her son was describing
her as 'better than I' (*Corr.*, III, 141, 185). Hence despite the accumulation
of complaints with the years – rheumatism, jaundice, fevers, diarrhoea, loss
of memory – the impression is one of change without development. Although
Pope's favourite image for her life, that of a guttering candle, implies that she
could flicker out at any moment, she survived fifteen years after his first use
of the image in 1718.

In addition to her physical complaints she was often depressed, or as Pope
puts it, in 'that dispirited State of Resignation, which is the effect of long Life,
and the Loss of what is dear to us', and since she evidently needed the constant stimulus of company, Pope made sure that she was never long parted
from him and had plenty of visitors (I, 455, 517; II, 263). In 1723, for
example, when illness confined her to her room she liked 'to enjoy a few particular Friends when they have the good Nature to look upon her', and in
general Pope felt that it was 'so melancholy to her to be quite alone' that he
often cancelled visits to friends in order to be at home with her (II, 162, 484).
Yet towards the end, although he attended her as assiduously as ever, he had
to admit that she was 'now no companion' (III, 141, 185, 228).

Most of what we know about Edith's interests and activities comes from
Pope's correspondence; for she evidently had no aspiration to make a figure
in the fashionable world. Basic to her personality was the Roman Catholic
piety which she shared with her husband and passed on to her son. Both his

---

[24] *Corr.*, I, 340; Sherburn, 'New Anecdotes', p. 348.
[25] See the draft of *To Arbuthnot* in *The Last and Greatest Art: Some Unpublished Poetical Manuscripts
of Alexander Pope*, edited by Maynard Mack (London, 1984), p. 434.

parents, he told Spence, would have suffered 'a great deal of pain' had he converted to the Church of England, and after his father's death he repeated to
his friend Francis Atterbury, Bishop of Rochester, that she 'would think this
separation more grievous than any other'.[26] Yet she must have come to
terms with the fact that half of her sisters were Protestants, and her faith was
never a bar to friendship with non-Catholics – although Swift speculated,
perhaps accurately, as to what she really thought:

I thank Mrs. Pope for her prayers, but I know the mystery. A person of my acquaintance who used to correspond with the last great Duke of Tuscany, shewing one of the
Duke's letters to a friend, and professing great sense of his Highnesses friendship, read
this passage out of the letters, *I would give one of my fingers to procure your real good*. The
person to whom this was read, and who knew the Duke well, said, the meaning of *real
good* was only that the other might turn a good Catholick: pray ask Mrs. Pope whether
this story is applicable to her and me? I pray God bless her, for I am sure she is a good
christian, and (which is almost as rare) a good Woman.

(Corr., II, 394)

All observers seem to have reached the same conclusion. Almsgiving, which
made her 'a parent to the poor', was a religious duty all could admire; and
when Patty, after Pope's death, paid tribute to his charitable disposition it
seemed natural to her to relate it to his mother's example:

He did not know anything of the value of money, and his greatest delight was in doing
good offices for friends. I used to know by his particular vivacity, and the pleasure that
appeared in his looks, when he came to town on such errands or whilst he was
employed in them, which was very often. You knew his mother, and how good a
woman she was.[27]

Where observance was more specifically religious than ethical Pope preferred
the spirit to the letter to an extent which may perhaps have given his parents
some uneasiness, although his tact no doubt tempered his behaviour to them,
just as it led him in an early letter to an elderly town wit to minimise his attachment to the family religion:

I had written to you sooner but that I made some Scruple of sending Profane Things
to You in Holy week. Besides Our Family wou'd have been Scandalizd to see me
write, who take it for granted I write nothing but ungodly Verses; and They say here
so many Pray'rs, that I can make but few Poems: For in this point of Praying, I am
an Occasional Conformist. So just as I am drunk or Scandalous in Town, according
to my Company, I am for the same reason Grave & Godly here.   (Corr., I, 81)

Yet for his mother, prayer was a basic routine: in her late eighties 'she sleeps
not ill, eats moderately, drinks water, says her prayers; this is all she does'
(III, 117). Whatever his yearnings for a simpler, more inclusive style of

[26] For Atterbury, see G. V. Bennett, *The Tory Crisis in Church and State, 1688–1730: The Career
of Francis Atterbury, Bishop of Rochester* (Oxford, 1975). For Pope's general view of his inherited
faith see Chester Chapin, 'Alexander Pope: Erasmian Catholic', *Eighteenth-Century Studies*,
6 (1972–73), 411–30.
[27] *Essay on Man*, IV.110 (*TE*, III.i, 138); Spence, no. 358.

religion, filial piety effectively reinforced his allegiance to Catholic ritual:
in 1729 he asked Lord Oxford not to call on a particular day 'for my Mother
is to do a Christian duty that day at which I attend'. On his deathbed it was
the suggestion that he should 'die as his father and mother had done' that
prompted him to send for a priest, on whose arrival 'he exerted all his strength
to throw himself out of his bed, that he might receive the last sacraments
kneeling on the floor'.[28]

Christian charity came easily to Edith: she liked people and they liked her;
so that her son's friends would visit even when he was away.[29] Once introduced as the mother of a celebrity, she was able to consolidate friendships
with people as varied as Wycherley, Parnell, Lord and Lady Oxford, the Har-
courts, Molly Lepell, Digby, Atterbury, Broome, the Duchess of Buckingham, Swift, Gay and even Lady Mary Wortley Montagu, who made her the
double-edged compliment 'that (tho' I only knew her very old) she allways
appear'd to me to have much better sense than himselfe' (Corr., III, 449). Yet
especially for Pope's less intimate acquaintances she derived her appeal largely
from him: Abel Evans explicitly locates her merit in 'furnishing the world
with you' (II, 8). This is one factor in reducing our impression of her
individuality, but another is perhaps in the end more pervasive: she lived
happily absorbed in the concerns which the age held to be the realm of a good
woman, and it would hardly have been appropriate for her son to have
expressed his devotion by discussing the details of that privacy. Close friends
already knew her, and those less close were the less likely to be told about her
except in the most general terms.

As well as the friends that her son brought into their home Edith mixed in
local Catholic society: the Dancastles of Binfield, the Blounts of
Mapledurham, and their cousins the Carylls (with whom the Popes, probably
under their son's influence, sided during the controversy over Mrs Weston)
were particular friends. She also corresponded with Lady Swinburne, a
maternal aunt of Patty and Teresa Blount who had married into a Northum-
brian family.[30] She liked to have women friends within easy reach: for example, Pope writes to Caryll about Lady Seaforth, Caryll's relation by marriage,
'who is the best neighbour she has, and the only one she cares to visit, since
poor Mrs Stonor's death' (II, 117). Later he tells Broome that his mother
'wishes we were near enough to be neighbours to Mrs. Broome' (II, 296).
Magdalen, by her own account, spent time sitting with Edith. Her account
of Edith's fall into the fire makes an interesting contrast with her brother's,
for while she stresses that he was not in the room and did not notice the

[28] Corr., III, 11; Spence, no. 655.
[29] For appreciative remarks see for example Corr., I, 58–59, 253, 490, 491; II, 26, 47, 108–9,
114, 115, 193, 296, 355, 393–94, 498; III, 43.
[30] Corr., I, 171, 177; Howard Erskine-Hill, 'A New Pope Letter', Notes and Queries, 218 (1973),
207–9.

uproar, his accounts give no hint of this.[31] His perception of his care for his mother is that it is close and constant, but Magdalen seems resentful of the fact that he gets on with his own work in a separate room. Both perspectives are understandable.

Not surprisingly, the only extant sample of Edith's writing is a letter concerned with the comings and goings, pleasures and troubles of her friends and relations. It is a busy and unfocused account of her world which shows vividly (and not only in its old-fashioned female spelling) her distance from her son's literary poise. Typical of her female privacy, this solitary scrap, written in a bold hand of distinctively old-fashioned conformation, survives only because Pope wrote part of his *Iliad* on the back:

My Deare, – Just now is Come and gone Mr mannock and Charls Rackitt to take his leeve of us, but being nothing in itt doe not send it, he will not faile to Cole here one friday morning, and take Ceare to Cearrie itt to mr Thomas Doncaster he shall dine wone day with Mrs Dune in Ducke Street but the day will be unsirton, soe I thinck You had better to send itt to me, he will not faile to Cole here, that is mr mannock, Your Sister is very well but Your brother is not, There Mr Blunt of mapill Durom is ded the Same day that mr Ingilfild died, my Sirvis to mrs Blunts, and all that aske of me, I hope to here from You and that you are well, which is my dalye prayres, this with my blessing I am Your loveing mother Ed Pope[32]

This, the sole literary remains of a person whose fame rests on her relationship with a writer, raises the question of how far they shared each other's mental worlds. Mack has focused the problem by asking how far she can have understood the aggression and personal abuse which her son both suffered and inflicted, and has noted in particular that by early 1733 senility would most probably have prevented her from knowing anything about *Verses Address'd to the Imitator of Horace* – an attack on her son by their former friend Lady Mary, assisted by the husband of Molly Lepell, whom Edith had once welcomed into their home to convalesce from a serious illness (Mack, *Life*, pp. 548–49). Even before this Pope had been involved in plenty of public unpleasantness, and it is hard to imagine that he was willing to bring any of this into his mother's life, although his sister at least knew of the hostility he aroused and thought him foolhardy to go out with only his dog for protection (Spence, no. 365). Quite apart from the emotional and ethical problems of his career, there were specifically literary barriers between him and his mother: without classical learning she could have had only a limited idea of what he was doing when he translated Homer, wrote mock-epic or imitated Horace, and except for a hint that she had some books of Catholic devotion, there is no evidence of what, or how much, she read.[33]

---

[31] For the accident, see Sherburn, 'New Anecdotes', p. 348. Pope's accounts are found in *Corr.*, III, 141, 142, 144, 153, 155.

[32] *Corr.*, II, 29–30: the original is bound up with Pope's *Iliad*, BL Add. MSS 4808, f. 194v.

[33] The following anecdote, recorded by George Steevens, is not borne out by BL Add. MSS 4808 and may simply represent a misunderstanding of the fact Pope had written part of the

Perhaps the fact that her voice is heard only twice in Spence's *Anecdotes* means that she said little to interest the poet's biographer. One of these recollections, perhaps the more characteristic, shows her maternal pride: referring to a portrait of Pope at the age of seven, Spence notes, 'I have often heard Mrs. Pope say that he was then exactly like that picture, as I have been told by himself that it was the perpetual application he fell into, about two years afterwards, that changed his form and ruined his constitution' (no. 9). If she believed this, she may have resented the study that had blighted his early beauty; yet in her other recorded remarks, on the origin of his interest in poetry, she seems affectionately amused as she points the irony that her much-loved husband, so ignorant of the art that he did not even know its terms, had yet been able to set their son on the road to literary distinction:

> Mr. Pope's father who was an honest merchant and dealt in Hollands wholesale was no poet, but he used to set him to make English verses when very young. He was pretty difficult in being pleased and used often to send him back to new turn them. 'These are not good rhymes' he would say, for that was my husband's word for verses.
>
> (no. 11)

Although she was obviously alert, perhaps exaggeratedly so, to such details of usage, she seems to accept that his poetic training was properly left to his father.[34] Despite the fact that it was one of her sisters who had initiated him into the mysteries of the written word, Edith gives no sign that she saw a role for herself in this side of his development, although it is hard to imagine that she was anything less than enthusiastic about his achievements.

It is unfortunate that Edith's claim to be related by more than mere blood to the great satirist rests on a single utterance, though a telling one. It is reported by the Duchess of Buckingham, who writes to Pope on his return from a journey, 'I hope You found Your Mother in very good Health & made your peace with the old woman for staying abroad soe long she will probably describe You by the Gadder as she did Mr Compton by the Prater' (*Corr.*, II, 303). Sir Spencer Compton, whom Edith may have known personally, was at that time Speaker of the House of Commons: if this kind of verbal play was at all typical it helps to explain why her son's friends found her so much more than an old lady they felt obliged to be polite to, especially if they shared the Popes' disillusion with the political status quo.

Iliad on the back of Edith's only extant letter: 'It appears from manuscripts of Mr. Pope, that he occasionally indulged his affectionate and aimiable mother in transcribing some part of his *Iliad* for the press; and the numerous corrections made in his own hand, sufficiently shew, that her mode of spelling gave him more trouble than the subsequent inacuracy [*sic*] of his printers' (*Additions to the Works of Alexander Pope*, [edited by George Steevens], 2 vols. (Dublin, 1776), II, 88). For speculation about her books of devotion, see Owen Ruffhead, *The Life of Alexander Pope, Esq., Compiled from Original Manuscripts, with a Critical Essay on his Writings and Genius* (London, 1769), p. 171.

[34] Pope himself occasionally uses 'rhymes' in this sense, e.g. *Imitations of Horace*, Satires, II.i.146.

The only parallel to Edith's sharpness about Compton is a remark about
her son passed on by Magdalen:

Mrs *Pope* complain'd that most Children plagu'd their Parents with Neglect; that
He did so as much with perpetually teasing her with his Over-fondness & Care, &
pressing her to Eat this or that; and Drink another Glass of Wine; & so assiduous as
never to let her be at Liberty, & chuse for her self. Gave her great Uneasiness this
way.[35]

With a certain wit in pointing the irony, she could apparently stand back from
the relationship by which alone history knows her and declare her desire,
however trivial, to 'be at Liberty, & chuse for her self'. Muffled as they are,
such echoes of a critical, independent voice help to suggest why so many
people found her not only good, but also good company.

4

Whatever 'uneasiness' Edith may have felt from her son's fussiness, she
obviously loved him deeply, and was probably sensitive enough to realise, in
Mack's words, 'that good sonship occupied, in his case, a position of some
importance in that more or less edifying conception of the self by which we
all live' (Mack, *Garden*, p. 29). In other words, as in the case of Mary Beach,
his devotion reflected in part a deliberate cultivation of virtue. Two notable
images summed up what the relationship had meant to him, one created during her last illness, the other after her death.

The first of these is his commitment, finally placed near the end of *To
Arbuthnot*, to 'the tender Office . . . / To rock the Cradle of reposing Age'.
The second is embodied in the portrait by Richardson in which Pope is posed
'in a mourning gown with a strange view of the garden to shew the obelisk
as in memory to his mothers Death'.[36] This fixed in paint the daily reality of
his meditative presence in a garden where the obelisk had become the principal focus. Together the two images reveal something of the impulses and
perceptions underlying his devotion.

At the most obvious level, his devotion arises from gratitude: as he sets
himself 'to rock the Cradle of reposing Age' he remembers how his mother
once rocked him; as he contemplates the obelisk he remembers her as
'Matrum Optima, Mulierum Amantissima'. Yet this return of love has the
circularity of a dead end, for he has no wife or child to carry his family affections into another generation: his mother's 'Cradle' prepares her not for

---

[35] Sherburn, 'New Anecdotes', pp. 348–49.
[36] Described by William Kent, cited in John Riely and W. K. Wimsatt, 'A Supplement to *The
Portraits of Alexander Pope*', in *Evidence in Literary Scholarship: Essays in Memory of James Marshall
Osborn*, edited by René Wellek and Alvaro Ribeiro (Oxford, 1979), pp. 123–64 (pp. 141–44).
The portrait is reproduced both in Riely and Wimsatt (no. 56x) and in Martin (frontis-
piece).

maturity but for death; and although the obelisk leads his eye to heaven it does so by pointing to the emptiness of a world without her. There is, however, an ambiguous gain to set against his loss, as he grows into a sensibility compounded of gloom and tenderness: in the painting he is dedicated to mourning; while in the suggestive reversal implicit in the 'tender Office' of rocking the cradle he takes on a distinctively female role, as like a mother with an infant he faces the appeal to 'explore the Thought, explain the asking Eye'.

A crucial statement is one made to Swift in 1728:

> I am many years the older, for living so much with one so old; much the more helpless, for having been so long help'd and tended by her; much the more considerate and tender, for a daily commerce with one who requir'd me justly to be both to her; and consequently the more melancholy and thoughtful; and the less fit for others, who want only in a companion or a friend, to be amused or entertained.
>
> (*Corr.*, II, 480)

Here as so often he reveals a shifting balance of loss and gain as he expresses contempt for anyone shallow enough to value his lost gaiety above the restraining altruism he has learned.

One aspect of this restraint was his confinement, whatever his personal inclinations, to Roman Catholicism, with all the (to him) uncongenial practices and civil disabilities which it entailed. To Atterbury, who pressed him to convert to the Church of England after his father's death, he replied in terms of his care for his mother. Even after her death he practised the faith they had validated (as he no doubt saw it) by their lives:

> A rigid divine may call it a carnal tye, but sure it is a virtuous one: at least I am more certain that it is a duty of nature to preserve a good parent's life and happiness, than I am of any speculative point whatever . . . For she, my Lord, would think this separation more grievous than any other.   (*Corr.*, I, 453)

Yet even in confinement there are gains: not only is it a relief not to have to engage in doctrinal logic-chopping, but also, and far more importantly, it is a privilege to have experienced a relationship which he knows intuitively to be as sacred as religion itself. He defines this privilege most clearly when he recognises his mother as the stable centre of his inner life, a blessed contrast with the (in his view) silly mother and dissolute sister his friend Patty was doomed to waste her life with:

> I wish you were as free as I; or at least had a tye as tender, and as reasonable as mine, to a relation that as well deserved your constant thought, and to whom you wou'd always be pull'd back (in such a manner as I am) by the heart-string.   (II, 236)

Edith was no less a light to him for defining the shadows closing around him: in another letter to Swift in 1727 the thought that no one can replace her leads him to a simple expression of gratitude:

Yet so short and transitory as this light is, it is all I have to warm or shine upon me; and when it is out, there is nothing else that will live for me or consume itself in my service. But I wou'd have you think this is not the chief motive of my concern about her: Gratitude is a cheap virtue, one may pay it very punctually for it costs us nothing, but our memory of the good done. And I owe her more good, than ever I can pay or she at this age receive, if I could.   (II, 436)

Yet the perception has a darker side, most pointedly expressed to Caryll: 'my life is not half the consequence to anybody that hers is to me' (II, 352).

Such pessimism draws on his sense of having been a special burden to his mother because of his sickness and deformity, and he contrasts her love with the 'difficulty, or art' with which 'any body else' would have to brace herself for so disagreeable a task. This recognition of the possibility of pretence and constraint in intimate relationships goes as far to explain his steadfast avoidance of marriage as any of his more explicit remarks on the subject:

I am so unfashionable as to think my Mother the best friend I have, for she is certainly the most partial one. Therefore as she thinks the best of me, she must be the kindest to me. And I am morally certain she does that without any difficulty, or art, which it would cost the devil and all of pains for any body else to do.   (II, 265–66)

On one occasion when Pope was prevented from visiting the second Earl of Oxford by his mother's illness, Oxford wrote, with reference both to his friendship for Pope and his apprehensions for Edith, 'I could almost talk like a fond woman upon this occasion.' Pope in return declares: 'Your own heart will bear me testimony that no Woman's Tenderness can exceed that of a Reasonable & Grateful man, who loses a kind Parent' (II, 268, 270). Extreme emotion of this kind is thus seen by both men as typically feminine, but appropriate to men in particular situations. Without calling into question Pope's primary commitment to the rules laid down for men – as writer, public figure, head of the family, friend to his male friends and protector to his female friends – it is easy to see how the opportunities (or disabilities) which enabled him to experience so wide a range of less positive and assured roles, including the melancholy duty of caring for his mother, are connected with his willingness in *Eloisa* and the *Elegy to the Memory of an Unfortunate Lady* to enter into the gloom and passion of female confinement.

In describing himself to Swift as 'tender', 'melancholy' and 'thoughtful' he depicted a figure less like his public self than like his friend, the depressive poetess Judith Cowper, whose troubles were themselves reminiscent of the scornful doctrine laid down in *The Rape of the Lock* that splenetic creativity is a specifically female perversion (see chapter 4.1). Hence, despite the imaginative benefits conferred by the female sensibility he had embraced in the image of rocking the cradle, he was bound to disapprove at some level of his departure from the lucid world which was his native realm. We are reminded of this resistance by his reaction to something trivial, even comic: despite his childhood experience of an elderly, predominantly female household, his habitual submission to the routine of an invalid and his long confinement with a sick old lady, there was a limit to his tolerance of domestic distractions; and it was reached when he found himself pushed into the role of housekeeper. Unlike rocking the cradle, housekeeping resisted idealisation, and irritation is uppermost as he finds himself 'forced to attend to every thing, even the least cares of the family, which you'll guess, to me is an inexpressible trouble, added to the melancholy of observing her condition' (III, 53). His exasperation at finding himself burdened with such trivia shows his distance from literal identification with the everyday lives of women: his expansion of sensibility into the female sphere is something altogether more elevated.

His position with regard to his mother sometimes seemed to be one of pure loss. He is unusually specific in writing to Gay in 1729:

I have now past five weeks without once going from home, and without any company but for three or four of the days. Friends rarely stretch their kindness so far as ten miles. My Lord *Bolingbroke* and Mr. *Bethel* have not forgotten to visit me; the rest (except Mrs. *Blount* once) were contented to send messages. I never pass'd so melancholy a time.   (III, 3)

In preparing this letter for publication in 1735 he seems to have added some lines that he had written on his birthday in 1724, later to be included in a revision of his 1723 birthday poem for Patty (*TE*, VI, 244–47). There they function as a contrast with her 'gay Conscience of a life well spent', but here they point to the dead end of his own life:

> With added Days if life give nothing new,
> But, like a Sieve, let ev'ry Pleasure thro;
> Some Joy still lost, as each vain Year runs o'er,
> And all we gain, some sad Reflection more!
> Is this a Birth-day? – 'Tis alas too clear,
> 'Tis but the Funeral of the former Year.

Magdalen later recalled that Edith finally became 'quite childish', and that she once nearly 'choak'd her self with eating Asparagus, Ends & all'.[37] Although Pope never describes anything as painfully undignified as this, he confesses to Caryll that by 1729 her memory had decayed to the extent that she took in letters and forgot to pass them on: 'I found it by chance among linen 2 days ago' he apologises (*Corr.*, III, 30). In 1731 he finally had to confess that she was 'now no companion', and in the next year he reported that 'she is weak to such a degree as not to speak, even to me, thrice in 24 hours' (III, 228, 288). The poignancy of 'even to me' shows how he had become, in his own eyes and probably in hers, the sole figure in her field of vision, and in 1733, the year of her death, he still notes with relief that she 'is yet awake and sensible to me, tho' scarce to any thing else' (III, 349). He was still in what he had described as 'that most dismal situation of wishing for what can-

[37] Sherburn, 'New Anecdotes', p. 348.

not be, her recovery', and he confessed that the thought of her death 'confuses my whole frame of mind' (III, 274, 336). Yet although the prospect of a life beyond hers seemed empty, there were friendships which would carry him forward. Even in the same letter in which he finds his 'whole frame of mind' assailed by the prospect of her death, he makes himself put the thought of her aside as he asks Patty and Bethel to dine with him: 'you may, and she know nothing of it; for she dozes much, and we tell her of no earthly thing lest it run in her mind which often trifles have done' (III, 336). She finally died in June 1733, the month of her ninetieth birthday.[38]

5

Magdalen meanwhile, less alive to elevated sentiment and ever observant of consolations such as those her brother is seen arranging in the letter cited above, had formed the opinion that his emotional needs were thoroughly provided for, and in a way that did little credit to him and Patty: 'thought by many would declare his Marriage with her on his Mother's Death', she remarked to Jonathan Richardson.[39] Magdalen was certainly not the only one to draw this conclusion; but the letters Pope wrote to Patty show that the emotion with which he turned to her was far from the confidence of an accepted lover.

In 1728, for example, writing to Patty during a trip to Bath forced upon him by illness, he links his fear of separation from his mother with his fear that Patty is growing away from him:

I set out with a heavy heart, wishing I had done this thing the last season; for every day I defer it, the more I am in danger of that accident which I dread the most, my Mother's death (especially shou'd it happen while I am away.) And another Reflection pains me, that I have never since I knew you been so long separated from you, as I now must be. Methinks we live to be more and more strangers, and every Year teaches you to live without me: This absence may I fear, make my return less welcome and less wanted to you, than once it seemed, even after but a fortnight.

(*Corr.*, II, 511–12)

Here he is fearful that her feeling for him is on the wane; yet a few days later, cheered by a letter from her giving a good account of his mother's health, he makes her care for Edith a link between them: 'To think that a person whom we wish so much our friend as to take a concern in all that concerns us, should be cordially affected with things, is a greater and more tender pleasure than any of the same cares or testimonies from others' (II, 513). This, with its stress on 'wish', is surely too laborious, too insecure, for established intimacy.

---

[38] *Corr.*, I, 463. Pope and most of his biographers have been mistaken about her age: although Sherburn gives her date of birth as 1642, she was baptised on 18 June 1643, which means that she was almost certainly born that month (*Corr.*, III, 117; Mack, *Life*, p. 821, note 4; Rumbold, p. 27). For her death, see *Gentleman's Magazine*, 3 (1733), 326.

[39] Sherburn, 'New Anecdotes', p. 348.

The only other letter extant between this and his mother's death is the one in which he proposes that Patty and Bethel should dine with him without his mother's knowledge (III, 336). It is written in response to Patty's letter breaking the news of Gay's death: 'Let us comfort one another', he urges her, 'and if possible, study to add as much more friendship to each other, as death has depriv'd us of in him: I promise you more and more of mine, which will be the way to deserve more and more of yours.' Again, he seems less than assured of the intimacy he craves.

The secret marriage theory was attractive insofar as it accounted for Pope's attachment to Patty without challenging conventional ideas of the relations between the sexes. Although the nature of their relationship is ultimately mysterious, two obvious points can be made about Patty's role at this time. First, bereavement made him turn to his friends, whether in act or imagination: he hoped that Bolingbroke or Lyttelton would one day be to him what he was to his mother, he lamented Gay's death and Swift's exile, and he spent as much time as possible in the summer following her death staying at the homes of friends.[40] It says as much about the assumptions of the age as it does about Pope and Patty that her position as sole woman among his intimates was seen as a puzzle best explained by her being his wife or his mistress. Secondly, it was natural for him to turn to a person who echoed in so many ways the one he had lost, and had indeed, as far as we can tell, enjoyed an affectionate relationship with her (*Corr.*, I, 482; II, 17, 513). Patty belonged to the same world of Catholic piety as Edith, and could like her be idealised as one who despised public glamour and lived a quiet life devoted to friendship.

A strong reason for rejecting the secret marriage theory lies in its implication – at least as recounted by Magdalen – that in some sense Pope saw his mother as an impediment. In fact, his letters breathe no hint of relief at her death: rather they show him insisting on her continued importance. As he contemplated her corpse, he found her moral beauty captured in 'such an expression of Tranquillity nay almost of pleasure, that far from horrid, it is even amiable to behold it', and he asked Richardson to preserve in a drawing this 'finest Image of a Saint expir'd' (*Corr.*, III, 374). In another gesture which similarly goes beyond the obligations of filial piety he erected the obelisk two years later. Far from putting the past behind him he set it before him as a model, and as a sign pointing to a life beyond the grave (III, 453). Indeed, the position of the obelisk as the culminating focus of his long, narrow garden may even suggest that the spot was set aside for her before her death, and that the less eye-catching 'green theatre' which seems to have occupied the site previously was an inconspicuous way of reserving this privileged

---

[40] Bolingbroke and Lyttelton are respectively mentioned and addressed in the original draft of the passage which became lines 406–19 of *To Arbuthnot*; see *TE* note. For Gay and Swift see *Corr.*, III, 385; for visits in the summer of 1733 see pp. 375, 381.

space.[41] The obelisk was not completed until two years after her death, and her son's continuing commitment to remembrance is further underlined by Richardson's picture, completed five years after her death and showing Pope in a gown of 'second' or 'half' mourning (Riely and Wimsatt, pp. 143–44). Although he immediately recognised that her death marked 'a great and new Æra of my life' he also confessed that 'my whole amusement is in reviewing my past life, not in laying plans for my future' (pp. 375, 384). His home was so suggestive of his mother's presence that he could not settle to living there alone for several months: 'my home is uneasy to me', he told Bethel in August 1733, 'and I am therefore wandring about all this summer' (p. 381).

In September he wrote to Patty of the 'uneasiness . . . I find at Twitnam, whenever I pass near my Mother's room' (p. 385). It was Patty who came closest to filling the void, and at the end of this letter Pope turns his attention to her problems, which for the rest of his life were to provide an alternative focus for the solicitude fostered by his long care for his mother. Patty took on his mother's role as the fixed point in his relations with the opposite sex, and despite his contacts with many more obviously fascinating women, it was to her abiding presence that he inevitably returned.

[41] For the relative positions of theatre and obelisk, see Martin, pp. 48–49, 55–57, 59–60.

3

Reigning beauties

1

Pope entered the world he was to immortalise in *The Rape of the Lock* via his friendship with Teresa and Patty Blount, whom he had known since he and Teresa were about nineteen and Patty seventeen.[1] His parents had lived at Binfield from about 1700, and it was at Whiteknights, nearby home of Anthony Englefield, that he was introduced to his host's granddaughters, first Teresa and later Patty (Spence, no. 101). Their home at Mapledurham was also nearby, and they rapidly became his central point of contact with the world of fashionable young Catholics.

For some years before Pope met the Blounts he had been experimenting with inherited styles of writing to and about women. When only 'a Youth of 13' he produced imitations of Waller and Cowley in which a woman's slightest look or action casts the poet into slavery and despair. If, to quote Johnson, Cowley's love poetry 'might have been written for penance by a hermit, or for hire by a philosophical rhymer who had only heard of another sex', these youthful imitations are yet further removed from amorous passion – the real passion is Pope's desire to master yet another poetic mode.[2]

Radically different was the tone of bawdy insinuation which Pope learned from the elderly town wits who became his mentors in his late teens. In his letters to Wycherley and Henry Cromwell all females, the muses included, are discussed as sexually available, and it is interesting that even the Catholic patriarch Anthony Englefield, Teresa and Patty's grandfather and Pope's 'vir facetissimus, juventis meae deliciae', was quite at home with the language of the rakes insofar as he aimed, as 'a great lover of poetry and poets', to share the world of the wits.[3] He thought nothing of asking the young Pope to transmit to Cromwell the message that 'he hopes the Ladies of Drury are no less favorable to you now than those of Paris were formerly' (*Corr.*, I, 91). Yet Englefield, whose daughter Helena was a nun in the convent where his granddaughters were educated, was to introduce Pope not only to them, but probably also to the pious John Caryll, Patty's godfather; and if Pope was to joke

---

[1] *Corr.*, I, 258; *TE*, III.ii, 47. [2] Johnson, I, 42; *TE*, VI, 7–14.
[3] EC, I, ix; Spence, no. 101.

with Caryll's son about the 'one or two Dozen' women required for 'my ordinary Occasions' and the ruse of avoiding family prayers by retreating to the privy, it was equally Englefield's son who was to make a stand in the face of the penal laws by declaring his faith in the Real Presence when registering his land for double tax.[4] This easy accommodation between a fashionably rakish lifestyle and religious and domestic duty suggests a natural context for the pose of Pope's 'Farewell to London' of 1715:

> This Year in Peace, ye Critics, dwell,
> Ye Harlots, sleep at Ease!

(line 3; TE, VI, 128)

According to William Cheselden, the physician who attended Pope in his later years, the pose was not purely rhetorical:

He had been gay, but left it on his acquaintance with Mrs. Blount. He had been in fear of a clap, but even that was without grounds.

(Spence, no. 252)

Even when in the 1740s he was outraged by Colley Cibber's claim to have rescued him in youth from the embraces of an infected whore, his comment to Spence was suggestively equivocal:

He [Lord Warwick] carried me and Cibber in his coach to a bawdy-house. There was a woman there, but I had nothing to do with her of the kind that Cibber mentions, to the best of my memory – and I had so few things of that kind ever on my hands that I could scarce have forgot it, especially so circumstanced as he pretends.

(no. 251)

Mediating between the style of the rake and that of the enraptured lover was the epistolary gallantry derived from seventeenth-century French models. As an accepted mode of politeness, particularly associated with letters to ladies, it was a necessary part of Pope's repertoire. One of his first extant letters is a specific imitation of a letter from Vincent de Voiture to his patroness, the celebrated *précieuse* Mme de Rambouillet. Both letters are intended to accompany the gift of a book on drawing:

The Painters are a very vain generation, and have a long time pretended to rival Nature; but to own the truth to you, she made such a finish'd piece about three and twenty years ago, (I beg your pardon Madam, I protest I meant but two and twenty) that 'tis in vain for them any longer to contend with her. I know You indeed made one something like it, betwixt five and six years past: 'Twas a little girl, done with abundance of spirit and life; and wants nothing but time to be an admirable piece: But not to flatter your work, I don't think 'twill ever come up to what your Father made. However I wou'd not discourage you; 'tis certain you have a strange happiness, in making fine things of a sudden and at a stroke, with incredible ease and pleasure.

(*Corr.*, I, 4)

---

[4] Blount Papers, c. 63; Mack, *Life*, p. 89 and ' "My Ordinary Occasions": A Letter from Pope', *Scriblerian*, 9 (1976–77), 1–7 (p. 4); Howard Erskine-Hill, 'Alexander Pope: The Political Poet in his Time', *Eighteenth Century Studies*, 15 (1981–82), 123–48 (p. 143).

Emile Audra, the most detailed analyst of Pope's links with Voiture, finds this clumsy in comparison with its original.[5] It is certainly typical of Pope's compulsion to push a style of refined compliment towards *double entendre*.

Although indecency might be expected to flourish in his correspondence with elderly survivors of the Restoration, it is perhaps more surprising when addressed to ladies, particularly to an unmarried girl like Betty Marriott. Pope cultivated her and her mother under the auspices of their vicar, William Broome, his collaborator on Homer; yet he can open a letter by likening correspondence to seduction and develop a comic fantasy of her inflammable sexuality:

It is too much a rule in this town, that when a Lady has once done a man a favour, he is to be rude to her ever after. It becomes our Sex to take upon us twice as much as yours allows us: By this method I may write to you most impudently, because you once answer'd me modestly; and if you shou'd never do me that honour for the future, I am to think (like a true Coxcomb) that your silence gives consent. Perhaps you wonder why this is address'd to you rather than to Mrs. M— with whom I have the right of an old acquaintance, whereas you are a fine Lady, have bright eyes, &c. First Madam, I make choice of you rather than of your Mother, because you are younger than your Mother. Secondly, because I fancy you spell better, as having been at school later. Thirdly, because you have nothing to do but to write if you please, and possibly it may keep you from employing your self worse: it may save some honest neighbouring Gentleman from three or four of your pestilent glances. Cast your eyes upon Paper, Madam, there you may look innocently; Men are seducing, books are dangerous, the amorous one's soften you, and the godly one's give you the spleen: If you look upon trees, they clasp in embraces; birds and beasts make love; the Sun is too warm for your blood, the Moon melts you into yielding and melancholy.

(Corr., I, 205–6)

The fact that Betty's mother is included in the fun testifies to Pope's faith in its acceptability, although he confided later to Broome that he was concerned that he might have said something 'unpardonable' as 'I was not quite sober' (I, 227).

Betty was a relatively casual acquaintance, but in cases where his feelings went deeper Voiture could offer a specific if severely limited precedent for sophisticated indecency; for despite the decorum insisted on by Mme de Rambouillet, he occasionally permitted himself the kind of allusions which Pope, with his nudging insistence on the sexual aspirations behind the wit of his letters, took as precedent for his own indecencies. He declares as much in his imitation of a rondeau which he sent to Cromwell in 1710:

> You know where you did despise
> (T'other day) my little Eyes,
> Little Legs, and little Thighs,
> And some things, of little Size,
> You know where.

[5] E. Audra, *L'Influence français dans l'oeuvre de Pope* (Paris, 1931), pp. 330–32.

> You, tis true, have fine black eyes,
> Taper Legs, and tempting Thighs,
> Yet what more than all we prize
> Is a Thing of little Size,
>   You know where.   (*Corr.*, I, 90; *TE*, VI, 61)

This was his revenge on 'a Lady, who rally'd my Person so much, as to cause a total Subversion of my Countenance' (to judge by her physical attributes, probably Teresa Blount). In order to make a triumphant joke out of what must have been hurtful he takes what is unusually indecent in Voiture and makes it more so: there is nothing here of Voiture's ostensibly respectful opening, and hence nothing of the poignancy of the final *double entendre*:

> Ou vous sçavez tromper bien finement,
> Ou vous m'aimez assez fidelement,
> Lequel des deux, je ne le sçaurois dire,
> Mais cependant je pleure et je soupire,
> Et ne reçois aucun soulagement.
>
> Pour vostre amour j'ay quitté franchement
> Ce que j'avois acquis bien surement;
> Car on m'aimoit, et j'avois quelque empire
>   Où vous sçavez.
>
> Je n'attens pas tout le contentement
> Qu'on peut donner aux peines d'un Amant,
> Et qui pourroit me tirer de martyre,
> A si grand bien mon courage n'aspire;
> Mais laissez-moy vous toucher seulement
>   Où vous sçavez.[6]

This, however, is only one limited aspect of the way in which the potentially mocking hyperboles of French gallantry came to the aid of his deformity. Of far more general use was the licence to express attraction without giving the addressee any potentially embarrassing evidence which could be made to bear the weight of a literal reading. Moreover, the sheer wit of his complimentary fantasies would naturally focus attention on the one attraction in which he outdid all other suitors. As he notes in his *Guardian* papers on 'The Club of Little Men', in which he parodies himself as the diminutive Dick Distick, Voiture had also been 'petit et d'une complexion délicate', and had been able to joke elegantly about it, but Pope's need for wit in this respect was far greater. He writes to the Blounts, 'I am pretty sensible, that if I have any wit I may as well write to show it, as not; because any Lady that has once seen me will naturally ask, what I can show that is better?'[7] The joke is typically

---

[6] Vincent de Voiture, *Poésies*, edited by Henri Lafay, 2 vols., Société des textes français modernes (Paris, 1971), II, 141.
[7] Maynard Mack, *Collected in Himself: Essays Critical, Biographical, and Bibliographical on Pope and Some of his Contemporaries* (London, 1982), p. 374; Audra, p. 325; *Corr.*, I, 426.

disarming. In another letter, this time to Teresa, he playfully belittles his
talents at the opening of a letter much of which is calculated to dazzle by its
wit:

I have so much Esteem for you, and so much of the other thing, that were I a handsome fellow I should do you a vast deal of good: but as it is, all I am good for is to
write a civil letter, or to make a fine Speech. The truth is, that considering how often
& how openly I have declared Love to you, I am astonished (and a little affronted)
that you have not forbid my correspondence, & directly said, *See my face no more.*

(Corr., I, 350)

Everything about this style is double-edged: it would be ludicrous for Teresa
to take offence at such declarations as Pope pretends she ought to; yet the fact
that she does not is referable to his physique as well as to a literary convention
which discounts the literal, hence the underlying reality of the affront which
is ostensibly just part of the joke. His correspondence with women he found
attractive is full of such wit, as he deploys what he takes to be his only lure:
ultimately he was to define himself with some pride not as Patty's husband
or lover, but as her poet.[8]

This is not to say that his aspirations to the former roles were easily laid
aside. In the letters to the Blounts written in his twenties, and even more in
his letters to Lady Mary Wortley Montagu, a more than Voiturean licence
persists (see chapter 6.2). In his correspondence with the Blounts, however,
this is only one aspect of the broadening out from gallantry into an easier style
which can be both clever and bawdy, and more importantly both complimentary and expressive of real intimacy.[9] As early as about 1715 he could
address Patty as 'a friend that will think a kind letter as good as a diverting
one' *(Corr.,* I, 280).

Indeed, a degree of alienation from the Voiturean world of witty flattery
for the ladies is apparent as early as 1710, when Pope completed the poem
now known as 'Epistle to Miss Blount, with the Works of Voiture' *(TE,* VI,
62–64). As Audra notes, the poem's central passage on the wrongs of women
is not only irrelevant to the characterisation of Voiture, but antithetical to his
outlook; for much as Pope admires Voiture, he cannot share his complacency
about the role of women in the polite world:

> Too much *your Sex* is by their Forms confin'd,
> Severe to all, but most to Womankind;
> Custom, grown blind with Age, must be your Guide
> Your Pleasure is a Vice, but not your Pride
> By nature yielding, stubborn but for Fame;
> Made Slaves by Honour, and made Fools by Shame.
> Marriage may all those petty Tyrants chace,

[8] *Characters of Women,* line 292 *(TE,* III.ii, 74).
[9] For this evolution see James A. Winn, 'Pope Plays the Rake: His Letters to Ladies and the
Making of the *Eloisa',* in *The Art of Alexander Pope,* edited by Howard Erskine-Hill and Anne
Smith, pp. 89–118.

But sets up One, a greater, in their Place;
Well might you wish for Change, by those accurst,
But the last Tyrant ever proves the worst.
Still in Constraint your suff'ring Sex remains,
Or bound in formal, or in real Chains;
Whole Years neglected for some Months ador'd,
The fawning Servant turns a haughty Lord.

(line 31; Audra, p. 329)

Teresa – the likely addressee – was surrounded by men who played 'the fawning Servant', but Pope recognised that insofar as any of them might mean it seriously they were inviting her into a relationship at least potentially oppressive to her. As a landless cripple who could hardly hope to possess such a woman it was possible, even tempting, for him to risk insights at odds with the vested interests of more fortunate men.

Meanwhile, Patty and Teresa and their friends were playing out their own variations on the world of French gallantry. Educated in France, the sisters read in French throughout their lives, continuing to acquire French books long after they returned to England. Although their library included works in French on a variety of topics, including history, devotion and etiquette, the majority were romances, and of these the majority belonged to Patty.[10] The only romance inscribed with Teresa's name is marked 'Given me by Cap[tn] Bagnell' (whom family tradition suggests was the married lover with whom she shocked respectable opinion in the late 1720s); and the few other books which bear her name suggest an unsentimental outlook, notably *Réflexions sur les grands hommes qui sont morts en plaisantant*, placed on the index of prohibited books shortly before her death, and *Le Moyen de parvenir*, an irreverently satirical collection of obscene tales in the manner of Rabelais.[11] Nevertheless, it was the fantasy world of the French romances that provided the model for the epistolary game which both sisters, but especially Teresa, played with their Catholic friends and cousins. Like the members of the Rambouillet circle, these young people assumed the kind of names familiar from romances and bound themselves into a mock order of chivalry (*Corr.*, I, 252). To judge from the letters written by 'Silvia' to 'Parthenissa' (Patty), the game began in about 1708, when Patty was eighteen and Teresa twenty, and lasted, if only in a vestigial form, into the next decade.[12]

[10] See the catalogue of the Blount library down to the present day compiled by Richard Williams. Romances inscribed with Patty's name – mostly in French but including some translations – include works by Madeleine de Scudéry, Marie-Madeleine Comtesse de la Fayette, Gauthier de Costes de La Calprenède and Honoré d'Urfé.

[11] I am indebted to Richard Williams for the suggestion that Captain Bagnall may have been Teresa's lover (see chapter 9.2). The book he gave her is [Marie-Madeleine Comtesse de la Fayette], *Zaide: Histoire espagnol* (Paris, 1705). See also André François Boureau-Deslandes, *Réflexions sur les grands hommes qui sont morts en plaisantant* (Rochefort, 1714), and François Béroalde de Verville, *Le Moyen de parvenir* (Chinon, no date).

[12] Like most of the letters to Teresa and Patty among the Blount Papers, Silvia's have been bound into the three-volume set hereafter referred to as Blount Letters (III, 91–95).

At the beginning the formalities of the game were prominent: in a letter of 4 October 1709 Silvia reports from London that Lord Waldegrave 'tells me that in less than a months time he will send us a hundred seals of our order to distribute amongst our brothers and sisters, but he has so often broke his word in ye affair y^t I begin now to have no faith in what he sayes'.[13] At least one of the vows imposed on the members is implied in Silvia's apology for the dullness of her letters: 'but our order obligeing us to charity I am in hopes you will have so much as to forgive my nonsence and let me hear from you very soon'. As well as charity there was to be romance, whether simply as imitation of the familiar rhetoric of literary romances, or more ambiguously as a way of handling the excitement of emergence from a cloistered education into mixed society. A draft of a letter concerning Silvia, perhaps by one of the Blount sisters, shows both the literariness and the possible real-life application, as the writer warns that just as Silvia was once Octavio's slave, she is now in danger of becoming Damon's:

> & is Sillvia so Little skilled in Love to Declair her self a nenimey to the Sex; she once adored . . . trust to y^r frosen hart no Longer: Sence Like a river soe it Loosens from y^r Side & Longs to be mellte'd with Damons Beams Shun him as Death heatte every thought of him & know he is y^r Bain.

(Blount Letters, III, 91)

The whole group, who called each other brother and sister, presumably helped to choose each other's names. Certainly the Blounts' names suggest vividly the different attractions their friends found in them: Teresa's 'Zephalinda' suggests freshness and perhaps flightiness (the suffix has connotations of coquetry), and Patty's 'Parthenissa', perhaps borrowed from the would-be romantic heroine of Steele's *The Tender Husband*, captures a quality of maidenly shyness, as well as echoing her familiar diminutive.[14] Unfortunately, Patty's role in the game is less clear than Teresa's, and it is impossible to tell whether this is because Patty was less involved, or because her letters were not preserved. The letters now extant comprise three to Parthenissa from Silvia, one from Alexis, and one from Henry Jernegan, but no drafts of her replies; while in addition to three drafts of Zephalinda's replies to Alexis and one to Typographate there remain twenty-two letters to her from Alexis and five from Typographate.[15] However, since letters to one sister

---

[13] This is ironic in view of Lord Waldegrave's later renunciation of Catholicism in favour of a career as courtier and diplomat: see G.E.C., *The Complete Peerage*, revised by Vicary Gibbs *et al.*, 13 vols. (London, 1910–40).

[14] For the suffix '-linda' see Robert N. Gosselink, 'Pope's Belinda: The Very Name of Coquette', *Papers on Language and Literature*, 14 (1978), 218–23. For Steele's Parthenissa (alias Biddy Tipkin), see *The Plays of Richard Steele*, edited by Shirley Strum Kenny (Oxford, 1971), pp. 223, 239.

[15] These correspondences are found as follows: Blount Letters, III, 91–95 (Silvia to Parthenissa); I, 191–92 (Alexis to Parthenissa); II, 108 (Henry Jernegan to Parthenissa); III, 148, 153–54, 156 (Zephalinda to Alexis); III, 153 (Zephalinda to Typographate); I, 189–90, 193–232 (Alexis to Zephalinda); III, 115–24 (Typographate to Zephalinda).

generally mention the other, the collection sheds light on the circle in which both sisters moved.

All the correspondents are enthusiastic participants in the diversions of fashionable society, and within that society they belong to a clearly defined subgroup as sons and daughters of the old landed Catholic families. Silvia has Stonor and Fermor cousins and attends functions given by the Duke of Norfolk; Alexis is in real life Henry Moore of Fawley, of the same family as Teresa and Patty's great-grandmother Blount; and Typographate, probably named for the print-like regularity of his italic hand, is thoroughly at home in the Fermors' house at Tusmore.[16] Henry Jernegan, who uses the sisters' romance names but signs his real name, is a younger son of Sir Francis Jernegan of Costessey in Norfolk who became a distinguished goldsmith and jeweller.[17] Like Pope, who used the Blounts' romance names in verse but conducted his prose correspondence under their and his real names, Jernegan seems to have been on the fringes of the game. It may be more than coincidence that the younger Jernegans (another practised as a doctor) were, like Pope, outside the charmed circle of Catholics who relied entirely on landed property for their livelihood.

The brothers uniformly begin their letters by striking a pose of hopeless passion, but none gives the slightest grounds for belief, since their writing tends invariably to self-parody, whether by inflating hyperbole to the point of collapse or by bringing it into explicit contrast with more down-to-earth attitudes. Teresa too begins from the romantic role assigned her sex – in the first instance heroines are outraged by professions of love and command their lovers to repress their unruly passions – only to reveal herself as less obsessively pure and tougher than a heroine. The playing out of the game can be observed between her and Typographate. Teresa insists that his professions of love must cease, and the reader of her sharp-tongued letters can only agree with her that he has 'choose a wronge person to be imposed upon in thatt kind', since all that interests her is to know 'what opra was acted or whatt town news ther was'. In his reply Typographate repeats her words with mock ruefulness ('You say, *Correspondence is a thing as unfitt for me to desire as you to Permitt*') and insists that if she did write to him as he begs her to, he would never compromise her reputation by showing her letters: 'no I would be hack'd in ten thousand pieces, before I would doe such a base thing'. Needless to say, there is nothing in any of Teresa's letters to justify any such scruple.

[16] James T. Hillhouse, 'Teresa Blount and "Alexis" ', *MLN*, 40 (1925), 88–91; Sir Alexander Croke, *The Genealogical History of the Croke Family, Originally Named Le Blount*, 2 vols. (Oxford, 1823), II, table 14 facing p. 278.

[17] The spelling of the name varies: details of Henry and his family are given by John Kirk, *Biographies of English Catholics in the Eighteenth Century*, edited by John Hungerford Pollen and Edwin Burton (London, 1909) ('Henry Jerningham') and in *The Jerningham Letters*, edited by Egerton Castle, 2 vols. (London, 1896), 'A Descent from Three Martyrs' at the front of I.

Whenever Teresa affects the severity of a heroine, her forthright self-assertion and coquettish consciousness of her charms reveal both the artificiality of the game and the piquant licence it conferred on the participants. In a letter to Alexis, written, she declares, 'neither . . . to devert my selfe nor you', she demands that he should send immediately 'those stokins that you were imploy'd about' and adds a teasing ultimatum: 'these I ware begin to be very thinn . . . I shall get an ugly way ellce of hiding my feet and legs when I step out of a Coach, thro the custom of haveing Darns above my shooe'. In a sense, her indelicacy is simply a strategy for survival among young men intent on reducing her to blushing confusion: when, for example, she asks Alexis to make an appointment for her and her sister with Mr Gibbons the hairdresser, his automatic response is, 'Mr Gibbions was allways a great man with the Ladys of Covent Garden'. Teresa's riposte is that Alexis is a procurer (i.e. because he has to contact the hairdresser), and he ought to know. In return he labels her readiness in bawdy repartee as 'Malice':

> You are grown I suppose so scrupulous nice a Lady, since you were last in Town, that you would no more take a Pen between your Fingers to write to a Man than – Now will I leave your Imagination to frame a bawdy Similitude, wch I am certain your Malice will suggest to you.

If these were the terms on which intimacy with her male peers was to be had, Teresa was not one to be forced blushing into a corner. Perhaps this is one reason why Patty, whose blushing response to *double entendre* so delighted Pope, is scarcely represented in the writings of the brothers and sisters (*Corr.*, I, 143, 256, 375).

Teresa's wit certainly impressed Alexis, to judge by her success in engaging his own. Like Pope in his relationships with witty women, he was both fascinated by her sharpness and uneasy at its relation to her sex: 'there is a happiness in all you say or write that glitters & is as valuable as gold to our understandings: But I must desire you not to attack me in Verse . . . if you turn Poet I will turn Fop, not at all doubting but my finery will prove as destructfull to your eyes, as your Verses to my understanding'. Although writing is man's domain and dressing woman's, it is an aphorism of Teresa's which sets him off on a fantasy of writing a proof that the deadly sins are really virtues. This treatise is to be 'founded on a Principle & Tenet of y^r own viz: That buying a lac'd Head, tho' there·may be pride & vanity in the wearing of it, is one of the highest acts of Charity that can be exerciz'd towards our Neighbour'. Teresa was in fact exhorted by one of the nuns who had educated her in Paris to patronise some of her nieces, 'poor Catholick gentlewomen' who were trying to earn their living by millinery, so her excuse for buying finery may not be as specious as it appears (Blount Letters, II, 146). Alexis, however, takes her remarks as confirming her female vanity, and he goes on to separate her sphere from his by the proviso that while his contribution to

the new ethics is to write, theirs is to seduce: 'those men that I cannot over-
come by argument you shall by temptation, a Woman's surest & readiest way
of confuteing, for I ever found better reason in a Woman's face than in her
dialect'. Although Teresa was well able to put him down by pretending to
stand on her dignity ('The vain and sensuall man appears before you proceed
ten lines; for the very first query you proposed was only to excuse yᶜ vanity
of your head, & the latter to gratify the loose inclinations of your hart'), this
was a game which insisted on woman's role as gilded bait for mankind.

Town gossip, which gives pride of place to the success or failure of girls in
the search for husbands, is the subject of overriding interest in this circle. The
plays, operas, balls and card parties attended by the brothers and sisters provide the scene in which the drama is played out, and the writers' employment
of the formula of romantic passion provides a framework for correspondence
and a means of filling out letters when the town is dull. Typographate makes
comedy out of the juxtaposition of his opening pose of hopeless love with the
trivia of fashions, marriages and deaths, 'yᶜ chatt of yᶜ town', which is the
real stuff of his friendship with Teresa. Alexis makes her interest in match-
making yet more explicit: 'You desire to know how Lovers thrive in Town,
if you mean as to constitution I will inform you, if as to success I must beg
your pardon, for I am sworn to Secresy & intrusted by half a dozen well lookt
& well fed Couple'. Even the more naive Silvia assures Patty that 'I hear
nothing but complaints for the absence of fair parthenissa who is justly accused
of robbing the gentlemen of there hearts'; and she gives accounts of the shops,
balls and parties which provide the context for these artificial yet nonetheless
exciting approaches to courtship. Given these delights in town there is a pleasant though innocent irony in Silvia's remark to Patty that 'I think as you do
that london air is very refreshing some times and believe you will find it
nessessary for your health for the country in cold weather is certainly very
unwholesome'. Thus not even the relatively shy Patty was immune to the
charms of the flirtatious social life which absorbed so much of the energy of
the young Catholic circle. Alexis feigns to concur with Teresa's mock denun-
ciation of 'that teizing disgustfull impertinence Love' and declares that he
finds it merely 'a ready subject when a Man has nothing else to say'.
However, the hard facts of his writing are just as concerned with sexual pursuit, although in the very different world of the marriage market, as the
romantic flights which he derives from the fantasy world of chivalry. Politics
is mentioned by the members of the order only in passing and there is the
merest sprinkling of anecdote about the non-Catholics whom they met socially,
but the bulk of comment concerns the marital prospects of girls like Teresa
and Patty.

Pope was later to write of a woman skilled in refinements learned from the
romances (her name is reminiscent of Rambouillet-style pseudonyms), and of
her shocking capitulation to less ideal compulsions:

> Philomedé, lect'ring all mankind
> On the soft Passion, and the Taste refin'd,
> Th'Address, the Delicacy – stoops at once,
> And makes her hearty meal upon a Dunce.[18]

The crucial compulsion for girls like the Blounts was not so much sex as money – in the context of a religious community which depended for survival on the continuing wealth of its constituent families.

2

In the perspective of the marriage market the glitter of a Belinda and the gloom of an Eloisa or an Unfortunate Lady are intimately linked, as Pope was able to observe from his privileged position on the sidelines.

Despite the zest with which girls like the sisters of the order of chivalry embraced town life, there were troubling contradictions beneath the surface. As Catholics they were offered conflicting accounts of what they were in the world to do. On the one hand routines supervised by nuns at school and by chaplains at home emphasised spiritual priorities, but on the other hand their duty of disposing of themselves for their families' best interest was made more urgent by the special needs of a religious minority which now felt its persecution most keenly in financial terms. Thus dressing well, deploying their charms to advantage in the world of 'Courtly Balls and Midnight Masquerades' and learning a due respect for the wealth of prospective suitors could ironically be necessary virtues in girls whose confessors urged (to quote a priest's advice to Teresa and Patty's mother) 'a separation as much as possible from ye amusements, divertisements, and vain intertaiments of creatures'.[19] As Pope noted in 'With the Works of Voiture', the matrons who guided girls in the marriage market had made certain adjustments in the direction of expediency: 'Your Pleasure is a Vice, but not your Pride' (line 34).

If a glittering marriage to a substantial heir symbolised the forces pulling in one direction, the example of the nuns who educated Catholic girls was a reminder of more austere demands. Although Elizabeth Meynell, Teresa and Patty's teacher in the English Benedictine convent in Paris, found them quite adorable and fussily chose Teresa a new damask coat when her old one 'was so very ragged 'twas not fitt for her to appear in before any Strangers', the fact remained that such teachers had renounced the world for which their pupils, for the most part, were being prepared, and this renunciation was far more easily reconciled with the religion they were taught than the fashionable life that awaited them on their return to England (Blount Letters,

---

[18] *Characters of Women*, line 83 (*TE*, III.ii, 57).
[19] *Rape*, I.72 (*TE*, II, 151); Blount Letters, II, 149 (the priest is J. Witham, probably the James Witham O.S.B. described by Kirk).

III, 137). The point was sharpened for Teresa and Patty by the presence in the same convent of their maternal aunt Helena Englefield, who continued to write to them after they had returned home, wistfully regretting that neither of her nieces felt the call of the monastic life:

You are much coveted amongst us, but I dare not flatter myself with such agreable thoughts, fearing the world will rob you of us, but however since you are not yet fixt in Babylon Ile still hope to see you on Mount Sion; Certainly your parts of the world are much corrupted to afford soe few vocations, for never was our house soe slenderly furnishd with white heads as now.   (Blount Papers, c. 63)

Aunt Helena's distrust of the wickedness of England perhaps gestures towards the frivolities to which one at least of her nieces rapidly became addicted: as a nun she could only have been alarmed had she been able to read a letter to Teresa from her friend Miss Trevor, addressed to her at Grinstead, where Teresa was staying with the Carylls:

But tho your Description is amusing, It Convinces me but too plainly, that Dr Terry is not suited to her present situation, nor can her society at home, or her unanimated hardships a broad, support that uninterrupted flow of spirits, wch the most unhappy of our acquaintance could never see without some degree of satisfaction.
                                                          (Blount Letters, III, 165)

Teresa's captivating liveliness evidently turned to satirical dissatisfaction when confined to the pious routine of the type of household into which she should have aspired to marry: what was intended as the means – a social whirl in which to charm eligible Catholic heirs – had become her end in life. In the light of Miss Trevor's perception, the sympathy expressed in Pope's 'Epistle to Miss Blount, on her Leaving the Town, after the Coronation' (1714) is highly specific:

> She went, to plain-work, and to purling brooks,
> Old-fashion'd halls, dull aunts, and croaking rooks,
> She went from Op'ra, park, assembly, Play,
> To morning walks, and pray'rs three hours a day.
>   (line 11; TE, VI, 125)

The understanding between poet and addressee may be further implied in a line of what is probably part of a rejected draft, 'Some strangely wonder you're not fond to marry': anyone who wonders at her lack of enthusiasm for the duties of a wife hardly knows Teresa.[20] In contrast, Patty was far better

---

[20] The Twickenham editors first published this fragment under the title 'Lines suppressed at the End of the Epistle – To Miss Blount, on Leaving the Town, etc.'; but later, in the one-volume edition, they changed the title to 'Epistle to a Lady'; whom, influenced by Ralph N. Maud, 'Some Lines from Pope', *Review of English Studies*, 9 (1958), 146–51, they surmised to be one of the maids of honour (*TE*, VI, 232; *The Poems of Alexander Pope: A One-volume Edition of the Twickenham Text*, edited by John Butt, corrected edition (London, 1968), p. 308). To summarise briefly, Maud's arguments fall under three main heads: since the alleged

adapted to the role of mistress of a Catholic household. If an early letter from Mrs Howard is any guide, she found it positively wearisome to dress up for formal occasions, and her love of rural retirement and long walks is a constant theme of her correspondents, who include throughout her life admiring clergy both Catholic and Anglican.[21]

It is impossible to be sure whether the Blounts remained unmarried through choice or necessity, but the likelihood is that after their father's death in 1710, when it became clear that the estate could not meet the obligations laid down in his will, their lack of adequate dowries prevented them from receiving offers equal to their expectations – or, it may be, any offers at all.[22] There is thus a poignant contrast between the rhetoric of the order of chivalry, which insists on their irresistible beauty, and the evident ability of their correspondents to resist them. Even if there were tentative proposals – Alexis hints at an imminent change of their names to their advantage, though he may be joking; and it has been suggested that Pope wrote 'With the Works of Voiture' when it seemed that Teresa was 'destined Hymen's victim' – there is a definite sense of declining prospects as they advance into their twenties (Mack, *Life*, p. 247).

In the earliest letters after their return from school, Sylvia's to Patty in 1708, Patty's power over men is a constant theme: Sylvia tells her, for example, that she had a visit from a gentleman who could not talk about anything else. Around 1711, as the sisters prepare for a London season, Alexis hints that even the young Lord Petre (later the Baron of *The Rape of the Lock*) need not be out of their reach: 'I shall expect shortly to hear of some great Conquest in the Kingdome of Love since Zephalinda's & Parthenissa's Forces are taking the Field; if the young Ld P. that is just entring Cupids Lists should happen to be made y^r Prisoner, treat him wth generous clemency & compassion.' Hereafter he repeatedly teases them with their supposed disappointment as one eligible man after another chooses a bride. For example, in 1713, 'Mr Crathorn is goeing to be married to a great Fortune, I shall prepare a

original is lost, it cannot be proved that these lines run continuously with the 'Coronation'; Zephalinda is too innocent to be addressed in such bawdy terms; there is no logical connection between the last line of the poem and the first of the fragment. Of these arguments the strongest is the first; no reader of the Zephalinda–Alexis letters could maintain the second; and the third could suggest simply that the fragment parted company from the poem before it reached its final form. The view that the fragment was composed for Teresa remains plausible: it is no bawdier than other epistles she was happy to read – and to write; the sentiments on marriage suit her; she was on intimate terms with Gay (see his letter in the person of her horse in Maynard Mack, 'The Happy Houyhnhnm: A Letter from John Gay to the Blount Sisters', *Scriblerian*, 11 (1978), 1–3); 'B—' may, as the Twickenham editors first suggested, stand for the Blounts' friend Bethel; and 'Sir Harry', not an uncommon name, could be, for example, Sir Henry Tichborne, soon to be Michael Blount's father-in-law. Whilst certainty is impossible, the fragment is probably what it purports to be.

21 Blount Letters, III, 160 and *passim*.
22 Several documents among the Blount Papers allude to the shortfall: see for example Helena Englefield to her nieces in 1715: 'I know you are sensible of how much short y^r dear fathers estate fell of what he computed' (c.63).

willow Riband for a certain Lady of my acquaintance.' The term 'fortune' in this context is telling.

Already Teresa, whether from distaste for a career as wife, mother and housekeeper or from hurt pride, is hinting that marriage is a business deal best stripped of its sentimental pretensions. When Alexis reports that a lady has fallen for his new suit, Teresa says he cannot do better than marry her; and she is so scornful of the idea of marrying a young husband that she prompts him to propose to her a brisk old man of his acquaintance. Such a rejection of sentiment may be simply putting a brave face on her own failure to attract proposals: for however often Alexis makes the formal tender of his heart he does not hide from the sisters that he is involved in serious marriage negotiations. When his current scheme falls through, his silence as to any ambitions in their direction speaks for itself: they are fun to flirt with, but not rich enough to marry. Viewed in this perspective, some of his writing is tactless if not positively cruel. Having written an attack on Teresa under the name of Olinda, he pretends to draft her reply in the form of a will in which she bequeathes such qualities as 'unspotted reputation', 'wit & understanding' and 'my voice & my shape' to rivals who need them. The closing stroke is to will 'all the portion my father design'd me' to a girl who is gambling hers away. The phrasing suggests that the money is as fictitious as the proposed disposition of it; and the bitterness of the satire against Teresa's peers that Alexis puts into her mouth hints at a jealousy of their popularity that is no secret to male observers.

When Alexis quotes Pope's 'Two or Three; or, A Receipt to Make a Cuckold' and notes that it 'has no Relation to Ladys in their virginall capacity' since 'there must be more than two or three things to bring them to ye matrimoniall lure', his rhetoric of marriage as a male conquest for which he is unqualified mocks their real disadvantage in attracting serious suitors (*TE*, VI, 104–5). In the same vein he rhapsodises on the 'Witchcraft' by which they entrance beholders but wonders 'if it extends so far, as to have any efficacy of powerfull operation upon Matrimoniall Love, because I cannot find hitherto that either of you have practis'd it that way'. He is more frank when he teases Teresa with being 'a Maid & that too shrewdly against your will & inclination'; or when, describing a lady who 'would give up all her former, present & future Admirers, to confine one Man in sacramentall fetters', he hints that 'some other Ladys of my acquaintance' are in the same position. His most outspoken comment on the discrepancy between Teresa's pretensions and prospects reflects the surprising freedom of expression between the cousins: 'Faith I cannot but think Zephalinda your Face some winters hence will be in London just like a rich old fashion'd silk in a shop, which every Body has seen & nobody will buy.'[23] But Teresa is not to be ruffled by such reminders: she embraces his comparison and declares herself 'a rich admired

---

[23] The final word is illegible, but the sense is obvious.

Brocade' too good 'to be Cut out or made up to any ones Humour'. Whatever the element of sour grapes, her assurance is impressive.

The attractions of marriage as a social triumph are summed up for this circle by the glittering match made in 1713 between Thomas Gage and Benedicta Hall.[24] Alexis relays the Blounts' invitation and afterwards teases them with their inevitable jealousy:

> I hope this will find you all safe return'd from ye Celebration of ye great Wedding, and if you have no Temptations of Pride Vain Glory or Concupiscence, I pronounce you the greatest Stoicks and Platonists, that this Age or any former has given Examples off in any of your Sex.

The malicious wit of Teresa's friend Mrs Nelson exposes the contrast between the wealth which 'our Empress' (apparently Patty) has lost to a rival loaded with 'embroideries, lace, brocades, and Diamonds . . . which woud have shone much brighter about your fair Neck' and the dubious character of the bridegroom, who, already compromised by his sponsorship of a match between one of Teresa's friends and a fraudulent marquis who turned out to be penniless ('your dear Beau M^r gage was father to this happy Couple', comments Mrs Nelson), is prepared to jest cynically about his own marriage:

> M^r gage has made himself a black Coat, wch came into his Lodgings when a freind of mine was by; He ask'd him whether he woud mourn at his Wedding no (he told him) he woud wear his weding suit upon ye day, but mourn a month after because he was married.

He later renounced his faith for a career at court, becoming Viscount Gage, and his extra-marital exploits made him a byword for sexual immorality. An equally colourful figure was his brother Joseph, remembered as Pope's 'modest Gage', the speculator disappointed in his attempt to buy the throne of Poland; but more important to Pope was their sister, estranged wife of Mr Weston, whose reliance on her brother is sympathetically discussed by Mrs Nelson in these same letters.[25] In general, however, Mrs Nelson is maliciously witty about the Gages and their connections: she calls the wedding a 'Centre of Noise, Vanity, and Nonsense', and promises Teresa that she has some delicious scandal about the bride's mother – apparently involving bigamy – to share when next they meet. Yet the wedding is still a major event in their world: whatever fun they have at the participants' expense they

---

[24] Accounts of the Gages are in *DNB*, Kirk, G.E.C., *Peerage* (which misdates the Gage–Hall marriage) and Romney Sedgwick, *The House of Commons 1715–1754*, 2 vols., The History of Parliament (London, 1970). Mrs Nelson's letters to Teresa about the match are in Blount Letters, II, 171–81. For Thomas and Benedicta Gage after their marriage, see *Corr.*, I, 119, 260, 309; and for a joke against his sexual conduct see *Letters to and from Henrietta, Countess of Suffolk and her Second Husband the Hon. George Berkeley*, edited by J. W. Croker, 2 vols. (London, 1824), I, 343 (hereafter *Suffolk Corr.*).

[25] Joseph Gage is mocked in *To Bathurst*, lines 129–30 (*TE*, III.ii, 103); and Mrs Weston's predicament is described in Charles Wentworth Dilke, *The Papers of a Critic*, 2 vols. (London, 1875), I, 141–49.

always treat the wealth and status which is at stake absolutely seriously.

By 1737, when Teresa's brother Michael was worried about his heir's desire to marry the unsuitable Mary Eugenia Strickland (although a Catholic, she was tainted insofar as her father was a practising lawyer), Teresa had decided that love was for fools and marriage for the propagation of family and estate: 'I hope at thirty I shal hear of y^r sons wedding; & til then —' (Blount Papers, c. 63). In a spirited letter she indulges her contempt for the Stricklands ('to have such odd folks darc to think of him; is to great a humiliation I shal Laugh em to scorn in al Companys') and takes a casual view of her nephew's claim to have fallen in love: 'these sorts of ammours being extreemly Common with young men of his age, I hope he wil have 10 such befor he is ty'd for life'. Finally she comforts her brother with the unsentimental observation that 'ours is not a wedding family, I date our good sense from it'. She firmly associates this hard-headed social creed with London society, as she warns her brother specifically against keeping his son in Winchester, which 'is a County town & wil only add to a Boy wrong notions of good Company & ye world'.

Her own 'notions' apparently suggested to her that married love was an infantile delusion; and that it was better (if Pope's later allegations are taken at face value) to take a lover, or (if they are exaggerated) to dress and flirt in a manner which became less acceptable as she advanced into her thirties and forties. Her teacher Elizabeth Meynell had been well aware of the gaiety, even sensuality, which made her so attractive as an adolescent, but Mrs Meynell was over-sanguine about the capacity of Catholic society to absorb and direct her pupil's energies: 'I would gladly hear my D^r, that you are well setled, for I'm perswaded you have no Nuns flesh, and I know 'twould be a great ease to y^r Mother' (Blount Letters, II, 146). But instead of finding a husband in the London whirl, Teresa had found a congenial lifestyle: the priest whose advice to her mother has already been cited could have pointed to Teresa as an example of his fear that without the quasi-conventual discipline he recommends 'piety not only languishes, but often perishes in persons of y^r state' (I, 149). In contrast, her nephew (the second Michael Blount) actually did marry Mary Eugenia Strickland, and together they established an idyll of connubial piety which would have driven Teresa to distraction.[26]

Thus, whether from disinclination or lack of opportunity, Teresa turned away from the idea of marriage, but what her sister felt, we cannot know for lack of evidence. Although Alexis's tactless banter expressed social pressures which both must have felt, they were at the same time receiving letters from Pope which suggested less narrow criteria for valuing themselves. Despite his frequent testimony to their attractiveness (which is in any case frequently undercut by parodic exaggeration), he refuses to present himself as a candidate

[26] See Mary Eugenia's letters to her husband, Blount Papers, c.65.

for the hand of either; but he differs from Alexis in that he never aspires to the full-blown romance rhetoric of the order of chivalry and increasingly abandons the postures of courtship for the confidence of friendship. An early letter to Patty accompanying a presentation copy of *The Rape of the Locke* (i.e. the version of 1712) claims, much as Alexis would, that 'our Virtue will be sooner overthrown by one Glance of yours, than by all the wicked Poets can write in an age, as has been too dearly experience'd by the wickedst of 'em all' (i.e. himself). However, the tone of his writing to them for the future is on the whole better summed up in a comment of 1714 prompted by Patty's passion for romances: 'You will both injure me very much, if you don't think me a truer Friend than ever any Romantic Lover, or any Imitator of their Style, could be' (*Corr.*, I, 143, 252). Pope is probably thinking specifically of Alexis and the order of chivalry.

Although girls like the Blounts were in many ways extremely privileged, Pope, as a relative outsider, was struck by the potential sterility of the goals that town life set before them. One victim of such values is Paméla in 'With the Works of Voiture' (first of the gallery of female horrors to culminate in *Characters of Women*), who has set her heart on the trappings of a 'good' marriage, the kind of match which might have appealed most to Teresa – or to the Belinda of *The Rape of the Lock*:

> The Gods, to curse *Paméla* with her Pray'rs,
> Gave the gilt Coach and dappled *Flanders* Mares,
> The shining Robes, rich Jewels, Beds of State,
> And to compleat her Bliss, a Fool for Mate.
> She glares in *Balls*, *Front-boxes*, and the *Ring*,
> A vain, unquiet, glitt'ring, wretched Thing!
> Pride, Pomp, and State but reach her outward Part,
> She sighs, and is no *Dutchess* at her Heart.   (line 49; *TE*, VI, 63)

What this marriage offers is status and luxury: there is nothing in it to sustain the heart. Pope's point is not that the only good life for a woman is to be the pious and hardworking mistress of a Catholic family – Paméla need not be a Catholic at all, and Pope, like Teresa, could apparently find life with a family like the Carylls less than entirely congenial – but rather that without a stable sense of personal identity all other gratifications are ineffectual.[27] Girls like Paméla presumably wanted to be happy, but the poet who was to conclude that 'God in externals could not place Content' could only see their aims as pathetically wide of the mark.[28] As more realistic provisions for happiness he proposes either 'the free Innocence of Life' as a spinster, which he characterises as solid 'Ease' as opposed to insubstantial 'Joy', or marriage based on the quality which was to become his touchstone of female excellence, the 'good humour' which transfigures the aims of the coquette as it 'still

---

[27] For Pope's reservations about the Carylls, see Erskine-Hill, *Social Milieu*, pp. 87–97.
[28] *Essay on Man*, IV.66 (*TE*, III.i, 134).

makes new Conquests, and maintains the past' (lines 45–48, 57–68). This
stress on good humour is another pointer through *The Rape of the Lock* towards
Characters of Women, in which Teresa is forgotten and Patty exalted for precisely
this quality. Furthermore, the poems are connected by the implication that
the woman who attracts to herself the language of brilliance ('gilt', 'shining',
'glares', 'glitt'ring') is worth less than the woman of unpretentious good
humour, that dimmer but constant figure, later identified with Patty, to whom
he will finally say with confidence, 'Ah Friend! to dazzle let the Vain
design'.[29]

An alternative route to misery was almost the opposite of Paméla's: the
marriage for which there was not much to be said beyond the fact that the
bride's family was no longer responsible for her support. Since profitable matches were increasingly hard to find in a community which was double-taxed,
heavily reliant on unprofitable French stocks, barred from placing its younger
sons in the professions and largely reluctant to place them in trade, girls who
were not heiresses had to be prepared to deplete their family stocks as little
as possible by taking their relatively small dowries either into convents or into
the hands of suitors insufficiently eligible to bid for richer brides. This was
probably the dominant factor in the wretchedness of Anne Cope, whose
feckless brother Philip Caryll was a semi-dependent cousin of Patty Blount's
godfather, Pope's friend John Caryll.[30] It is hard to believe that Cope had
ever looked like a good catch: he was a soldier posted abroad who swiftly committed bigamy and refused his wife maintenance despite the two arduous
journeys she made to plead with him. The way in which Pope and John Caryll
discuss her case brings out the dominance of financial considerations in marriage: if her husband will not provide for her and the brother who thought
he was rid of the burden cannot, she becomes a genteel pauper, dependent
on remoter relations like John Caryll and friends like Pope. Mrs Weston too,
although she had voluntarily left her husband, depended on friends and relations: both women demonstrated within Pope's early experience how irrelevant women's intrinsic qualities – as he perceived them – could be to their
happiness in marriage. Since society defined them as dependent on men, pro-
pertiless or under-age women faced with protectors who were greedy, stupid
or lazy were without any recognised means of averting disaster. In the heady
fiction of the *Elegy to the Memory of an Unfortunate Lady*, however, the narrator
was to endorse suicide as one method of taking control. This understandably
shocked Johnson, who felt that 'poetry has not often been worse employed
than in dignifying the amorous fury of a raving girl' (Johnson, II, 101).

Less dramatic than the anguish of a Paméla or a Mrs Cope, but closer to
Pope's heart as the fate of the Blount sisters, was the insecurity of women who
did not marry at all. With the only productive career for women closed to

---

[29] *Characters of Women*, line 249 (*TE*, III.ii, 70).   [30] Erskine-Hill, *Social Milieu*, pp. 74–77.

them, widows and spinsters lived on jointures and allowances often perceived by heads of families as a drain on embarrassed estates. Indeed, the accumulation of obligations to female dependants played an important role in the disintegration of the substantial Caryll estate within a mere thirty years of John Caryll's death.[31] Yet the Blounts' difficulties made Pope see such problems entirely from the dependants' point of view: although he had been their brother's friend, he showed remarkably little consideration for his predicament when he inherited the embarrassed Mapledurham estate in 1710 and realised the impossibility of paying his mother and sisters the sums laid down in his father's will. The situation was aggravated when Michael married Mary Agnes Tichborne in 1715, since the marriage settlement further injured his female dependants by preventing him from raising money on the greater portion of the estate: his father-in-law could insist on such conditions only because Michael was already in a weak position (Blount Papers, c.59).

With this settlement we return to the paradox of piety and pragmatism in the Catholic marriage market. The Tichborne aim was to ensure the status of the match both in the person of their daughter, who must have an ample jointure if widowed, and in the continuing status of the representative of the family into which she had married, which meant concentrating the Blount estates in the hands of her eldest son instead of dispersing them among all the children. Hence Michael and Mary Agnes, who took legal advice on the issue in 1736, were limited in the provision they could make for daughters or younger sons, and there were always problems about paying allowances to Michael's mother and sisters (c.59, c.63). Although Mary Agnes's son and daughter-in-law were too devoted to see it in this light, her exceptional longevity increased the burden, for she drew her jointure for nearly forty years after her husband's death (Blount Papers, Mortuary Book).

The Tichbornes could not be faulted for breeding and piety, but their estates were dwindling. In the deathbed memoir which Mary Agnes's grandfather, Sir Henry Tichborne, composed for her father's guidance, he dwells regretfully on their past greatness:

Although we now Posses scarce a Quarter of that Large Revenue, w[ch] once belonged to our Family, yet I had drawn the Map of all or most of it, to shew you where it is, & how we parted from it. Not but that it is in vain to shew the rock when the ship is split, yet I had marked it to make you take the more care of w[t] yet remains.

(c.65)

Yet at the same time as he laments their losses, he warns against the most obvious means of repairing them: families are 'too often vitiated for sordid interest of a Rich Mecanick's Daughter'. Blood is all in all: he praises the breeding and associated virtue of the brides chosen by his ancestors, and provides a pious justification of his concern by pointing out that 'Our Lord himself, tho He would be born of a meeke, & Humble Virgin, yet would He

[31] Erskine-Hill, *Social Milieu*, p. 101.

have Her, & His Human Blood, Descend From the Royall, & Prophetical House of David'. The only way forward was thus to drive the hardest possible bargain with a good family, as his son did in the case of Mary Agnes's settlement.

Sir Henry, who had been imprisoned during the Popish Plot, can hardly be accused of a shallow or consciously self-seeking commitment to his faith, for as well as the pious resignation which colours all his writing, he left more specific evidence in his rule of life, a routine of prayer and meditation testifying to sincere and unremitting devotion. For him there is no conflict between this self-denying devotion and the quest for noble alliances, but it is hard when contemplating his son's management of Mary Agnes's marriage not to think of Clarissa's lament, 'What then is this narrow selfishness that reigns in us, but relationship remembered against relationship forgot?', the 'forgetting' the more poignant when the exploited were members of the same tiny and oppressed Catholic community (*Clarissa*, p. 62). Yet beyond the distress the settlement caused to those who lived directly under its shadow we may glimpse something of the grand design pursued by families like the Tichbornes, for today a Roman Catholic descendant of Michael Blount and Mary Agnes Tichborne still owns Mapledurham.

3

To Teresa and Patty, Sylvia and Alexis, the 'Cosen Bell' who appears in the Blount Letters is simply one of the host of cousins resulting from intermarriage between Catholic families; but the modern reader recognises her with something of a shock as Arabella Fermor, the original of Pope's Belinda. The mundanity of Bell's presence in the Blount Letters is a salutary reminder that *The Rape of the Lock* does not simply represent the world it immortalises: to her peers she was nothing out of the ordinary. Indeed, her cousins' letters reveal her as humiliatingly vulnerable to the pressures of being eldest daughter but not heiress of one of the 'best' families.

In this respect as in others she was in a similar position to Teresa, whose interest in her doings hints at an understandable rivalry. They were about the same age; both attended convent schools in Paris at about the same time; both were accustomed to extravagant praise of their beauty, yet both, for whatever reasons, entered their twenties without, apparently, receiving acceptable proposals.[32] Moreover, Bell, like Teresa, enjoyed high life and the role of inexorable beauty:

[32] Bell was born around 1688–90, she had brothers and she was with the English Augustinian Canonesses in Paris from 1693 to 1704 (and note that Mrs Fermor and Bell's grandmother Lady Browne are mentioned in the English Benedictine nuns' letters to Mrs Blount cited above). Four poems praising her beauty survive in print (see Geoffrey Tillotson's biographical appendix to the *Rape* in *TE*, II, 371–75).

major Generall ross declairs publickly he will shoot himself if cosen Farmer will not marry him which I think she resolves not to doe soe I suppose in my next I shall tell you the newes of his Death. I danced tother day at Mrs Cresswells till six in the morning the room being little we were but five-coupple. Mrs Chettwin the beauty was one of our Ladys and you may be sure bell was another our men was the Duke of beaufort Lord Fredrick howard Mr Chettwin and brother tipografatt.

(Blount Letters, III, 93)

This glimpse comes from one of Sylvia's letters to Patty, probably written in 1708 or 1709. Only in the most baldly literal sense is this the world of the poem ('In various Talk th'instructive hours they past, / Who gave the *Ball*, or paid the *Visit* last'), since for Sylvia the rituals of society are simply the way life is, and Bell is just a girl like any other (III, 11–12). For Bell's peers to find her transformed in Pope's poem into a goddess-like marvel must have been deliciously funny – and perhaps provoking.

While Pope knew so many people who knew Bell that it would have been difficult for him not to have known her at least slightly, there is no evidence that she meant enough to him to inspire what Mack rightly calls 'the poem's deep currents of affection and sexual attraction', which he convincingly traces to the girls Pope knew best, 'the sparkling young women at Mapledurham' (*Life*, p. 257). Indeed, Bell seems to be a kind of shadow through which, in the character of Belinda, Pope explores the confusing sensations of his attraction to the type of femininity represented by reigning beauties. Chief among such women for him is Teresa, whose ringlets really were, as Bell's were apparently not, the fashionable 'sable'.[33]

Pope's reason for lavishing his powers – nominally at least – on Bell was purely circumstantial:

The stealing of Miss Belle Fermor's hair was taken too seriously, and caused an estrangement between the two families, though they had lived long in great friendship before. A common acquaintance and well-wisher to both desired me to write a poem to make a jest of it, and laugh them together again.

(Spence, no. 104)

This approach from John Caryll marked the beginning of a project which was to stretch over six years (1711–17), developing from a specific commission through three versions of increasing elaboration and independence and a cluster of associated material into the literary object now familiar as *The Rape of the Lock*.[34]

It is not clear whether the theft itself was the disastrous climax of a troubled courtship or a simple practical joke; but whichever it was, it had connotations which could make it deeply offensive. A context for understanding Petre's act

[33] *Rape*, IV.169; and see Mack's comment on Teresa's portrait in *Life*, p. 257.
[34] The poem exists in three principal versions, published in 1712, 1714 and 1717. The first, distinguished by the spelling 'Locke', is printed in *TE*, II, 127–37. As the second differs relatively little from the third it is not separately printed in *TE*. Unless otherwise specified, references are to the third version, printed on pp. 144–212.

emerges from other exchanges in Pope's circle. In July 1711, just a few weeks previously, Pope had written to the town wit Henry Cromwell, who had impressed the ladies around Binfield with many 'civill things' during a recent visit: 'The Trophy you bore away from one of 'em, in your Snuffbox, will doubtless preserve her Memory, and be a Testimony of your admiration, for ever' (*Corr.*, I, 125). Here, apparently, was a woman sufficiently detached to take Cromwell's vacuous gallantry in good part; and although the verses on the incident which Pope includes in the letter anticipate the *Rape* in some detail, they are as yet wholly free from implications of triumph on the one side or disgrace on the other (compare *Rape*, III.159–70). Another playful incident, though doubtless one in which Teresa enjoyed the sensation of arbitrary power, is commemorated by Typographate. Even if he had read the *Rape* when he wrote this undated letter, he at least shows how well the motif fitted his experience of Teresa:

I desir'd a lock of your hair, but it t'was refus'd me, I had no sooner got out of your room, but another (ten millions of times happyer y^n me) askt Y^e same favour & to him t'was granted: no Tongue can expresse ye grief I had, in seeing ye lock in another mans hands: Ye Gods! what a sight to one y^t loves to distraction.

(Blount Letters, III, 118)

Another letter, from Alexis in 1713, hints more directly at the traditional link between virginity and uncut hair. He has made an appointment for Teresa with Mr Gibbons the hairdresser, who, he says, 'has orders to treat with you for your Virginity' (Blount Letters, I, 205).

Lord Petre, as Alexis had hinted to the Blounts, was a catch of the highest order; and whether or not Bell seriously thought that they might marry, indeed whether or not such a proposal would have pleased her, it was offensive to be robbed of a token which could be read as pre-empting the issue. Even while Pope strove to disarm such an interpretation, he articulated it with dangerous clarity:

> Methinks already I your Tears survey,
> Already hear the horrid things they say,
> Already see you a degraded Toast,
> And all your Honour in a Whisper lost!
>
> (*The Rape of the Locke*, II.25)

Although Pope told Spence that his initial version of the *Rape* 'was well received and had its effect in the two families', a passage like this, which runs the risk of stimulating the very gossip it seeks to ridicule, shows the difficulty of his task (Spence, no. 104). Moreover, it was impossible to write humorously about the events without implying that some of the actors had behaved, at the very least, foolishly. Sir George Browne, the real life Sir Plume – who had apparently tried, to his credit, to make Lord Petre apologise – becomes the victim of a sense of fun that has nothing to do with the reconciliation sought by Caryll. The caricature hurt the more for being 'the very picture of the man'. It earned Pope his lasting enmity, and it calls into serious question Pope's sense of how far a joke could be carried without doing more harm than good (Spence, no. 106, quoting Patty). As he warmed to the task his ostensible purpose of reconciliation gave way to a joyous fantasy based less on observation than on such tempting stereotypes as the pompous ass, the hypocritical gossip, and, crucially, the coquette who has only herself to blame for male rapacity. Yet, of the three versions Pope was to produce, *The Rape of the Locke* is the one best adapted 'to laugh them together': indeed it is so genial in effect as to obscure the oddity of choosing satire as a tool of reconciliation. The offended Bell is flattered by the beauty of her fictional equivalent; her assailant's pretensions are belittled by reference to 'Flavia's Busk that oft had rapp'd his own'; and male arrogance is ridiculed by the opening allusion to '*Little Men*', by the contrast between the ineffectual Sir Plume and his vigorous lady, and by the weighing of 'the Mens Wits against the Lady's Hair' which heralds the apotheosis of the lock. The less complimentary aspect of the poem's treatment of women, hinging on the space it gives to assumptions not unfavourable to Lord Petre's act, was not likely to attract comment in a society in which such assumptions were commonplace. In any case, with very few exceptions, Pope's irony places the tactless question of whether or not he privately endorses these assumptions – which to an extent he clearly does – firmly beyond the scope of the poem to answer.

In the invocation, for example, Pope's pose of affected wonderment defies simple clarification:

> Say what strange Motive, Goddess! cou'd compel
> A well-bred *Lord* t'assault a gentle *Belle*?
> Oh say what stranger Cause, yet unexplor'd,
> Cou'd make a gentle *Belle* reject a *Lord*?   (*Rape of the Locke*, I.7)

The first question is presumably meant to be answered in terms of the naturalness of male desire. However, the question that follows, which the poet declares more difficult, presumably because it hinges on perversity, seems to demand an answer in terms of the woman's failure to understand, or to admit to, her real desire. Yet this desire apparently includes an essentially feminine attraction to the wealth and status of 'a *Lord*' that complicates the whole structure of values so far worked out – for if female desire is materialistic ambition, what merit can there be in being true to it? This is typical of the difficulty, perhaps the absurdity, of pursuing a clear moral path through a poem that prefers any mode to unequivocal affirmation.

When challenged, even the most dazzling compliments reveal damaging possibilities:

> Yet graceful Ease, and Sweetness void of Pride,
> Might hide her Faults, if *Belles* had Faults to hide:

If to her share some Female Errors fall,
Look on her Face, and you'll forgive 'em all.

(*Rape of the Locke*, I.31)

This is the kind of crux at which interpretations diverge: although for many
readers such a compliment seems entirely charming and appropriate, for
others it cloaks much that is questionable. Since, for example, we can hardly
imagine Pope locating the Baron's offence in '*male* errors' (though modern
readers may wish to do exactly that), the reference to 'Female Errors' suggests that poet and audience are united in seeing the sex as peculiarly flawed.
Moreover, beauty that pre-empts moral judgement opens the door to
meretricious deception, suggesting that women inhabit a realm of physical
witchery dangerous to the moral world of men. It is telling that in letters Pope
uses a similar rhetoric to evoke his pleasure in authors about whom he has
serious reservations: Ovid, he writes, 'has an agreeableness that charms us
without correctness, like a mistress whose faults we see, but love her with
them all'.[35] Interesting in this connection is Pope's repudiation to Teresa of
'the strict Life of graver Mortals' in favour of 'an innocent gay Farce'
characterised by 'native Ease and Grace' (compare the first line of the quotation above): he excuses what he recognises as a frivolous perspective by the
observation that 'Criticks in Wit, or Life, are hard to please', which is a striking concession from one as concerned as Pope with correctness in life and
art.[36] Mack is surely right to claim that this 'may be the finest compliment
Teresa Blount ever received', a testimony to the power of her charm, like that
Pope ascribes to Belinda, to make him shut his eyes to breaches of the rules;
yet in a culture in which the rules enjoy such prestige, such compliments place
women in a questionable position (*Life*, p. 247).

From general praise of Belinda's beauty Pope goes on to focus on her hair
(so like Teresa's), while the language works to blame her for arousing male
desire: we are told that she 'Nourish'd' the ringlets 'to the Destruction of
Mankind'; that they 'conspir'd' to set off the whiteness of her neck; that they
are like the snares by which humans 'betray' and 'surprise' animals (*Rape of
the Locke*, I.35–44). The active verbs underline the description's affinities with
the classic rapist's defence that women ask for it; and such a passage, placed
just before the Baron's decision 'by Force to ravish, or by Fraud betray', has
the effect of deflecting attention from his unexplained reluctance to consider
legitimate methods. Furthermore, Pope reminds us that the belief that all is
fair in love and war is widely shared – although he is too discreet to confirm
whether he shares it himself:

For when Success a Lover's Toil attends,
Few ask, if Fraud or Force attain'd his Ends.

(*Rape of the Locke*, I.49)

---

[35] *Corr.*, I, 92; for the same remark applied to Spenser, see p. 316.
[36] 'With the Works of Voiture', lines 21–30.

The assumption that the luring of men is women's definitive role is crucial:
Canto II, for example, opens with a pointed comparison of men in heroic
situations of distress with women piqued by the shortcomings of their
appearance (II.2–10). At the crisis of the poem, Pope underlines the implications of the language with which he had praised Belinda's hair by making the
furious Thalestris declare that women have no objection at all to men who rise
to the bait, so long as the public facade of chastity is maintained:

> O had the Youth but been content to seize
> Hairs less in sight – or any Hairs but these!
> Gods! shall the Ravisher display this Hair,
> While the Fops envy, and the Ladies stare!
> *Honour* forbid! At whose unrival'd Shrine
> Ease, Pleasure, Virtue, All, our Sex resign.
>
> (*Rape of the Locke*, II.20)

Amusing as this inadvertent self-revelation is, it obviously affects our estimation of Belinda's good faith, or at least of her self-knowledge; and the
insistence on surrender to a man as her natural destiny is continued by the
'dying' Baron, who points out that she is sure to attract some other suitor who
will reduce her to sexual and marital obedience:

> Boast not my Fall (he said) insulting Foe!
> Thou by some other shalt be laid as low.   (II.142)

The theme of male triumph is continued, though with an ironic twist, in
the apotheosis of the stolen lock that ends the poem:

> Then cease, bright Nymph! to mourn the ravish'd Hair
> Which adds new Glory to the shining Sphere!
> Not all the Tresses that fair Head can boast
> Shall draw such Envy as the Locke you lost.
> For, after all the Murders of your Eye,
> When, after Millions slain, your self shall die;
> When those fair Suns shall sett, as sett they must,
> And all those Tresses shall be laid in Dust;
> *This Locke*, the Muse shall consecrate to Fame,
> And mid'st the Stars inscribe *Belinda's* Name!
>
> (*Rape of the Locke*, II.183)

The compliment leaves the poet holding the stage – not without justice, we
may feel, at the conclusion of such a performance – as mortality, putting
a date to all (apparently) that is remarkable in Belinda, enables him to
appropriate the beauty whose implicit challenge to male desire can, as he has
shown, be read as justifying the predatory ruse for which he consoles her.
Whether Pope himself so reads it is a question he prefers not to raise; and to
insist too much on the evidence of the passages quoted above is to risk the flat-
footedness of John Dennis's condemnation of the doctrines he deduced with

remorseless logic from the version of 1714.[37] Yet the reader may perhaps be forgiven a smile at the contrast between the poet, left flourishing *The Rape of the Locke* in triumph, and Lord Petre, whose relatively crude tactics leave him a very poor second as regards his trophy.

4

At first, Bell must have been unaware that the poem posed any danger to her reputation, for she not only circulated copies in manuscript, but also gave Pope permission to publish this first version in May 1712 (*TE*, II, 94–95). Yet soon after *The Rape of the Locke* was in print Pope was telling Caryll that 'the celebrated lady herself is offended, and, which is stranger, not at herself, but me' (*Corr.*, 151). It may well be that he blames her not only because her vanity in circulating copies has made publication necessary, but also because he feels that he has done nothing but bring out the true implications of her conduct towards Petre (*TE*, II, 375).

An intriguing sidelight on Bell's situation is shed by Alexis's playfully malicious letters to Teresa at this time.[38] She is evidently not expected to react with sorrow to the news that 'the only lean Beauty I descry about Town is Mrs Belinda, whose charms & Gallants desert her so fast that I wonder despair & the spleen have not quite eaten her up'. Like Teresa, Bell was older than many brides (if Tillotson's conjectures are right, she was between twenty-three and twenty-five in 1713, while Teresa was definitely twenty-five); and Alexis's use of the name adopted (though not necessarily invented) by Pope points the contrast, whether or not Alexis intends it, between the fantastic claims made for Belinda and the everyday reality of Bell. Although Alexis may be exaggerating, her diminished popularity may well be related to suspicions, derived from the poem, that she had compromised herself by flirting with Lord Petre.

In another letter Alexis projects a scene which could almost be a parody of the glamour of Pope's poem: here is Bell with her lapdog – but in the poem there is no indefatigable grandmother to chaperone the heroine, no indifferent young man to call her powers into question:

If Lady Brown Bell or her Dog will divert you, I can tell you I had the pleasure of seeing them all three last Saturday, & all the news I can send you of them is that Lady Brown looks as if she would not quit this mortall life till about the year 1715. As to Bell Mr Douty, from whom I just now parted, assures me he makes no pretensions, nor has any designs upon her. Fidelle is mightily in fav^r & barks as loud as ever at all strangers.   (Blount Letters, I, 201–202)

Teresa's interest in all this could be excused as a kind of family curiosity

---

[37] *Remarks on Mr. Pope's Rape of the Lock* (London, 1728); *TE*, II, Appendix D.
[38] Blount Letters, I, 221–22. Although this letter is not dated, it is grouped with others dated 1713.

(Bell's grandmother, Lady Browne, née Englefield, was Teresa's great-aunt and daughter-in-law of Ellinor Browne, née Blount of Mapledurham; while a Mr Doughty was to marry a sister of the Mary Agnes Tichborne who in 1715 married Teresa's brother), but Alexis clearly senses over and above this her desire to hear that her cousin is doing no better than she is.[39]

By 1713 the *Rape* had definitely taken on a life of its own, for despite Lord Petre's death in March, Pope was still elaborating his poem, and by the end of the year he had completed the new machinery of sylphs and gnomes. Yet he still took care to consult Bell, and his method of dealing with her illuminates his understanding of the awkwardness caused by his original response to Lord Petre's offence.

In December 1713 Pope told Caryll, 'I have some thoughts of dedicating that poem to Mrs Fermor by name, as a piece of justice in return to the wrong interpretation she has suffered under on the score of that piece' (*Corr.*, I, 203). No doubt the interpretation was 'wrong' principally because readers who shared the assumptions present in the passages cited above had jumped to the conclusions about Belinda and therefore about Bell from which Pope had been commissioned to divert them, and in addition, the Latin motto he had chosen could be taken by the malicious to imply either that she had herself prompted the theft, or that she had been vain enough to ask him to write the poem in her praise.[40] It was easy enough to change the motto; but the drafting of a preface that would undo any harm that the poem itself had done to her reputation demanded considerable ingenuity. He had two options: he could either make it clear that he regarded Belinda as blameless, or he could cut the knot which tied the fictitious Belinda to the real Bell.

He tried both methods. In the verses later entitled 'To Belinda on the Rape of the Lock' he addresses Bell as Belinda (as he does at the opening of the *Rape* in all its versions) and likens her to Lucretia, type of the blameless rape victim:

> Nature to your undoing arms mankind
> With strength of body, artifice of mind;
> But gives your feeble sex, made up of fears,
> No guard but virtue, no redress but tears.
> Yet custom (seldom to your favour gain'd)
> Absolves the virgin when by force constrain'd.
> Thus *Lucrece* lives unblemish'd in her fame,
> A bright example of young *Tarquin*'s shame.
> Such praise is yours – and such shall you possess,
> Your virtue equal, tho' your loss be less.

---

[39] *TE*, II, 377; William Berry, *Pedigrees of the Families in the County of Hants*, County Genealogies (London, 1833), p. 30.

[40] Nolueram, Belinda, tuos violare capillos. / Sed juvat hoc precibus me tribuisse tuis' ('I had not wished, Belinda, to damage your hair, / But I am delighted to have yielded this to your entreaties': *TE*, II, 125). For hostile interpretations, see EC, V, 93–95.

Then smile Belinda at reproachful tongues,
Still warm our hearts, and still inspire our songs.
(line 15; *TE*, VI, 108)

In the event Bell preferred the prose dedication, which simply if unconvincingly proclaims that 'the Character of Belinda . . . resembles You in nothing
but in Beauty' (*TE*, II, 143). In comparison, the verse preface comes too close
for comfort to the gossip it seeks to discredit, playing too insistently with the
notion of rape, and ending with a less than tactful echo of the notorious 'hairs
less in sight':

Who censure most, more precious hairs would lose,
To have the *Rape* recorded by his Muse.
(line 29; compare *Rape*, IV.175–76)

It may be, however, that Pope believed that Bell's reasons for preferring the
prose dedication were based less on close reading than on the vanity of being
addressed by name:

As to the *Rape of the Lock*, I believe I have managed the dedication so nicely that it can
neither hurt the lady, nor the author. I writ it very lately, and upon great deliberation;
the young lady approves of it; and the best advice in the kingdom, of the men of sense
has been made use of in it, even to the Treasurer's. A preface which salved the lady's
honour, without affixing her name, was also prepared, but by herself superseded in
favour of the dedication. Not but that, after all, fools will talk, and fools will hear 'em.
(*Corr.*, I, 207)

He is quite unabashed at the inconsistency between on the one hand addressing Bell as Belinda and on the other denying any identity between them. This
is not a matter of truth, but of politeness.

The dedication to the expanded *Rape* of 1714, which Bell chose in
preference to the verses, is to the modern eye more openly patronising than
anything in any version of the poem. Bell is reminded that the project began
as satire aimed at 'a few young Ladies, who have good Sense and good
Humour enough, to laugh not only at their Sex's little unguarded Follies, but
at their own'. The ancient epicists are playfully compared to 'many modern
Ladies', in that 'let an Action be never so trivial in it self, they always make
it appear of the utmost Importance'; the poet apologises for using 'hard
Words before a Lady', and the source of his machinery is said to be 'in its
Title and Size . . . so like a *Novel*, that many of the Fair Sex have read it for
one by Mistake'. In addition, the reader is presented with a frontispiece, conceived or at least approved by Pope, which is loaded with traditional
iconography of woman as vain and lascivious: Belinda is shown at her mirror
(vanity) with thigh provocatively exposed, watched by a satyr (lewdness) and
by an ominously shadowed figure crouched behind the mirror (perhaps

denoting the inner darkness of repressed sexuality connected with Spleen and Umbriel).[41]

With the tone thus set, Pope embarks on his expanded version, which includes a wider selection of traditionally anti-feminist themes, whilst maintaining for the most part a tongue-in-cheek reticence as to what the reader is to make of them. The newly-invented sylph Ariel, for example, praises the childish credulity he expects to find in Belinda ('the Fair and Innocent shall still believe') and invokes as an authority not philosophy but 'all the Nurse and all the Priest have taught' (I.27–40). We are free to infer that women never grow up, but at the same time Pope takes the opportunity to tease the judicious reader with such eminently respectable precedents as Jesus's 'of such is the kingdom of God', and the conventional disdain of the gentleman for the pedant:

> Some secret Truths from Learned Pride conceal'd,
> To maids alone and Children are reveal'd.   (I.37; Luke, 18:16)

The principal 'Truth' on which Ariel insists, in line with the tradition which sees women as essentially vain, is 'thy own Importance' (*Rape*, I.35). Belinda is commanded to a vanity which elevates every detail of her appearance and comfort to the level of the things her society officially holds sacred; yet while the poem lasts the reader is brought to a surprising extent to share this heightened perception, not least because of the dubious light the juxtaposition sheds on official pieties:

> Whether the Nymph shall break *Diana*'s Law,
> Or some frail *China* Jar receive Flaw,
> Or stain her Honour, or her new Brocade,
> Forget her Pray'rs, or miss a Masquerade,
> Or lose her Heart, or Necklace, at a Ball;
> Or whether Heav'n has doom'd that *Shock* must fall.   (II.105)

Religion is eclipsed when Belinda is presented as both goddess and worshipper at her own dressing table ('the sacred Rites of Pride'), and later when she issues her own divine fiat: '*Let Spades be Trumps*! she said, and Trumps they were' (I.121–28; III.46). In fact, despite a gesture towards Dryden's scheme for reconciling epic machinery with Christian doctrine (II.89–90), Christianity has no place in a world whose 'angels' are immortal souls without any conventionally spiritual dimension: scratch the surface of woman's life, Ariel admiringly tells us, and you find only a deeper superficiality:

> Think not, when Woman's transient Breath is fled,
> That all her Vanities at once are dead:
> Succeeding Vanities she still regards,
> And tho' she plays no more, o'erlooks the Cards.   (I.51)

---

[41] Robert Halsband, *The Rape of the Lock and its Illustrations, 1714–1896* (Oxford, 1980), pp. 18–21.

Even more crucial than neglect of religion is the denial of sexuality by women actually engrossed in a ritual of sexual attraction. Ariel encourages girls to entice only to reject: under the rule of the sylphs procreation would cease, since it is their aim to keep girls chastely threading the ornate mazes of the London season immune to male approaches – presumably including proposals of marriage (I.67–78, 91–104). The comedy lies in the way that Ariel's ideal overlaps to such a large extent with the preoccupations of Bell's world while frustrating its overriding aim: this, Pope is surely suggesting (though it may be rash to be sure of anything), is how girls like Bell (we may think of Teresa) learn to be coquettes. Ariel mentions marriage only in relation to the gnomes, who – so complete is the futility of the metaphysical world Pope has invented – oppose the sylphs only to do the same job in a different way, through pride instead of denial of sexuality:

> Some Nymphs there are, too conscious of their Face,
> For Life predestin'd to the *Gnomes'* Embrace.
> These swell their Prospects and exalt their Pride,
> When Offers are disdain'd, and Love deny'd.
> Then gay Ideas crowd the vacant Brain;
> While Peers and Dukes, and all their sweeping Train,
> And Garters, Stars, and Coronets appear,
> And in soft Sounds, *Your Grace* salutes their Ear.   (I.79)

Girls who succumb to 'the *Gnomes' Embrace*' do not marry either: they reject each match in hope of a better, becoming in time the spiteful prudes that gnomes adore. Thus, unlike Boileau's *Le Lutrin* and Garth's *Dispensary*, which conclude by introducing personifications of positive values, Pope's machinery offers only alternative perversities, each equally dependent on the vanities encouraged in Bell and her peers; for if the gnomes use ambition to gain their ends, the sylphs distract their protégés from amorous engagement with endless diversification of the social surface:

> With varying Vanities, from ev'ry Part,
> They shift the moving Toyshop of their Heart.[42]

Pope seems least elusive when he suggests that it is natural for a girl to be attracted to men and a dangerous denial of nature for her to pretend otherwise. Belinda's dream, for example, is rich in hints: Pope allows (or instructs?) the illustrator to depict the leg of her dressing stool as the leg of a satyr, concealed and ready to spring; he focuses on the lapdog (who 'leapt up, and wak'd his Mistress with his Tongue'), a motif with accepted sexual connotations in anti-feminist satire; and he emphasises her amorous susceptibility to 'a Youth more glitt'ring than a *Birth-night Beau*, / (That ev'n in Slumber caus'd her Cheek to glow)' – a complicated moment, since Ariel is not only

---

[42] *Rape*, I.99; Boileau, *Le Lutrin*, VI (*OEuvres*, edited by Jérôme Vercruysse, 2 vols. (Paris, 1969), I, 223–27); Samuel Garth, *The Dispensary*, 9th edition (Dublin, 1725), Canto VI, pp. 58–71.

the advocate of chastity but originally, despite appearances, a woman himself.[43] Indeed, as Pope makes clear in the dedication, although he is too discreet to highlight it in the poem, the sylphs of his immediate source attend women in order to achieve 'the most intimate Familiarities', raising the possibility that Ariel's motives may be just as objectionable as the Baron's. In any case, Ariel's doctrine of chastity makes only a transient impression on Belinda: she is so extremely susceptible that the moment she picks up her billet-doux she is inflamed by its hackneyed language of '*Wounds, Charms*, and *Ardors*' (so close to the raptures simulated in letters to Teresa and Patty), and goes to her dressing-table intent on conquest: 'Now awful Beauty puts on all its Arms', Pope writes, likening the process to the arming of the epic hero (*Rape*, I.117–20, 139). Later, a game of cards provokes an ambiguous warmth, and the hubris of her challenge, which signals by the standards of the time a markedly unfeminine desire for fame and conquest, supports this hint, since female lust and insubordination traditionally go hand in hand:

> *Belinda* now, whom Thirst of Fame invites,
> Burns to encounter two adventrous Knights,
> At *Ombre* singly to decide their Doom;
> And swells her Breast with Conquests yet to come.[44]

Pope's intention seems most transparent at the dramatic moment when Ariel, who can protect her only while she 'rejects Mankind', is forced to fall back and leave her to the Baron (I.68):

> Sudden he view'd, in spite of all her Art,
> An Earthly Lover lurking at her Heart.
>
> (*Rape*, III.143)

It is hard to avoid the conclusion that the 'Earthly Lover' is the Baron himself, and Pope apparently shows his hand further when he transfers to the victim herself what had previously been Thalestris's lines on the preferability of a real but concealed seduction, placing them for increased emphasis at the conclusion of Canto IV. Yet we are still not obliged to read this as conscious hypocrisy: Belinda may after all intend only the innocent half of the *double entendre*:

> O hadst thou, Cruel! been content to seize
> Hairs less in sight, or any Hairs but these! (IV.175)

Whether or not we believe that Belinda means the full implications of her words, this reallocation effectively cuts more ground from under her feet; and Pope continues to emphasise suggestions of her moral flimsiness and lack of self-knowledge by associating her for the rest of the poem with the gnomes and

---

[43] Halsband, *Illustrations*, pp. 10–11; *Rape*, I.23–24, 116; Felicity A. Nussbaum, *The Brink of All We Hate: English Satires on Women, 1660–1750* (Lexington, 1984), pp. 29, 140–41.

[44] *Rape*, III.25; Nussbaum, pp. 15, 19–20, 148–50.

with the Cave of Spleen, an allegory which gives pride of place to specifically female perversities (see chapter 4.1).

In the light of the *Rape*'s common ground with anti-feminist satire it is a mark of Pope's special skill in handling potentially offensive attitudes and of his infectious pleasure in Belinda's charms that the *Rape* has been read with such pleasure by so many women: in Brean Hammond's words, 'Anyone who is disposed to see this as a misogynist satire should compare it with the real thing'.[45] Yet, compared with a misogyny that offends by its very excess, gallantry can be a subtle and effective method of keeping women in their place; and in this respect the *Rape* belongs very much to the world of *The Spectator* and of its compliments to the sex defined as companions to men and ornaments of the creation.[46] This was not, however, an issue to concern Bell, who was apparently pleased with the 1714 expansion of the *Rape*. Her niece, Abbess Fermor, later recalled that 'Mr. Pope's praise made her aunt very troublesome and conceited', and she implied that he was a welcome visitor despite the inconvenience caused by his poor health (*TE*, II, 100). It may have been Bell herself who had his lines about her diamond cross inscribed on the portrait made on her marriage; and the poet himself felt sufficiently confident to represent her in April 1715, in *The Key to the Lock*, as accepting 'the Character of *Belinda* with much Frankness and good Humour' (pp. 99, 102).

By this time, however, Bell was finally married to Francis Perkins of Ufton Court in Berkshire, who, if not a lord, was at least a gentleman of landed property and impeccable antecedents.[47] Congratulations were obviously in order, yet Pope's insinuations on the occasion were in disturbing contrast to the amused detachment of the *Rape*. As Geoffrey Tillotson remarks with striking understatement, 'the tone is not pleasant' (*TE*, II, 101):

It was but tother day I heard of Mrs Fermor's being Actually, directly, and consummatively, married. I wonder how the guilty Couple and their Accessories at Whiteknights look, stare, or simper, since that grand Secret came out which they so well conceald before. They conceald it as well as a Barber does his Utensils when he goes to trim upon a Sunday and his Towels hang out all the way: Or as well as a Fryer concealed a little Wench, whom he was carrying under his habit to Mr Colingwood's Convent; Pray Father (sayd one in the Street to him) what's that under your Arm. A Saddle for one of the Brothers to ride with, quoth the Fryer. Then Father (cryd he) take care and shorten the Stirrups – For the Girls Legs hung out –

(*Corr.*, I, 269)

Patty, the addressee, was a safe repository for such confidences, but to Bell herself Pope was guardedly respectful, composing a letter on her marriage

[45] Nussbaum, pp. 137–43; Hammond, *Pope*, Harvester New Readings (Brighton, 1986), p. 167.
[46] For a forceful account of the *Rape* as a brilliant but insidious mythologising of these assumptions, see Pollak, chapter 3 (pp. 77–107).
[47] See A. Mary Sharp, *The History of Ufton Court* (London, 1892).

which, while polite, emphatically puts aside the high life which was of the essence in her poetic transformation and sets out the opposite demands of her new career, beginning with a pious assumption which, for a girl anything like the fictional Belinda, is at least questionable:

You are by this time satisfy'd how much the tenderness of one man of merit is to be prefer'd to the addresses of a thousand . . . It may be expected perhaps, that one who has the title of Poet, should say something more polite on this occasion: But I am really more a well-wisher to your felicity, than a celebrater of your beauty. Besides, you are now a married woman, and in a way to be a great many better things than a fine Lady; such as an excellent wife, a faithful friend, a tender parent, and at last as the conse-quence of them all, a saint in heaven.   (*Corr.*, I, 272–73)

He concludes with a reminiscence of the appropriation enacted in the closing lines of the *Rape*, calling himself 'a man who will certainly be spoken of as your admirer, after he is dead'. He also refers to the 'good humour' which ensures she will make her husband happy, a compliment which takes on a shade of irony from the final addition made to the *Rape* for its appearance in the *Works* of 1717; for in a new speech, Clarissa, provider of the fatal scissors, makes precisely this quality the touchstone of Belinda's moral failure.[48] Despite signs in the text that Clarissa is offensively self-righteous and over-eager to show herself to advantage (signs which tend to preserve the detach-ment from moral judgements which is so marked a feature of the poem), Pope tells the reader in a note added in 1736 that the passage was 'introduced . . . to open more clearly the MORAL of the Poem, in a parody of the speech of Sarpedon to Glaucus'; and it remains the only course for a woman who wants to achieve peace of mind without challenging the structures of Bell's society:

> But since, alas! frail Beauty must decay,
> Curl'd or uncurl'd, since Locks will turn to grey,
> Since painted, or not painted, all shall fade,
> And she who scorns a Man, must die a Maid;
> What then remains, but well our Pow'r to use,
> And keep good Humour still whate'er we lose?
> And trust me, Dear! good Humour can prevail,
> When Airs, and Flights, and Screams, and Scolding fail.
> Beauties in vain their pretty Eyes may roll;
> Charms strike the Sight, but Merit wins the Soul.
>
> (*Rape*, V.25)

Sheila Delany, insisting on the *Rape*'s basis in institutionalised injustice, neatly describes this as 'useful advice for a ruling class to offer those whom it exploits'.[49] Readers who take a hard line will see Pope setting the seal on Belinda's failure; yet he could have done it so much more clearly by making

[48] See John Trimble, 'Clarissa's Role in *The Rape of the Lock*', *Texas Studies in English*, 15 (1974), 673–91.

[49] Delany, 'Sex and Politics in Pope's *Rape of the Lock*', *English Studies in Canada*, 1 (1975), 46–61 (p. 59).

Clarissa a less ambiguous character. Precisely in this refusal to be simple as
his letter to Patty is simple lies the continuing fascination of the poem, whose
virtuoso art of evasion saves him, in Ellen Pollak's words, from 'ever having
to take direct responsibility for an unchivalrous poetic act' (Pollak, p. 83).

It is clear from the letter to Patty that Pope saw Bell as in some sense compromised, and the family manoeuvrings over her marriage as sordid and
discreditable. His is not the only voice to suggest that there is something
amiss with a match so secretive, for Teresa, writing to a female cousin, dwells
on the same point, suggesting also that Bell has been lucky to find a taker for
her dangerously mature charms. Whether Bell's 'superiour merit' is ironically
meant is hard to tell; for Teresa's wit is evidently of a kind that runs into
satire even of those she likes. Despite the complimentary flourishes and self-
consciously humorous style of reporting which help to show why Pope found
her so fascinating, the letter also reveals something of the caustic frivolity that
finally revolted him.

> I have a thousand thanks to return for your good natured concideration of me, its cer-
> tain nothing coud soe well resign me to Mr Perkins wedding with my Cosen Bell; as
> ye Leave you gave me on that occation to writ to you; to have but one Authodox Bat-
> chelor in ons neightbourhood & see him marry'd to a Lady of superiour merit is I con-
> fess a very mellencoly circumstance for me; yet Madam in this great trial I have a
> pleasure to think it may perhaps devert you to hear an account of this matter.
>
> He spends a great Part of his time with her but its Obsarvable he comes commonly
> att [an] evening & stays tell latte: Now whether his reason be ye old Provabe that
> women & Linnen Look Best by Candles, or that in Lovers ther is a Gleam that Pleases
> it selfe in moonshine, I dont know. t'was by chance I met him ther once & thro his
> great care to hide it I coud Plainly perceive how Terribly he was charmed, I had much
> adoe to give civillity ye Preference to my Curiosity immagining to have seen what
> happened in a soft interview and to have Lett you know but I left em very soon when
> I reflected that I mortifyed em with being ther & that tho it was an new thing for me
> to see a man make Love it was not soe to you; nor coud I hope to entertain you with
> ye reharsall of a Passage your selfe has soe often bein A Party consarned in. its
> ungenerous I think in em not to marry in the Country its ye Least they can doe to
> soften as much as in em lays ye afflctions of all ye single people in this neightbourhood
> of Both Sexes by deverting us one day, the writtings are certainly in hand, for y^e
> grave face of a Councellor ye Busse on of a Trustee & ye gay on of a Bride ever meets
> one att her hous; Mrs Harret Brown I remmember woud not believe the Wedding
> when I saw her; I beg leave to tell her she dose not know my Cosen Bell soe well as
> I doe, for when I found her make a secret to   (Blount Letters, III, 155)

At this tantalising point Teresa reaches the foot of the page, and the second
page is lost.

This document is doubly poignant, both for what it says about Bell's final
if unspectacular success and for the light it sheds on the predicament of the
woman in whom Pope found more of Belinda's charm than in Bell herself.
By her marriage Bell has just escaped temptations remarkably close to the
preoccupations ascribed to Teresa in 'After the Coronation':

Garters, Stars, and Coronets appear,
And in soft Sounds, *Your Grace* salutes their Ear.   (*Rape*, I.79)

Before you pass th'imaginary sights
Of Lords, and Earls, and Dukes, and garter'd Knights.

('Coronation', line 35)

Teresa is, in effect, dangerously close to 'the *Gnomes'* Embrace', as with her characteristically satirical eye she observes the cousin whose status and security, if nothing else, she can hardly have escaped envying. However, she does not seem to have been the kind of person who could have admitted, even if it had been true, that she would have liked what she had never been offered.

It is particularly piquant that the commentator on this one solid triumph of Belinda's original should be Teresa; for the poem through which Bell is known to posterity celebrates and criticises precisely that glittering and ambitious style of femininity which touched Pope most closely in the bolder and more striking of his favourite sisters.

4

Rebellious sympathies

1

In retrospect Pope's development tends to look as if it could never have been otherwise, but in the case of the *Rape*, perhaps best-loved of all his works, events conspired peculiarly neatly to give him the opportunity for what now seems so characteristic. The affair of the lock specifically invited him to involve himself with the 'little unguarded Follies' of female behaviour as he saw it, unleashing his imagination on the intimate everyday concerns of fashionable women (Dedication, 1714). Thus licensed, he gives the impression of apprehending with imaginative gusto the kind of detail many of his sex would hardly notice. Not only does he elaborate such set pieces as the ritual of the toilette or the discomforts of sylphs stuck in various cosmetics, but he also fills the poem with appreciation of the small-scale, fragile and highly-finished artefacts of this predominantly indoor world. Although the real life equivalents of these interiors also contained men – men who were moreover expected to adorn themselves and their surroundings in a brilliant style since redefined as a female prerogative – for Belinda (and for Teresa) this interior world is the world itself, where life's truly important events occur. For the men, however, there exists a range of outside worlds (even for Catholics there are coffee houses, taverns, field sports), each allowing in its different way some relaxation of the constraints of the tea-table. Although it is arguable that Pope, being barred from the more robust activities of his sex, necessarily had more time and energy than many men for the delicate indoor world of the ladies, what really distinguishes his approach is the poet's interest in giving full imaginative realisation to experience, even to those aspects which others might see but not notice.

The issue of Pope's imaginative relation to a distinctively feminine aesthetic presents difficult problems of balance. It would be relatively simple to make a case for the feminine as an especially fertile area in the context of an old-fashioned Age of Reason, in which judicious men could be represented as fencing out passion and imagination to such a degree that the poet's vitality depended on escaping into realms governed by the inferior sex or by the conventions of inferior genres such as Gothic romance or vision and Oriental

tales. Emrys Jones comes close to this in his suggestive account of Pope's
pleasure in creating Belinda's world:

What women of this kind provided for a poet like Pope, a poet working in a *milieu* of
somewhat narrow and dogmatic rationalism, was a means of entry to a delightful world
of folly and bad sense . . . Women are closer than men to the fantastic and fabulous
world of older poetry, such as that of *A Midsummer Night's Dream* . . . *The Rape of the
Lock* is full of the small objects and appurtenances of the feminine world which arouses
Pope's aesthetic interest.[1]

Later he speaks more generally of a culture driven to escape:

In this period of somewhat exaggerated politeness, correctness, rationalism, there
existed a correspondingly strong interest in the low, the little, the trivial, the mean,
the squalid, and the indecent – to the extent of giving all these things expression in
imaginative writing.   (p. 234)

Although this tends to overstate the repressiveness of current norms, in comparison with Pope's previous major projects (the *Pastorals* and the *Essay on
Criticism*) Caryll's commission virtually commanded a romp; and as Emrys
Jones suggests, the context would not be simply the material world of lapdogs
and china jars, but would extend into the mental world attributed to the
fashionable coquette, which he rightly identifies as having special affinities (in
contemporary eyes at least) with the imaginative territory of folklore and
fantasy.

    The notion of such a link is in line with current beliefs about the nature
of the mind and of the sexes. Sanity was traditionally seen as a balance between various mental powers:

According to faculty psychology men possessed three souls: the rational, the sensitive,
and the vegetative. Because the vegetative soul was the province of such involuntary
functions as growth, nutrition, and generation, discussion of mental health focused on
the relationship between the rational soul, containing the will and the understanding,
and the sensitive soul, containing the corporeal agencies of knowledge (imagination,
memory, the common sense, and the senses) and the passions . . . Rational and sensitive souls are thus interdependent, and mental health is determined by how har-
moniously they work together.[2]

The powers of the sensitive soul thus posed a challenge: if not properly
ordered by the rational soul they could result in madness. Traditionally the
passions were the greatest threat, but in Hobbes's formulation fancy takes on
this role. Fancy (which Hobbes does not distinguish from imagination) acts
by perceiving similarities and summoning one image to follow another; but
it needs to be balanced by judgement, which by perceiving differences sorts

---

[1] Emrys Jones, 'Pope and Dulness', Chatterton Lecture on an English Poet, 1968, *Proceedings
  of the British Academy*, 54 (1968), 231–63 (p. 242).
[2] Michael V. DePorte, *Nightmares and Hobbyhorses: Swift, Sterne, and Augustan Ideas of Madness*
  (San Marino, 1974), p. 12.

thoughts into order.[3] It followed that wholesome creativity relied on similar
balances: hence in early eighteenth-century criticism the dynamic faculties
(imagination, invention, wit) are regularly subject to discipline (reason,
judgement, probability).[4] Although Pope, for example, reveres the '*Grace*
beyond the Reach of Art' which 'without passing thro' the *Judgment*, gains /
The *Heart*', this remains the privilege of one who has mastered the '*vulgar
Bounds*': it is no sanction for the simple abdication of judgement which produces 'One *glaring Chaos* and *wild Heap* of *Wit*'.[5] Thus the literature of times
and places remote from contemporary views of what was reasonable (notably
Gothic and Oriental fiction) was generally convicted of formal shortcomings,
resulting, as contemporary critics saw it, from imaginative flights ungoverned
by any organising principle. The test case for respectability by this standard
must be Homer, who so impressed Pope with 'amazing Invention', 'unequal'd
Fire and Rapture' and 'the Force of . . . *Imagination*' that he may appear from
Pope's Preface alone as a prodigy in whom only the imaginative and emotional pole of creativity was active; but it is only necessary to read the notes
to Pope's translation to realise his faith in Homer's governing moral intention, which is in his view to demonstrate the evil effects of anger.[6] In comparison with this structural coherence the Gothic Shakespeare is like 'an
ancient majestick piece of *Gothick* Architecture' in which, for all its awe-
inspiring qualities, 'many of the Parts are childish, ill-plac'd, and unequal to
its grandeur'.[7] Yet, for all his concessions, he profoundly admires
Shakespeare; and this admiration is part of his long-standing interest in fantastic genres markedly at odds with stereotypes of neoclassical taste. When it
came to enhancing Belinda's world with the metaphysical dimension provided
by his sylphs and gnomes, his imagination was well stored, not only with the
Rosicrucianism of *The Count of Gabalis*, which provided the original of the
sylphs, but also with the faery lore of Chaucer and *The Flower and the Leaf*, the
miniature fairy world of *A Midsummer Night's Dream* and *Romeo and Juliet*, and
the intriguing servant spirits of *The Tempest* and the Oriental tales.[8]

---

[3] DePorte, pp. 12–19; David Fairer, *Pope's Imagination* (Manchester, 1984), pp. 54–55.
[4] See the range of evidence analysed in Donald F. Bond, ' "Distrust" of Imagination in
    English Neo-classicism', *PQ*, 14 (1935), 54–69.
[5] *Essay on Criticism*, lines 141–57, 292 (*TE*, I, 255–58, 272).
[6] Preface to the *Iliad*, *TE*, VII, 4; *Iliad*, I, note to 155.
[7] Preface to Pope's edition of Shakespeare (*Prose Works*, II, 25–26).
[8] Pope mentions *Gabalis* as his principal source in the Dedication to the 1714 *Rape* ([Nicolas de
    Montfaucon, Abbé de Villars], *The Count of Gabalis; or, The Extravagant Mysteries of the Cabalists,
    Exposed in Five Pleasant Discourses on the Secret Sciences*, translated by P. A[yres] (London, 1680)).
    He was from childhood a careful reader of Chaucer and Chaucerian apocrypha (see Maynard
    Mack, 'Pope's Copy of Chaucer', in *Evidence in Literary Scholarship; Essays in Memory of James
    Marshall Osborn*, edited by René Wellek and Alvaro Ribeiro (Oxford, 1979), pp. 105–21); and
    fairies act as machines both in his version of *The Merchant's Tale* ('January and May', lines
    617–709; *TE*, II, 45–46) and in the Wife of Bath's tale, which Dryden had translated in the
    Fables and to which Pope translated the prologue (*The Poems of John Dryden*, edited by James
    Kinsley, 4 vols. (Oxford, 1958), IV, 1703–17; *TE*, II, 57–78). He discusses medieval dream

In parallel to these beliefs about thought and creativity runs the ancient assumption that women are mentally as well as physically softer and weaker than men: in terms of traditional psychology, their rational soul is inadequate to discipline an overactive sensitive soul. Although it is sometimes admitted that 'feminine' mental problems occur less frequently in women who do physical work, the implication that these 'female' characteristics are less natural than acquired is not one that investigators down to the time of Pope are eager to pursue.[9] Thus it remains axiomatic, even for a female apologist like Mary Lady Chudleigh, that women are weak in judgement and correspondingly strong in imagination.[10] As evidence from daily life contemporaries could point to examples of fickle and superficial female behaviour like those regularly complained of by the periodical journalists, or to the kind of emotional disproportion which cannot distinguish between a lover and a lapdog, a lock of hair and a rape.[11] In literature not only women's failure to produce good examples of major genres but also their apparent preference, both as readers and as writers, for extravagant and unrealistic novels and romances could be cited. They could also be blamed for perpetuating an outmoded world view in the 'old wives' tales' to which they clung despite the new science. All such observations were suggestive in a culture relatively unused to asking, for example, how far social pressure on girls to market themselves and in the process consume the products of commerce contributed to their vanity and frivolity; and how far their exclusion from schools, universities and coffee houses influenced the divergence of masculine and feminine taste and outlook.

In the absence of such questioning, women remained associated with mental indiscipline in art as in life. When Atterbury reacted against the elaborately descriptive style of some Oriental tales Pope had lent him, he found it natural to suggest that they might be the product of 'some Womans Imagination' (*Corr.*, II, 56). Oriental tales are again connected with a woman in a complex passage from one of Pope's letters to his friend Judith Cowper; and it is suggestive that the genre is cited together with another non-standard form, the Gothic allegorical vision:

I could wish you tryd something in the descriptive way on any Subject you please, mixd with Vision & Moral; like the Pieces .of the old Provençal Poets, which

poems (in the same breath as Oriental tales) in *Corr.*, II, 202–3. He singles out Mercutio's Queen Mab speech for praise in his edition of *The Works of Shakespear*, 6 vols. (London, 1725, vols. II–VI misdated 1723), VI, 260–62. His use of Shakespeare's traditional superstitions is discussed by Pat Rogers in 'Faery Lore and *The Rape of the Lock*', *Review of English Studies*, 25 (1974), 25–38. Pope's enthusiasm for Oriental tales emerges from *Corr.*, II, 56; from Spence, no. 340; and from Sherburn, 'New Anecdotes', p. 345.

9 For similar obstacles to the recognition of hysteria as common to both sexes see Ilza Veith, *Hysteria: The History of a Disease* (Chicago, 1965), p. 127.

10 For Mary Lady Chudleigh see Fairer, pp. 83–90.

11 See for example *The Spectator*, I, 191–95, 311–15; II, 8–11; III, 345–46.

abound with Fancy & are the most amusing scenes in nature. There are 3 or 4 of this kind in Chaucer admirable: The Flower & the Leaf every body has been delighted with. I have long had an inclination to tell a Fairy tale; the more wild & exotic the better, therfore a *Vision*, which is confined to no rules of probability, will take in all the Variety & luxuriancy of Description you will. Provided there be an apparent moral to it. I think one or 2 of the Persian Tales would give one hints for such an Invention: And perhaps if the Scenes were taken from Real places that are known, in order to compliment particular Gardens & Buildings of a fine Taste, (as I believe several of Chaucer's descriptions do, tho tis what nobody has observd) it would add great beauty to the whole. – I wish you found such an amusement pleasing to you; If you did but, at leisure, form descriptions from Objects in nature itself which struck you most livelily, I would undertake to find a Tale that shoud bring em all together: which you'l think an odd undertaking, but in a Piece of this fanciful & Imaginary nature I am sure is practicable.   (pp. 202–3)

This is a fine example of the flexibility which enriched Pope's sensibility in ways the narrower Atterbury would have thought corrupting. Although Pope finally retains the role of judicious organiser (a poetic role analogous to the physiological role of male form acting on female matter in the Aristotelian account of conception) he reveals in the process a feeling for undisciplined invention summed up in his suggestion that the moral need only be 'apparent', not generating description but masking its effective independence. Only in such genres, which he is ostensibly recommending as appropriate for a woman's amusement, could such a reversal of orthodox values achieve even this specious plausibility.[12] Moreover, writing to a woman offered a peculiarly safe context for confiding his urge to write outside the rules in which he so deeply believed.[13]

A further dimension of the situation is opened up by the realisation that Judith suffered from depression.[14] Since women were believed to be especially liable to a cluster of afflictions (melancholy, spleen, vapours, hysteria) in which depression led through distorted perception to (in extreme cases) madness, Judith's tendency made her as it were quintessentially feminine, a perfect match in her inner disorder for the literary disorder which Pope finds it so easy to discuss with her. His comments to her about the similar problems of their mutual friend Mary Howe show how easily the diagnosis of such mental imbalances follows from the assumption that a woman's physical constitution is less robust than a man's:

There is an Air of sadness about her which grieves me, & which I have learnt by experience, will increase upon an indolent (I won't say an affected) Resignation to it. It will do so in Men, & much more in Women, who have a natural softness that sinks them even when Reason does not.   (*Corr.*, II, 202)

[12] For a similar reading see Fairer, pp. 15–16.
[13] For his commitment to the claims of judgement, see for example Spence, nos. 73, 380, 384, 391, 402.
[14] This is hinted at in Pope's letters (*Corr.*, II, 137, 141–42, 155, 174). For further evidence see Falconer Madan, *The Madan Family* (Oxford, 1933), pp. 77–78.

Physicians agreed: weakness of constitution was, for example, an obvious replacement for the finally discredited theory of migration of the womb as an almost equally gender-specific explanation of hysteria (Veith, pp. 131–33). Yet as Pope handles it, physical constitution is not the whole story: he also hints at a refusal to fight the disease which can verge on affectation; and he goes so far as to suggest that he has caught himself lapsing into this kind of state.

In the Cave of Spleen episode in the 1714 *Rape* Pope makes this kind of perversity prominent, personifying Affectation alongside Ill-nature as one of the goddess's handmaids (IV.25–38). Women dominate the scene, and it is telling that the one specifically male affliction among the 'Throngs . . . chang'd to various Forms by *Spleen*' is the delusion of being in a uniquely female condition: 'Men prove with Child, as pow'rful Fancy works' (IV.47–54). It is reserved for the gnome Umbriel to bring out the most damaging implications of the connection between spleen and women, a connection which he tellingly locates in the female reproductive cycle:

> Hail wayward Queen!
> Who rule the Sex to Fifty from Fifteen,
> Parent of Vapours and of Female Wit,
> Who give th'*Hysteric* or *Poetic* Fit,
> On various Tempers act by various ways,
> Make some take Physick, others scribble Plays;
> Who cause the Proud their Visits to delay,
> Who send the Godly in a Pett, to pray.   (line 57)

This, of course, is all a gnome *would* know about poetry; yet behind the speech is the assumption that women's writing is sufficiently anomalous to make sense of the parallel, however ironic, with disagreeable symptoms of bad health and temper. So, at least, thought Anne Finch, Countess of Winchilsea, who as poet and sufferer from spleen took issue with Pope over the passage (see chapter 6.5).

Read in this spirit, however, there may seem to be some inconsistency between this passage and Pope's other pronouncements on the relationship between mental illness, creativity and gender. In the *Art of Sinking*, for example, he applies a similar criticism to bad poets in general when he makes Scriblerus define poetry as 'a natural or morbid Secretion' arising from 'Titillation of the Generative Faculty of the Brain', and has him recount cases in which writing has acted as a wholesome purge: 'I have known a man thoughtful, melancholy and raving for divers days, who forthwith grew wonderfully easy, lightsome and cheerful, upon a discharge of the peccant humour, in exceedingly purulent Metre' (*Prose Works*, II, 189). Although the hint at frustrated sexuality recalls the Cave of Spleen, there is no mention of women; yet when Pope does consider female creativity, as for example in various attacks on women writers in the *Dunciad*, it is typically associated with offensive matter voided from the body, in line with the traditional association of the female with the grosser aspects of physicality and the male with the higher realm of mind.[15] This obviously expresses male ambivalence towards women's fertility, which Umbriel defines as coterminous with the empire of Spleen, and which is highlighted again in Pope's treatment of the maternal monster Dulness. In her 'Cave of Poverty and Poetry', which is predictably located next to Bedlam, she fosters monstrous conceptions assimilated by the language to the warm fleshiness of the fertile womb:

> Here she beholds the Chaos dark and deep,
> Where nameless somethings in their causes sleep,
> 'Till genial Jacob, or a warm Third-day,
> Call forth each mass, a poem, or a play:
> How Hints, like spawn, scarce quick in embryo lie,
> How new-born Nonsense first is taught to cry,
> Maggots half-form'd, in rhyme exactly meet,
> And learn to crawl upon poetic feet.[16]

Such imagery is more revealing of his underlying attitude than any of his compliments, qualified as they usually are, to women who write.

The connection between women, morbid secretion and bad writing was not, however, without its problems for Pope, since it brought him into implicit conflict with another tradition, which recognised that melancholy often went with genius and that the madness of a bard or prophet could communicate truths beyond ordinary sanity.[17] Although Pope and other writers of the early eighteenth century can be cited as showing unusual hostility to this tradition, this is by no means the whole truth. As Max Byrd has argued, the hostility seems kindled by the danger of man's having to recognise the sources of madness in himself: without his sense that there might be truth in the tradition the rage for sanity would be less intense (Byrd, pp. 12–57). It should not, therefore, be surprising that Pope recognises, if only in less guarded moments, a degree of involvement with some of the mental states and types of creativity associated with the milder forms of imbalance, and therefore with femininity. In his intense yet confining relationship with his mother, he felt the gloom and emotional sensitivity engendered by caring for a helpless woman less as a deviation from some ideally positive cheerfulness than as an expansion into a valuable moral and aesthetic sensibility; he used his correspondence with women to explore his interest in Gothic and Oriental fantasy; and in his friendship with Patty he shared an appreciation of landscape more 'romantic' (to use his word) than he revealed to any of his male

---

[15] For this theme see chapter 6.7, and Susan Gubar, 'The Female Monster in Augustan Satire', *Signs*, 3 (1977), 380–94.

[16] *Dunciad A*, I.32, 53 (*TE*, V, 64, 66).

[17] For creative melancholy see Lawrence Babb, 'The Cave of Spleen', *Review of English Studies*, 12 (1936), 165–76 (pp. 170–75). For divine madness see Max Byrd, *Visits to Bedlam: Madness and Literature in the Eighteenth Century* (Columbia, 1974), pp. xi–xv.

friends.[18] In his late twenties, moreover, he showed particular sympathy with that resentment of control which contemporary theory represented as the tension between the sensitive soul and its rational counterpart; and he expressed this sympathy by focusing on female distress.

2

This theme emerges in two poems included in the *Works* of 1717, *Verses to the Memory of an Unfortunate Lady* and *Eloisa to Abelard*. In an early transcript of *Eloisa* Pope actually included lines which were later to appear at the close of the *Unfortunate Lady*, thus underlining the imaginative affinity between the two poems.[19] In both he testifies to the triple association between women, sub-standard literary modes (in this case the Gothic) and vividness of imagination and feeling, setting a female protagonist in intolerable confinement, surrounding her with Gothic trappings (ghosts, curses, monasteries, gloomy forests) and exploring with sympathy her attempts to master her situation. This was in part a natural development of his early interest in Ovid, whose *Heroides*, which comprise for the most part letters from abandoned heroines, were then assumed to have as their primary aim the dramatic representation of passion.[20] These women are, for the most part, the abandoned partners of famous heroes; and while in their outpourings, as Rebecca Ferguson notes, 'sheer extremity of emotion can represent the feminine equivalent of valorous action', so that the poet seems to vindicate the dignity of women, the assumption that the love which forms an interlude in the crowded career of a hero is a heroine's occupation for life is a confining reassertion of an age-old distinction.[21] Certainly Ovid's heroines, along with the tragic female victims of Rowe's drama and other manifestations of the vogue for distressed women that was to lead to the mid-century fascination with Clarissa's flight from perverse sexuality, offered Pope a map of the sexual world on which he meditated deeply; and if, as Mack has suggested, Pope's juvenile tragedy 'built on a very moving story in the legend of St Genevieve' was actually about the legendary persecuted wife Geneviève of Brabant, he had responded creatively to this vein of sentiment from a very early age.[22]

---

18 See chapters 2.4, 5.4, 6.2, 9.1.

19 Mack, *Collected in Himself*, pp. 322–23 and note.

20 For an account of the contemporary reading of Ovid and an impressive case for the artistic success of Pope's 'Eloisa' see Hoyt Trowbridge, 'Pope's *Eloisa* and the *Heroides* of Ovid', *Studies in Eighteenth-Century Culture*, 3 (1973), 11–34.

21 Ferguson, *The Unbalanced Mind: Pope and the Rule of Passion* (Brighton, 1986), p. 15. For the wider context see Gillian Beer, ' "Our Unnatural No-voice": The Heroic Epistle, Pope, and Women's Gothic', *Yearbook of English Studies*, 12 (1982), pp. 125–51. For the repressive aspects of the 'fashion for troubled females' which 'tended to confirm . . . a stereotype of woman's anarchic slavery to her passion' see Mack, *Life*, p. 324.

22 For female pathos see Brown, 'Defenceless Woman', and, by the same author, *English Dramatic Form, 1660–1760: An Essay in Generic Form* (London, 1981), pp. 148–54. For Pope's tragedy see Spence no. 34; Mack, *Collected in Himself*, p. 323 and note.

Mack has shown how several of the poems of Ovid which Pope translated in adolescence enabled him to explore the plight of lovers too unrefined, even monstrous, to please – a situation uncomfortably close to the increasingly deformed youth, whose sensitivity to the possible identification between himself and such figures seems to have led him to delete from his pastorals a passage in which the spurned shepherd Alexis lamented the apparent loss of charms once equal to those of his rival.[23] This line of interest coincided with the interest in specifically female flights of despair in the letter translated by Pope as 'Sapho to Phaon', in which the heroine, like Pope, feels deeply hurt that her poetic gift cannot atone in the eyes of her beloved for her lack of physical beauty.[24] Her letter also shows how directly Ovid fed the tradition of women's Gothic: he provides for his impeccably classical heroine dreams of fruitless wandering, a gloomy grotto, a supernatural voice and a jutting crag from which to leap to her death (lines 155–66, 185–200).

The *Metamorphoses* as well as the *Heroides* provided examples of women pursued and confined. Although Pope makes little of it, this is Galatea's situation as Polyphemus chases her in jealous rage; but in the wily courtship of Pomona by the disguised Vertumnus he focuses on the situation of a determined virgin confronted in her walled garden by a lover prepared for rape – and also by the complicity of her own emotions, which, unlike Belinda, she does not attempt to deny:

> Force he prepar'd, but check'd the rash Design;
> For when, appearing in a Form Divine,
> The Nymph surveys him, and beholds the Grace
> Of charming Features and a youthful Face,
> In her soft Breast consenting Passions move,
> And the warm Maid confess'd a mutual Love.[25]

The pathos of a different kind of helplessness is the focus of 'The Fable of Dryope', in which the heroine's innocent act of picking flowers for her baby causes her to be transformed into a tree:

> But when she backward wou'd have fled, she found
> Her stiff'ning feet were rooted in the ground:
> In vain to free her fasten'd feet she strove,
> And as she struggles, only moves above.[26]

Her dying speech is a poignant race against time:

> 'My son, thy mother's parting kiss receive,
> While yet thy mother has a kiss to give.

[23] Maynard Mack, *Collected in Himself*, pp. 380–83.
[24] 'Sapho to Phaon', lines 37–42 (*TE*, I, 395).
[25] 'Polyphemus and Acis' (*TE*, I, 365–73); 'The Fable of Vertumnus and Pomona', line 118 (*TE*, I, 382).
[26] 'The Fable of Dryope', line 39 (*TE*, I, 387).

> I can no more; the creeping rind invades
> My closing lips, and hides my head in shades.'

('Dryope', line 94)

The less innocent implications of fascination with female helplessness are interestingly hinted at in *Windsor Forest*, when, as Pan pursues Lodona, Pope notes succinctly that 'her Flight increas'd his Fire', and goes on to describe the excitement of his approach in sensuous detail:

> And now his shorter Breath with sultry Air
> Pants on her Neck, and fans her parting Hair.[27]

This anticipates the ambiguous excitement dear to Richardson and the Gothic novelists – ambiguous because it is true of the writer and reader as well as of the fictional pursuer; and, as the rake would argue, perhaps even of the victim too.[28] For Pope, however, perhaps rather more convincingly than for some exploiters of the theme, the primary enthusiasm is for the kind of sympathy which in life leads to solidarity with the oppressed, as his practical concern for the 'originals' of his Unfortunate Lady was to demonstrate. If 'her Flight increas'd his Fire' represents one aspect of the charm of women under stress in his writing, the words with which Dryope's sister introduces her tale may stand for his dominant concern in real life: 'kindly sigh for sorrows not your own' ('Dryope', line 4). These words also provide an apt epigraph for the two poems of female distress in the 1717 *Works*.

Although the *Unfortunate Lady* was not at first entitled *Elegy*, but simply *Verses*, it is clearly in the tradition of funeral elegy inherited from Roman poetry and developed by English Renaissance writers.[29] Yet for all the familiarity of many of its themes and strategies, there is an element of outrageousness about it which declares itself quite independently of any allegations about the events behind it.

To an extent we are prepared for wild, uninhibited speech by discovering the speaker startled by a bloody apparition in a moonlit wood. His rush of feeling is captured by exclamations and rhetorical questions, as the reader, recollecting ghostly lore which for many then as now would centre on the role of the ghost in *Hamlet*, begins to speculate on the meaning of the apparition and on the relation of the speaker to the woman whom he addresses so fervently:

> What beck'ning ghost, along the moonlight shade
> Invites my step, and points to yonder glade?
> 'Tis she! – but why that bleeding bosom gor'd,
> Why dimly gleams the visionary sword?   (line 1; *TE*, II, 362)

[27] *Windsor Forest*, lines 184, 195 (*TE*, I, 167–68).

[28] Compare *Pastorals*, 'Spring', lines 57–60 (*TE*, I, 66).

[29] Ian Jack analyses its generic character in relation to contemporary theories in 'The Elegy as Exorcism: Pope's "Verses to the Memory of an Unfortunate Lady" ', in *Augustan Worlds: Essays in Honour of A. R. Humphreys*, edited by J. C. Hilson *et al.* (Leicester, 1978), pp. 69–83 (75–79).

The reader's inference that she is a suicide is confirmed by the speaker's fear
that she may be damned:

> Oh ever beauteous, ever friendly! tell,
> Is it, in heav'n, a crime to love too well?   (line 5)

Thus by the end of the first verse paragraph Pope has indicated his controversial territory. Against the background of the belief that suicide entails damnation, Pope makes his ghost signal by her beckoning that she has something
to tell, perhaps like Hamlet's father a tale of crime committed against her,
which told, she will presumably (if inconsistently) rest in peace. Meanwhile
the speaker's rhetorical questions press for defiant answers: no, one can never
love too well; yes, there must be a heavenly reward for courage.

Perhaps, although he never offers any clear narrative of her love, the
speaker himself is the man whom she loved too well. Whatever his relation
to her, he embarks on a justification of her conduct which insists on a defiance
of ordinary standards: although he repeatedly begins by conceding that a different commentary is at least conceivable ('Why . . . else, ye Pow'rs!',
'perhaps', 'if eternal justice rules'), once the scaffolding is in place he kicks
it away, moving to unqualified assertions which rest only on the status of her
brilliance of soul as an ultimate value recognised by the forces that govern the
universe.[30] Thus the framework of Christian folklore, with its dichotomy of
salvation and damnation, is set in tension with the notion of spiritual energy
as a value in itself. Although the very force of the speaker's insistence on such
transcendent energy may reveal his need to drown out the warning voice of
conventional religion, his references to 'a *Roman*'s part' and 'the glorious fault
of Angels and of Gods' remind the reader that there have been more ways
than one of ordering the moral universe (lines 8, 14). Yet Milton's classic
account of Lucifer's rebellion provides a troubling precedent for a 'glorious
fault', preventing the poem from moving smoothly into the classical decorum
that the coming of age of the Olympians might suggest. The tension seems
deliberate: a classical moral decorum might simply suggest another kind of
respectability.

There were, as the Twickenham commentary demonstrates, numerous
modern examples of admiration for lawless ambition: an additional instance
is the self-justification offered by Marlowe's Tamburlaine:

> The thirst of reign and sweetness of a crown,
> That caus'd the eldest son of heavenly Ops
> To thrust his doting father from his chair,
> And place himself in the imperial heaven,
> Mov'd me to manage arms against thy state.
> What better precedent than mighty Jove?
> Nature, that fram'd us of four elements

---

[30] *Unfortunate Lady*, lines 11, 23, 35; 13–22, 25–28, 37–46.

> Warring within our breasts for regiment,
> Doth teach us all to have aspiring minds.
> Our souls, whose faculties can comprehend
> The wondrous architecture of the world,
> And measure every wand'ring planet's course,
> Still climbing after knowledge infinite,
> And always moving as the restless spheres,
> Wills us to wear ourselves and never rest
> Until we reach the ripest fruit of all.[31]

These connotations of ambition are clearly part of the tradition on which Pope draws, for the speech evokes from one of Tamburlaine's followers a remark highly pertinent to the *Unfortunate Lady*:

> And that made me to join with Tamburlaine;
> For he is gross and like the massy earth
> That moves not upwards, nor by princely deeds
> Doth mean to soar above the highest sort. (II.7.30)

This is precisely the justification to which Pope turns, replacing dichotomies of virtue and vice, salvation and damnation, with a contrast between the free, bright soul of the suicide and the dull earthiness of ordinary people:

> Most souls, 'tis true, but peep out once an age,
> Dull sullen pris'ners in the body's cage:
> Dim lights of life that burn a length of years,
> Useless, unseen, as lamps in sepulchres;
> Like Eastern Kings a lazy state they keep,
> And close confin'd to their own palace sleep. (*Unfortunate Lady*, line 17)

On this basis the speaker proceeds to transform the act of suicide: perhaps it was fate that rescued her from such earth-bound society; yet in one of the dismissals of the framework of possible concession noted above, he immediately abandons suggestion for assertion backed by chemical analogy:

> From these perhaps (ere nature bade her die)
> Fate snatch'd her early to the pitying sky.
> As into air the purer spirits flow,
> And sep'rate from their kindred dregs below;
> So flew the soul to its congenial place,
> Nor left one virtue to redeem her Race. (line 23)

This 'congenial place' belongs to no Christian scheme; and in the light of the speaker's earlier fear that she was damned, his language seems particularly eager to deflect attention from the fact that she wilfully stabbed herself: instead of the 'bleeding bosom gor'd' we see fate intervening, spirits evaporating and the soul taking wing.

[31] *The Plays of Christopher Marlowe*, edited by Roma Gill (Oxford, 1971); *Tamburlaine the Great, Part I*, II.7.12.

The persistent tension between a Christian and a classical scheme is sharpened by the comparison which Pope specifically invites with Jonson's 'Elegie on the Lady Jane Pawlet':

> What gentle Ghost, besprent with *April* deaw,
> Hayles me, so solemnly, to yonder Yewgh?
> And beckning wooes me, from the fatall tree
> To pluck a Garland, for her selfe, or mee?[32]

Unlike Pope's elegy, this is a consolation addressed to real mourners, and unlike the suicide, Lady Jane is celebrated as a Christian paragon, whose less demanding apparition requires of her poet not justification but simply a 'Garland' of commemoration. Yet the qualities Jonson claims for her centre in a similar brilliance of soul, which renders her genealogy insignificant by comparison and qualifies her to be attended in death by angels.[33] Even from his explicitly Christian perspective Jonson senses the same spiritual chemistry that consoles the speaker in Pope's poem:

> It is too neere of kin to Heaven, the Soule,
> To be describ'd! Fames fingers are too foule
> To touch these Mysteries! We may admire
> The blaze, and splendor, but not handle fire! (line 29)

Moreover, Lady Jane displays a similar contempt for the dross of the body, not in the impious act of suicide, but in obedient submission to medical torture:

> 'Tis but a body which you can torment,
> And I, into the world, all Soule, was sent! (line 55)

There is of course much here that Pope cannot imitate, all that follows from exemplary Christian piety and from the dead woman's solidarity with her family, yet central to both poems is the assertion of a woman's vividness of spirit transcending the material world as if by a natural law. By imitating Jonson's opening so closely, Pope invites the reading of one poem against the other, sharpening the tendentiousness of his claim that a suicide, shameful in the sight of the world, belongs to the same spiritual elite as a noblewoman distinguished by religious and family piety.

One mark of Pope's distance from the harmonious functioning of soul and society which Jonson finds compatible with spiritual distinction is the violence with which the suicide's guardian and his family are denounced. Their offence is left deliberately vague: the uncle is a 'mean deserter of thy brother's blood', while his family are 'cursed with hearts unknowing how to yield'; and

---

[32] *Ben Jonson*, edited by C. H. Herford, Percy and Evelyn Simpson, 11 vols. (Oxford, 1925–52), VIII, 268–72, lines 1–4.

[33] This is not to deny significant differences in the treatment of these themes: compare Pope, lines 71–74, 67–68, with Jonson, lines 19–22, 63–64.

only hints in the opening lines ('to love too well', 'a Lover's . . . part') suggest
the supposed interference in their ward's marriage with which criticism of the
poem has too often been entangled (lines 30, 42, 6, 8). Apparently circumstantial detail is less important than the generic failing of such people,
'whose breast ne'er learn'd to glow / For others' good, or melt at others' woe'
(line 45). They are evidently to be classed with the 'dull sullen pris'ners in
the body's cage' in whom soul is deadened by stubborn respectability, and
the pomp of endless funerals seems both image and consequence of their
spiritual state. Indeed, Pope comes strikingly close to the complex of feelings
about innocence oppressed which was to flourish later in the century as he
adumbrates not only the stress on redeeming sensitivity but also the kind of
plot and atmosphere typical of what would later be called Gothic fiction:

> Thus, if eternal justice rules the ball,
> Thus shall your wives, and thus your children fall:
> On all the line a sudden vengeance waits,
> And frequent herses shall besiege your gates.
> There passengers shall stand, and pointing say,
> (While the long fun'rals blacken all the way)
> Lo these were they, whose souls the Furies steel'd,
> And curs'd with hearts unknowing how to yield.   (line 35)

The speaker then continues in tendentious vein as he offers an atonement of
a kind – presumably the exorcism her ghost requires to rest in peace – which
is simply a defiance of all that society represents by its deathbed and funeral
customs (lines 46–62). Dismissing as worthless all that she was denied, he asserts
that her grave, though in unconsecrated ground, is 'sacred by thy reliques
made', attended by angels and the rejuvenating powers of nature, and that
she 'peaceful rests' (lines 63–70). Insofar as the apparition represents the
speaker's anguish at the cutting off of her life, this transfiguration of the meaning
of the suicide is indeed all that is needed to lay the ghost. Yet the tension caused by retaining in the poem hints of a Christian scheme and the modern world
of guardians and midnight dances alongside the pagan universe of noble Roman
suicide is essential to this arresting treatment of deliberately outrageous claims.
Pope is evidently not interested in creating a moral universe in which the
heroine's action would be unequivocally wise and noble.

This tension is, however, set in a light closer to that of common day at the
close of the poem, where, with the ghost laid, the speaker leaves his talk of
the fiery soul's aspiration and contemplates mortality:

> A heap of dust alone remains of thee;
> 'Tis all thou art, and all the proud shall be!   (line 73)

The poet too will come to dust; and just as there is now no talk of the suicide's
transcendence, so there is no hint of immortality for him or his work. All in
the end will be revealed as vanity:

Life's idle business at one gasp be o'er,
The Muse forgot, and thou belov'd no more!   (line 81)

Yet what kind of reality is it that will expose this vanity? Without logical
extrapolations alien to the developing tone of the poem, it can hardly be the
world to come as conceived by Christians, dominated by the choice between
salvation and damnation which it was the speaker's concern to dismiss; nor
does it sound like the realm of elemental fire evoked by his praise of the
suicide: it seems, in effect, more like the consolation of nonentity, an alternative assurance that the distress figured in the ghost's walking will indeed
have an end. Moreover, as at the close of *Eloisa*, the voice that delivers the
valediction seems increasingly to blend into that of its creator, as if in some
respect the fiction is so personally important to him that it requires this final
signature.

In the *Unfortunate Lady* Pope contrives a poem of consolation as indeter-
minate about the moral nature of the universe as about the state of the
suicide's soul. The view most strongly presented, that a distinguished soul is
a rebellious fire naturally drawn to heaven from the dregs of earth, emerges
with dubious logic from a grammatical context of potential concession which
is never directly faced and answered, and the dusty close seems to dismiss
such claims without comment. Yet to extrapolate from these inconsistencies
and from the known views of the poet a logic which proves the speaker's passion to be simply wrong is to deny the poem its special ambivalence.[34] While
the speaker is logically distinct from the historical Pope, he speaks for an
aspect of the poet's nature not usually allowed to dominate, that resentment
of good sense and rational compromise which he feels particularly through his
compassion for people put into intolerable situations by a society which professes these values. Such resentment and compassion, rather than any of the
circumstantial fantasies which later accumulated round the poem, constitute
its strongest link with its creator's experience (Jack, pp. 69–74).

In comparison with a poem in which the poet appears to defend suicide,
the poem in which Eloisa speaks for herself is less obviously shocking. She
asserts herself with the pen, not the sword; she attempts to take the balanced
view of her situation that good sense requires; and she brings herself by the
end to some kind of accommodation with her misery. She also gains a kind
of literary respectability from her status as modern successor to the forsaken
heroines of Ovid's *Heroides*, as her memory and imagination work with
obsessive impotence over the brief portion of her experience made significant
by love. This Ovidian conception, as suggested above, led naturally into the
Gothic mode in which physical oppression becomes the symbol of female
powerlessness. Pope contributes to this development by selecting a character
who is literally Gothic (i.e. lived in what we call the Middle Ages) and

---

[34] For the view that Pope convicts the speaker of error see Howard D. Weinbrot, 'Pope's *Elegy
to the Memory of an Unfortunate Lady*', *Modern Languages Quarterly*, 32 (1971), 255–67.

incarcerating her in one of the distinctive institutions of Gothic culture, haunted by monitory ghosts and surrounded by gloomy forests. In countless novels this is to be recognised as the distressed woman's natural setting, and Eloisa's recognition of 'Black Melancholy' as the spirit of the landscape provides a link with the physiological doctrines of the Cave of Spleen, image of the complex of beliefs which made the female Gothic plausible.[35]

The richness of feminine passion and imagination are everywhere apparent in a poem structured on exclamatory shifts between one imagined scene and another; but Pope places particular emphasis on the subjectivity of perception which, as the teapots of the Cave of Spleen remind us, was recognised as a first step on the path to madness. Although Eloisa is far from mad, it is clear that emotion colours her perception of the Paraclete and its surroundings. At first it is a 'darksom round' with 'rugged rocks' and 'grots and caverns shagg'd with horrid thorn', but later, although its 'awful arches make a noonday night' she remembers how when Abelard was there his 'eyes diffus'd a reconciling ray' (lines 17–20, 143–46). Later still, in a celebrated passage, she observes the process by which her mood darkens the tone of the landscape:

> The darksom pines that o'er yon' rocks reclin'd
> Wave high, and murmur to the hollow wind,
> The wandring streams that shine between the hills,
> The grots that eccho to the tinkling rills,
> The dying gales that pant upon the trees,
> The lakes that quiver to the curling breeze;
> No more these scenes my meditation aid,
> Or lull to rest the visionary maid:
> But o'er the twilight groves, and dusky caves,
> Long-sounding isles, and intermingled graves,
> Black Melancholy sits, and round her throws
> A death-like silence, and a dread repose:
> Her gloomy presence saddens all the scene,
> Shades ev'ry flow'r, and darkens ev'ry green,
> Deepens the murmur of the falling floods,
> And breathes a browner horror on the woods.   (line 155)

In contrast, when she imagines happy lovers visiting the tomb in which she is reunited with Abelard, she visualises through their eyes '*Paraclete*'s white walls, and silver springs' (line 348). As befits the age's conception of a woman in the grip of emotion, gloom and brightness are very much in the mind of the beholder.

In dreams that typify the traditional apprehension of what the imagination might do while the rational soul was suspended in sleep, Eloisa is tormented both with interrupted repetitions of past intimacies and with fantasies of frightening symbolism:

[35] *Eloisa to Abelard*, line 165 (*TE*, II, 333).

> To dream once more I close my willing eyes;
> Ye soft illusions, dear deceits, arise!
> Alas no more! – methinks we wandring go
> Thro' dreary wastes, and weep each other's woe;
> Where round some mould'ring tow'r pale ivy creeps,
> And low-brow'd rocks hang nodding o'er the deeps.
> Sudden you mount! you becken from the skies;
> Clouds interpose, waves roar, and winds arise.   (line 239)

Although this suggestibility, with its Gothic overtones, is in line with contemporary notions of gender, Pope is equally concerned to mark out his heroine, by her magnanimity and struggle towards a disciplined spirituality, as far above any lowest common denominator of female nature. His introductory account of 'those celebrated letters . . . which give so lively a picture of the struggles of grace and nature, virtue and passion' shows his fascination with the energy of her efforts and the power of the feelings she has to combat. The drama focuses on conflict between the two poles of mental activity which in a healthy life would support and balance each other; for to Pope it is axiomatic that the passions are the only faculty that can rouse the mind into action, although they need the restraining hand of reason to operate for the best:

> In lazy Apathy let Stoics boast
> Their Virtue fix'd; 'tis fix'd as in a frost,
> Contracted all, retiring to the breast;
> But strength of mind is Exercise, not Rest:
> The rising tempest puts in act the soul,
> Parts it may ravage, but preserves the whole.
> On life's vast ocean diversely we sail,
> Reason the card, but Passion is the gale;
> Nor God alone in the still calm we find,
> He mounts the Storm, and walks upon the wind.
>   (*Essay on Man*, II.101)

Eloisa, however, favours a more rigorous view, in which religion's role is to stamp out the influence of passion and the flesh altogether. As David Morris points out, she is in effect victim of the 'subtle schoolmen' (exemplified by Abelard, although this irony is not taken up in the poem), whose 'rash dexterity of Wit' has made faculties which ought to work in harmony regard each other as enemies:[36]

> In vain lost *Eloisa* weeps and prays,
> Her heart still dictates, and her hand obeys.   (line 15)

> All is not Heav'n's while *Abelard* has part,
> Still rebel nature holds out half my heart.   (line 25)

> There stern religion quench'd th'unwilling flame,
> There dy'd the best of passions, Love and Fame.   (line 39)

[36] *Essay on Man*, II.81–90; Morris, *Alexander Pope: The Genius of Sense* (London, 1984), pp. 140–47.

Yet, implicitly at least, she knows that it is the lively, sensitive heart which
has potential for religious ecstasy:

> But let heav'n seize it, all at once 'tis fir'd,
> Not touch'd, but rapt; not waken'd, but inspir'd!   (line 201)

Typically, this recognition merges into a plea for Abelard's spiritual
assistance complicated by the belief that she must cease to love him in order
to love God; whereas at the end of the poem she is able to transform her old
passion into a concern which, for all its ambiguity, points to a more realistic
absorption of the lesser in the greater love:

> Then too, when fate shall thy fair frame destroy,
> (That cause of all my guilt, and all my joy)
> In trance extatic may thy pangs be drown'd,
> Bright clouds descend, and Angels watch thee round,
> From opening skies may streaming glories shine,
> And Saints embrace thee with a love like mine.   (line 337)

In conceiving of heaven as a place 'where flames refin'd in breasts seraphic
glow' she has already implied such a possibility; and although images of light
and warmth often speak to her of the sinful past she has no other effective
language for divine love, as she speaks of the 'sun-shine' of holiness and the
'dawning' of grace (lines 207–16, 280). It is not the poem's purpose to allow
her to *articulate* a satisfactory synthesis, for as Morris suggests, it is part of her
predicament that she looks to one pole of her being to cancel out the other;
but her handling of her situation allows the reader not only to see the potential
for the conversion of passion by grace, but also to glimpse that at a less than
conscious level she sees it too. There is poignancy in her description of
Abelard's passionless tranquillity, apparently to her a state of enviable
holiness, yet also, if more clearly for Pope and for the reader than for her, one
slightly sinister and inhuman, its imagery reaching back to the blank before
the spirit of God moved on the face of the waters:

> For thee the fates, severely kind, ordain
> A cool suspense from pleasure and from pain;
> Thy life a long, dead calm of fix'd repose;
> No pulse that riots, and no blood that glows.
> Still as the sea, ere winds were taught to blow,
> Or moving spirit bade the waters flow;
> Soft as the slumbers of a saint forgiv'n,
> And mild as opening gleams of promis'd heav'n.   (line 249)

Moreover, as Eloisa is too generous to stress, Abelard neglects her, even if
he is judged merely as founder of her order. It is as if for him loss of sexuality
means loss of sympathy, and however uncomfortably Eloisa's sensual dreams
and memories sit with her profession, the reader could hardly wish her to
aspire to such blankness. When heaven looks for flames to refine, there will

be little found to the purpose in Abelard, and although Eloisa herself ultimately
despises the flesh in a dusty aside reminiscent of the close of the *Unfortunate
Lady* ('What dust we dote on, when 'tis man we love'), her truth to her passionate experience has in effect been revealed as the necessary condition of her
heroism (line 336). As in the *Unfortunate Lady*, Pope sustains tension and
ambiguity in order to define – and to question – the peculiar kinds of daring
and integrity he celebrates.

Moral courage and purity, striking in relation both to the less exemplary
heroines of the *Heroides* and to Pope's potentially denigrating emphasis on the
'feminine' weaknesses of passion and imagination, are everywhere apparent
in Eloisa, who is moreover unusually strong in the self-analysis essential to
moral vision (Trowbridge, p. 24). She instantly disallows her appeal to
Abelard to tend his flock because she sees that she has spoken disingenuously,
and she is conscious that pious ejaculations may be nothing more constructive
than a rhetoric of despair (lines 129, 179). Her ethical fervour even carries
the poem over the awkwardness, for contemporary readers, of her refusal of
marriage, which Rebecca Ferguson usefully compares with the more embarrassed discussion by John Hughes in the introduction to his translation of the
letters (Ferguson, p. 21). Like the speaker of the *Unfortunate Lady*, who used
brilliance of soul to cut across the Christian dichotomy of salvation and damnation, Eloisa cuts across the distinction between virtuous and fallen
womanhood with an integrity in love unbuttressed by 'fame, wealth, and
honour' (lines 73–98). More magnanimous, however, than the defender of
the Unfortunate Lady, she is far from condemning respectable people who
have chosen to do otherwise:

> Let wealth, let honour, wait the weded dame,
> August her deed, and sacred be her fame;
> Before true passion all those views remove,
> Fame, wealth, and honour! what are you to Love?   (line 77)

Most generous of all, she never thinks of blaming the man who, as her
recollections unwittingly reveal, has from the beginning manoeuvred her into
increasing confinement and isolation. Through her Pope offers a better-
substantiated version of the claim which is equally crucial to the *Unfortunate
Lady*, that respectability and goodness may be poles apart.

Eloisa also approaches the tendentiousness of the *Unfortunate Lady* in setting
up a female character agitated by the rebellion of passion and imagination as
an object of admiration, an admiration which is demanded irrespective of
Eloisa's success in bringing the cooler judgement of religion to bear on her
situation.[37] Readers differ in their estimate of how far and how convincingly
this does in fact happen, for possibilities of sexual implication persist even in

---

[37] For objections to this aspect of the poem see Patricia Meyer Spacks, *An Argument of Images: The
Poetry of Alexander Pope* (Cambridge, Massachusetts, 1971), p. 236.

the pious resolution with which she comes to rest, and her closing reflections on their posthumous fame speak less of repentance than of satisfaction in having achieved exemplary status: 'Oh may we never love as these have lov'd!', she imagines future lovers saying (lines 317–42, 343–52). In this stress on the value of the capacity for feeling the speaker's dramatic presence seems to fade before her creator's preoccupations. Not only is Eloisa's love presented as the object of pilgrimage and the subject of the poet's healing art, but it also requires a similar emotion in that poet: 'He best can paint 'em, who shall feel 'em most' (line 366).

The notion of a real history behind these poems has in different ways interfered with the reading of both. Johnson, for example, believing what he had been told about the supposed Unfortunate Lady, wished that Pope had told her story more clearly, and that he had not prostituted his talent by 'dignifying the amorous fury of a raving girl'; but since Abelard and Heloise were 'known from undisputed history' for their 'eminence of merit', and since 'they both found quiet and consolation in retirement and piety' he is predisposed to enjoy the poem as a commentary on an edifying reality (III, 101, 226, 235). Although the scandal he received about the Unfortunate Lady allowed him to put his finger on a scandalous quality actually characteristic of the poem, the pious perspective history provided for Eloisa obscured for him the centrality of her sensuality and ambivalence. Even without the critical problems raised by assimilating these texts to historical originals, it would be important to stress as a matter of fact that there simply was no real Unfortunate Lady in the sense that there was a real Belinda, although readers, including Caryll, persisted in believing otherwise. (Eventually Warburton obliged them with a misleading note, attributed to Pope, to the effect that she might have been the same person as a lady to whom he had written a letter and the Duke of Buckingham a poem on her decision to enter a convent.)[38] The fact that there was a real Heloise is hardly any more helpful, especially since Pope's source bears little resemblance to her actual writings.[39] In both cases the interesting connections between life and art involve not originals for the heroines but complexes of feeling consolidated through a variety of experiences. Jack, rightly concerned to dismiss the distracting shades clustered around the *Unfortunate Lady*, characterises it instead as 'the product of his imagination working upon his reading', yet the kind of imagination which sets this and *Eloisa* apart from the rest of Pope's output is shaped and focused by experience as well as by books.

---

[38] *TE*, II, 355; Jack, pp. 69–70.

[39] Compare Pope's source, *Letters of Abelard and Heloise*, translated by John Hughes, 4th edition (London, 1722) with the genuine writings of the lovers, *The Letters of Abelard and Heloise*, translated by Betty Radice (Harmondsworth, 1974).

3

The eager, even combative advocacy of wronged women which animates the two poems of female distress in the 1717 volume was to cause friction between Pope and less radically sympathetic friends throughout his life. His own family life, like that of his friends John and Elizabeth Caryll, offered him an ideal of affection and mutual support, and where he saw men in authority failing in their responsibility to female dependants his indignation found a ready literary channel in Ovid's rhetoric of female suffering. Although in real life he was never alone in his concern, his partisanship was typically extreme, even offensive to others. Although he argues less that men should not have power over women than that they should live up to the responsibility which goes with that power, some of the remarks prompted by his sympathy with individuals reveal the more radical chafing against women's legal and customary confinement already familiar from 'With the Works of Voiture'. This is a line of argument which, we may suspect, a young man materially and physically attractive to girls like Teresa would have had less stimulus to develop, but whatever its origins, his passionate advocacy of oppressed wives in a society where the rights of a husband were paramount implies considerable moral courage.

The women who contributed most directly to the distresses of Eloisa and the Unfortunate Lady were Elizabeth Weston (née Gage) and Anne Cope (née Caryll), both of whom first appear as objects of Pope's concern in 1711.[40] Both belonged to great Catholic families; both their fathers were dead; and when their marriages failed, both were helped by John Caryll.

Mrs Weston is first mentioned in Pope's correspondence in June 1711: Caryll has been consulting her former guardian, Sir William Goring, and Pope, with a touch of the officiousness which often marked his dealings with those he cared for most, offers to pass on to her the result of the interview (*Corr.*, I, 119). He also offers a characteristic rationale for his concern, a specifically, religious complement to the emotional sympathy which was to become a moral and aesthetic ideal in the poems of 1717: 'To relieve the injured . . . is no less than to take the work of God himself off his hands, and an easing Providence of its care' (*Corr.*, I, 119; compare I, 130). Goring, however, proved unable or unwilling to act on Mrs Weston's behalf, although later the same month Pope still looked to him to prevent Mr Weston's removal of his daughter from his wife's custody (I, 123). By August Pope was blaming Goring directly for his part in arranging his ward's marriage: 'And he who put so valuable a present into so ill hands shall (I own to you) never have my good opinion, tho' he had that of all the world besides. God grant he may never be my Friend! and guard all my friends from such a guardian!'

[40] For Mrs Weston see Dilke, I, 131–40; for Mrs Cope see Erskine-Hill, *Social Milieu*, pp. 64, 74–78, 88–90. Unless otherwise stated, all material on Mrs Cope and Mrs Weston is taken from these sources.

(I, 132). The curse laid on the Unfortunate Lady's unfeeling guardian clearly
reflects Pope's exasperation with Goring, and the violence of the poetry suggests how easily his advocacy of Mrs Weston – who had in conventional
terms compromised herself by leaving her husband – could give serious
offence. Indeed, Pope had at the outset alienated his sister and brother-in-law,
who supported the husband, probably because he was related to their chaplain
(I, 426). Pope's comment on their attitude further highlights his resistance to
uncritical family solidarity, as well as the value he set on sensitivity to others'
woes. The letter also raises the intriguing possibility that it was he who had
brought Caryll into the affair in the first place:

> I cannot . . . excuse some near allies of mine for their conduct of late towards this lady,
> which has given me a great deal of anger as well as sorrow. All I can say to you of
> them at present is, that they have not been my relations these two months – The con-
> sent of opinions in our minds is certainly a nearer tie than can be contracted by all
> the blood in our bodies; and I am proud of finding I've something congenial with Mr
> Caryll in me. Will you permit me, dear sir, in friendship to confess to you, that all
> the favors and kind offices you have shown towards me have not so strongly cemented
> me yours, as the discovery of that generous and manly compassion you manifested in
> the case of this unhappy lady? Nothing (without flattery) ever touched me more than
> the sentiment you expressed on my first opening that matter in your coach as we past
> on the road.   (I, 143–44)

Like the *Unfortunate Lady*, the Weston affair shows Pope asserting the worth
of someone who has transgressed oppressive rules. He writes to Caryll that
'I cannot but join with you in a high concern for a person of so much merit,
as I'm daily more and more convinced by her conversation that she is; whose
ill fate it has been to be cast as a pearl before swine' (I, 132). In May 1712,
when she was on a visit to an aunt (whom she approached with a 'mixture
of expectation and anxiety' which increased his sympathy), he reflected that
if her welcome was 'such as is due to her merit . . . it must be as good as ever
woman found' (I, 143). Never does he refer to her as a wrong-doer, simply
as 'unfortunate', and as such it is his duty, in accordance with the importance
of sympathy in his morality, to console her: 'The unfortunate of all people are
the most unfit to be left alone; yet we see the world generally takes care they
shall be so, by abandoning 'em: whereas if we took a right prospect of human
nature, the business and study of the happy and easy, should be to divert and
humour, as well as pity and comfort, the distressed' (I, 143). This is far from
the scant charity many would have felt appropriate to a wife who had left her
husband.

Although others regarded her sympathetically – the Carylls, Mrs Nelson,
presumably her correspondent Teresa, and Mrs Weston's brother, Thomas
Gage – none apparently felt as Pope felt. Caryll, for example, hoped to patch
up the marriage, whereas Pope, typically putting an attractive individual
before the forms of society, cautions that 'I am very confident they can't be

united, tho' they may be brought together: 'Tis an easy thing (we daily find) to join two bodies, but in matching minds there lies some difficulty' (I, 123). His sense of Mrs Weston as a superior being who ought not to be in the power of her moral inferior (called in the same letter 'the tyrant') is reminiscent of the advice he had given Teresa in 'With the Works of Voiture', before Mrs Weston's plight had sharpened the issue for him: that 'the free Innocence of Life' as a spinster is preferable to living under the power of a 'Tyrant' in marriage (lines 36–48). In that poem he had presented oppression as the norm, 'the fawning Servant turns a haughty Lord'; and in the letter to Caryll cited above, even while he praises the Carylls for their exemplary harmony, he stresses that they are unusual: their example, he teases, may lead others who are unsuited to marriage to attempt 'that hard science to which so very few are born with a genius' (I, 123). As a man conscious of his ineligibility it was perhaps easier for him to adopt this perspective, but in confronting the normative status of marriage he was setting out on a course that diverged from respectable opinion.

It is not clear precisely why other observers, notably Mrs Nelson and Mrs Englefield, fell out with Pope over the case. A probable explanation is a sense that the concern which was proper in Mrs Weston's women friends, or in Caryll as head of one of the great Catholic families, was somehow excessive in an unmarried man of her own generation, and one who stood in any case outside the charmed circle of Catholic intermarriage.[41] A suspicion that Pope was capitalising on Mrs Weston's need offers a plausible motive for the injured husband, who is reported as 'gloomy upon the matter, – the tyrant meditates revenge' (I, 151). Perhaps the eagerly helpful Mr Pope looked too much like an insinuating, if platonic, candidate for his erring wife's affections; and when we read further in the same letter that 'the distressed dame herself has been taught to suspect I served her but by halves, and without prudence' it becomes clear that there has been an attack on Pope's character rather than a simple disagreement over tactics. True, he had, perhaps indiscreetly, told Caryll that Mrs Weston thought one of Mrs Nelson's suggestions ill-judged, but when he says of Mrs Nelson's gossip that it would not 'be any concern to me if every married man were as wise as Mr Caryll' it seems fairly clear that the husband's jealousy has been aroused. Mrs Nelson, whose 'poetry and sense' Pope nonetheless respected – the witty malice of her correspondence with Teresa flares out amidst the amiable commonplace of the Blounts' letters from women friends – was a powerful adversary in a gossips' war, as the nuns of a convent where she stayed in Paris found to their cost; and Pope blames her by implication for the fact that the Englefields later broke off

---

[41] In addition to his general standing in the Catholic community, Caryll may have been related to Mrs Weston by marriage, although it is not true as suggested by *DNB* that Joseph Gage had been married to Caryll's daughter Catherine (who in fact died unmarried: see Erskine-Hill, *Social Milieu*, p. 101).

relations with his parents.[42] Clinging to his consciousness of innocence, he
professes that he would rather let Mrs Nelson and Mrs Englefield 'worry his
character together very comfortably' than 'take inglorious pains of a chatter-
ing eclaircissement with women (or men) of weak credulity' (*Corr.*, I, 171).
Yet in 1717, by which time the Westons were reunited, he described to the
Blount sisters how he had avoided the embarrassment of meeting them in
terms which probably correspond, in jest, to the earlier gossip about his interest in Mrs Weston: 'I arrived at Mr Dancastles on Tuesday-noon, having
fled from the face (I wish I could say from the horned face) of Mr Weston,
who dined that day at my Brother's' (I, 426, 428).

Hence it is not difficult to imagine angles from which gossips might have
approached this agreeable subject. Certainly, as *Eloisa* and the *Unfortunate
Lady* and Pope's subsequent involvement with similar cases were to show,
estranged wives and other oppressed women held an incomparable emotional
appeal for him; yet his satisfaction in offering himself in a climate of emotional
intensity he was unlikely ever to generate as a lover does not undermine either
his sincerity or the value of the services he undertook for these women.
Recognising 'Wild Nature's vigor working at the root' of all active virtue, he
dismissed the gossips' understandable suspicions with contempt.[43] Indeed,
Mrs Nelson's slander is reminiscent of his reading of La Rochefoucauld, who
similarly irritated him by his assumption 'that all virtues are disguised vices'
(Spence, no. 517). In contrast, Pope would have liked to show 'all vices to
be disguised virtues', yet he was honest enough to admit that 'neither, indeed,
is true'. The insight is probably as applicable to his feeling for distressed
women as to any of his moral enthusiasms.

The history of Pope's concern for Mrs Cope is in some respects similar, but
in this case even Caryll was to an extent alienated by his friend's zeal. It was
Caryll, Mrs Cope's cousin, who first introduced her to Pope in July 1711, and
at once he recognised her as a superior woman. His remarks, typically
dismissive of the sex as a whole, are a salutary reminder of the context of such
admiration: 'I am infinitely obliged for your bringing me acquainted with
Mrs Cope, from whom I heard more wit and sense in two hours than almost
all the sex ever spoke in their whole lives' (*Corr.*, I, 129). In this case there
was no suspicion that the unfortunate lady had acted improperly – indeed
she twice travelled abroad to remonstrate with her bigamous husband – and
her problems, which ended only with her death in 1728, were as much financial as emotional (I, 416–17). In this context Pope's concern, which he
expressed by giving her money and helping her to put legal pressure on her
husband as well as by supportive visits and letters, was intrinsically less controversial than his involvement in the Westons' marital crisis, despite the
element of excess in his sense of her spiritual distinction:

---

[42] *Corr.*, I, 171, 177; EC, VI, 180, note.   [43] *Essay on Man*, II.184 (*TE*, III.i, 77).

I ever was of opinion that you wanted no more to be vindicated than to be known: and like Truth, cou'd appear no where but you must conquer . . . Tho' you modestly say the world has left you, yet I verily believe it is coming to you again as fast as it can: For to give the world its due, it is always very fond of Merit when 'tis past its power to oppose it . . . Wheresoever Providence shall dispose of the most valuable thing I know, I shall ever follow you with my sincerest wishes, and my best thoughts will be perpetually waiting upon you, when you never hear of me or them. Your own guardian Angels cannot be more constant, nor more silent. I beg you will never cease to think me your friend, that you may not be guilty of that which you never yet knew to commit, an Injustice.[44]

Although he presents his feelings so as to give the maximum encouragement to an 'extremely dejected' woman, he is evidently sincere in classing her among his select band of superior souls (*Corr.*, II, 380).

This time Pope caused unease not so much by his feeling for the victim as by his pressure on Caryll to do more for her. Caryll's obligations to Mrs Cope arose from his status as head of the only reasonably prosperous branch of his family. Until she married Cope, Anne Caryll had received £50 a year from him, an implicit recognition that the head of her branch of the family, her brother Philip, was not able to support his dependants. There is thus a strong probability that her marriage had been something of a desperate venture, and it is probably significant in this connection that her sister, Mrs Blewet, whose maxims of patience Pope admired, was also unhappily married (*Corr.*, I, 158). Meanwhile, Philip gave further evidence of unreliability. In 1712 he tried to bully his invalid son into breaking the entail on the estate; in 1723 he became a government informer against neighbours of his cousin and benefactor John Caryll; and although in 1725 he promised his sister that he would join her in France, he kept her waiting in poverty and depression for nearly a year before he arrived.

Pope's response, apart from helping Mrs Cope himself, was to put pressure on John Caryll to provide for her, yet his tendency to idealise his friend's patriarchal role made him rather less than realistic about its financial practicability. The estate was only superficially prosperous, and as head of the family Caryll evidently felt obliged to live in a style more lavish than his finances warranted.[45] Indeed, Pope's urging of Mrs Cope's claims was part of this pressure towards extravagance: the patriarch's duty to poor relations is part of the same ideal as the open-hearted hospitality and generosity to tenants which Pope delighted to praise, and it was in the long term a moral luxury that the estate could not afford (*Corr.*, I, 457). Soon it became clear that Mrs Cope was suffering from cancer of the breast and required surgery, and Pope constantly referred to her need in a way which was evidently

---

[44] Pope frequently mentions his donations, e.g. *Corr.*, II, 361; he outlines a legal scheme in I, 522. The quotation is from II, 367–68: see Erskine-Hill, *Social Milieu* for evidence that the letter is in fact addressed to Mrs Cope (p. 75).

[45] Erskine-Hill, *Social Milieu*, pp. 63–64, 101–2.

irritating to Caryll. Only after her death did Pope learn that, though still modest, Caryll's contributions had been larger and more regular than he had realised. The feeling remained, however, that Caryll could have done more, and Pope evidently found it particularly inappropriate that he should be the one to pay the medical bills incurred during her last illness (*Corr.*, III, 13, 17–18).

Although Pope was not the only one to imply criticism of Caryll (Mrs Cope's younger brother John made similar points though in guardedly respectful terms) his urgency, as with Mrs Weston, provoked the slander of less enthusiastic observers. This time the calumny, circulated by Caryll's 'Sussex acquaintance' was apparently that Pope's pleas were hypocritical, since he was himself the agent through whom Caryll was paying Mrs Cope an annuity (III, 13). This was just as untrue as the assurances Pope had received from a third party that she was getting no substantial help at all from Caryll, assurances that prompted Pope to give her an annuity of £20 (III, 18). Clearly the case evoked in all concerned the kind of tension that bred recrimination. It was not for a full year after Mrs Cope's death that Pope and Caryll were fully reconciled, with Pope 'Glad we were both in the right, nay not sorry if I was a little otherwise since it has occasioned the knowledge of that dependence which I ought and am to have on your friendship and temper' (III, 35–36). This is an especially appropriate form of submission in the context of his somewhat burdensome insistence on the image of his friend as patriarch.

In his analysis of Pope's friendship with Caryll, Erskine-Hill makes an important link with an incident which troubled the last years of Pope's life:

It is interesting that a rather similar estrangement, sharp but temporary, was to occur between Pope and Ralph Allen, a man on whom the poet was to lavish, not without justification, much the same kind of praise for his public, patriarchal role, that he had bestowed on Caryll. In both cases the source of the estrangement was the lack of due consideration by the other man for a woman whom Pope considered to be helpless or vulnerable, and to whom (in the case of Allen, Martha Blount) Pope was deeply attached.   (*Social Milieu*, pp. 77–78)

Thus the closest to him of his unfortunate ladies had the power even at the end of his life to evoke the same anger which had complicated his relation to Catholic society as a young man and animated his fictions of female rebellion.

Insofar as these poems reflected his response to individual unfortunate ladies in his own religious community, they spoke out on behalf of women who were in life quietly dependent. On the other hand, by the time he wrote *Eloisa* and the *Unfortunate Lady*, he had met a woman who fascinated him by qualities very much more assertive than those he discerned in Mrs Cope or Patty – though possessing an ability to act out of desperation which perhaps links her with Mrs Weston – and who also came to play a part in the poems. Lady Mary Wortley Montagu – who knew Latin, wrote satire and took a lively interest in politics – had eloped in order to marry, and was later to leave her husband to follow a young Italian author across the continent (although her motive was a well-kept secret).[46] She thus represented a very different image of the distinguished woman from that valued by pious Catholics, and while the detailed correspondences between her and the Unfortunate Lady are striking – her 'beauty, titles, wealth and fame', her defiance of authority in choosing whom to marry, and her exile in Constantinople, imaged in her letters and in Pope's as a kind of death – her greatest contribution to the poems of 1717 is surely the example she gave of self-confident unconventionality, a kind of assertiveness hardly characteristic of the virtuous Catholic victims of the marriage market whose difficulties might seem better able to justify it.[47] Indeed, in the light of the structural unease shown in the *Unfortunate Lady* about the speaker's claims for uninhibited self-assertion, and of the short continuance and bitter conclusion of Pope's admiration for Lady Mary, it is plausible to suggest that the esteem enjoyed by his real life unfortunate ladies – and there were to be more of them – was in effect conditional on their conformity in manners and conversation with more conventional feminine ideals.[48]

It is paradoxical that Lady Mary became blended in Pope's imagination with such radically different women. The most striking example of his passionate indeterminacy is presented by *Eloisa*, which as we now have it draws to a close as if its poet has Lady Mary uniquely in mind (Eloisa looks forward to finding a poet 'Condemned whole years in absence to deplore, / And image charms he must behold no more', alluding to Lady Mary's absence in Constantinople). Yet there are strong hints that 'the conclusion I once intended for it' had implied a dedication to Patty that she had been unwilling to receive (*Corr.*, I, 338). In *Eloisa*, as in the *Unfortunate Lady*, he had transcended the conflict between Lady Mary's self-assertion and the dutiful passivity typical of his unfortunate ladies by imagining heroines whose outrageous self-expression was offset by impressive moral strength. In life, however, there was to be no such resolution, and in relation to the Blount sisters and Lady Mary he was to face choices whose consequences would be painful for all parties.

[46] For a fuller discussion of Lady Mary's relationship with Pope see chapter 6.
[47] For correspondences between Lady Mary and the Unfortunate Lady see Geoffrey Tillotson, 'Lady Mary Wortley Montagu and Pope's *Elegy to the Memory of an Unfortunate Lady*', *Review of English Studies*, 12 (1936), 401–12.
[48] For other women whose misfortunes appealed to his sympathy, see chapters 7 and 8.

5

A choice of sisters

1

The Blount sisters were never far away from the focuses of female fascination explored in previous chapters. In their very different, often ambiguous ways, *The Rape of the Lock*, *Eloisa* and the *Unfortunate Lady* testify to the potential for something both refined and impressive to be made out of the female condition, and in their own cruder way Pope's relationships with Teresa and with Patty reveal the criteria by which in his personal life he came to judge achievement in this narrow arena. Although the financial problems which afflicted them were milder than those which reduced Mrs Cope's life to an exercise in endurance, and although their fruitless flirtations in the order of chivalry led to nothing as embarrassing as Bell's quarrel with Lord Petre, they were under similar pressures. As poorly endowed girls of good family they failed to attract acceptable suitors, and their brother's inability to support them as their father had intended, which was exacerbated by the terms of his own marriage settlement, did nothing to deter him from requiring his mother and sisters to move out of Mapledurham on his marriage. Though never actually penniless, nor subject to male tyranny in its cruder forms, the sisters' lives were nonetheless constrained by the actions of their father and brother, and young men like Alexis who enjoyed teasing them about their marital ambitions did nothing to reconcile them to almost inevitable failure. Fortunately the Blounts also had reliable men friends who did much to lighten their difficulties. Caryll, Patty's godfather, was one, and so, at the beginning, was Pope, but he later became disgusted by what he came to see as Teresa's corruption, and correspondingly impressed by Patty's superior qualities. Yet it was apparently his judgement rather than the girls' characters that changed, as over the years he increasingly polarised their differences.

The sisters' charm as children is captured in a pair of portraits still preserved at Mapledurham, certainly the most attractive images of them to survive. A few letters too suggest the delight they gave to the adults around them, the first dating from 1693, when their brother Michael was born: as Teresa was five and Patty only three at the time it is presumably Teresa who is described by her schoolmistress in Paris:[1]

[1] The Blounts had six children in all: a son William died as an infant before Teresa's birth,

Your Dear Jewel here is the pretiest creature aliue she . . . has great delight in makeing
us read letters as from you and her papa, sometimes we read shes a naughty girl that
she does not like, but when 'tis that shes a good girl she must hear it ouer and ouer
again . . . mis sends her papa and you her duty, she's a principle woman at Madam
Pees as she calls R^d Mother who is extreamly fond of her, and indeed so is euery
body.   (Blount Letters, III, 138)

The make-believe about letters from home is touching, but more indicative
of Teresa as an adult is her ability, even at five years old, to make herself such
'a principle woman' in the establishment that she could give Reverend
Mother a nick-name with impunity.

    When Patty was a little older she joined Teresa in Paris: another letter from
Elizabeth Meynell, sent to meet their mother at Calais after she had left them
at the convent, assures her that they are settling well:[2]

I can with truth assure you the tears you left us in were blown ouer in a quarter of
an hour & your two dear little ones as brisk and merry euer since, as if their Mama
were still here. mis Teresa you know has many charms, and the command she had
ouer her self, in parting so discreetly with what with reason she loues aboue all things
in ye world, was a considerable one to all your Bons amis . . . dont fear Dear M^{rs}
Blount y^r orders being contradicted in anything, or that she [another of the nuns]
and I won't doe for 'em as if they were our owne, & I hope in God you'l find 'em
improu'd in all things, at y^r next meeting: I am perswaded they'l proue very tract-
able and good. I intend mis Teresa shall put in a word or two, so I need say nothing
from her. mis Patty will put her scratch, [she] desires me to tell you she loues D^r
mama with [all] her hart, & asks her blessing. . . .
    [In Teresa's hand] dear mama I being in haste to goe to my master I heaue only
time to tell you how dearly I loue you and how sorry I am to hear you haue soe bad
places [in the coach] but I hope you haue now beter . . . belue me I will be a good
garl and that I am your dutyful child TB
    [In Mrs Meynell's hand] mis Patty [Patty makes a squiggle]
                                    (Blount Papers, c. 63)

Presumably it was Patty who cried most when her mother left, since the nuns
admired Teresa's 'discreet' leave-taking. Although Teresa was two years
older and probably felt she had an example to set, there may be a hint here
of her later hardness.

    A letter from Mrs Blount to Patty, then aged about 14, at Mrs Cornwallis's
school in Hammersmith, apologises for not having written and asks how she
enjoyed Christmas. It is now the middle of January, and her parents have not
seen her for some time:

My Dear I haue this day writ to London to haue Lodgings taken against Saterday Sen-
net, I hope nothing will alter your fathers Resolution hee comes with us I Long to see
you; and assure you twas for your good I parted with you; and hope you'l improue

    after Michael a daughter Anne also died an infant, and after her a son Richard survived to
    the age of 5, dying in 1702. I am grateful to Richard Williams for his transcription of Mrs
    Blount's record of her children from her copy of the Office of the BVM.
  [2] This sequence of letters shows that both sisters were educated in Paris, and that it was after-
    wards that Patty went to school in Hammersmith (compare Mack, *Life*, p. 243; Ault, *New
    Light*, p. 354).

in euery thing as you doe in writing, which is a true Content to mee . . . My Saruice
to Mrs Cornwallis tho unknown and to all that Loue and are kind to you. Lett your
father knew what Mrs Cornwallis has lay'd out for you before wee come to London
and what elce you want writ to him your owne stile and hand.   (c. 63)

   In contrast with the sparse but convincing evidence of the affection between
the girls and their parents, the history of Pope's feeling for the sisters is as difficult to reconstruct as it is to understand. Four overlapping periods can be
broadly distinguished: the happy years up to 1715 or 1716; an intermittently
troubled period from then until his last extant letter to Teresa in 1720; a
period of silence about her which lasts until his first direct condemnations of
her to Caryll in 1725 and 1726; and the long years following in which she
stood for all that was bad in woman and Patty for very nearly all that was
good.[3] As Magdalen was later to put it: '*Patty Bl* the fair one, Mr. *Pope*'s,
the other he did not love, call'd Bitch, Hoyden'.[4]

   From the beginning Pope was fascinated by Teresa, the elder sister and the
one whom he met first. Given her satirical disposition and the good looks of
which she was so well aware, she may well have prompted 'You know where'
in 1710. It was for her that Pope wrote 'With the Works of Voiture' in the
same year, and it was for her too that he wrote 'After the Coronation' in
1714.[5] Yet even in this poem, by a strategy that soon becomes familiar, he
avoids any suggestion that he favours one sister to the exclusion of the other:

> Just when his fancy points your sprightly eyes,
> Or sees the blush of soft *Parthenia* rise.
>
>   (line 45; *TE*, VI, 125)

2

In the years up to 1716 Pope's letters show that in his eyes each sister has her
endearing traits: Patty her blushes and modest hatred of puns, her appetite
for French romances and her fear of thunder; Teresa her less straight-laced
appreciation of gossip and *double entendre*, and her readiness to confess an
interest in going 'a Rakeing with me in Man's Cloathes', although it is
interesting that Pope, never particularly drawn to music, never mentions her
singing or playing, talents in which she apparently outshone her sister.[6]
Nevertheless, so even-handed does he seem in his letters that the evidence of
his initial preference for Teresa does not lie at all on the surface of a period
that contains his happiest, most intricately graceful epistolary games with

---

[3] For the dating of individual letters I follow Sherburn's notes in *Corr.* unless otherwise
stated.

[4] Sherburn, 'New Anecdotes', p. 348.

[5] For 'You Know Where', see chapter 3.1; for 'With the Works of Voiture' see Mack, *Life*, pp.
247–48. (Ault had argued that it was addressed to neither sister: *New Light*, pp. 49–56.)

[6] *Corr.*, I, 143, 252, 257, 261. Teresa was painted at the keyboard by Kneller, and a
manuscript book of songs and other music belonging to her was recently on the market (Mack,
Life, plate 32; private information from Richard Williams).

women.[7] Patty too had a poem, if a relatively slight one, written for her: the risqué 'To a Lady with the Temple of Fame', which was sure to make her blush becomingly. Later, her dangerous attack of smallpox threw him into emotional turmoil, and he saw new charms in her cheerful acceptance of having missed the coronation because of her illness.[8] In each sister too he found grounds for teasing criticism: Teresa was apparently already showing by her attitude that she would respect him more if he had his own coach, and she professed a distaste for reading which could hardly be pleasing to a poet, while Patty failed to write to him as often as he would have liked and seemed less eager to see him than he had hoped.[9] Amidst all his teasing, however, there is no serious attempt to play one off against the other: to Teresa he writes in 1714 that 'my *violent* passion for your fair self and your sister has been divided with the most wonderful regularity in the world. Even from my infancy I have been in love with one after the other of you, week by week' (*Corr.*, I, 258). A few months later he boasts that 'everyone values Mr Pope, but every one for a different reason . . . Mrs Teresa for his Reflections on Mrs Patty, and Mrs Patty for his Reflections on Mrs Teresa' (I, 269). Often he addresses them jointly, and several times he praises them without distinction for the openness to others' troubles that was to be crucial in his poems of unfortunate ladies. In one especially interesting fragment he thanks them for their 'Humanity' and 'Sincerity' in refusing to listen to slander against him, concluding that 'I must ever have that Value for your Characters, as to express it for the future on all Occasions, & in all the Ways I am capable of' (I, 182; see also pp. 327, 336).

Although a teasing flirtation with both sisters kept the triangular relationship stable in these years, Pope was already committed to the criteria which in the long term he would use to differentiate them:

There are but two things in the World which can make you indifferent [i.e. objects of indifference] to me which I believe you are not capable of, I mean Ill nature & Malice. I have seen enough of you not to resent any frailty you coud have, & nothing less than a Vice can make me like you less. (I, 261)

Ironically the day was to come when he accused Teresa of precisely such a vice. On the other hand, the qualities he praised in Patty at this time were to be the focus of his admiration throughout his life:

That [letter] which begins with Dear Creature, and my charming Mr Pope, was a delight to me beyond all Expression. You have at last entirely gaind the Conquest over your fair Sister; 'tis true you are not handsome, for you are a Woman and think you are not; but this Good humor and Tenderness for me has a charm that cannot be resisted. (I, 268)

---

[7] Dilke was justly sceptical, given the limited evidence known to him, that there ever was any such preference. It remains true that the evidence is cumulative and that some of its components are too doubtful to stand alone (Dilke, I, 205).

[8] *Corr.*, I, 280, 264–65, 268.

[9] *Corr.*, I, 173, 252, 293, 280.

Plate 1   Martha and Teresa Blount by Charles Jervas, *c.* 1716

Something of what the sisters meant to him in the days before his conviction
of Teresa's malice and Patty's good humour had made choice inevitable is
communicated in a picture which Charles Jervas probably painted early in
1716, apparently under Pope's direction (see plate 1). Jervas writes:

The Poets will give you lively Descriptions in their Way, I shal only Acquaint you with
that which is directly my own Province. I have just set the last hand to a Couplet, for
so I may call two Nymphs in One Piece. They are Pope's Favorites & therefore you
will guess must have cost me more pains than any Nymphs can be worth.

(I, 332)

We can indeed read the picture as a couplet, displaying visually something
of the tension between similarity and difference from which Pope's couplet art
draws its power: the sisters stand together, strikingly similar although one is
fair, one dark. Teresa reaches her arms towards Patty yet looks out of the picture, while Patty's gaze is on her sister and her arms lead the eye away from
the group. The composition has a centrepiece which, like the rhyme in a
couplet, ties its elements together: Teresa holds a wreath entwined with rib-
bon, on which is the legend, 'Martha Teresa Blount, Sic positae quoniam
suaves' (Mack, *Life*, p. 243). The allusion, which Mack convincingly
attributes to Pope rather than to Jervas, is to lines from Virgil's *Eclogues* in
which the shepherd Corydon gathers laurel and myrtle because their per-
fumes are complementary:

> et vos, o lauri, carpam et te, proxima myrte,
> sic positae quoniam suaves miscetis odores.[10]

In the picture Patty holds laurel, Teresa myrtle. Thus Teresa, who gazes
assertively at the beholder, proclaims her commitment to Venus, while Patty,
confining her gaze modestly within the composition, holds the plant beloved
by Apollo god of poetry, once the obstinately virgin Daphne. Pope's fascination is more than the sum of its parts: were the girls not 'sic positae' as sisters
it would be impossible to hover teasingly between them, to proclaim that he
was alternately in love with each, to use one as insurance against a courtship
of the other which could only lead to humiliation. Indeed, Pope's epigraph
signals his recognition of precisely this constraint, for Virgil's shepherd knows
that for all his skill in song he cannot succeed in love:

> rusticus es, Corydon; nec munera curat Alexis,
> nec, si muneribus certes, concedat Iollas.   (*Eclogues*, II, 56)

Thus, in an allusion neither sister could understand, Pope commemorated
their charm and his frustration.

It was predictable that in life the couplet should break down under the
stress. In retrospect, possible reservations about Teresa are implied even in

---

[10] *Virgil*, with an English translation by H. Rushton Fairclough, 2 vols., Loeb Classical Library
(London, 1935), *Eclogues*, II, 54–55.

Pope's humorous and affectionate verses 'After the Coronation' (1714), which in so many ways evoke the happiness of these early years:

> As some fond virgin, whom her mother's care
> Drags from the town to wholsom country air,
> Just when she learns to roll a melting eye,
> And hear a spark, yet think no danger nigh;
> From the dear man unwilling she must sever,
> Yet takes one kiss before she parts for ever:
> Thus from the world fair *Zephalinda* flew,
> Saw others happy, and with sighs withdrew;
> Not that their pleasures caus'd her discontent,
> She sigh'd not that They stay'd, but that She went.
>
> (line 1; *TE*, VI, 124)

Although Warton found fault with the opening simile, a reading along the lines he suggests reveals a very particular point to the passage:

There is so much likeness (to use Johnson's words on another poem) in the initial comparison, that there is no illustration. As one lady lamented the going out of London, so did another.[11]

Yet whereas the girl in the simile is all sexual spontaneity, 'fond', 'melting' and credulously infatuated with her 'spark', betraying the warm physicality that appeals to the libertine in Pope, Zephalinda is grieved in contrast not by the loss of love but by her exile from 'the world', an ironically narrow world which comprises only the pleasures of a season in town. When she dreams of 'triumphs' it is not as the 'fond virgin' smitten with her spark, but as the coquette to whom male glamour is an unindividualised commodity associated with rank and display:

> In some fair evening, on your elbow laid,
> You dream of triumphs in the rural shade;
> In pensive thought recall the fancy'd scene,
> See Coronations rise on ev'ry green;
> Before you pass th'imaginary sights
> Of Lords, and Earls, and Dukes, and garter'd Knights;
> While the spread Fan o'ershades your closing eyes;
> Then give one flirt, and all the vision flies.
> Thus vanish sceptres, coronets, and balls,
> And leave you in lone woods, or empty walls.
>
> ('After the Coronation', line 31)

What a lover is to the 'fond virgin', high life is to Teresa; and, if what purports to be the poem's suppressed conclusion really is so, she herself is to Pope: 'And if poor *Pope* is cl-pt, the Fault is yours'.[12] At this early stage,

---

11 *The Works of Alexander Pope, Esq.*, edited by Joseph Warton, 9 vols. (London, 1797), II, 323.
12 'Lines Suppressed', lines 41–50 (*TE*, VI, 232); for the problems surrounding this fragment, see chapter 3.2.

however, addiction to the town is a topic for teasing, not condemnation: in the same year he teases Betty Marriot in terms which anticipate the poem without implying any darker side to the joke:

You sigh out, in the ardour of your heart, Oh Play-houses, Parks, Opera's, Assemblies, *London*! I cry with rapture, Oh Woods, Gardens, Rookeries, Fishponds, Arbours! Mrs. *Betty M—*.   (*Corr.*, I, 206)

Teresa's personality in these early years is further illuminated by letters she received from correspondents other than Pope. At some unspecified period after her return from school in Paris Mrs Meynell became dissatisfied with her slowness in replying to letters, but once she did exert herself her old teacher declared herself impressed by her 'solid reason' and 'good sense' (Blount Letters, II, 147–48). Mrs Meynell's letters illustrate one aspect of the social pressures to which Teresa had been schooled: she is exhorted to charity to her old nurse, now destitute, which she accordingly sends, and she is urged to employ Mrs Meynell's nieces, Catholic milliners in difficult circumstances, which may relate to the comment about the 'Charity' of 'Buying a lac'd Head' repeated by Alexis (I, 199–200). Another religious duty that fell to Teresa's lot was that of describing the death of her grandfather Anthony Englefield in 1712 to her Swinburne cousins, a task which she evidently performed in the proper terms, enabling them to give thanks for 'his pious and happy end he made' (III, 59). In these respects she could show herself, when she took the trouble, as an exemplary product of her religious upbringing.

Teresa's skill with words, evident both in her drafts of letters and in the satisfaction of her more solemn correspondents, brings into question the impression Pope gives that she was utterly uninterested in literature. Her professions of uninterest were perhaps meant to excuse her from expressing an admiration of *his* writings which would enmesh her further in a problematic relationship (*Corr.*, I, 252). Alexis had after all lent her a book of poetry and warned her not to attack him in verse; and there is a poem signed 'Zephalinda' among the sisters' papers.[13] Although its subject is unrequited love the use of the fantasy name may suggest a piece of role-playing; but if it is indeed by Teresa it is an interesting demonstration of her competence in metre, if not of her perseverence in rhyme:

> Know whatt thow art & Love as Maidens ought
> & Drive these golden wisshes from thy thought
> Thou Canst not hope thy fond dessiers to gain
> Where hope is wanting wisshes are in vain
> & yett no guards against our Joys Conspire
> Or Jeallous husband, hinders our dessier

---

[13] Blount Letters, I, 195; III, 187. The book of poetry Teresa had borrowed was by Hopkins. Likely candidates, both writers of amorous verse and versions of Ovid, are Charles Hopkins (*Epistolary Poems*, London, 1694) and John Hopkins (*Amasia; or, The Works of the Muses*, London, 1700).

> My Parents are propitious to my wish
> & I my Self Consenting to the Bliss
> All things concur, to prosper our dessire
> All things to prosper any Love butt mine
>
> (Blount Letters, III, 187)

What is clear is that Teresa did not share Patty's compulsive absorption in books, particularly romances.[14] Mrs Nelson may indeed have Patty's fantasy world in mind when she remarks in a postscript to Teresa, 'Pray let ye Empress know (that to add to her present affliction) I am credibly inform'd ye Emperour of Morrocco is upon his marriage to his 15th Wife'.[15] Pope too connects the love of romances with 'the Want of a Lover', perhaps sensing the advantage of not having to force a way to her heart through the crowd of beaux so deliberately sought by Teresa, whose correspondence shows how much she preferred the flirtations of the present to those of the fabulous past (*Corr.*, I, 375). Although Teresa's friend Mary Dering, who writes from America in 1718 and 1719, enjoys the novelties of the New World ('amongst pritty things there is Alegators & rattle Snakes enough'), she concludes with what was evidently nearest both their hearts: 'may you meet with pleasures & plays, & Assemblyes, your Cloathes sett well, & your Eyes Command who you bid them'.[16] Back in England in 1721 she retails just the kind of gossip from Bath and Bristol that Teresa seems to have enjoyed.

Yet however delightful membership of a gossiping community might be, it had its difficulties for Teresa. Acquaintances who enjoyed her detraction of others might not enjoy being teased themselves, and they might easily decide that she was more fun as a victim than as a conspirator. A poem preserved among the sisters' papers seems to record a third party's amusement at her situation with regard to Pope: entitled 'Bardillo's Fate' it seems to be a gallant but ultimately bawdy joke about the bard best known at Mapledurham (Blount Papers, III, 214). When Teresa surprises the shepherd Bardillo asleep on the bank of the Thames she proves alluring as Cynthia but elusive as Daphne. As she flees with skirts flying he is enslaved by the sight of 'her legs and snowy thighs / And more, but what I dare not say'. This humorous commentary suggests a new angle on a pursuit which literary history has usually approached from the point of view of the celebrated pursuer. Teresa had to bear in mind that to be seen as the object of such an ineligible, even ludicrous suitor could make her a laughing-stock, a consideration which probably fuelled the bad temper he later complained of. For all her vivacity, she had

---

[14] Lady Charlotte Radcliffe borrowed romances from Patty. Pope and the Hanoverian diplomat Louis Schrader teased her about them (Blount Letters, II, 220; III, 48, 51; *Corr.*, I, 252).

[15] The joke is apparently that Patty must be heartbroken at Thomas Gage's decision to marry someone else (Blount Letters, II, 81; and see chapter 3.2).

[16] Blount Letters, II, 52–57. This is probably the Mary Dering, cousin to Lord Egmont, who in 1730 became dresser to the Princess Royal. For numerous references, see index to *Diary of Viscount Percival, Afterwards First Earl of Egmont*, 3 vols., Manuscripts of the Earl of Egmont, Historical Manuscripts Commission (London, 1920–23).

always sensed that her position among her peers was far from secure, and remarks made by Mrs Nelson, another wit whose talent turned easily to scandal, help to suggest the common ground between these two prickly women:

You tell me you have met wth many false friends, and seem therefore once to have resolvd to Trust no more; Believe me, Madam, I have shar'd your Fate, & Experienc'd [illegible] there are such Vices as falsehood, & ingratitude, but that Sincerity I know to be in your Nature, & wch I Value Equal wth any of your other perfections, shall be still ye more esteemd ye more I find other people Treacherous.[17]

3

In addition to these underlying factors, the second phase of Pope's relationship with the Blount sisters (roughly defined as from 1715 to 1720) was complicated by more tangible problems: Michael Blount's marriage and the consequent displacement of his sisters from Mapledurham, the punitive measures taken against Catholics in the wake of the Jacobite rising of 1715, the Popes' move from their Binfield home, the watershed in Pope's career constituted by his *Works* of 1717 and his father's sudden death later the same year. Sometimes the old tone of gaiety is recaptured, and sometimes the letters, often undatable, hint at quarrels imperfectly smoothed over; but amid the apparent chaos recurrent themes point towards the new configuration of the 1720s.

A grave letter to Patty, probably of 1717, shows how Patty's charms were to increase in these years of public and private stress; for Pope, as so often talking of preparation for death, praises country life (which he and she enjoy) and condemns town life (which absorbs Teresa): 'A true relish of the beauties of nature is the most easy preparation and gentlest transition to an enjoyment of those of heaven; as on the contrary a true town life of hurry, confusion, noise, slander, and dissention, is a sort of apprenticeship to hell and its furies' (*Corr.*, I, 349). He makes no invidious applications – indeed, as if to prove to posterity that Patty too was human he teases her about her new gown – yet this sharing of her serious concerns to the extent of advising her that meditation on the life to come 'will make you the happier and the easier at all times' would be inconceivable in his correspondence with Teresa. He confirms the high degree of friendship to which Patty is elected by his conclusion:

This is an odd way of writing to a lady, and I'm sensible would throw me under a great deal of ridicule, were you to show this letter among your acquaintance. But perhaps you may not your self be quite a stranger to this way of thinking.

This perhaps paves the way for his declaration of his first intention for *Eloisa* early in 1716, yet in August 1715 he is still able to declare, 'I am in love with you both as I am with myself' (I, 315, 338).

---

[17] Undated, probably about 1713 (Blount Letters, II, 180–81).

On the face of it, a more daring vein of teasing in his dealings with Teresa may suggest a camaraderie not unlike that which she shared with Alexis, but in retrospect it is significant that the characteristics which later disgusted him become topics for increasingly frank humour in these years. Typical is a brief note referring to the death by lightning of the Stanton Harcourt lovers in 1718:

Madam. Since you prefer three hundred pound to two true Lovers, I presume to send you the following Epitaph upon them, which seems to be written by one of your Taste.

> Here lye two poor Lovers, who had the mishap
> Tho very chaste people, to dye of a Clap.

I hope Miss Patty will not so much as smile at this: if she does, she may know, she has less pity than I.[18]

This is intriguingly close to the way Pope was to use this incident as a test of another woman whom he perceived in rather similar terms: like Teresa, Lady Mary Wortley Montagu failed to be moved and was in due course rejected.[19] A few months later, in a letter to Teresa which partly recaptures the old effervescence, he fastens on the obsession with news to which her correspondences with Alexis and Mrs Nelson also bear witness: 'You have askd me News a thousand times at the first word you spoke to me, which some would interpret as if you expected nothing better from my lips' (Corr., I, 350). Her addiction to town pleasures offers Pope later the same year a contrast for Patty's affectionately parodied preference for rural seclusion:

Let your faithless Sister triumph in her ill-gotten Treasures; let her put on New Gowns to be the Gaze of Fools, and Pageant of a Birth-night! While you with all your innocence enjoy a Shady Grove without any leaves on, & dwell with a virtuous Aunt in a Country Paradise.   (I, 375)

In comparison, the wit of the 'Verses Sent to Mrs. T. B. with his Works' in 1717 is less forgiving (TE, VI, 189–90). He stresses her excessive regard for dress (and for the other gallingly unattainable graces comprehended in the author's 'bare Outside') and for money. He also records her 'peevish Fits' of rudeness to him as a loyal friend. Moreover, he seems to hint by references to 'G—ge', 'S—te' and 'a *Fool in Red*' at her uncritical adulation of the glamour of an establishment under which her community suffered. It was after all only a year since her cousin Edward Swinburne, condemned (though later reprieved) for his part in the rising of 1715, had written to ask the Blounts' prayers that 'our Behaviour may be becoming the Christian Catholique and Old English firmness'.[20] In all Teresa's attitudes, but most pain-

---

[18] I follow Ault in referring the epigram to the Stanton Harcourt affair, TE, VI, 201. For Sherburn's earlier dating see Corr., I, 349.

[19] Lady Mary's response to Pope's emotion at the deaths is discussed in chapter 6.2.

[20] Blount Letters, III, 62–64. For the suggestion that the '*Fool in Red*' may have been one Captain Bagnall, see chapter 3.1.

fully with regard to himself, Pope records a superficiality which he professes
to have seen through once and for all:

> This Book, which, like its Author, You
> By the bare Outside only knew,
> (Whatever was in either Good,
> Not look'd in, or, not understood)
> Comes, as the writer did too long,
> To be about you, right or wrong;
> Neglected on your Chair to lie,
> Nor raise a Thought, nor draw an Eye;
> In peevish Fits to have you say,
> *See there! You're always in my Way!*
> Or, if your Slave you think to bless,
> *I like this Colour, I profess!*
> *That Red is charming all will hold,*
> *I ever lov'd it − next to Gold.*
>
> Can Book, or Man, more Praise obtain?
> What more could *G—ge* or *S—te* gain?
>
> Sillier than *G–ld–n* cou'dst thou be,
> Nay, did all *J–c–b* breath in thee,
> She keeps thee, Book! I'll lay my Head,
> What? throw away a *Fool in Red*:
> No, trust the Sex's sacred Rule;
> The gaudy Dress will save the Fool.   (line 1)

Yet he did not make the clean break that he seems to promise: the currents
of emotion continue to eddy confusingly until the end of the decade.

Obsession with 'Gold' was an understandable if undesirable development
in a woman whose life had been conditioned from her mid twenties by financial disappointment. Indeed, because of Michael's difficulties in paying his
sisters' allowances and his insistence that they should leave Mapledurham,
they were well qualified to join Mrs Weston and Mrs Cope as examples of the
unfortunate ladies who so readily evoked Pope's love and sympathy. Even
before Michael's marriage Pope declares to Patty that 'I cannot heartily wish
him married', and believing himself in danger of death, he writes to her that
'I cannot think without tears of being separated from my friends, when their
condition is so doubtful, that they may want even such assistance as mine'
(*Corr.*, I, 315, 319). If Teresa and Patty were enhanced in his eyes by their
misfortunes, their brother incurred the same contempt that Pope had
previously expressed for feckless or self-seeking guardians: in 1718 he twice
attacked Michael in letters to Caryll (I, 472, 475–76). His anger could easily
have annoyed Teresa, for although she could be sharp with her brother when
he kept her waiting for money, her frank and lively letters to him show that
they remained close; and as a lover of town life she may even have been pleased
to leave Mapledurham for London (Blount Papers, c.63).

Teresa however voiced her need for assistance – largely owing to her extravagant tastes – rather more decidedly than most of Pope's unfortunate ladies; and he, with a naivety which was perhaps wilful, took her at her word, both by acting as her financial consultant (as he did also for Patty) and by making substantial gifts (*Corr.*, I, 375–76, 379, 517). It is perhaps indicative of his activities in the former role that it was he, together with Henry Jernegan, who on 7 May 1716 witnessed three agreements between Michael and his sisters. Each sister endorsed a statement that Michael had paid her arrears, and Michael committed himself to give Patty £1,000 and an annuity of £50 (Blount Papers, c.65). There is no record of such a grant to Teresa, despite the fact that she was apparently Michael's favourite sister; and if she was put at a disadvantage in this way it would help to explain why in March 1718 Pope risked her displeasure by settling on her an annuity of £40.[21] The condition attached, that the payments should cease if she married, is presumably intended to prevent embarrassment between Pope and any more favoured suitor, but what enraged Teresa in Pope's action may be guessed from the comment of a nineteenth-century chaplain at Mapledurham, to whom it seemed obvious that the annuity indicated their intention to marry.[22] Yet Pope's hurt at her reaction seems to speak of a deeper and probably correct intuition that beneath any social embarrassment he might cause Teresa lay revulsion at finding herself obliged to a deformed cripple whose friendship had always had an unwelcome amorous element. A letter written just before the settlement was made seems to refer to her resentment:

You exprest your self desirous of increasing your present income upon Life: I proposed the only method I then could find, & you encoragd me to proceed in it – when it was done, you received it as if it were an Affront. – Since when, I find the very thing, in the very manner you wishd, & mention it to you; You don't think it worth an answer.

If your meaning be, that the very things you ask, and wish, become Odious to you, when it is I that comply with 'em, or bring 'em about; pray own it, & deceive me no longer with any thought, but that you Hate me. My Friendship is too warm & sincere to be triffled with; therfore if you have any meaning, tell it me, or you must allow me to take away That which perhaps you don't care to keep.

(*Corr.*, I, 468)

Pope's grappling with such suspicions lay at the heart of the developing crisis. Late in 1716 his letters had begun to allude, though teasingly, to his unattractiveness: 'I wish I were the handsomest fellow in England for your sakes'; yet he remained wary of the vulnerable role of rejected lover, declaring next summer, 'I know no Two Things I would change you for, this hot weather, except Two good Melons' (I, 379, 409). In 1717, however, revisiting the Berkshire and Oxfordshire landscape which now that he and the sisters

---

[21] I am indebted to Richard Williams for this suggestion. Pope's indenture is in Blount Papers, c.65, transcribed in Mack, *Life*, p. 876.

[22] For the chaplain's comments, see Dilke, I, 211.

are exiled to London takes on the poignancy of a lost Eden, he acknowledges
that the Muses are the only women who will ever woo him, and even as he
pays tribute to the sisters as friends he implies in lines both humorous and
elegiac how much more they could have been:

I . . . past the rest of the day in those Woods where I have so often enjoyd – an Author
& a Book; and begot such Sons upon the Muses, as I hope will live to see their father
what he never was yet, an old and a good Man. I made a Hymn as I past thro' these
Groves; it ended with a deep Sigh, which I will not tell you the meaning of.

> All hail! once pleasing, once inspiring Shade,
>   Scene of my youthful Loves, and happier hours!
> Where the kind Muses met me as I stray'd,
>   And gently pressd my hand, and said, Be Ours.
>
> Take all thou e'er shalt have, a constant Muse:
>   At Court thou may'st be lik'd, but nothing gain;
> Stocks thou may'st buy & sell, but always lose;
>   And love the brightest eyes, but love in vain!

On Thursday I went to Stonor, which I have long had a mind to see since the romantic
description you gave me of it. The Melancholy which my Wood, and this Place, have
spread over me, will go near to cast a cloud upon the rest of my letter, if I don't make
haste to conclude it here. I know you wish my happiness so much, that I would not
have you think I have any other reason to be melancholy: And after all, He must be
a beast that is so, with two such fine women for his friends. Tis enough to make any
creature easy, even such an one as Your Humble Servant.   (I, 428–29)

During the same visit he writes from Oxford, more bluntly, yet still avoiding
the embarrassment of utter gravity:

Methinks I do very ill, to return to the world again, to leave the only place where I
make a good figure, and from seeing myself seated with dignity on the most conspicuous Shelves of a Library, go to contemplate this wretched person in the abject
condition of lying at a Lady's feet in Bolton street.
    I will not deny, but that like Alexander, in the midst of my Glory, I am wounded,
& find myself a meer man. To tell you from when the Dart comes, is to no purpose,
since neither of you will take the tender care to draw it out of my heart, & suck the
poison with your lips; or are in any disposition to take in a part of the venome
yourselves, to ease me. Here, at my Lord Harcourt's, I see a Creature nearer an Angel
than a Woman . . . and he gravely proposd her to me for a Wife . . . I told him his
Lordship could never have thought of such a thing but for his misfortune of being
blind, and that I never cou'd till I was so. But that, as matters now were, I did not
care to force so fine a woman to give the finishing stroke to all my deformities, by the
last mark of a Beast, horns.   (I, 430–31)

Any progress towards a realistic attitude towards the sisters was complicated by the sudden death of Pope's father in October 1717. Pope breaks
the news to them in a note of moving brevity:

My poor Father dyed last night. Believe, since I don't forget you this moment, I never
shall.   (I, 447)

Both sisters are kind to him: Patty writes, 'My sister and I shall be at home all day: if any company comes that you dont like; I'll go up into my room with you; I hope we shall see you' (I, 452). Perhaps Teresa is somewhat unwilling to put off her gossiping friends, while Patty shares his mourning more readily. Soon, however, the old tensions with both sisters, given a new twist by Pope's grief, became intolerable, and he declared his frustration in terms which highlight the preposterous indeterminacy of the relationship. This is language which no reader would guess to be addressed to two people simultaneously:

I think myself obligd to desire, you would not put off any Diversion you may find, in the prospect of seeing me on Saturday, which is very uncertain. I Take this occasion to tell you once for all, that I design no longer to be a constant Companion when I have ceas'd to be an agreable one. You only have had, as my friends, the priviledge of knowing my Unhappiness; and are therefore the only people whom my Company must necessarily make melancholy. I will not bring myself to you at all hours, like a Skeleton, to come across your diversions, and dash your pleasures: Nothing can be more shocking than to be perpetually meeting the Ghost of an old acquaintance, which is all you can ever see of me.

You must not imagine this to proceed from any Coldness, or the least decrease of Friendship to you. If You had any Love for me, I should be always glad to gratify you with an Object that you thought agreable. But as your regard is Friendship & Esteem; those are things that are as well, perhaps better, preservd Absent than Present. A Man that you love is a joy to your eyes at all times; a Man that you Esteem is a solemn kind of thing, like a Priest, only wanted at a certain hour to do his Office: Tis like Oyl in a Sallet, necessary, but of no manner of Taste. And you may depend upon it, I will wait upon you on every real occasion, at the first summons, as long as I live.

Let me open my whole heart to you: I have some times found myself inclined to be in love with you: and as I have reason to know from your Temper & Conduct how miserably I should be used in that circumstance, it is worth my while to avoid it: It is enough to be Disagreable, without adding Fool to it, by constant Slavery. I have heard indeed of Women that have had a kindness for Men of my Make; but it has been after Enjoyment, never before; and I know to my cost you have had no Taste of that Talent in me, which most Ladies would not only Like better, but Understand better, than any other I have.

I love you so well that I tell you the truth, & that has made me write this Letter. I will see you less frequently this winter, as you'll less want company: When the Gay Part of the world is gone, I'll be ready to stop the Gap of a vacant hour whenever you please. Till then I'll converse with those who are more Indifferent to me, as You will with those who are more Entertaining.   (I, 455–56)

The composite personality he portrays has what he later came to see as Teresa's characteristics.

Even after such an outburst the final breach is delayed, and a cluster of undated notes, principally to Teresa, hints at a variety of tensions, even quarrels, unconvincingly smoothed over.[23] Because Teresa seems to be the focus

[23] *Corr.*, I, 456, 458, 459, 517; II, 25, 57.

of the trouble, it is tempting to see her as still Pope's favourite, and thus presumably the 'One' of another letter that presumably belongs to this period:

You will please to consider that my Coming or not is a thing Indifferent to both of you. But God knows, it is far otherwise to me, with respect to One of you.

I scarce ever come but one of two things happens, which equally afflicts me to the Soul. Either I make her Uneasy, or I see her Unkind.

If She has any Tenderness, I can only give her every day Trouble and melancholy. If she has none, the daily sight of so undeserved a coldness must wound me to death.

It is forcing one of us, to do a very Hard and very unjust thing, to the other.

My continuing to see you, will, by turns, teize all of us. My Staying away can at worst be of ill consequence only to myself.

And if One of us is to be sacrific'd, I believe, we are all three agreed, Who shall be the person.   (*Corr.*, I, 460)

Yet the same letter that deals with Teresa's resentment of the annuity, presumably written in February 1718, raises another possibility:

You told me if such a thing was the Secret of my heart, you shoud entirely forgive and think well of me. I told it, & find the contrary – You pretended so much generosity, as to offer your Services in my behalf: the minute after, you did me as ill an office as you could, in telling the party concern'd, it was all but an Amusement occasiond by my Loss of another Lady.   (I, 468)

Pope's obliquity makes it impossible to be certain; but his grievance seems to have been that Teresa had led him into confessing his attraction to Patty, and had offered to do what she could to help; but that she had later betrayed him by telling Patty that he was only consoling himself with her because she, Teresa, would not have him. If this is correct, it shows Teresa in a thoroughly unpleasant light; yet it is impossible not to feel the injustice of the pressure to which Pope had for so long subjected the sisters simply because they were not disposed to fall in love with him. Moreover, if it was Patty for whom he finally declared his love under such inauspicious circumstances, the letter reminds us forcibly how little we know of her feelings for him after his abandonment of Teresa, at a time when it seemed to others, perhaps to Patty too, that he was intent on physical consummation of his love.

Once more it seems that after such a letter his friendship with Teresa cannot go on, yet once again the old tone of teasing flattery is fleetingly recaptured. This time, however, the long echo of the happy years up to 1716 is finally drawing to a close. In 1719 letters are sparse and in 1720 Pope writes his last extant letter to Teresa, which plays with *double entendre* and flattery, alludes to her preference for the town, and concludes with a humorous description of a flood at Twickenham (*Corr.*, II, 59). It has no reference, however, to any aspirations on the writer's part.

4

At this point a new era begins, and Pope probably meant to declare as much when in the next year he allowed 'To Mrs. TB with his Works' to appear in print (*TE*, VI, 191). Patty alone figures in his letters over the next five years, although in a very muted way in comparison with the frequency of his former references to the sisters.

At the same time Patty, encouraged by Pope and Gay, was embarking on a friendship with Henrietta Howard, the Prince of Wales's mistress, whose projected house at Marble Hill enabled Pope to combine the satisfactions of landscaping and of assisting an unfortunate lady. Despite the superficial incongruity of his attempting to protect Patty from her sister's dubious morals only to encourage her intimacy with a kept mistress, there were factors which set Mrs Howard well above Teresa in his estimation.[24] Her husband, who had proved brutal, grasping and feckless, had promoted her connection with the Prince and Princess, and when he decided that he had sold his wife at too low a price the royal couple constituted her only protection against his violence. Moreover, far from being held in sensual thrall by her charms, her royal master hardly even liked her: he held opinions contrary to hers on all important subjects and encouraged his wife to humiliate her. Under this provocation she won admiration for her quiet dignity and behaved with such circumspection that some observers doubted 'the King's ever having entered into any commerce with her, that he might not innocently have had with his daughter'.[25] Such a woman, Pope's most enduring friend from the years when, incongruously for a man of his faith, he frequented the court and teased the maids of honour, was to him a wronged heroine whose friendship could only do Patty good.

Patty's early letters to Mrs Howard show just how deep was the diffidence that distinguished the younger from the elder sister:

Your letters say so much, and Mr Pope says so much more from you . . . at the same time I fear (my old fault) that my nearer approach will put you out of love wth me. I may be better in prospect then in possession (Just the contrary to Marble Hill). I begin to wish my self one of the trees of y[t] place; that, since I find I must always belong to you, I might be always in y[r] eye.[26]

This is less polite reserve than a habitual lack of confidence that makes her constantly seek reassurance. Mrs Howard feels bound to reprove her: not only does Patty let her diffidence, 'a fault that has many beauty's', call Mrs Howard's sincerity into question; she also lets the 'compliance to other people's humour' (here presumably Teresa's) which is a 'distinguish'd part of Your Character' prevent her from taking the country holiday she needs.[27]

[24] For Mrs Howard see chapter 7.2.
[25] *Lord Hervey's Memoirs*, edited by Romney Sedgwick (London, 1952), p. 41.
[26] BL Add. MSS 22627 (Suffolk Papers), II, 7.
[27] Blount Letters, II, 94; III, 61.

These exchanges foreshadow the irony of Pope's later attempts to persuade her to stand up for herself: the characteristics fostered by standing in 'the shade' cast by her sister made her in his eyes not only 'fairest' but also infuriating.[28]

In contrast, another correspondence of these years brings out the positive side of this softness of character. Patty's friend Bridget Floyd, who lived with her brother at St Germains because of his involvement with the Jacobite court, pays some attention in her letters to society gossip, but unlike Teresa's correspondents she is really seeking a sympathetic ear for her personal problems: her confidences about an obscure but terrifying conspiracy against her by her brother and his suspected mistress are at times almost Richardsonian in their intensity (Blount Letters, II, 117a–41). Patty's cowardice, expressed in her fear of crossing the Channel to join her friend, may have unfitted her for dramatic intervention, even supposing this had been possible; but her willingness to listen and comfort was something Teresa's friends would probably have looked for in vain. Moreover, the passive, depressive tendencies which Bridget and Patty shared were accompanied by a love of landscape that gave them more common ground with Pope – once *The Rape of the Lock* and his fascination with Teresa were behind him – than the brash urban delights in which Teresa centred her life: as 'an admirer of Nature' Bridget 'wished for Mr Popes genious when I was upon the borders of the Loire', and when she had to disembark in a storm on a wild shore scattered with crabs and shellfish she wished that Patty had been there to admire the scene.

Pope often calls Patty's response to landscape 'romantic'; and the allusion to her favourite books is not far beneath the surface. Both tastes suggested at once an aspiration to something nobler than the everyday world and a difficulty or fatigue in coping with its demands. They were tastes which fostered intimacy with the poet who had set the unfortunate ladies of his poetry in a context of licensed subjectivity amid sympathetic landscape, and as the relationship matured he became on one hand the guide and protector that Patty's indecision and ill health required and on the other the imaginative companion who could interpret landscape in the 'romantic' spirit that she herself brought to it.[29] In the light of the descriptions he was to send her in the years to come there cannot be much doubt which of the sisters had given him 'the romantic description' of Stonor which made him so anxious to see it in 1717, and which apparently fed a melancholy once pleasurable but now sharpened by exile:

Nothing could have more of that Melancholy whch once us'd to please me, than that days journey: for after having passd thro' my favorite Woods in the forest, with a thousand Reveries of past pleasures; I rid over hanging hills, whose tops were edgd with Groves, & whose feet water'd with winding rivers, listening to the falls of

---

[28] *Characters of Women*, line 202.
[29] George S. Rousseau, 'A New Pope Letter', *PQ*, 54 (1966), 409–18; Nicolson and Rousseau, pp. 211–18; Brownell, pp. 86–94.

Cataracts below, & the murmuring of Winds above. The gloomy Verdure of Stonor
succeeded to these, & then the Shades of the Evening overtook me, the Moon rose in
the clearest Sky I ever saw, by whose solemn light I pac'd on slowly, without company,
or any interruption to the range of my thoughts. About a mile before I reachd Oxford,
all the Night bells toll'd, in different notes; the Clocks of every College answerd one
another; & told me, some in a deeper, some in a softer voice, that it was eleven a clock.

(*Corr.*, I, 429–30)

From about 1722 it was generally observed that Pope had dropped Teresa,
and rumours began to circulate that he had either married Patty secretly or persuaded her to become his mistress.[30] Patty's note of 1723 that 'I begin to take it
a little ill that you come so seldom to me' suggests that it was not the time they
spent together that fuelled the gossip (*Corr.*, II, 134, 191). The real source is
plausibly indicated in a letter of 1725, in which Pope refers to an explanation
which took place between Patty and her godmother Elizabeth Caryll in about
1723. The scandal as he reports it to Caryll is patently false, since Mrs Caryll's
corroborative reply to Patty is still extant, but what is interesting is the way in
which he begins to represent Teresa and, to a lesser degree, Mrs Blount as
malicious and immoral companions from whom Patty needs to be separated:[31]

A very confident asseveration has been made, which has spread over the town, that
your god-daughter Miss Patty and I lived 2 or 3 years since in a manner that was
reported to you as giving scandal to many: that upon your writing to me upon it I consulted with her, and sent you an excusive alleviating answer; but did after that,
privately and of myself write to you a full confession; how much I myself disapproved
the way of life, and owning the prejudice done her, charging it on herself, and declaring that I wished to break off what I acted against my conscience, &c.; and that she,
being at the same time spoken to by a lady of your acquaintance, at your instigation,
did absolutely deny to alter any part of her conduct, were it ever so disreputable or
exceptionable. Upon this villanous lying tale, it is farther added by the same hand,
that I brought her acquainted with a noble lord, and into an intimacy with some
others, merely to get quit of her myself, being moved in consciousness by what you
and I had conferred together, and playing this base part to get off.

   You will bless yourself at so vile a wickedness, who very well (I dare say) remember
the truth of what then past, and the satisfaction you expressed I gave you (and Mrs
Caryll also expressed the same thing to her kinswoman) upon that head. God knows
upon what motives any one should malign a sincere and virtuous friendship! I wish
those very people had never led her into any thing more liable to objection, or more
dangerous to a good mind, than I hope my conversation or kindness are. She has in
reality had less of it these two years past than ever since I knew her; and truly when
she has it, 'tis almost wholly a preachment, which I think necessary, against the ill consequences of another sort of company, which they by their good will would always
keep; and she, in compliance and for quiet sake keeps more than you or I could wish.

[30] For a full account of this gossip see Sherburn, *Early Career*, pp. 291–93.
[31] Mrs Caryll's letter is in Blount Letters, III, 44–45, transcribed in Sherburn, *Early Career*, pp.
    292–93. For evidence that Mrs Blount may have embarrassed Patty, see a friend's promise
    'to have a watchful Eye over her conduct' if Patty comes to Bath with her (Blount Letters,
    III, 167–69).

To deal with you like a friend, openly: you know 'tis the whole misfortune of that family to be governed like a ship – that is, the head guided by the tail, and that by every wind that blows in it.

God is my witness I am as much a friend to her soul as to her person: the good qualities of the former made me her friend. No creature has better natural dispositions, or would act more rightly or reasonably in every duty, did she act by herself, or from herself.   (*Corr.*, II, 353–54)

This is in many ways an intriguing statement. Teresa had always found the Carylls tedious, and would perhaps feel little compunction about involving them in gossip which shows at the very least a wilful misinterpretation of the facts; yet Patty too had expressed dissatisfaction with her reception by the Carylls, and Pope had been angry with them for not being readier to invite her (I, 481, 512). At this point, however, he is prepared to sink whatever annoyance he felt – and it had never been expressed to Caryll himself – and invoke Caryll's undoubted care for Patty. Indeed, if the sisters' visits to Ladyholt had been less than pleasant, Teresa's contempt for the retired life may well have been responsible. Interesting too is Pope's progress from teasing Teresa about her taste for high life to insinuating that her friends are actually corrupt and corrupting: his play on 'tail' plainly hints at lewdness as the mainspring of the social set she has imposed on her mother and sister.

Teresa's character as revealed by her own writings makes Pope's accusation of slander only too credible. Despite her impatience with his protestations of esteem, jealousy on her part need not be ruled out: although only physically attractive, well-dressed young men about town qualified for her serious interest, it must have been galling to realise that the little cripple whose work others rated so highly would not submit for ever to be teased like an monkey or lapdog – however deeply he might feel that his deformity qualified him for little else.[32] Her whole outlook is implicitly swept aside in the poem which he wrote for her sister's birthday in 1723, a poem in which any amorous feeling for Patty is tactfully muted, yet which allows for a place in her life which he will make his own:

> Oh be thou blest with all that Heav'n can send!
> Long Health, long Youth, long Pleasure – and a Friend.
> Not with those Toys the Woman-World admire,
> Riches that vex, and Vanities that tire:
> Let Joy, or Ease; let Affluence, or Content;
> And the glad Conscience of a Life well-spent,
> Calm ev'ry Thought, inspirit ev'ry Grace,
> Glow in thy Heart, and smile upon thy Face!
> Let Day improve on Day, and Year on Year,
> Without a Pain, a Trouble, or a Fear!
> And ah! since Death must that dear Frame destroy,
> Die by a sudden Extacy of Joy!

[32] Mack, 'My Ordinary Occasions', pp. 3–4.

> In some soft Dream may thy mild Soul remove,
> And be thy latest Gasp a Sigh of Love.[33]

This sets the direction for his idealisation of Patty. Emphasis on happy, even pious virtue enables the conclusion to be read in the sense to which he later revised it ('Peaceful sleep out the Sabbath of the Tomb, / And wake to Raptures in a Life to come'); yet as it stands it hints a discreet hope that in the end she will return his love as unreservedly as it is offered. In these obscure years of adjustment both agree that they do not see as much of each other as they would like, and Mrs Pope, who would surely not have encouraged a woman she suspected of fornication with her son, seems to have been a major link between them. Patty's nervous regard for decorum may have enjoined a discretion frustrating to both; or perhaps she was disturbed to find herself the object of feelings which still had much in common with the amorous friendship that had alienated her sister (*Corr.*, II, 191, 354, 236). Moreover, she was still living with that sister, whom in spite of all Pope's pleading she never repudiated.

Pope's verdict on Teresa, Belinda's sister in pride, dress, assertiveness and most of all in her 'sprightly eyes', was clear and final ('After the Coronation', line 45). The first of his female suns had set in a tawdry glare. In his view, she, like Belinda, had refused tenderness and intimacy to the man she had captivated. The pattern was to be repeated in his more notorious quarrel with Lady Mary Wortley Montagu.

---

[33] This is the text actually sent to Patty, printed by Ault in *New Light*, p. 196: for revisions see *TE*, VI, 244–47. An earlier autograph with slight variations, apparently Pope's draft, is described in R. M. Schmitz, 'Two New Holographs of Pope's Birthday Lines to Martha Blount', *Review of English Studies*, 8 (1957), 234–48.

6

Female wit

1

The complexities of Pope's manoeuvres with Patty and Teresa were only a part of the painfully experimental amorous fencing of his late twenties. Given the apparent depth of the drama unfolding between him and the sisters, it comes as something of a surprise to discover that at the same time, most intensely from 1715 to 1718, he was going over much of the same ground with Lady Mary Wortley Montagu. Moreover, the sisters knew her at least slightly and knew also that Pope was her friend. Typographate had earlier, before her marriage, regaled Teresa with news of Lady Mary's father's refusal to pay her gambling debts; she is most probably the 'Lady Mary' whom Pope cites to Patty as a suitable 'historian' for his project of going 'a Rakeing' with Teresa 'in man's Clothes'; he makes no secret of her role in gathering the highly imaginative gossip he relays from the town in 1715; and he provided the sisters with evidence of her literary abilities in a copy which he made for them of her verses on Constantinople.[1] There is no evidence to suggest, however, that they realised anything of the intensity of Pope's feeling for her. Because Lady Mary's life and writings have long been available in print, she has always been a much more immediate presence in Pope's biography than the Blounts, whose self-revelations are largely confined to unpublished correspondence and whose connection with Pope's poetry has often been doubted or deliberately obscured.[2] Despite tantalising gaps, the great need in relation to Lady Mary's impact on Pope is less for information than for interpretation.

In the broader pattern of Pope's dealings with women, Lady Mary represents two connected themes. Most obviously, she is a woman who is not only physically attractive but also intellectually challenging, a writer, a wit, and a politician, and his response to her is so violent and lasts so long that it exposes the structure of his feeling about such women more clearly than any other single encounter. The second theme which centres on her extends this pattern into the realm of imagery and association: like Belinda and Teresa,

[1] Blount Letters, III, 122; Corr., I, 261, 309; Blount Letters, III, 189–91.
[2] Warburton denied that Patty was the ideal lady of Characters of Women (TE, III.ii, 46–47), and Ault argued that neither sister was connected with 'With the Works of Voiture' (New Light, pp. 49–56).

131

she is associated with brightness and with the sun, and like them also her brilliance is ultimately tarnished. Her striking appearance – she too had dark hair and eyes – and her sharp tongue suggest that, with the added advantages of rank and literary assurance, she burst on Pope's consciousness as a more impressive, less intimately known version of Teresa. Just as his homage to Teresa's sister prevented the embarrassment of being seen as a suitor, his courteous regard for Lady Mary's husband seemed to declare that his fascination was merely polite gallantry. As counterpart to this parallel between Teresa and Lady Mary, he evolved his characteristic moon imagery – later to be his ultimate compliment to Patty – out of his meditation on Judith Cowper, whose milder poetic manner he came to prefer to Lady Mary's.

2

When Pope met Lady Mary, probably in 1715, she was consoling herself for the aridity of her marriage by pursuing her husband's interest at court, a field which offered stimulating opportunities for her charm and shrewdness.[3] Her history to date had been a rehearsal for the pattern of attempted duty and final rebellion that was to characterise her marriage. To her father, a neglectful, pleasure-loving aristocrat, she had tried to play the role of submissive daughter, courting the approval of his intellectual friends by avowing the inferiority of the female mind and emphasising to her future husband that her hand was entirely at her father's disposal.[4] This effort finally collapsed under the stress of her father's attempt to marry her to a suitor who offered better financial terms than Edward Wortley: she made up her mind and eloped (*LM Essays*, pp. 16–18). Yet even after her own children were born, she knelt for her father's blessing when he surprised her at her dressing table (p. 31). She entered on marriage with similarly demanding but equally doomed ideals, committed to a 'passive Obedience' which 'makes me cautious who I set for my Master', and giving the impression that she had thoroughly internalised the demands of authority: 'What is Liberty to one that carrys her gaoler in her breast? My Duty is more a chain to me than all others that could be impos'd upon me' (*LM Letters*, I, 54, 125). Yet against this must be set the ominous acrimony of what in other courtships would be called their loveletters. After their marriage in 1712 Wortley expected her to live mainly in the country while he pursued his career in London, partly perhaps from considerations of economy, but also, according to Lady Mary, because he was so

---

[3] Compare her evaluation of court personalities with her husband's analysis of party politics in *The Letters and Works of Lady Mary Wortley Montagu*, edited by Lord Wharncliffe and revised by W. Moy Thomas, 2 vols. (London, 1861), I, 123–41.

[4] Lady Mary Wortley Montagu, *Essays and Poems and Simplicity, a Comedy*, edited by R. Halsband and I. Grundy (Oxford, 1977), pp. 8–9 (hereafter *LM Essays*); *The Complete Letters of Lady Mary Wortley Montagu*, edited by Robert Halsband, 3 vols. (Oxford, 1965), I, 45, 64 (hereafter *LM Letters*).

jealous that he 'would have made me invisible to all but himselfe'.[5] Unfortunately, jealousy seems to have been the only passion she aroused in him: whilst he expected her to write by every post, he wrote brief, unaffectionate notes only when it suited him (I, 154–55, 170–244). Finally, in November 1714, when their son was eighteen months old, she spoke her mind:

I have taken up and laid down my pen several times, very much unresolv'd in what style I ought to write to you. For once I suffer my Inclination to get the better of my reason . . . But I am very sensible I parted with you in July, and tis now the middle of November. As if this was not hardship enough you do not tell me you are sorry for it. You write seldom and with so much indifference as shows you hardly think of me at all. I complain of ill health and you only say, you hope tis not so bad as I make it. You never enquire after your Child . . . Own to me your Inconstancy, and upon my word I will give you no more trouble about it. I have conceal'd as long as I can the uneasyness the nothingness of your letters have given me, under an affected Indifference, but Dissimulation allways sits aukardly upon me . . . If your Inclination is gone, I had rather never receive a Letter from you, then one which in leiu of comfort for your absence gives me a pain even beyond it. For my part, as tis my first, this is my last complaint, and your next of that kind shall go back enclos'd to you in blank paper. (I, 236–37)

Thus she was left in the position of trying to fulfil her duty to an unsatisfactory husband just as she had tried previously with an unsatisfactory father (*LM Essays*, pp. 157–67). Finally, as with him, she failed, and giving as excuse her need to travel for her health she fled to the continent in 1739, intent on her secret hope of a new life with a young Italian writer.[6] Even when he failed to meet her she stayed abroad, using her new freedom to enjoy (by her own account) such modest pleasures as new friends, reading, writing and gardening, until her daughter persuaded her to come home a few months before her death in 1762. Whilst abroad she wrote her husband kind, dutiful letters, full of news of health, weather and local curiosities, but she retained a keen sense of the wasted effort of her married life. On hearing that their daughter was staying with him she wrote:

I hope her obedience and affection for you will make your life agreable to you. She cannot have more than I have had; I wish the succcss may be greater.
(*LM Letters*, II, 271)

Pope first appeared on her social horizon soon after the marital crisis of November 1714, for it was early in the following year that she returned to London and began her career as an attender at court. Her wit made her the natural ally of Pope and Gay. According to Pope, it was Gay who inspired her to write her town eclogues:

Lydia, in Lady Mary's poems, is almost wholly Gay's, and is published as such in

[5] *LM Essays*, p. 83; *LM Letters*, I, 58, 78.
[6] Robert Halsband, *The Life of Lady Mary Wortley Montagu*, corrected edition (Oxford, 1961), pp. 153–78 (hereafter *LM Life*).

his works. There are only five or six lines new set in it by that lady. It was that which gave the hint and she wrote the other five eclogues to it.[7]

Even in the years of her hostility to Pope she admitted that the eclogues 'were first thought of in company with Pope and Gay'.[8] Her texts are lavishly adorned with allusions to Pope's pastoral rhetoric, and it must have been a literary as well as a personal delight for him to suggest revisions and make a fair copy annotated with the Latin originals which they had both imitated.[9] Some of the bathos put into the mouths of her characters is highly reminiscent of the examples in the Scriblerian *Peri Bathous*, and it was no doubt intended as a compliment when in 1717 Pope and Gay echoed one of her resoundingly flat-footed couplets in the farce *Three Hours after Marriage* (*LM Essays*, p. 188). Thus for a time she became almost a Scriblerian, and when we remember how the members of that circle looked back on the period of its meetings as a golden age we may see further into the bitterness of her later insistence that Pope, Swift, Gay and Arbuthnot were both socially and artistically contemptible.[10]

The town eclogues preserve something of this brief intimacy. Lady Mary shows herself able to take up Gay's hint in true Scriblerian manner: her poems are witty, elegant and artfully insinuating. Perhaps even a plain woman could have fascinated Pope with wit of this calibre; but Lady Mary compounded her charm by her beauty. In Pope's *Epistle to Mr. Jervas* (written in the autumn of 1715 he had praised '*Wortley*'s' eyes'; and when she caught smallpox later that winter he must have been further impressed by the way she could transform her fears for the loss of 'the radiant bloom / That promis'd Happyness for Years to come' into a poem which, despite its humour, recognises the superficiality of all that women hope from beauty:

> Monarchs, and Beauties rule with equal sway,
> All strive to serve, and Glory to obey,

[7] Spence, no. 236. Pope's belief was the same even before he quarrelled with Lady Mary, since he omitted 'Lydia' (also called 'Friday' or 'The Toilette') from the fair copy he made for her, which is reproduced with commentary in Lady Mary Wortley Montagu, *Court Eclogs Written in the Year, 1716*, edited by Robert Halsband (New York, 1977). Halsband supports Gay's authorship in 'Pope, Lady Mary, and the *Court Poems* (1716)', *PMLA*, 68 (1953), 237–50. Vinton A. Dearing and Charles E. Beckwith adduce metrical evidence for Gay's authorship in John Gay, *Poetry and Prose*, 2 vols. (Oxford, 1974), I, 181–85; II, 572–73. Their copy text is Gay's revision of 1720. His status as pioneer of the sub-genre is considered by Dearing (I, 83–86; II, 508–9) and Halsband (*Court Eclogs*, p. 63). Isobel Grundy prints as Lady Mary's a version from her album in *LM Essays*, pp. 182, 198–200. For a comparison of the two versions, see Ann Messenger, *His and Hers: Essays in Restoration and Eighteenth-Century Literature* (Lexington, 1986), chapter 4, pp. 84–107.

[8] *The Yale Edition of Horace Walpole's Correspondence*, edited by W. S. Lewis, 48 vols. (London, 1937–83), XIV, 242 (hereafter *HW Corr.*).

[9] See commentary in *LM Essays* and Pope's fair copy reproduced by Halsband in *Court Eclogs*.

[10] This is a frequent theme: see *LM Essays*, 98, 247–51, 265–70, 273–76, 280–84; *LM Letters*, II, 71–72; III, 57, 83.

> Alike unpity'd when depos'd they grow,
> Men mock the Idol of their Former vow.[11]

As Pope lovingly transcribed her poem on the smallpox he was far from guessing that one day he would use 'Flavia', the name she gave herself in the poem, to express disgust, or that he would change the name 'Wortley' to 'Worsley' in order to deprive her of the compliment in *To Jervas*. Nor could he predict that he would try to make her look ungrateful by implying that, purely to protect her, he had decoyed the unauthorised publisher of two of her eclogues into swallowing an emetic.[12] Yet it is something of a puzzle to know whether the lines on her wit in 'Sandys's Ghost', which he was drafting soon after this clandestine publication, are a playful compliment dating from this period, or ironic belittlement added when he revised the poem in the late 1720s (*TE*, VI, 174). Although they seem admiring, their context – Pope is arguing ironically that the field of translation is equally open to the competent and incompetent – is ambiguous:

> Ye *Ladies* too draw forth your Pen,
> I pray where can the Hurt lie?
> Since you have brains as well as Men,
> As witness Lady *W—l—y*.

> In your French Dictionaries look,
> Ye Fair ones that are able
> For tho ye seldome write a book,
> Ye all can tell a Fable.   (line 65)

Pope chose not to print the latter stanza – yet Lady Mary *did* write in and translate from French. Her wit was to prove quite as ambiguous in her relationship with him as the lines which appear to praise it, but in their brief time at court together it was an unqualified attraction. Although Teresa probably matched her in assurance, she had neither the skill nor the classics for a project like the town eclogues, nor did she take any serious interest in affairs of state.

The decisive event in Lady Mary's relationship with Pope was her departure in August 1716 for Constantinople, where her husband was to be ambassador. At first it seemed that the post would last at least five years, perhaps as long as fifteen, but her response was enthusiastic, typifying the unconventional flair which fascinated Pope: ' 'twas a sort of dying to her friends and country: but 'twas travelling, 'twas going farther than most other people go'.[13] From being fellow wits and frequenters of the court, he and Lady Mary were to be

---

[11] *To Jervas*, line 60 (*TE*, VI, 158); 'Satturday', lines 7–8, 84–87 (*LM Essays*, pp. 201–4).

[12] *Characters of Women*, 1735 reading of lines 24–25 (*TE*, III.ii, 51–52); *To Jervas*, line 60. Halsband, 'Pope, Lady Mary and the *Court Poems*', argues convincingly that the emetic was meant to protect Gay, although Pope later tried to make it look as if he had had Lady Mary's interest at heart.

[13] Joseph Spence, *Letters from the Grand Tour*, edited by Slava Klima (London, 1975), p. 357.

separated by an immensity of time and distance which in his eyes transposed their relationship to a different plane. Armed with the conventions of epistolary flattery, he was able to express the element of sexual attraction in his feeling for her without committing himself. Such rhetoric was in any case usually discounted, and he could also tell himself that his fantasies would not be subject to the shock of a face-to-face meeting for several years. Even before her departure he had told her, 'if I thought I shou'd not see you again, I would say some things here, which I could not to your person' (*Corr.*, I, 345). As she advanced eastwards his inhibitions relaxed further: 'Let us be like modest people, who when they are close together keep all decorums, but if they step a little aside, or get to the other end of a room, can untye garters or take off Shifts without scruple' (I, 384). Protestations of seriousness are frequent; but in such a context it is impossible to judge their sincerity. Yet the fantasy is undoubtedly serious insofar as it reflects his excitement at meeting a lovely, aristocratic woman who could, to however limited an extent, do the things which mattered most in his own life. The problem he would later have to confront, and not as much later as he had expected, would be the return from the freedom of separation to the constraint of daily contact.

From the beginning he treats her as a phenomenon because of her (to him) miraculous combination of masculine wit and feminine softness:

You may easily imagine how desirous I must be of a Correspondence with a person, who had taught me long ago that it was as possible to Esteem at first sight, as to Love; and who has since ruin'd me for all the Conversation of one Sex, and almost all the Friendship of the other. I am but too sensible thro' your means that the Company of Men wants a certain Softness to recommend it, and that of Women wants every thing else.   (I, 353–54)

Already he associates her with the sun, at this point a warm, creative presence: 'May you appear to distant Worlds like a Sun that is sunk out of the sight of our Hemisphere, to gladden the other'.[14] At this stage he can also liken her to the moon, although later he was to reserve what came to be his highest compliment for less forceful women:

I lye dreaming of you in Moonshiny Nights exactly in the posture of Endymion gaping for Cynthia in a Picture. And with just such a Surprise and rapture should I awake, if after your long revolutions were accomplishd, you should at last come rolling back again, smiling with all that gentleness and serenity (peculiar to the Moon and you) and gilding the same Mountains from which you first set out on your solemn, melancholy journey.   (*Corr.*, I, 439–40)

Beneath such fanciful comedy there often runs a vein of more frankly erotic implication. Earlier, for example, the topic of sincerity had developed into a scenario of souls bared for Judgement Day in which the physical connotations

---

[14] *Corr.*, I, 389; see also 369, 382, 406, 440.

of nakedness are never far beneath the surface. Moreover, the motif is introduced by a biblical allusion redolent of exotic sensuality:

I think I love you as well as King Herod could Herodias, (tho I never had so much as one Dance with you) and would as freely give you my heart in a Dish, as he did another's head. But since Jupiter will not have it so, I must be content to show my taste in Life as I do my taste in Painting, by loving to have as little Drapery as possible. Not that I think every body naked, altogether so fine a sight as yourself and a few more would be: but because 'tis good to use people to what they must be acquainted with; and there will certainly come some Day of Judgment to uncover every Soul of us. We shall then see how the Prudes of this world owed all their fine Figure only to their being a little straiter-lac'd, and that they were naturally as arrant Squabs as those that went more loose, nay as those that never girded their loyns at all.   (I, 353)

It is ironic to find Pope backing, even metaphorically, the looseness of corsets and of morals which he was later to use against her. By that time he was content to follow the prudes; but at the beginning, decorum was more an obstacle than an ideal.[15] The word 'decency' is constantly on his lips, and such telling reminders as his inability to dance with Lady Mary highlight his sensitivity to the special decorum entailed in his deformity, in comparison with which the impropriety of making court to a married woman is as nothing. Part of the function of the fanciful allusions, often delightful in themselves, is to provide contexts in which the various restraints of real-life decency can be set aside.

From this point of view, the fact that Lady Mary had gone to the East was the happiest of coincidences, for Oriental fantasy led him effortlessly into the areas which preoccupied him. His reading in the genre made the atmosphere of refined yet brutal sensuality which Lady Mary evoked in her reports familiar imaginative territory:[16]

But what can you expect from such a country as this, from which the muses have fled, from which letters seem eternally banished, and in which you see, in private scenes, nothing pursued as happiness but the refinements of an indolent voluptuousness, and where those who act upon the publick theatre live in uncertainty, suspicion, and terror . . . The luscious passion of the Seraglio is the only one almost that is gratified here to the full, but it is blended so with the surly spirit of despotism in one of the parties, and with the dejection and anxiety which this spirit produces in the other, that to one of my way of thinking it cannot appear otherwise than as a very mixed kind of enjoyment.   (Corr., I, 422)

In order to provide an acceptable focus for his fascination with Lady Mary and its erotic implications he introduces the fantasy that she should buy him a Circassian slave-girl as like herself as possible: 'I have detested the Sound

---

15 Corr., I, 363, 389, 440, 469.
16 For his knowledge of the Arabian Nights, see Sherburn, 'New Anecdotes', p. 345. He lent the Persian and Turkish tales to Atterbury in 1720 (Corr., II, 56). The background is discussed by Martha Pike Conant, The Oriental Tale in England in the Eighteenth Century, Columbia University Studies in Comparative Literature (New York, 1908), pp. 1–29, 269, 273.

of *Honest Woman*, & *Loving Spouse* ever since I heard the pretty name of Odaliche' (I, 364, 441, 496). This topic is closely connected with his delight in believing that, according to Islam, women have no souls. With typical urbanity, however, he accommodates even her husband in the humour which licenses his fantasy (as he writes, she is still in Vienna):

> You have already (without passing the bounds of Christendom) out-traveld the Sin of Fornication, and are happily arrived at the free Region of Adultery: in a little time you'l look upon some other Sins, with more Impartiality than the Ladies here are capable of . . . I doubt not but I shall be told, (when I come to follow you thro' those Countries) in how pretty a manner you accomodated yourself to the Customes of the True-Believers . . . How happy will it be, for a gay young Woman, to live in a Country where it is a part of Religious worship to be giddy-headed? I shall hear at Belgrade, how the good Basha receivd the fair Convert with tears of joy, how he was charm'd with her pretty manner of pronouncing the words Allah, and Muhammed, and how earnestly you joind with him in exhorting Mr Wortley to be circumcised. But he satisfies you by demonstrating, how in that condition, he could not properly represent his Brittannick Majesty. Lastly I shall hear how the very first Night you lay at Pera, you had a Vision of Mahomet's Paradise, and happily awaked without a Soul. From which blessed instant the beautiful Body was left at full liberty to perform all the agreeable functions it was made for.   (I, 368–69)

Lady Mary reduced to 'the beautiful Body' would not have been the fascinating woman she was, but having been fascinated Pope revels in speculating on a relationship as unfettered by decorum as by her intellectual assertiveness. Similar possibilities also shape his anticipation of her return: he attributes to her body a pure sexual expressiveness besides which ordinary souls (with their irksome inhibitions) are nonentities:

> I long for nothing so much as your Oriental Self. You must of necessity be *advanced* so far *Back* into true nature & simplicity of manners, by these 3 years residence in the East, that I shall look upon you as so many years Younger than you was, so much nearer Innocence (that is, Truth) & Infancy (that is Openness.) I expect to see your Soul as much thinner dressd as your Body; and that you have left off, as unwieldy & cumbersome, a great many damn'd Europoean Habits. Without offence to your modesty be it spoken, I have a burning desire to see your Soul stark naked, for I am confident 'tis the prettiest kind of white Soul, in the universe – But I forget whom I am talking to, you may possibly by this time Believe according to the Prophet, that you have none. If so, show me That which comes next to a Soul; you may easily put it upon a poor ignorant Christian for a Soul, & please him as well with it: I mean your Heart; Mahomet I think allows you Hearts: which (together with fine eyes & other agreeable equivalents) are worth all the Souls on this side the world. But if I must be content with seeing your body only, God send it to come quickly: I honour it more than the Diamond-Casket that held Homer's Iliads. For in the very twinkle of one eye of it, there is more Meaning, than in all the Souls that ever were casually put into Women since Men had the making them.   (I, 494)

As noted above, the Oriental and the Gothic were often associated as literary modes which, like the weaker sex, tended to allow imagination to slip the leash of judgement.[17] In this correspondence whimsical Gothic allusion suits the decorum of addressing a court lady who is to an extent (though a limited one) Belinda's sister, and there is real charm in the consequent re-entry into the imaginatively fertile world of 'all the Nurse, and all the Priest have taught' (*Rape*, I.30). Bishop Atterbury's impatience with the licence of Oriental fiction has already been cited; but it was less dangerous to credit a woman with the taste for Gothic or Oriental absurdity, and Pope is at ease in his letters to Lady Mary with allusions which both license and mock his feelings. He can even invoke aspects of Roman Catholic theology which would usually embarrass him: thus he presents himself as a hermit or visionary, while she is a saint or separated spirit, with a troop of guardian angels to complete the scenario.[18]

It is only a small step from this to the outright whimsy of 'the man in the Alchymist that has a passion for the Queen of the Faeries'.[19] Perhaps too the sex of his correspondent stimulated him to respond more fully than we might have expected of a disciple of Burlington to the Gothic manor at Stanton Harcourt, 'a House that seems to be built before Rules were in fashion'.[20] Here again the tone is whimsical – the layout suggests to him that 'twenty Cottages had taken a dance together, were all Out, and stood still in amazement ever since', but it is clear that some less conventional strain in his personality is genuinely stirred by the dusty spectacle of its chaotic grandeur. On another occasion he is similarly stirred by the Gothic extravagance of a celebrated poet:

If you are really disposed to embrace the Mahometan religion, I'll fly on Pilgrimage with you thither, with as good a heart and as sound devotion, as ever Jeffery Rudel the Provençall Poet, went after the fine Countess of Tripoly to Jerusalem. If you never heard of this Jeffery, I'll assure you he deserves your acquaintance: He livd in our Richard the first's time, put on a Pilgrims weed, took his voyage, and when he got ashore, was just upon the point of expiring. The Countess of Tripoly came to the Ship, took him by the Hand: He lifted up his eyes, said, that having been blest with a sight of her, he was satisfied; and so departed this life. What did the Countess of Tripoly upon this? She made him a Splendid funeral, built him a Tomb of Porphyry, put his Epitaph upon it in Arabic verse, had his Sonnets curiously copied out and illumind with letters of gold, was taken with Melancholy, and turnd Nun . . . As for the rest,

---

[17] For attempts to link the two cultures historically, see Samuel Kliger, *The Goths in England: A Study in Seventeenth and Eighteenth Century Thought* (Harvard, 1952; reprinted New York, 1972), pp. 210–17; Arthur Johnston, *Enchanted Ground: The Study of Medieval Romance in the Eighteenth Century* (London, 1964), pp. 13–19, 53–56; *The Works of Alexander Pope Esq.*, edited by William Warburton, 9 vols. (London, 1751), III, pp. 266–69; Paul Frankl, *The Gothic: Literary Sources and Interpretations through Eight Centuries* (Princeton, 1960), pp. 363–65, 391–92.

[18] *Corr.*, I, 356, 363, 469. 471.

[19] *Corr.*, I, 439; Ben Jonson, *The Alchemist*, edited by F. H. Mares, The Revels Plays (London, 1967), I.2, III.5, V.3–4.

[20] *Corr.*, I, 505. Pope printed a very similar letter as sent to the Duke of Buckingham. Even if it was really sent, it is most probably based on one conceived with Lady Mary in mind (*Corr.*, I, 508–9).

if I have not followed you to the ends of the earth, 'tis not my fault; if I had, I might possibly have dyd as gloriously as Jeffery Rudel.   (*Corr.*, I, 440–41)

At one level Pope is using this bogus tale simply to mock himself, but he has also found a mode of expression for aspirations too embarrassing to discuss openly: a sea voyage would have killed him in fact just as love killed the Gothic lover of the fiction.[21] This see-sawing between what is too weighty to utter and what is too silly to take seriously is typical of these letters. Ultimately, whatever balance is achieved, he has to recognise that only in imaginative worlds outside his native decorum can he find a context for the aspirations other people take for granted: when he reminds Lady Mary of the pseudo-Gothic romance of a queen who fell in love with a dwarf he is also reminding himself that only in a grotesque world could his body be other than repulsive.[22] At this point Gothic and Oriental meet, for he offers in the same breath to follow her 'to those parts of India, where they tell us the Women best like the Ugliest fellows, as the most admirable productions of nature, and look upon Deformities as the Signatures of divine Favour' (*Corr.*, I, 364).

Pope's literary construction of the relationship faced two challenges from real life: the first was Lady Mary's response by letter, the second their mutual re-adjustment to face-to-face contact. As to the first, although it was not to be expected that she would take up the flirtation in earnest, the detachment of her replies comes as a shock. This may be partly because the copies now extant seem to have been written up very much as a potential book of travels. Even so, despite Pope's repeated appeals to her to forget about the monuments and write about herself, the letters addressed to him betray hardly a hint of warmth: those addressed to her women friends are positively extravagant in comparison. Indeed, the crisis to come is foreshadowed in the letters exchanged during her homeward journey. Pope is obviously concerned at her refusal to show the tenderness that he insists on as part of her charm (crucial for example in the moon image), and when two lovers were killed by lightning near Stanton Harcourt he saw it as just the topic to bring out the latent softness in which he still believed. He sent accounts of the lovers to several friends, but for Lady Mary he framed the affecting circumstances in his fantasy of her 'Oriental self', concluding with an appeal to her tenderness which subtly alludes to her supposed freedom from the conventional qualities that left her when she put off her soul:

The greatest honour people of this low degree could have was to be remembered on a little monument; unless you will give them another, that of being honourd with a Tear from the finest eyes in the world. I know you have Tenderness; you must have it: It is the very Emanation of Good Sense & virtue: The finest minds like the finest

---

[21] Pope had the tale from Thomas Rymer, *A Short View of Tragedy* (London, 1693), pp. 70–72, who had it from the fraudulent Jean de Nostredame: see Nathan Edelman, *Attitudes of Seventeenth-Century France toward the Middle Ages* (New York, 1946), pp 343–46.

[22] *Corr.*, I, 365. For the source of the allusion, see Winn, p. 99.

metals, dissolve the easiest. But when you are reflecting upon Objects of pity, pray do
not forget one, who had no sooner found out an Object of the highest Esteem, than
he was seperated from it: And who is so very unhappy as not to be susceptible of Consolation from others, by being so miserably in the right as to think other women what
they really are. Such an one can't but be desperately fond of any creature that is quite
different from these. If the Circassian be utterly void of such Honour as these have,
and such virtue as these boast of, I am content.   (I, 496)

Pity, as the Chaucerian echo reminds us, is the key to the courtly lover's
hopes: Pope is making a last attempt to win her to a friendship more sentimental than she was prepared to countenance. For this he would have needed
to find in her a little of that softness he insisted on believing in, but here he
failed, as he had also failed with Teresa. In her reply she drives home the
point that much as she esteems Pope as a poet, his sentimentalism leaves her
cold:

> Who knows if 'twas not kindly done?
> For had they seen the next year's sun,
> A beaten wife and cuckold swain
> Had jointly curs'd the marriage chain;
> Now they are happy in their doom,
> FOR POPE HAS WROTE UPON THEIR TOMB.   (I, 523)

This was not a warning he was prepared to take.

3

The story of the relationship after her return in 1718 is one of gradual decline.
At first Pope lent his somewhat officious aid to the Wortley Montagus by helping them to look for suitable houses, and once they were settled at
Twickenham the two households had several friends in common.[23] Despite
this return to the reality of social life, Pope could not entirely relinquish the
fantasy world of the letters, and as late as 1720 he put into effect a plan for
acquiring a permanent image of her 'Oriental self'. He writes twice to her to
arrange her sittings with Kneller, emphasising both the erotic aspect of the
possession he designs for himself ('allow me as much of your Person as Sir
Godfrey can help me to') and the deference which is being paid to her:

To give you as little trouble as possible, he proposes to draw your face with Crayons,
& finish it up, at your own house in a morning; from whence he will transfer it to the
Canvas, so that you need not go to sit at his house. This I must observe, is a manner
in which they seldom draw any but Crown'd Heads; & I observe it with a secret pride
& pleasure.   (Corr., II, 22)

The episode in their relationship was also commemorated in verses of which
Lady Mary kept Pope's autograph:

[23] Corr., II, 6, 12, 26, 41; LM Letters, II, 8, 13.

> The play full smiles around the dimpled mouth
> That happy air of Majesty and Youth.
> So would I draw (but oh, 'tis vain to try
> My narrow Genius does the power deny)
> The Equal Lustre of the Heavenly mind
> Where every grace with every Virtue's join'd
> Learning not vain, and wisdom not severe
> With Greatness easy, and with wit sincere.
> With Just Description shew the Soul Divine
> And the whole Princesse in my work should shine.

(TE, VI, 211–12)

This picture, in which Lady Mary was symbolically assimilated to the fantasy of the Circassian slave, hung in Pope's best room until his death, looking down on a situation which made its existence increasingly ironic (Mack, *Garden*, p. 250).

The surviving evidence of their contacts after 1718 reveals nothing serious enough to cause their later hostility: where their correspondence in these years important, it is inexplicit; where explicit, it is trivial. In August 1720 Pope advised Lady Mary to buy South Sea Stock, advice which may have contributed to their falling out; for she was buying on behalf of a Frenchman, Rémond, who had been persecuting her with a platonic and probably calculated passion for some years. When the stock fell, as it did continuously from the date of Pope's letter, Rémond accused her of dishonesty and gave her the choice of paying him off or having their correspondence exposed to Wortley, which would, Lady Mary confided to her sister, have caused 'inevitable eternal misfortunes'.[24] Yet meanwhile Pope had won her approval for Broome's project of honouring her in a poem on the inoculation for smallpox which she had been popularising since her return from the East (*Corr.*, II, 77). His last extant letter to her was written in September 1721 to apologise for having to go back on his promise of lending her a harpsichord. There is no air of final breach about it: he offers his own house for her consort, is pleased that she liked his gardens, passes on an invitation from Lord Bathurst and closes with an impenetrable private joke (II, 82–83). By April of 1722 she tells her sister that she sees him 'very seldom' – but she encloses his latest verses in her honour, which relate like his last letter to the completion of his gardens:

> Ah Freind, tis true (This Truth you Lovers know),
> In vain my Structures rise, my Gardens Grow,
> In vain Fair Thames refflects the double Scenes
> Of hanging Mountains and of Slopeing Greens;
> Joy lives not here, to happier seats it flys,
> And only dwells where W— casts her Eyes.
> What is the Gay Parterre, the chequer'd Shade,

24 *Corr.*, II, 52; *LM Letters*, II, 9.

The morning Bower, the Evening Colonnade,
But soft recesses of uneasy Minds,
To sigh unheard in to the passing Winds?
So the struck Deer in some sequester'd part
Ly's down to dye, the Arrow at his Heart,
There, stretch'd unseen in Coverts hid from Day,
Bleeds drop by drop, and pants his Life away.

(LM Letters, II, 15–16)

It seems from this letter that she has not even seen the improvements he has made to the grotto, so a report from a hostile witness a few months later that 'she and Pope keep so close yonder that they are a talk to the whole town' can probably be discounted.[25] In May 1723 she mentions a ballad 'which has been laid firstly to Pope and secondly to me, when God knows we have neither of us Wit enough to make it', a comment that suggests she still sees him as a fellow wit. Later in the year she returns a borrowed book and asks for another, although her tone suggests possible reluctance on Pope's part (LM Letters, II, 23, 27). Her last letter, late in that year, still suggests intimacy: 'If you are not well enough to come hither, I will be with you to-morrow morning, having something particular to say to You' (II, 28). On this enigmatic note the documented friendship ends.

Behind the breach lay some greater undisclosed problem: in part it must have arisen from Pope's impossible desire to be treated as a potential lover, and in part from the growing incompatibility of his aims as a Tory poet and hers as a leading court wit. For both the amorous and the political elements in their estrangement a suggestive if not literally accurate explanation survives. A version of the rejected passion theory was current in contemporary satire, but it is best known as told by Lady Louisa Stuart, Lady Mary's granddaughter:

At some ill-chosen time, when she least expected what romances call a declaration, he made such passionate love to her, as, in spite of her utmost endeavours to be angry and look grave, provoked an immoderate fit of laughter; from which moment he became her implacable enemy.   (LM Essays, p. 37)

In this form the tale is incredible: it hardly matches Pope's usual defensiveness with women, and such a dramatic scene is inconsistent with the gradual cooling that the letters suggest. What does ring true, however, is the laughter.

Their comradeship was in any case becoming harder to sustain, as their political attitudes diverged and hardened. At first it had hardly mattered that Lady Mary was by birth and marriage a Whig, for in the early years after the death of Queen Anne Pope still had many Whig friends and was quite at home on the fringes of court society, but as time went on she identified herself

[25] LM Letters, II, 15, note. The witness was the mother of Griselda Murray, with whom Lady Mary had recently quarrelled (pp. 14, 49–50).

more and more closely with an administration that he found increasingly offensive. While Lady Mary became a close personal friend of the king's minister Sir Robert Walpole and of the leading courtier Lord Hervey, Pope identified himself more and more clearly with the opposition. Moreover, as Lady Mary increasingly distanced herself from her husband's mediocre career and associated with the most powerful of the Whigs, she in effect admitted to an interest in politics that could no longer be masked by the pretence of marital duty. Disapproval of this unfeminine ambition may well have combined with Pope's jealousy of her new friends. In this context a story which Lady Mary repeated but tried to discredit is suggestive:

> I then got Dr. Arbuthnot to ask what Lady Mary had done to him? He said that Lady Mary and Lord Hervey had pressed him once together (and I don't remember that we were ever together with him in our lives) to write a satire on some certain persons, that he refused it, and that this had occasioned the breach between us.
>
> (Spence, no. 751)

Whether or not she and Hervey issued such a challenge, Pope must have realised that their targets were no longer his. Moreover he can only have been jealous that Hervey was now occupying the role which had once been his. Then Pope and Lady Mary had shared what Addison called 'an appetite to satire': henceforward they would indulge it at each other's expense. Addison had apparently warned her, perhaps even before she went to Constantinople, that she should drop Pope's acquaintance, because 'he will play you some devilish trick else'.[26] Such advice would have had great weight with her, for Addison was not only her political ally and her husband's friend, but also the writer she was to hold up as Pope's superior in her replies to the *Dunciad*.[27] An additional factor in the estrangement may have been her intimacy in the 1720s with the brilliant but unreliable Lord Wharton, for she confided to a friend that Pope was jealous. This sheds an interesting light on Pope's characterisation of Wharton as ruined by his need for the praise of 'women and fools'.[28]

Pope's conviction that Lady Mary was not only slandering him but also circulating her lampoons under his name grew steadily from about 1724. Where his allusions can be identified he is sometimes wrong, but more often probably right. For her part Lady Mary was behaving quite as disingenuously as Pope ever did, at the very least lampooning him and his friends in private, and almost certainly circulating the verses at court (Mack, *Life*, pp. 555–57). While Pope was working on the *Epistle to Dr. Arbuthnot* (published 1735) he experimented with hints at the cause of the estrangement:

[26] Spence, no. 748; Ault, *New Light*, pp. 112–13.
[27] *LM Essays*, pp. 14, 253–54.
[28] Spence, no. 751; *LM Letters*, II, 42, 44–45, 52–53; *Characters of Men*, lines 180–83 (*TE*, III. ii, 30).

Once, & but once, my heedless Youth was bit,
And lik'd that dang'rous Thing, a Female Wit;
Safe, as I thought, tho all ye Prudent chid;
I writ no Libels, but my Lady did.
Great odds! in Am'rous or Poetic Game,
When Woman's was the *Sin*, & Man's the *Shame*.

(Mack, *Last and Greatest*, p. 454)

In the published version, however, he is more discreet:

Yet soft by Nature, more a Dupe than Wit,
Sapho can tell you how this man was bit.

(line 368; *TE*, IV, 123)

This version has no unbecoming contempt for women in general, no embarrassing hint at the nature of his sufferings at her hands. Instead he vindicates himself by emphasising her unwomanliness. 'Soft', the womanly epithet he had laboured to attach to her, is now ironically his, while she, to her disgrace, is the biter, aggressive in her brilliance. His 'female wit' had at first been a glorious paradox, but once she showed herself more a wit than womanly she became a 'dang'rous Thing', the monstrous Sappho of his later poetry.

Yet Lady Mary was hardly a defenceless victim, as an anecdote of her meeting with a young traveller in 1757 makes clear:

She shew'd him her Commode, with false back of books, the works of Pope, Swift and Bolinbroke; said she knew them well. They were the greatest Rascals, but she had the satisfaction of shitting on them every day.[29]

4

Meanwhile, if Lady Mary had found more congenial friends, Pope had already tasted the pleasures of correspondence with Judith Cowper, a melancholic poet nearly fifteen years his junior. He probably saw her first when she sat to Jervas for her portrait; but they were already linked by common friends, notably Mary Howe, one of Princess Caroline's maids of honour, and the Jacobite activist Mary Caesar.[30] This suggests a political tolerance far more sympathetic to Pope than Lady Mary's keen party spirit. Judith herself was to marry into a family in high favour at court, but it is suggestive of her acceptability to Pope that in the 1730s her husband, like him, was drawn into the Prince of Wales's opposition.[31] The crucial event in her literary development had been the publication of Pope's *Works* in 1717, and henceforth she delighted in praising and imitating him:

[29] Robert Halsband, 'New Anecdotes of Lady Mary Wortley Montagu', in *Evidence in Literary Scholarship: Essays in Memory of James Marshall Osborn*, edited by René Wellek and Alvaro Ribeiro (Oxford, 1979), pp. 241–46 (p. 245).
[30] *Corr.*, II, 136, 139, 293. For Mary Caesar, see chapter 8.3.
[31] Madan, pp. 65–68, 75–76, 276.

High on the radiant List, Great *Pope* appears,
With all the *Fire* of Youth & *Strength* of Years,
Wher'e're Supreme he points the Nervous Line,
Nature & Art in bright conjunction shine.[32]

In contrast with Lady Mary, she consistently preferred celebration to satire, and her emphasis on humility, retirement and friendship would have had an attraction for Pope far less problematic than Lady Mary's brilliance:

An humble Cottage, or a Chrystal Flood,
A silent Grotto, or a leafy Wood,
More strike the Sense of this insipid Creature,
Than all the rich Magnificence in Nature,
Yet to this Merit may the Wretch pretend,
That *Howe* and *Pope* vouchsafe to call her Friend.

(f. 158)

Judith's experience of depression is reflected in the most successful of her longer poems, 'Abelard to Eloisa'.[33] The melancholy passion of Pope's poem struck a chord in Judith; yet ironically, while Pope relished the licence of imitating a feminine sensibility, Judith, knowing its dangers from the inside, welcomed the opportunity to assert a masculine firmness. Although she imitates in her impersonation of a tormented Abelard 'the struggles of grace and nature, virtue and passion' which remain at best ambiguously resolved at the end of Eloisa's letter, she permits no postscript which would confer glamour on what she resolutely calls their 'crimes'. Abelard merely commends to Eloisa the remedies which have failed in his own case:

---

[32] 'The Progress of Poetry', BL Add. MSS 28101, ff. 154–57 (modern numbering). For Judith's depression see chapter 4.1 and Madan, pp. 77–78, 86, 88.

[33] 'Abelard to Eloisa' first occurs in a family album where it is attributed to Judith although not in her hand, with the date of composition given as 1720 (BL Add. MSS 28101). In print, however, it first appears in the posthumous *The Poetical Works of Mr. William Pattison* (London, 1728), pp. 67–77. While it is just possible that the copyist of Add. MSS 28101 mistook a copy by Judith of a poem by Pattison for one of her own, the date of 1720 makes this unlikely: Pattison was then fourteen at most, whereas Judith was eighteen (Pattison, p. 2). The likelihood of a deliberately fraudulent attribution to the dead Pattison is increased by the fact that he was at the time of his death living in the household of Edmund Curll (pp. 44–45). Numerous variations between the two texts furnish no conclusive evidence as to which is the author's original – indeed both could be author's variants – although the MS is generally more convincing. The MS text appears as 'by a lady' in 1747, as 'by Mrs. C—er' in 1755, and again as 'by Mrs. Madan' in the same year: see Lawrence S. Wright, 'Eighteenth-Century Replies to Pope's *Eloisa*', *Studies in Philology*, 31 (1934), 519–33 (pp. 522–23); but Wright shows no knowledge of the MS and assumed that the version attributed to Judith is 'a very ill-disguised revision of Pattison's "Abelard to Eloisa" '. F. W. Bateson also thought Pattison to be the originator, apparently without having seen the MS: see John Wilson Bowyer, *The Celebrated Mrs Centlivre* (Durham, NC, 1952), p. 247. Slight but convincing evidence that 'Abelard' was known as Judith's as early as 1723 comes from Lady Mary, who echoes the line 'Nor can you pity what you never felt' (addressed by Abelard to the saints) in a satirical heroical epistle supposed to be from Judith to her inconstant lover: 'Cheiffly from you, I should the pain conceal, / Who cannot pity, what you cannot feel' ('Miss Cooper to —', line 17; *LM Essays*, p. 228).

> Let Love divine, frail mortal Love, dethrone,
> And to your Mind immortal Joys make known;
> Let Heav'n, relenting, strike your ravish'd View,
> And still the bright, the blest Pursuit, renew:
> So, with your Crimes, shall your Misfortunes cease,
> And your rack'd Soul be calmly hush'd to Peace.

It is clear in the poem that Abelard's peace will come only with death; but it is imperative for Judith that the poem should nevertheless end with a declaration of victory for the forces of grace and virtue, without any hint of their infiltration by nature and passion. There is thus no place for Pope's ambiguity in a poem whose somewhat unconvincing resolution reflects her own determination to live by rules she knows to be powerless to reduce her inner life to order.

This substantial tribute by a beautiful and well-connected young woman can only have been gratifying to Pope. Equally flattering were appreciative verses written in her copy of his *Works*, and it seems to have been these, passed on to him by a mutual friend, that prompted their correspondence (Madan, pp. 85, 265). Superficially there are similarities between his letters to Judith and those to Lady Mary, but when the texts are set side by side the letters to Judith appear altogether soberer, and there is a complete absence of sexual innuendo. He begins by stressing friendship: 'I am ready to Treat with you for your Friendship. I know (without more ado) you have a valuable Soul; & Wit, Sense & Worth, to make me reckon it (provided you will permit it) one of the happinesses of my life to have been made acquainted with you' (*Corr.*, II, 137). In his second letter he alludes to his deformity with a frankness quite different from his former innuendos about the strange charm of dwarfs and freaks: 'If you can Overlook an Ugly *Body* (that stands much in the way of any Friendship, when it is between different Sexes) I shall hope to find you a True & Constant Kinswoman in Apollo', and in his third he continues the theme of poetic comradeship: 'I like Parnassus much the better, since I found I had so good a Neighbour there' (II, 138, 141). His practical, sympathetic advice on the use of cheerful company in driving away melancholy shows a very different concern from the frenzy with which he had responded to news of Lady Mary's illness.[34]

The overlap between the imagery of the two correspondences is in fact rather limited. In 1722, for example, he sends Judith a stanza of the lament on Lady Mary's absence from his gardens which she had sent to her sister in the previous April: but the stanza sent to Judith refers explicitly only to melancholy, not to unrequited love, and is presented in the context of a warning not to blight her youth with the disillusion appropriate to (Pope's) age – although the flattering possibility of an unnamable passion is left open (*Corr.*, II, 142). The only other significant overlap is the image of himself as a hermit

---

[34] *Corr.*, I, 155–56, 201–2; compare II, 389.

or visionary devoted to a distant saint, spirit or fairy.[35] In the letters to Lady Mary this is the kind of extravagance most easily explained away, but in those to Judith it is the only even remotely erotic strain. Moreover it appears solely as a concluding formula with obvious reference to their difficulty in arranging to meet. The light, self-parodying version of the image used here ventures nothing as explicitly amorous as the passion of Endymion for Cynthia which he drew into the pattern when writing to Lady Mary.

The temperate warmth sustained between Pope and Judith is closely linked with her deference, so different from Lady Mary's impressive yet potentially threatening stance. While Pope was fascinated by a woman with the courage to believe in her own talents, to write satire, to intrigue at court and to revel in exploration, he had to fight his distrust of such self-sufficiency, and his worst misgivings seemed vindicated when Lady Mary turned on him: female wit and wickedness became indistinguishable. Judith represented a more acceptable version of female creativity insofar as she approached Pope with deference, eschewed satire, and testified by hypochondria and its disreputable literary associations that he need not fear her grasping at equality, still less her daring to ridicule him as Lady Mary had done. Verses he wrote for Judith early in their friendship mark the contrast:

> Tho sprightly Sappho force our Love & Praise,
> A softer Wonder my pleased Soul surveys,
> The mild Erinna, blushing in her Bays.
> So while the Sun's broad beam yet strikes the sight,
> All mild appears the moon's more sober Light,
> Serene, in Virgin Majesty, she shines;
> And un-observed, the glaring Sun declines.   (*Corr.*, II, 139)

This comparison artfully commends what in other contexts might appear as feebleness. Whilst Sappho, principal woman poet of antiquity and subject of her clause, represents Lady Mary, able to 'force' Pope's response, her less celebrated associate, Erinna, represents Judith, who is 'mild' and 'blushing' and grammatically merely the object on which he chooses to focus. Although writing is a kind of self-assertion, Judith, 'blushing in her Bays', shows a womanly shame at the activity which guarantees that she will never challenge real poets on their own ground. In the comparison of sun and moon Judith is complimented with the typically feminine connotations of the dimmer, reflected light: she is 'mild', 'sober', 'serene', 'Virgin', and she limits her actions to the most modest: she 'appears' and at her most active merely 'shines'.[36] In contrast, Lady Mary's more conspicuous gifts are associated to

---

[35] *Corr.*, II, 143, 196, 210; compare I, 356, 363, 469, 471.

[36] For sun and moon as male and female, see for example note on *Paradise Lost*, VIII.148–51, in *The Poems of John Milton*, edited by John Carey and Alastair Fowler (London, 1968); and Margaret Cavendish, Duchess of Newcastle, *The World's Olio* (London, 1655), 'Preface to the Reader', quoted by Angeline Goreau, *Reconstructing Aphra: A Social Biography of Aphra Behn* (Oxford, 1980), p. 33.

damaging effect with the original masculine vigour of the sun: she is 'broad' and 'glaring' and she 'strikes the sight'. Pope taught Judith what, subconsciously, she already knew: that weakness is a woman's best strength.

If Lady Mary had seen and taken offence at these lines it would help to explain her heroic epistle, 'Miss Cooper to —', written only a few months before Judith married Martin Madan in December 1723, in which Lady Mary makes Judith describe her attractions in such a way as to suggest intolerable self-conceit (*LM Essays*, pp. 227–30). Like Lady Mary's poems on her friend Griselda Murray, whose embarrassment over an attempted rape she turned into a wounding joke, 'Miss Cooper to —' gives point to the pun which circulated when Lady Mary had the smallpox (i.e. 'pitted/pitied'): 'she was very full & yet not pitted, but she'l live to be reveng'd on some more of her Sex'.[37] She uses her intimate knowledge of Judith's affairs with malicious precision: she knows that she writes poems to her lover as 'Lysander', that she suffers excessively from her emotions, that she suspects Lysander of preferring one of her closest friends and that she prides herself on a taste for virtuous retirement.[38] There is a hint of amusement in an allusion to Judith's 'Abelard', as Judith, in Lady Mary's view, finds herself in a situation in some ways similar to her own fiction (lines 17–18, perhaps 51–52). Lady Mary, like Pope, could seldom resist a literary joke at another's expense, but beyond that she was probably jealous. Merely to compare the fictional Judith's appraisal of her charms with 'the wretched Flavia' and her 'Glass revers'd' in Lady Mary's 'Satturday: The Small Pox' is to be reminded of one obvious cause of envy:

> The Croud still follows where I please to pass
> Nor need I dread the Censure of my Glass,
> The Heaven-born Muses in my Bosom dwell,
> Not Sapho's selfe express'd their sense so well.[39]

More explicit is literary jealousy: although the primary allusion is to the Greek Sappho whom Judith commemorated in 'The Progress of Poetry', it is hardly plausible that Lady Mary, whose preeminence as a female wit was undisputed, did not intend an implied sneer at herself, thus signalling her contempt for the superior attitude Pope was encouraging in her rival. Indeed, she subtly corroborates his reservations about her tendency to 'force' a response, when she attributes to Judith the confidence that her qualities 'would force Esteem from any Man but You' (line 28). This may be the way Lady Mary thinks, but it is as foreign to Judith's view of herself as it is to Pope's idealisation of her diffidence. Moreover, he was not alone in his reservations about Lady Mary, for Lord Peterborough makes essentially the same point in a poem praising Mrs Howard:

[37] *LM Essays*, pp. 216–24; James Brydges, quoted in Sherburn, *Early Career*, p. 204.
[38] 'Miss Cooper to —', lines 2, 7–16, 23, 33–34, 63–68; Madan, p. 87.
[39] 'Miss Cooper to —', line 3; compare 'Satturday', lines 1–3 (*LM Essays*, p. 201).

When our Sappho appears, whose wit's so refined,
I'm forced to applaud with the rest of mankind:
Whatever she says is with spirit and fire;
Every word I attend – but I only admire.[40]

Judith, had she known it, was to suffer further from Lady Mary's wit once open
war broke out between her and Pope. In a draft of 'Pope to Bolingbroke' (most
probably written in 1734) she makes Pope boast of his lies about his sexual
conquests:

When dear Miss Cooper my retreat has blest
How sweet her Lips! how downy was her breast!
(note to line 55; *LM Essays*, p. 282)

All this was in the future when Pope wrote the lines to Erinna which confess
the uncomfortable power of the woman who can 'force' not only his 'praise'
but also his 'love'. He needed to oppose to her a rhetoric which made
brilliance itself a questionable quality and which could celebrate a woman
who shared aspects of his inner life that more rigorous minds might have
found questionable. The ultimate type of such a woman was Patty, for whom
the lines to Erinna were later remodelled, and for whom he intended the birthday poem of which he ill-advisedly and somewhat disingenuously sent a copy
to Judith, who promptly assumed it was meant for her.[41] Although Patty
was by far the more important to him, they both attracted him as mild reflective moons in blessed contrast to the presumptuous glare of female wit.

5

A more distinguished woman poet was Anne Finch, Countess of Winchilsea,
whom Pope knew before either Lady Mary or Judith. Although no letters survive, this seems to have been a less intense relationship: Lady Winchilsea was
not only his social superior, but also twenty-five years his senior.[42] Nevertheless, their friendship in some respects foreshadowed the pattern of his dealings with Judith and Lady Mary.

It is not clear when they first met, although Swift had exchanged verses with
her (as 'Ardelia') as early as 1709.[43] In 1713, the year of her *Miscellany*

---

[40] 'I Said to my Heart', line 9, in *The New Oxford Book of Eighteenth Century Verse*, edited by Roger
Lonsdale (Oxford, 1984), p. 158. A version by Pope, turned as a compliment to Lady Mary,
neither includes this stanza nor uses the name Sappho. Isobel Grundy plausibly suggests that
Pope may have been Peterborough's model, and that some years may have elapsed between
Pope's compliment to Lady Mary and Peterborough's transformation, which appeared in
1723 (Isobel Grundy, 'Pope, Peterborough, and the Characters of Women', *Review of English
Studies*, 20 (1969), 461–68). This would fit the pattern of Pope's relations with Lady Mary as
outlined above. A less convincing alternative explanation is offered in R. M. Schmitz, 'Peterborough's and Pope's Nymphs: Pope at Work', *PQ*, 48 (1969), 192–201.
[41] *Corr.*, II, 180; III, 18; Schmitz, 'Birthday Lines', p. 157.
[42] For Biography, see Myra Reynolds' introduction to *Poems of Winchilsea*.
[43] *Swift Corr.*, I, 121; *The Poems of Jonathan Swift*, edited by Harold Williams, 2nd edition, 3 vols.
(Oxford, 1958), I, 119–21, 123.

Poems, Pope dined with her and stayed to hear a play read. Unfortunately he was too ill to enjoy it, but there is no evidence that his hostess or even the play (which may or may not have been hers) was to blame, for his account is typical of his precarious health – and of his tendency to make excuses to his correspondent, John Caryll:

The truth was this: I was invited to dinner with my Lady Winchelsea, and after dinner to hear a play read, at both which I sat in great disorder with sickness at my head and stomach. As soon as I got home which was about the hour I should have met you, I was obliged to goe directly to bed.   (*Corr.*, I, 203)

By this time, he had presumably read her published works; so it must have been unpleasant for her, a woman habitually apprehensive of criticism of her presumption in writing, to see Spleen, the malign deity of the enlarged *Rape of the Lock*, addressed in these terms:

> Hail wayward Queen!
> Who rule the Sex to Fifty from Fifteen,
> Parent of Vapours and of Female Wit,
> Who give th'*Hysteric* or *Poetic* Fit,
> On various Tempers act by various ways,
> Make some take Physick, others scribble Plays;
> Who cause the Proud their Visits to delay,
> And send the Godly in a Pett, to pray.   (IV.57; *TE*, II, 188)

To make things worse, Lady Winchilsea had herself made a connection between her tendency to spleen and her anomalous status as a writer:

> O'er me alas! thou dost too much prevail:
> I feel thy Force, whilst I against thee rail;
> I feel my Verse decay, and my crampt Numbers fail.
> Thro' thy black Jaundice I all Objects see,
>   As Dark, and Terrible as Thee,
> My Rymes decry'd, and my Employment thought
> An useless Folly, or presumptuous Fault:
>   Whilst in the *Muses* Paths I stray,
> Whilst in their Groves, and by their secret Springs
> My Hand delights to trace unusual Things,
> And deviates from the known, and common way.
>   ('The Spleen', line 74)

To her credit, Lady Winchilsea suppressed personal grievance and took up the general issue. From Pope's 'Impromptu' in reply to her remonstrance, now lost, it is clear that she had concentrated on his implicit claim that female wit was an aberration the world would be better without (*TE*, VI, 120). Hence she had insisted on the excellence of female 'Poetic Names of yore', asserting the value of women's writing irrespective of its causes. In his reply Pope uses her praise of others to sidestep the real issue – the value and legitimacy of women's writing – and revert to the common topics of compliment. In the second couplet, for example, the second line presents only one of a myriad conceivable ploys for drawing the sting of the first, but the amelioration is not a matter of doctrine, merely of politeness:

> Fate doom'd the Fall of ev'ry Female Wit,
> But doom'd it then when first *Ardelia* Writ.   (line 3)

Whilst the first line of the couplet says resoundingly what most people in any case assume, the second is simply flattering nonsense: although there is nothing amorous in the poem, it uses the method of gallantry, disguising its prejudices in compliment so exaggerated that it would be ungracious to argue.

Interestingly, Pope refers Lady Winchilsea to the conventional idea of a good woman by making a point of her modesty:

> Of all Examples by the World confest,
> I knew *Ardelia* could not quote the best;
> Who, like her Mistress on *Brittannia*'s Throne;
> Fights, and subdues in Quarrels not her own.   (line 5)

Yet however modest she may be in not mentioning her own work, many would have seen her writing and even more her publishing as immodest in themselves: Pope, probably without realising it, points her to a model which would ultimately enjoin silence. Although he intends a real compliment by comparing her to Queen Anne, queens, however revered *ex officio*, remain anomalous exceptions to a male succession. Moreover, the poem closes with a comparison which is, in retrospect, ominous:

> Light to the Stars the Sun does thus restore,
> But shines himself till they are seen no more.   (line 11)

Like Lady Mary, Lady Winchilsea is a sun, an originator, not one of Pope's ideal moons. The image reveals his sense of challenge, yet Lady Winchilsea's 'good humour', the easy yet possibly ironical tolerance which he advocated as the best response to woman's predicament, made it possible for him to stay on good terms with her as he could not with the acerbic Lady Mary.[44]

Typical of this 'good humour' is Lady Winchilsea's reply to the 'Impromptu', which, though critical, is also complimentary: Pope is like Orpheus (although the Greek is a burlesqued figure, lacking London polish and glad to be rid of his wife), and his women readers are always enthusiastic:

> Our Admiration, you Command,
> For all that's gone before;
> What, next we look for, at your Hand
> Can only raise it more.   (*TE*, VI, 122)

Having made the point that women rule the world by their sexual allure she proceeds tongue-in-cheek to hold up the fate of Orpheus as an awful warning:

[44] *Rape*, V. 15–34 (*TE*, II, 200–1); *To a Lady*, lines 257–68 (*TE*, III.ii, 71–72).

> Yett, ventring then with scoffing Rimes
> The Women to Incense,
> Resenting Heroines, of those Times
> Soon punished his Offence.

Yet although she presents her poem as an 'admonition' to him 'to be wise' she has to admit that there is no force behind her words, since Pope 'need not fear his awkward Fate'. Having located women's power in sexual attraction, she has admitted her sex's powerlessness when confronted with prejudice not to be dispelled by a pretty face. In fact she confesses as much at the beginning, conscious of conducting her argument in the never-never land of polite gallantry and of being obliged to submit to Pope's sidestepping of the real issue:

> Disarm'd, with so Genteel an Air,
> The Contest I giue ore.

She gracefully agrees to differ, more concerned for friendship than victory, embodying the good humour which prefers to make the best of relationships rather than risking a frankly feminist stance. Although her response illustrates the self-serving element in Pope's advice, she is nonetheless acute in identifying the problem in classifying what would in other hands be straightforward anti-feminist satire:

> But You, our Follies, gently treat,
> And spinn so fine the thread.   (line 25)

Here, identified by a contemporary, is one of the characteristic paradoxes of Pope's writing on women, the combination of uncommon delicacy with all too common prejudice.

The next evidence of their relationship confirms the prejudice rather than the delicacy. In January 1717 *Three Hours after Marriage*, a farce by Gay with help from Arbuthnot and Pope, ran for six nights at Drury Lane. Hostile commentators were quick to claim that Phoebe Clinket, supposedly a housekeeper but in effect preoccupied with ludicrous verse and unstageable dramas, was a caricature of Lady Winchilsea, the implication being that Pope was pretending friendship for a woman he actually despised.[45] In fact the character is an obvious composite, with clear hints of the notoriously eccentric Duchess of Newcastle as well as of Mrs Centlivre. Yet as one of the co-authors, Pope must be held responsible for satire which Lady Winchilsea

---

[45] For text of *Three Hours*, see John Gay, *Dramatic Works*, edited by John Fuller, 2 vols. (Oxford, 1983), I, 207–63. The most recent summary of the argument about Phoebe Clinket is by Fuller, pp. 440–41, representative contenders being George Sherburn, in 'The Fortunes and Misfortunes of *Three Hours after Marriage*', *Modern Philology*, 24 (1926–27), 91–109 (pp. 92–97), and Bowyer, pp. 197–206. For the character's place in a tradition of satire on learned ladies see *Poems of Winchilsea*, pp. lvii–lxx, and Jean Elizabeth Gagen, *The New Woman: Her Emergence in English Drama 1600–1730* (New York, 1954), pp. 78, 81. A complicating factor is the possibility, noted by Fuller, that Gay, rather than Pope, may have had a grudge against Lady Winchilsea.

could well have thought meant for her: at bottom he accepted the theatrical convention that women were legitimate figures of fun insofar as they looked beyond feminine accomplishments to male learning.

Such a parody may have been a way of airing unease which ordinarily had to be suppressed for the sake of friendship. The evidence, scanty as it is, suggests that they did remain on good terms: in June of the same year he prefaced her commendatory poem to his collective *Works*. As Myra Reynolds remarks, 'Either Pope liked the lady, or he liked the lady's verses, or he liked to have a countess speak well of him.'[46] Further evidence of his esteem came in July, when he published her reply to the 'Impromptu', to which he had made slight alterations, with seven more of her poems in the miscellany that he edited for Bernard Lintot.[47] Interestingly, although the other poems are attributed to her by name, her reply to the 'Impromptu' is given only as 'by a Lady of Quality' and its subject as 'a little Dispute upon four Lines in THE RAPE OF THE LOCK'.[48] As the 'Impromptu' itself, which used her pen-name of Ardelia, was not printed, she was protected from identification and hence from the possible embarrassment of being thought to be the butt of Pope's original satire (*TE*, VI, 120). Whether the concealment was prompted by her wish or his delicacy, it hardly suggests the eagerness to expose her to ridicule so readily ascribed to him by critics of *Three Hours after Marriage*.

One of the poems Pope chose to print is particularly revealing: 'The Mastif and Curs, A Fable inscrib'd to Mr. Pope', likens him to the mastiff, 'Strong, stately, true in ev'ry part', and his detractors to 'butchers curs' and 'the little dogs by ladies kept' (*Pope's Own Miscellany*, pp. 131–33). Perhaps Lady Winchilsea realised something of the importance of dogs to Pope, in particular his Great Dane's role as large and vigorous complement to an undersized and vulnerable master. By making the mastiff a fine physical specimen she gave Pope back in the fiction the qualities his real life appearance so conspicuously lacked:

> And each upon the masty falls,
> With distant noise and threat'ning grin,
> Tho' none durst fasten on his skin.
> So well his greater strength they knew,
> Who dirt and scandal on him threw.

The mastiff, 'Who when he careless tost or rowl'd, / Was still superior, stern and bold', wastes no energy on contemptible attackers, adopting an attitude which Pope must have found gratifying:

[46] Reynolds, *Poems of Winchilsea*, p. lvii.
[47] *Pope's Own Miscellany: Being a Reprint of 'Poems on Several Occasions' 1717*, edited by Norman Ault (London, 1935), pp. xix–xxi. The seven additional poems are 'An Invocation to the Southern Winds', 'An Epistle to the Honourable Mrs. Thynne', 'On a Double Stock July-flower', 'The Toad Undrest', 'The Mastif and Curs', 'A Fable' and 'The Fall of Caesar' (pp. 118–35, 165). None is included in *Poems of Winchilsea*.
[48] *Pope's Own Miscellany*, p. 79.

> But whilst I keep them all in awe,
> From their assaults this good I draw;
> To make you men the diff'rence see,
> Between this bawling troop, and me.
> Comparison your observation stirs,
> I were no masty if there were no curs.

In this clumsier version of the contrast made in 'Bounce to Fop', between little sneaking lapdogs and large dogs of sound morals, Lady Winchilsea shows herself content to take Pope at his own valuation, a recommendation which, together with her rank, her preference for studious retirement and her unpolemical Stuart sympathies, enabled him to overlook for the most part the unconventionality implicit in her dedication to writing (*TE*, VI, 366–70).

After 1717 there are no records of further contacts, but Gay's inclusion of '*Winchilsea*, still Meditating Song' among the crowds of well-wishers in *Mr. Pope's Welcome from Greece* is oblique confirmation that their friendship lasted until the completion of the *Iliad* in March 1720.[49] Although she died later that year, Pope was to remember her more than ten years later when he came to compose the *Essay on Man*. One of the characteristic nightmares by which he defends the system of the universe, 'Die of a rose in aromatic pain', echoes her evocation of splenetic over-sensitivity:

> Now the *Jonquille* o'ercomes the feeble Brain;
> We faint beneath the Aromatick Pain.[50]

Thus Pope takes a fitting leave of a woman whose position in his firmament was equivocal: sun-like in her creativity, yet moon-like in her diffidence and good humour, she explored and acknowledged that darker side of female sensibility which both fascinated him and at the same time confirmed the subordinate status of women's writing.

6

Poets are commonly remembered in connection with the women they have loved, but it is Pope's fate to have linked his name indissolubly to the one who came to represent all that disgusted him in the sex; for the expression of his hatred for Lady Mary has exercised a power over readers unmatched by anything he wrote about Patty. The development of his quarrel with Lady Mary from its mysterious origins into a public literary brawl has been amply documented, but it is important to realise the extent to which Pope's poetic campaign, often seen as an objective response to the presumed actions of his

---

[49] Gay, *Poetry and Prose*, I, 256. Myra Reynolds sees the inclusion in the same stanza of the actress who played Phoebe Clinket as a possible reminder that the Countess was her original, but as the two names are separated by others this seems unlikely (*Poems of Winchilsea*, p. lxx).

[50] 'The Spleen', line 40; echoed in *Essay on Man*, I.200 (*TE*, III.i, 40).

adversary, is in fact impelled by a rhetoric with a life of its own.[51] The consistency and accumulated venom of this rhetoric is best appreciated by bringing together the allusions which became almost a trademark of Pope's satire from the *Dunciad* onwards:

1a   See Pix and slip-shod W—— traipse along,
    With heads unpinned and meditating song.

 b   As the sage dame, experienc'd in her trade,
    By names of toasts retails each battered jade,
    (Whence hapless Monsieur much complains at Paris
    Of wrongs from Duchesses and Lady Mary's).[52]

2a   Or find some Doctor that would save the life
    Of wretched Worldly, spite of Worldly's Wife.

 b   Why starves the Peer his son? the cause is found:
    He thinks a loaf will rise to fifty pound.
    Why heaps lewd Lesbia that enormous sum?
    Alas! she fears a man may cost a plum.

 c   Why she and Sappho raise that monstrous sum?
    Alas! they fear a man will cost a plum.[53]

3   From furious *Sappho* scarce a milder Fate,
    P-x'd by her Love, or libell'd by her Hate.[54]

4   *Avidien* or his Wife (no matter which,
    For him you'll call a dog, and her a bitch)
    Sell their presented Partridges, and Fruits,
    And humbly live on rabbits and on roots:
    One half-pint bottle serves them both to dine,
    And is at once their vinegar and wine.
    But on some lucky day (as when they found
    A lost Bank-bill, or heard their Son was drown'd)
    At such a feast old vinegar to spare,
    Is what two souls so gen'rous cannot bear;
    Oyl, tho' it stink, they drop by drop impart,
    But sowse the Cabbidge with a bounteous heart.[55]

5a   The Tribe of Templars, Play'rs, Apothecaries,
    Pimps, Poets, Wits, Lord *Fanny*'s, Lady *Mary*'s . . .

[51] For a chronological account of their warfare, see *LM Life*, pp. 129–32, 135–37, 140–45, 147–52, 228–29.
[52] Draft of *Dunciad* A, III.141 (*TE*, V, 162); *Dunciad* A, II, 125 (*TE*, V, 112).
[53] Draft of *To Bathurst*, line 95 (*TE*, III.ii, 97); draft cited in *LM Life*, p. 140; line 123, changed from earlier 'Lesbia', 'she' being Lady Mary's friend and Walpole's mistress, Maria Skerret (*TE*, III.ii, 102).
[54] *Imitations of Horace*, Satires, II.i.83 (*TE*, IV, 13).
[55] *Imitations of Horace*, Satires, II.ii.49 (*TE*, IV, 57).

b   *Fufidia* thrives in Money, Land, and Stocks:
For Int'rest, ten *per Cent.* her constant Rate is;
Her Body? hopeful Heirs may have it *gratis.*
She turns her very Sister to a Job,
And, in the Happy Minute, picks your Fob:
Yet starves herself, so little her own Friend,
And thirsts and hungers only at one end:
A Self-Tormentor, worse than (in the Play)
The Wretch, whose Av'rice drove his *Son* away.

c   See wretched *Monsieur* flies to save his Throat,
And quits his Mistress, Money, Ring, and Note!

d   A Lady's Face is all you see undress'd;
For none but Lady M—— shows the Rest.[56]

6a   Still *Sapho* – 'Hold! For God-sake – you'll offend.'

b   Once, and but once, his heedless youth was bit,
And lik'd that dang'rous thing, a female wit.

c   Yet soft by Nature, more a Dupe than Wit,
Sapho can tell you how this Man was bit.[57]

7   Rufa, whose eye quick-glancing o'er the Park,
Attracts each light gay meteor of a Spark,
Agrees as ill with Rufa studying Locke,
As Sappho's diamonds with her dirty smock,
Or Sappho at her toilet's greasy task,
With Sappho fragrant at an ev'ning Mask:
So morning insects that in muck begun,
Shine, buzz and fly-blow in the setting-sun.[58]

8   As who knows Sapho, smiles at other whores.[59]

9   You laugh, half Beau, half Sloven if I stand,
      . . .
White Gloves, and Linnen worthy Lady Mary![60]

10a   But *Horace*, Sir, was delicate, was nice;
Bubo observes, he lash'd no sort of *Vice.*
Horace would say, sir Billy *serv'd the Crown,*

56 *Imitations of Horace*, 'Sober Advice from Horace' (*TE*, IV, 75–89), lines 1, 18, 53; line 124 as revised (previously 'show'd', alluding to an old story of Lady Mohun). An apparent reference at line 166 is convincingly dismissed in Aubrey Williams, 'The "Angel, Goddess, Montague" of Pope's *Sober Advice from Horace*', *Modern Philology*, 71 (1973–74), 56–58.
57 *To Arbuthnot*, line 101 (*TE*, IV, 103); draft of line 368, given in Mack, *Last and Greatest*, p. 454; line 368 (*TE*, IV, 123).
58 *Characters of Women*, line 21 (*TE*, III.ii, 50). 'Sappho' was originally 'Flavia'.
59 *The Second Satire of Dr. John Donne*, line 6 (*TE*, IV, 133).
60 *Imitations of Horace*, Epistles, I.i.161, 164 (*TE*, IV, 291).

Blunt *could do Bus'ness*, H—ggins *knew the Town,*
In *Sappho* touch the *Failing of the Sex* . . .

b   And at a Peer, or Peeress shall I fret,
Who starves a Sister, or forswears a Debt?[61]

At first the allusions are to her real name, and the misrepresentations of her
conduct focus on her real problems with her son, her sister, and Rémond; but
as the accusations of filth, lust and avarice become more familiar, Pope introduces the name 'Sappho', associated with her at least from the time of
Peterborough's 'I said to my heart'.[62] It was thus particularly cruel that
when she ill-advisedly complained to Peterborough in 1733 of the slander
which she suffered under the name, he should have chosen, as Pope's supporter, to pretend complete ignorance of the association, resorting instead to
Pope's favourite argument in convicting his victims out of their own mouths,
'If the cap fits, wear it':

He [Pope] said to me what I had taken the Liberty to say to you, that he wondered
how the Town could apply those Lines to any but some noted common woeman, that
he should yet be more surprised if you should take them to your Self, He named to
me fower remarkable poetesses & scribblers, Mrs Centlivre Mrs Haywood Mrs
Manley & Mrs Been, Ladies famous indeed in their generation, and some of them
Esteemed to have given very unfortunate favours to their Friends, assuring me that
Such only were the objects of his satire.   (*Corr.*, III, 352)

Soon it was necessary only to cite the faults to evoke the name Sappho and
its alleged original, as Pope triumphantly confirmed by inserting the name in
a revision of a passage which had already found its mark without it (see *TE*
notes on example 7 above).

The success of this vilification is impressive, yet it must be stressed that it
is essentially a rhetorical success. Although the impression has persisted that
these are objective accusations, properly annotated by confirmatory observations, it is important to notice how dependent this tradition is on the sole
authority of Horace Walpole, and how dependent he is on his recollection of
Pope's connection with the Wortley Montagus.[63] In effect Walpole is less an
independent witness than a commentator in the school of Pope, and his sensa-
tional allegations are calculated for the taste of correspondents who would
scarcely be interested in sober appraisal of an eccentric old woman. We are
not likely at this distance of time to discover how often Lady Mary changed
her smock, but until a better witness appears, there is no good reason to doubt

[61] *Epilogue to the Satires*, I, lines 11, 111 (echoed in II, line 20); *TE*, IV, 306.
[62] For a more favourable view of these painful relationships, see *LM Life*, pp. 38, 47–48, 101–5,
124–27, 133–35, 138–39. For Peterborough see chapter 6.4.
[63] Plausible motives for Walpole's evident malice are put forward by Halsband in 'Walpole versus Lady Mary', in *Horace Walpole: Writer, Politician, and Connoisseur*, edited by W. H. Smith
(New Haven, 1967), pp. 215–26 (216–17). For examples of Walpole's allegations, see *HW
Corr.*, X, 5; XIII, 234; XIX, 72; XXII, 3; XXX, 8, 10–11; XXXV, 268–69; XXXVII,
78–79.

that she did so about as frequently as other people. What we do discover, however, from other observers besides Walpole, is a radical unconventionality of dress, manifested, especially as she grew older, in her choice of 'undress' styles when 'dress' was expected, of garments more warm than fashionable, and of fabrics cheaper and coarser than was thought genteel.[64] She could certainly dress to captivate when she chose, as even Pope admitted (see example 7 above); but otherwise travel had produced its proverbial effect on a mind already disposed to question, and having seen the passionate yet arbitrary commitment of Parisians, Viennese and Turks to their respective sartorial imperatives, she was ill-disposed to respect the equally arbitrary demands of her own society.[65] This defiance explains the ready acceptance found by the sneers of Pope and Walpole: filth, meanness and lewdness were readily available metaphors for a rejection of the conventions that enabled a woman to be recognised as a respectable member of her sex and social class, and in this respect Lady Mary's nonchalance about dress merely underlined the immodesty implicit in her confidence in facing and commenting on the world.[66] Not content passively to reflect her society's assumptions, she acted boldly by her own lights: a sun rather than a moon. Moreover, Pope's transformation of the woman who had attracted him too strongly for his comfort into a loathsome hag clearly serves a consolatory function of a kind. Lady Mary's reading of Swift's 'The Lady's Dressing Room', in which she attributes the Dean's nastiness to impotence, may at first sight seem to offer a parallel to Pope's retributive construction of her own image; but her approach, though suggestive, is too narrowly constrained by her characteristically reductive mockery to engage with the subtle indirection of the ambitions Pope had cherished in her regard.[67]

The momentum which Pope's rhetoric of abuse displays in defiance of its dubious relation to biographical fact is less surprising when it is seen as a development in a well-established tradition of writing about women whose activities cause male resentment. Especially relevant to Pope are the Earl of Dorset's attacks on James II's mistress Catherine Sedley, whose sharp intelligence made her exceptionally annoying to those intent either on bypassing

[64] Aileen Ribeiro, *A Visual History of Costume: The Eighteenth Century* (London, 1983), p. 13. Plates 12 and 16 show undress styles, while 5 and 35 show the contrasting dress styles usual at court and other social gatherings. That Lady Mary's dress was eccentric (there is no suggestion of dirt) is testified by Lady Strafford, cited in *LM Life*, p. 150; and by a young Irish traveller in 'New Anecdotes of Lady Mary Wortley Montagu', p. 245. She boasts of a decent economy in dress in *LM Essays*, p. 299.

[65] By her granddaughter's account, Lady Mary annoyed Princess Caroline by adopting a predatory style of dress as part of her attempt to win the favour of George, Prince of Wales. For Lady Mary's judgement of foreign styles, see *LM Letters*, I, 265, 314, 440, 328; II, 159; Spence, *Grand Tour*, p. 360; *LM Essays*, p. 164.

[66] For the association between filth and female creativity see Gubar and chapter 4.1 above.

[67] 'The Reasons that Induced Dr S to write a Poem call'd the Lady's Dressing Room' (*LM Essays*, pp. 273–76); Robert Halsband, ' "The Lady's Dressing Room" Explicated by a Contemporary', in *The Augustan Milieu: Essays Presented to Louis A. Landa*, edited by Henry K. Miller *et al.* (Oxford, 1970), pp. 225–31.

or on harnessing her influence. Dorset anticipates Pope's ironically unpleasant characterisation of metaphorical brightness, usually an obvious compliment to beauty, intellect or vivacity; and the character of Dorinda, like
Sappho, combines acquisitiveness, lust and barely concealed filth:

> Tell me, Dorinda, why so gay,
>   Why such embroid'ry, fringe and lace?
> Can any dresses find a way
> To stop th'approaches of decay
>   And mend thy ruin'd face?
>
> Wilt thou still sparkle in the box,
>   Still ogle in the ring?
> Canst thou forget thy age and pox?
> Can all that shines on shells and rocks
>   Make thee a fine young thing?
>
> So have I seen in larder dark
>   Of veal a lucid loin,
> Replete with many a heatless spark,
> As wise philosophers remark,
>   At once both stink and shine.[68]
>
> Proud with the spoils of royal cully,
>   With false pretence to wit and parts,
> She swaggers like a batter'd bully . . .   (Dorset, III.1)
>
> Dorinda's sparkling wit and eyes,
>   United, cast too fierce a light,
> Which blazes high but quickly dies,
>   Warms not the heart but hurts the sight.
>
> Love is a calm and tender joy,
>   Kind are his looks and soft his pace;
> Her Cupid is a black-guard boy,
>   That runs his link into your face.   (II.1)

Pope had imitated this vein in Dorset in his 'Artimesia' and 'Phryne',
apparently aimed at favourites of George I:[69]

> Tho' *Artimesia* talks, by Fits,
> Of Councils, Classicks, Fathers, Wits;
>   Reads *Malbranche*, *Boyle*, and *Locke*:
> Yet in some Things methinks she fails,
> 'Twere well if she would pare her Nails,
>   And wear a cleaner Smock.
>
>   ('Artimesia', line 1; *TE*, VI, 48)

---

[68] 'On the Countess of Dorchester', IV, in *The Poems of Charles Sackville, Sixth Earl of Dorset*,
   edited by Brice Harris (London, 1979), pp. 45–46.
[69] See Kathleen Mahaffey, 'Pope's "Artimesia" and "Phryne" as Personal Satire', *Review of
   English Studies*, 21 (1970), 466–71; but see Ragnhild Hatton, *George I; Elector and King* (London,
   1978), pp. 23–24 for evidence that Madame Kielmannsegge was not George I's mistress but
   his illegitimate half-sister.

So have I known those Insects fair,
(Which curious *Germans* hold so rare,)
   Still vary Shapes and Dyes;
Still gain new Titles with new Forms;
First Grubs obscene, then wriggling Worms,
   Then Painted Butterflies.

                     ('Phryne', line 19; *TE*, VI, 50)

In the days of his friendship with Lady Mary he had laughed over at least one of these pieces with her; but it is a sobering thought in relation to the reception of his satires on Sappho, that if these early lampoons had been written later, we should probably be reading them as allusions to Lady Mary, so closely do their traditional gibes correspond to the rhetorical case against Sappho.[70]

7

The economically secure women writers so far discussed had an obvious advantage when it came to maintaining respectability: in contrast, the threat of real rather than metaphorical dirt, greed and promiscuity came primarily from the poverty that drove many women into Grub Street or the playhouse, into economic competition with men in a market place more interested in their bodies than their books. For such 'poetesses & scribblers', as Lord Peterborough called them, 'some of them Esteemed to have given very unfortunate favours to their Friends', life was as Laetitia Pilkington found it when she left her husband, a shifting world of unreliable acquaintances intent on sexual favours as often as literary commissions, in which money even when earned was next to impossible to keep from thieves and swindlers.[71] Here the largely metaphorical accusations which focused society's unease with unconventionally powerful and assured women were more likely to be literally true; yet however conveniently the activities of Grub Street women coincided with the myth, it did not rely on their individual lives for its existence any more than the character of Sappho lived by the accuracy of Pope's indictment. This is demonstrated by a passage from the *Dunciad* in which the accusations sound very specific, yet an examination of the various revisions shows that the targets shifted casually over the years. In 1729 the lines stood as follows:

Lo next two slip-shod Muses traipse along,
In lofty madness, meditating song,
With tresses staring from poetic dreams,
And never wash'd, but in Castalia's streams:
Haywood, Centlivre, Glories of their race!

                     (*Dunciad* A, III.141; *TE*, V, 162)

[70] A copy of 'Phryne' survives in Lady Mary's hand (*TE*, VI, 50).
[71] Pilkington, *Memoirs*, vols. II–III, *passim*.

In the previous year the last line had begun 'H— and T—', the latter presumably for Catharine Trotter or Elizabeth Thomas; and in an earlier manuscript version the first line had specified 'Pix and slip-shod W—', i.e, Mary Pix and Lady Mary. In addition, 'meditating song' echoes words that Gay had used of the Countess of Winchilsea and may therefore be a concealed allusion to her (*TE* notes). So Pope tells us nothing about how often any individual washed her hair, but rather more about the unease which makes the writer refer female writers as a species to the image of the slip-shod muse.

Within this broad framework, however, Pope's treatment of particular writers is shaped by specific grievances. In his attack on Eliza Haywood in the *Dunciad* he is fired by his anger at her slur on Patty, implausibly called 'the most dissolute and shameless of her Sex' and alleged to have poxed a number of lovers.[72] Scriblerus affects pained surprise at such slander from 'that sex, which ought least to be capable of such malice or impudence', suggesting a bland ideal as far from the erstwhile alluring Lady Mary of the *Court Eclogs* as from Mrs Haywood.[73] The principal attack on Mrs Haywood, however, is conducted within the poem, as much through context and implication as through direct accusation:

> See in the circle next, Eliza plac'd;
> Two babes of love close clinging to her waste;
> Fair as before her works she stands confess'd,
> In flow'r'd brocade by bounteous Kirkall dress'd;
> Pearls on her neck, and roses in her hair,
> And her fore-buttocks to the navel bare.
> The Goddess then: 'Who best can send on high
> 'The salient spout, far-streaming to the sky;
> 'His be yon Juno of majestic size,
> 'With cow-like udders and with ox-like eyes.
> 'This China-Jordan, let the chief o'er come
> 'Replenish, not ingloriously, at home'.
>
> (*Dunciad A*, II.149)

Mrs Haywood had certainly deserted her husband, and may well have had illegitimate children, although there is no independent confirmation of this; yet the real point of the two babies is to fix Pope's allusion to a line of Virgil describing a Cretan slave with twins at the breast, a reference which enables him to smear his victim with the proverbial Cretan vices of mendacity and sexual deviance.[74] Like Dorset's Dorinda she glitters in the spoils of her promiscuity (although her promiscuity is at least partly metaphorical, and the spoils entirely owing to the engraver of her portrait), and like Sappho 'fragrant at an ev'ning Mask' she emerges from a context of filth. Her writing,

---

[72] Mack, *Life*, p. 411; Guerinot, pp. 90–91.

[73] *Dunciad A*, II.149, note (*TE*, V, 119).

[74] *A Dictionary of British and American Women Writers, 1660–1800*, edited by Janet Todd (London, 1984), p. 157; note to *Dunciad A*, II.150.

like that of the male writers in Grub Street, is symbolically equivalent to sewage; but unlike them she is not represented as an active competitor, but as the prize of others' endeavour. As her new keeper leads her home she is 'pleas'd' and 'soft-smiling', demonstrating that as a woman she is more gen- uinely interested in sex than in writing. Finally, somewhat at a tangent from this attack on an undeniably scandalous writer, Pope uses her to undermine the pretensions of a very respectable female scholar who had annoyed him not only by remarks on his Homer but also by her general presumption as a classicist:

In the games of *Homer Il.*3, there are set together as prizes, a Lady and a Kettle; as in this place Mrs. *Haywood* and a Jordan. But there the preference in value is given to the *Kettle*, at which Mad. *Dacier* is justly displeas'd: Mrs. *H.* here is treated with distinction, and acknowledged to be the more valuable of the two.   (157, note)

The effect is complex: two women who have nothing in common but writing are brought together in such a way that even the irreproachable Mme Dacier is left looking rather silly. Writing, especially when it involves trespassing on a revered male tradition, lays her open to ridicule, if not to the violence pro- voked by Mrs Haywood's scurrility. Pope had always thought Mme Dacier trivial and imitative in comparison with her husband, André Dacier, and he believed that she owed her reputation more to her sex than to her abilities: 'It is great complaisance in that polite nation [France], to allow her to be a Critic of equal rank' (*Corr.*, I, 492).

There are, however, greater indignities reserved for other women writers in the *Dunciad*. Elizabeth Thomas, who inadvertently causes her publisher's downfall in the booksellers' race, is even more closely associated with excrement:

> Full in the middle way there stood a lake,
> Which Curl's Corinna chanc'd that morn to make,
> (Such was her wont, at early dawn to drop
> Here evening cates before his neighbour's shop,)
> Here fortun'd Curl to slide; loud shout the band,
> And Bernard! Bernard! rings thro' all the Strand.
> Obscene with filth the Miscreant lies bewray'd,
> Fal'n in the plash his wickedness had lay'd.
>
> (*Dunciad A*, II.65; *TE*, V, 106)

Assessment of Mrs Thomas's character is complicated by the irreconcilable claims of Pope and his editors (she was unchaste and, specifically, Henry Cromwell's mistress) and of her own circle (she was an impoverished gentlewoman, good to her mother and careful of her reputation).[75] In

---

[75] See James Sutherland's biographical summary in *TE*, V, 456, which relies on William Ayre, *Memoirs of the Life and Writings of Alexander Pope, Esq*, 2 vols. (London, 1745), I, 88–95. However, the letters which Ayre uses to blacken Mrs Thomas actually concern Teresa Blount (compare *Corr.*, I, 59–62, 137–39). Mrs Thomas's side of the case is set out in *Pylades*

addition, Edmond Malone, concerned to establish the reliability of her anecdotes about Dryden, convicted her of such circumstantial fabrication that it
is hard to credit her on any topic whatsoever, especially where her own
reputation is concerned.[76] If Pope and Malone are correct, she was at least
a convincing liar, for in her published correspondence she produced
testimonials from the Bishop of Durham, John Norris of Bemerton and Mary
Lady Chudleigh, as well as a series of letters between her and her suitor, a
grave but witty lawyer. According to the letters he was prevented from marrying her by her refusal to leave her dying mother, but by the time she died he
was already in the terminal stages of consumption. Both lovers satirise
Cromwell as a monster of conceit and affectation: if the letters are genuine,
it is hard to imagine that he was ever a threat to Mrs Thomas's chastity.

If her story is to be believed, there had been a time, at the height of Pope's
youthful intimacy with Cromwell, when Pope had been happy to show her his
work.[77] The cause of his later bitterness was the publication in 1726 of his
letters to Cromwell, which Cromwell had given to Mrs Thomas, and she, increasingly harassed by poverty after the deaths of her mother and fiancé, had
sold to Curll.[78] This provides the framework of Pope's allegory: Curll is
degraded by her act, but not without a glance at 'his wickedness' in encouraging her. Moreover, Pope may have been alluding to her actual medical problems, for she claimed that as a consequence of swallowing a chicken bone
she had suffered years of symptoms as disgusting as they were excruciating,
and although her account of her trials was not published until 1732, Pope
could perhaps have heard details from Samuel Garth, whom she names as one
of her physicians (*Pylades*, II, 93–96). Even more hurtful, because aimed at
her conception of herself as a writer, must have been her designation as
'Curl's Corinna'. The name Corinna was dear to her for having been given
her by Dryden: in the letter which she proudly sets before her correspondence
in *Pylades* he tells her:

Since you do me the Favour to desire a Name from me, take that of Corinna if you
please; I mean not the Lady with whom Ovid was in Love, but the famous Theban

*and Corinna; or, Memoirs of the Lives, Amours, and Writings of Richard Gwinnett Esq. . . . . and
Mrs Elizabeth Thomas Jun. . . .*, 2 vols. (London, 1731–32). For the Bishop of Durham,
see I, lxxix–lxxx; for Norris, II, 199–224; for Mary Lady Chudleigh, II, 47–55; for Gwin-
nett/Pylades, *passim*; for Cromwell, I, 96, 80–86, and what seems to be a parody of his style
at 86–87; for Mrs Thomas's concern for her reputation and care for her mother, II, 57–61.
Mrs Thomas is also taken seriously in Ruth Perry, *The Celebrated Mary Astell: An Early English
Feminist* (Chicago, 1986): for references, see index.

[76] *The Critical and Miscellaneous Prose Works of John Dryden*, edited by Edmond Malone, 3 vols.
(London, 1800), I.i, 337–419.

[77] Elizabeth Thomas alludes to visits from Pope (*Pylades*, I, 80–86), and in 1709 she claims to
have sent Gwinnet part of 'Of a Lady singing to her Lute' (II, 10). Pope several times mentions a 'Sappho' who may be Mrs Thomas in letters to Cromwell, occasionally in contexts
which could imply that she was his mistress (see *Corr.*, I, 57).

[78] *Dunciad A*, II.66, note; *Corr.*, II, 437, 440, 441.

Poetess, who overcame Pindar five Times, as Historians tell us. I wou'd have call'd you Sapho, but that I hear you are handsomer.[79]

Mrs Thomas adopted this letter as the basis of her literary identity; yet, as Dryden notes, the name Corinna could also suggest Ovid's mistress, the proverbial loose woman of anti-feminist satire. Thus the title 'Curl's Corinna' is well contrived to suggest primarily not the relation between a publisher and a poet, but between a man and his mistress.[80] Pope's heavily ironic endorsement of Curll's defence of her in his note on the passage ('our Poet had no thought of reflecting on her . . . she is a decent woman and in misfortunes') was dropped from later editions, probably because once Curll's words were forgotten it sounded dangerously like sympathy, especially since she had, as he believed, retaliated by collaborating with Curll in *Codrus*, a stupid travesty of his early life, family and friendships.[81]

The only woman in the *Dunciad* who is presented literally in her chosen role of writer is Susannah Centlivre – even if this is only because her prolific output shows a professionalism sufficient to qualify her for the trial of tedium which closes the heroic games with 'the soft gifts of Sleep'.[82] She had long been a member of the group of Whig writers centred on Edmund Curll, and in 1716 she contributed to his *State Poems*, in which he succeeded in blackening Pope's character by publishing 'To Mr. John Moore, Author of the Celebrated Worm-Powder'.[83]

Although this is the first hard evidence of her collusion in this campaign, Pope had already mentioned her earlier that year in his *A Full and True Account of a Horrid and Barbarous Revenge by Poison, On the Body of Mr. Edm. Curll*, his account of Curll's sufferings at his hands in revenge for the affair of the *Court Poems* (Bowyer, pp. 191–92). Curll, believing himself to be dying, is made to bequeath her a special legacy: Pope may be suggesting (falsely) that *she* rather than Gay, Lady Mary or himself, had written the *Court Poems* for which Curll had incurred the penalty of Pope's emetic; or perhaps the hint is simply that she, like Mrs Thomas, was the bookseller's mistress. She is mentioned again later in the year in Pope's *A Further Account of the Most Deplorable Condition of Mr. Edmund Curll*, where she is presented as so devoid of imagination that Curll has to keep her supplied with similes; but Pope's essentially political grudge surfaces in the accusation that she had contributed to *The Catholick Poet; Or, Protestant Barnaby's Sorrowful Lamentation*, an abusive ballad also published that year (Guerinot, pp. 38–40). He was unimpressed by Curll's claim that it was entirely the work of John Oldmixon and in future attributed it to Oldmixon without withdrawing the charge against Mrs Centlivre.[84]

---

[79] *The Letters of John Dryden*, edited by Charles E. Ward (New York, 1942; reprinted 1965), p. 126. For two further letters see pp. 127–28, 132.
[80] For other satirical applications of the name see Nussbaum, pp. 60–61, 66–69, 71–75, 107–12.
[81] *Dunciad A*, II.66, note; Guerinot, pp. 154–55.
[82] *Dunciad A*, II.387, 397.
[83] Bowyer, pp. 166–70; Mack, *Life*, pp. 296–97.
[84] *Dunciad A*, II.199, note; 379, note.

In his notes he dismisses her as prolific, precocious and prejudiced: 'She writ many plays, and a song . . . before she was seven years old. She also writ a Ballad against Mr. *Pope's Homer* before he begun it.' In 1717 he had a hand with Gay and Arbuthnot in mocking her in *Three Hours after Marriage*: the vogue for translations, her staple resource as a dramatist, is ridiculed, and there are allusions to her stratagem of getting a play accepted by pretending it was the work of a man, as well as to her problems in persuading the actors not to cut her work excessively (Bowyer, pp. 203–5). She had her revenge in *A Bold Stroke for a Wife* (1718) with allusions to an ape, which is introduced in conjunction with the mummy and the crocodile so notoriously crucial to the plot of *Three Hours*, and is thus easily recognisable as 'A. P—e' (p. 206).

The relative lack of stress on unchastity in Pope's attacks on Mrs Centlivre is unusual. More characteristic are his comments on two other women connected with the stage. One is Cibber's daughter, Charlotte Charke, whose promiscuity is insinuated when he is made to address the unsold copies of his works as 'My better and more Christian progeny! / Unstain'd, untouch'd, and yet in maiden sheets; / While all your smutty sisters walk the streets'.[85] The second is Aphra Behn: when Pope pays her the apparent compliment of inclusion in a catalogue of comic dramatists he criticises the other (male) writers for a variety of artistic lapses; but what offends him in Mrs Behn is merely the sexual licence universal in Restoration comedy:

> The stage how loosely does Astraea tread,
> Who fairly puts all Characters to bed.[86]

As so often in his assumptions about women's writing he echoes a vigorous tradition: this judgement of Mrs Behn was to persist into the twentieth century (Goreau, pp. 14–16).

Finally, as we move from allusions to individuals to the broader meanings of the *Dunciad*, it is striking that in a representation of a literary culture which characteristically excludes women, as many as two out of the three locations specified for the heroic games are associated with female delinquency.[87] The foot race begins from the Strand, where 'A Church collects the saints of Drury-lane'; and for the diving, 'by Bridewell all descend, / (As morning-pray'r and flagellation end.)' The promiscuous woman's refusal to know her place has become symbol not only of female writing, but also of writing by the dunces, on whom nature, in Pope's view, has enjoined a similar silence. It is an allusion far more effective than anything that can be said directly about bad writers because it draws on convictions about the duties and limitations of women far more emotive than beliefs about writing. Indeed, that Dulness herself is female is one of the most important facts about her: if her gender is a source of delight in opening up a world of capricious fantasy

[85] *Dunciad B*, I.228 (*TE*, V, 286).
[86] *Imitations of Horace*, Epistles, II.i.290 (*TE*, IV, 219).
[87] *Dunciad A*, II.26, 57: the odd one out is 'the gates of Lud' (II.332).

akin to the female world of *The Rape of the Lock*, it is also the key to her obscenity as, with her parody of a 'Son' and 'Holy Ghost', she opposes and undoes the work of God the Father (I.241–45). Her yawn, the formless yet potent opposite of the divine fiat, like her womb-like cave of pullulating literary monstrosities, draws on Pope's fundamental unease about female creativity; yet her very existence at the centre of his own creation testifies to his need for such a creature.[88] To over-simplify, she stands for what his mind abhors and his imagination craves.

[88] *Dunciad B*, IV.605–606; *Dunciad A*, I.53–82 (*TE*, V, 142).

Headstrong Duchesses

1

Two women who resembled Lady Mary in confidence and political ambition were Catherine Sheffield, née Darnley, Duchess of Buckingham (*c*. 1682–1743) and Sarah Churchill, née Jennings, Duchess of Marlborough (1660–1744). Each of these great ladies supported her rank with a physical presence and verbal assurance that impressed her identity on the imagination of the age, and each impinged most vividly on Pope's consciousness when, as a widow, her authority was further enhanced by the experience of controlling family estates and the destinies of children and grandchildren. When such women made overtures to a poet, there could be no doubt as to where the patronage and where the obligation lay: hence these assertive women escaped implication in the blend of literary and amorous aspiration that had so notably corrupted Pope's early fascination with his fellow wit Lady Mary. With her, as to a lesser degree with other women who presented a literary or sexual challenge, his revenge had been to confine the would-be wit within the satirical stereotype of woman as physically squalid and sexually insatiable. With the Duchesses, on the other hand, there was no competition for literary or sexual dominance to activate this painful level of anti-feminist resentment. Instead, his sense of their destructive arrogance in the exercise of their abilities found its expression in his vision of Atossa, which, although it is set in the balance against the possibility of a wholesome brilliance for women, approaches the tragic in its sense of waste and perversity:

> But what are these to great Atossa's mind?
> Scarce once herself, by turns all Womankind!
> Who, with herself, or others, from her birth
> Finds all her life one warfare upon earth:
> Shines, in exposing Knaves, and painting Fools,
> Yet is, whate'er she hates and ridicules.
> No Thought advances, but her Eddy Brain
> Whisks it about, and down it goes again.
> Full sixty years the World has been her Trade,
> The wisest Fool much Time has ever made.
> From loveless youth to unrespected age,
> No Passion gratify'd except her Rage.

So much the Fury still out-ran the Wit,
The Pleasure miss'd her, and the Scandal hit.
Who breaks with her, provokes Revenge from Hell,
But he's a bolder man who dares be well:
Her ev'ry turn with Violence pursu'd,
Nor more a storm her Hate than Gratitude.
To that each Passion turns, or soon or late;
Love, if it makes her yield, must make her hate:
Superiors? death! and Equals? what a curse!
But an Inferior not dependant? worse.
Offend her, and she knows not to forgive;
Oblige her, and she'll hate you while you live:
But die, and she'll adore you – Then the Bust
And Temple rise – then fall again to dust.
Last night, her Lord was all that's good and great,
A Knave this morning, and his Will a Cheat.
Strange! by the means defeated of the Ends,
By Spirit robb'd of Pow'r, by Warmth of Friends,
By Wealth of Follow'rs! without one distress
Sick of herself thro' very selfishness!
Atossa, curs'd with ev'ry granted pray'r,
Childless with all her Children, wants an Heir.
To Heirs unknown descends th'unguarded store
Or wanders, Heav'n-directed, to the Poor.

(Characters of Women, line 115; TE, III.ii, 59)

In this form, as it finally appeared in 1744 in Pope's final version of *Characters of Women*, 'Atossa' alludes most obviously to Catherine Sheffield, Duchess of Buckingham, a woman so notoriously eccentric that posterity has been largely content to repeat contemporary anecdotes in lieu of biography.[1] Her career, however, had far wider implications than are suggested by the catalogue of purely private excesses that Pope develops to such striking effect. Only by setting her life in the perspective of her own interests can we appreciate Pope's importance to her and hers to him.

The Duchess was the illegitimate daughter of James II by Catherine Sedley, most irrepressible of his mistresses; and from her proud parents the young Catherine, styled by royal decree Lady Catherine Darnley, inherited a spirit that, according to Horace Walpole, even her mother found hard to discipline: when she was difficult her mother would hint strongly that Colonel James Graham, not King James, was her father.[2] The 'loveless youth' commemorated by Pope reached its nadir in 1701, when only eighteen months

---

[1] For dating and identification see *TE*, III.ii, pp. 40–44, 159–70. The pioneering work on Pope's relations with the Duchesses of Buckingham and Marlborough was done by Dilke, I, 226–33, 269–87.

[2] For Catherine Sedley, see *DNB* and V. de Sola Pinto, *Sir Charles Sedley, 1639–1701: A Study in the Life and Literature of the Restoration* (London, 1927), pp. 132–40, 156–64, 205–6, 216–18, 236–38, 345–62. For doubts about her daughter's paternity see Horace Walpole, *Reminiscences*, edited by P. Toynbee (Oxford, 1924), pp. 91–92.

Plate 2   Catherine Sheffield, Duchess of Buckingham, and her son Robert, Marquis of Normanby
– funeral effigies in wax

after her marriage to James Annesley, Earl of Anglesey, she complained to
the House of Lords that he was trying to murder her.[3] The Lord Chief
Justice bound him over and while he was in the House complaining of this
breach of privilege she took the opportunity of escaping. Colonel Graham
received the news in a letter which concluded with the observation that
Anglesey was 'very deep in a consumption': in fact he died in January 1702,
having been separated from his wife by act of parliament since the previous
June. In March 1706 she embarked on a far happier period of her life, when
she married John Sheffield, Duke of Buckingham, already twice widowed and
nearly thirty-five years her senior.[4] Although there was some suspicion that
he had 'not . . . made a very good Husband to his first and second Wives',
his third wife soon gained a complete ascendancy:

Whenever she was very ill or in danger (which generally happen'd when she was with
child, or at her lying-in) he shew'd all possible marks of concern: and when there was
more than ordinary danger, his servants often found him on his knees at prayers: and
on those occasions he has made vows, in case she recover'd, to give in charities,
sometimes two hundred, sometimes three hundred pounds at a time, which he perform'd punctually. And I have been credibly inform'd, that the Dutchess herself has
said, that whenever they have had any Difference . . . he cou'd never stay till supper-
time, tho' pretty near, nor till she returned back of herself into his room, but constantly
left his books or business to come after her, and said, *Child, you and I should never fall
out; and tho' I still think my self in the right, yet you shall have it in your way.*

(*Character of Sheffield*, pp. 21–22)

The elderly husband's understandable tenderness for the mother of his only
legitimate children can only have confirmed for her the congenial lesson that
obstinacy pays.

Pope came to know the Duchess through his literary friendship with the
Duke. Buckingham had been one of the select group of elderly men of taste
who read the *Pastorals* before their publication in 1712; at some time before
1716 he asked Pope to compose choruses for his version of Shakespeare's
Julius Caesar; in 1717 he both contributed to Pope's miscellany and wrote commendatory verses for the *Works*; in about 1718 he joined with Pope, Gay, and
Erasmus Lewis in supporting Prior's publication of his poems; and in 1720
he consulted with Pope and Atterbury over his erection of a monument to
Dryden in Westminster Abbey.[5] Because of these shared interests, it seemed
appropriate for the Duchess to turn to Pope for help with her husband's
papers when he died in 1721.[6] Together with the Duchess and their mutual

---

3 *Tenth Report of the Royal Commission on Historical Manuscripts* (London, 1885), Appendix, vol. IV,
   pp. 335–36; G.E.C., *Peerage*, James Annesley, Earl of Anglesey.
4 G.E.C., *Peerage*, John Sheffield, Duke of Buckingham; *A Character of John Sheffield, Late Duke
   of Buckinghamshire* (London, 1729), pp. 20–23, 32.
5 *Corr.*, I, 17, 387, 521; II, 51–52, 54–55; *TE*, VI, 154.
6 For the complicated history of Pope's role as literary executor and editor of *The Works of John
   Sheffield . . . Duke of Buckingham*, 2 vols. (London, 1723), see Sherburn, *Early Career*, pp. 219–28.

friend Atterbury, Pope took charge of the memorial edition; but although he remarked to Caryll that the collection 'has many things in it you will be particularly glad to see in relation to some former reigns', and despite what looks like an attempt to limit his public responsibility for the volumes, he seems not to have realised the full danger of promoting the works of a friend who, though far from a committed Jacobite, held many of the views which had led less pragmatic politicians into that allegiance (*Corr.*, II, 117). Indeed, such realisation was hardly possible in advance, since the government suppression of the Duke's *Works* was apparently based on very minor indiscretions, and would probably never have taken place at all except for the hysteria surrounding the exposure of the Atterbury plot, which brought Pope and all the Bishop's associates under suspicion. Pope, though he probably realised that Atterbury was preoccupied with something of the kind, seems to have preferred to know as little about it as possible.[7]

The importance of the Duke's *Works* for the Jacobites is amply demonstrated by the Duchess's fervent supporter Mary Caesar:

About this time the Duke of Buckinghams Works came out. they had No sooner Appear'd but all the Rest was seiz'd at Jacob Tonsons. Mr Pope was Question'd About them As the Publisher, that they Dropt but the Books ware No more to be sold in Full Beauty. The first day sold Only by Permission to the Dutchessis Friends as the Duke [i.e. her son] came to tell me. I Immediatly Presented Lord Cowper with them and Next day he told me He had set up Allmost all Night He was so Pleas'd – But Not so when Lord Battarest [i.e. Bathurst] went to desire Him Not to Moue the House to have them Burnt. With Concern my Lord told it me, I was Astonish'd and said Could Battarest think your Lordship Lay'd down the Great Seal to be the Proposer of burning of Books, He is yong and Hutcheson some times a little Wild. Therefore desire you will give Admittance to One More of our Friends, the Earl of Strafford and Much He was delight'd . . . and With Him Convers'd with Freedome.[8]

In this circle the Duke's *Works* were evidently received almost as a sacred object, and Pope's involvement as editor implicated him in the eyes of Jacobites and government alike in political manoeuvres to which he was not and did

[7] For the plot, see Bennett, pp. 200–2, 206–7, 236–37, 269–70, 272. For Pope's probable attitude, see Howard Erskine-Hill, 'Life into Letters, Death into Art: Pope's Epitaph on Francis Atterbury', *Yearbook of English Studies*, 18 (1988), 200–20 (pp. 204–9).

[8] Mrs Caesar's manuscript book, BL Add. MSS 62558, f. 11 (for further discussion of her writings, see chapter 8.3). William, first Earl Cowper, former Whig Lord Chancellor and uncle of Judith Cowper, was assiduously cultivated by Mrs Caesar in his later years, and was widely suspected of involvement in the Atterbury plot (*DNB*, William Cowper, Mary Cowper; Bennett, pp. 231–32, 235, 254, 272). Mrs Caesar implies that Bathurst, who had withdrawn from active Jacobitism during the plot, should have known Cowper better than to have thought him capable of acting against the cause (Bennett, p. 230). For the MP Archibald Hutcheson, see Sedgwick. For Thomas Wentworth, third Earl of Strafford, see G.E.C., *Peerage*.

not wish to be a party. For any Tory whose status made him a desirable recruit to the Jacobite cause, associating with the Duchess was playing with fire: as Buckingham's wife she had been the channel for letters to him from the exiled court, and as his widow she was to enter into copious correspondence with the half-brother whom she worked ceaselessly to restore to the throne as 'James III'.[9]

Although Pope was later to resent her arrogance, in the years immediately following the Duke's death he evidently enjoyed her company: he stayed at her country house, dined with her together with Atterbury and Dr Chamberlain, the physician reputed to be her lover, and even subscribed in her name for a volume of music by her favourite Bononcini, rival of the court favourite Handel.[10] He was a key figure at her son Edmund Duke of Buckingham's seventh birthday celebrations in 1723, for which she organised a performance of the choruses which Pope had written for the late Duke's adaptation of *Julius Caesar*: the music was 'Performed with great Magnifisence and Order ye Musick being composed by Sig^r Bononcine sung ye best by ye best Voices M^{rs} A: Robinson & others & ye best Instruments of all sorts' (*TE*, VI, 155). The Duchess subscribed lavishly to Pope's *Odyssey*, arranged an annuity for him, and was on sufficiently easy terms with him and his mother to tease him about his rambles around the country by imitating one of his mother's jokes.[11] These were the years, as he recollected in his later disillusionment, when she had seemed 'a Woman of great honour & many generous Principles' (*Corr.*, IV, 446). Yet even at this early stage he had been forced to take a stand against some of her assumptions: writing to Atterbury about her plans for the prefatory inscription for Buckingham's *Works*, he had challenged both her demand for flattery and her inability to conceive that even commoners have their integrity:

I must keep clear of Flattery . . . I beg therefore you would represent thus much at least to her Grace, that as to the fear she seems touch'd with, (That the Duke's memory should have no advantage but what he must give himself, without being beholden to any one friend.) Your Lordship may certainly, and agreeably to your character, both of rigid honour and christian plainness, tell her that no man can have any other advantage: and that all offerings of friends in such a case pass for nothing. Be but so good as to confirm what I've presented to her, that an inscription in the antient way, plain, pompous, yet modest, will be the most uncommon, and therefore the most distinguishing manner of doing it: And so I hope she will be satisfied, the Duke's Honour be preserv'd, and my integrity also: which is too sacred a thing to be forfeited, in consideration of any little (or what people of quality may call great) Honour or distinction whatever, which those of their rank can bestow on one of mine;

---

[9] *Calendar of the Stuart Papers*, Historical Manuscripts Commission, 7 vols. (London, 1902–23), I, 307, 318, 321, 323, 325, 328; and see below.

[10] *Corr.*, II, 99, 121, 259, 297.

[11] This annuity is presumably the charge on Edmund's estate discussed by Dilke, I, 276–77. See also *Corr.*, II, 276, 303, 525.

and which indeed they are apt to over-rate, but never so much as when they imagine
us under any obligation to say one untrue word in their favour.

(II, 128)

Just how arrogant the Duchess could be is demonstrated by her remarks to
the Countess of Huntingdon on the teachings of the Methodists:

Their doctrines are most repulsive, and strongly tinctured with impertinence and
disrespect towards their superiors, in perpetually endeavouring to level all ranks, and
do away with all distinctions. It is monstrous to be told, that you have a heart as sinful
as the common wretches that crawl on the earth. This is highly offensive and insulting;
and I cannot but wonder that your Ladyship should relish any sentiments so much at
variance with high rank and good breeding.[12]

A clue to Pope's response to the Duchess's presumption is probably to be
found in an abandoned draft of a letter of thanks which breaks off, suggestively, just as the rhetoric seems to be leading inescapably to the implication that
she is the focus of a court in opposition to which he is pleased to belong (*Corr.*,
II, 225). He was more at ease with her when he could see her less as a patron
and more as an unfortunate lady.

Her principal problems arose from the administration of her husband's
estate on behalf of her son, who was still a minor: in particular she was obliged
to prosecute the fraudulent lessee of the family's alum works, the MP John
Ward, better known for his involvement in the South Sea scandal.[13] When
she wrote to Pope expressing her gratitude for Lord Harcourt's support
against Ward (which Pope had probably helped to solicit), her words show
how closely she conformed at this crisis to the irresistible model of the unfortunate lady: 'There is no Body who can be oblig'd Whose Gratitude, is soe
useless as a Woemans & a childs' (*Corr.*, II, 287). Pope could never dismiss
an appeal so suggestive of helplessness: henceforth he never missed a chance
to strike at Ward; but, as in the case of Mrs Weston, his concern laid him
open to slander, and he was accused of sharing the Duchess's favours with
Dr Chamberlain.[14]

Pope's developing reservations about the Duchess came to a head in 1729,
when she asked him to revise her own 'Character' of herself. As his father had
warned him, there was inevitably a risk in 'correcting' another's writing; but
when the work was the self-assessment of a notoriously proud woman, and the
reviser had already made up his mind against flattery, conflict was inevitable
(Spence, no. 82). Only after her death did he explain what had happened.
When asked in 1743 if he was responsible for the 'Character' of the Duke
printed in 1729, he replied that he was not, but added:

[12] *The Life and Times of Selina, Countess of Huntingdon*, 2 vols. (London, 1844), I, 27.
[13] *Corr.*, II, 287; IV, 65. For John Ward, see Sedgwick.
[14] *To Bathurst*, line 20 (*TE*, III. ii, 85); *Dunciad A*, III.26 (*TE*, V, 152); *Epilogue to the Satires*, I.
    119 (*TE*, IV, 306); Richard Morley, *The Life of the Late Celebrated Mrs. Elizabeth Wisebourn,
    Vulgarly Call'd Mother Wybourn* (London, 1721), p. 33; Sherburn, *Early Career*, pp. 294–95.

There was another Character written, of her Grace by herself, (with what help I know not) but she shewed it me in her Blotts, & press'd me, by all the adjurations of Friendship, to give her my Sincere Opinion of it. I acted honestly, & did so. She seem'd to take it patiently, & upon many Exceptions which I made, ingagd me to take the whole, & to select out of it just as much as I judg'd might stand, & return her the Copy. I did so. Immediately she pickd a Quarrel with me, & we never saw each other in five or six years. In the meantime, she shewed this character (as much as was extracted of it in my handwriting) as a Composition of my own, in her praise.

(*Corr.*, IV, 460)

If Pope's edited version is in fact the basis of the 'Character' now extant, it is easier to see why he felt obliged to strike out parts of her original than it is to understand how he managed to reconcile himself to what remains.[15] The reader is informed, for instance, that 'the nicest eye could find no fault in the outward lineaments of her face or proportion of her body'; and her notorious pride and obstinacy are presented as evidence of her superiority to her sex:

Her understanding was such as must have made a figure, had it been in a man; but the modesty of her sex threw a veil over its lustre, which nevertheless suppressed only the expression, not the exertion of it; for her sense was not superior to her resolution, which, when once she was in the right, preserved her from making it only a transition to the wrong, the frequent weakness even of the best women.

Whatever the substance of her composition, Pope's 'in her Blotts' is an evocative phrase to would-be readers of her unusually formless and impetuous handwriting: the very fact that she turned to him suggests that proud as she was, she had to recognise his superior skill; and her sense of having laid herself open to humiliating criticism no doubt contributed to the violence of her recoil.

During the estrangement following their quarrel, the Duchess used Caryll and Nathaniel Pigott (her legal adviser, Caryll's son's father-in-law and Pope's friend) to convey £100 to him in such a way that he could only guess at its origin.[16] Having guessed, he returned it 'with the contempt it deserved', explaining to Caryll his distaste for her assumption 'that I would receive reward for what I had formerly done out of pure friendliness', and hinting at her offensive treatment of him not as a friend but as an employee: she 'imagined she could acquit herself of an obligation by money, which she cared not to owe on a more generous account' (*Corr.*, III, 116, 122). The exiled Atterbury, who seems to have asked his son-in-law William Morice to mediate, commented from his knowledge of both parties that 'I almost despair of making up that matter; since the prejudices conceived are, I see, so strong, and so unlikely to be altogether removed'.[17]

---

[15] The extant 'Character', printed in EC, V, appendix IV, is excluded from Cowler's *Prose Works*. Although Pope may have revised it there is no question of its being his composition.
[16] *Corr.*, III, 91, 110, 116, 122.
[17] *The Epistolary Correspondence of Francis Atterbury*, 4 vols. (London, 1783–87), IV, 294–95.

For his part, Pope now expressed the strength of his prejudice by composing 'Atossa', a satirical counterpart to the Duchess's panegyric on herself which absorbed elements of an attack on Sarah Duchess of Marlborough that he had never printed.[18] Whether this early version of 'Atossa' was expressly designed for or simply absorbed into *Characters of Women*, it was certainly one of the scandalous passages which he felt obliged to omit when he published the poem in 1735, by which time he was either reconciled or on the brink of reconciliation with the Duchess. Yet despite the real sympathy he felt for her in her last years he apparently stood by his judgement of her character, for he was to include 'Atossa' in the unique copy of his works which he printed for Frederick Prince of Wales in 1738. While the Duchess, like her brother James, always assumed that the Stuarts were the obvious focus for dissatisfaction with George II, opposition was also centring on the Prince of Wales; and it was perhaps to be expected that he, who had already incurred her wrath by breaking her windows on a drunken spree a few years previously, should enjoy a joke at the expense of this eccentric zealot in his rival's cause.[19]

It was during the period of the Duchess's quarrel with Pope that her political career reached its peak, for in the early 1730s she was entrusted, along with Lord Cornbury and others, with the planning of a Jacobite rising backed by French troops.[20] Further testimony to her eminence in Jacobite politics is provided by the visits of the French envoy Chavigny to Buckingham House in these years, and by the constant reporting to the British government of her movements and contacts during her visits to the continent.[21] Her active part in the plot began when late in 1730 she escorted Cornbury to meet

---

[18] For the genesis of 'Atossa' see F. W. Bateson, *TE*, III.ii, xxxv–xxxvii, 159–70; Vinton A. Dearing, 'The Prince of Wales's Set of Pope's Works', *Harvard Library Bulletin*, 4 (1950), 320–38; Mack, *Life*, pp. 746–50; Frank Brady, 'The History and Structure of Pope's *To a Lady*', *Studies in English Literature*, 9 (1969), 439–62.

[19] For the calculated ambiguity of Opposition plans and rhetoric as handled by Bolingbroke, see Howard Erskine-Hill, 'Literature and the Jacobite Cause: Was there a Rhetoric of Jacobitism?', in *Ideology and Conspiracy: Aspects of Jacobitism 1689–1759*, edited by Eveline Cruickshanks (Edinburgh, 1982), pp. 48–69 (p. 56). For the Prince's attack on Buckingham House, see John Lord Hervey, *Some Materials towards Memoirs of the Reign of King George II*, edited by Romney Sedgwick, 3 vols. (London, 1931), I, 308–9 (entry dated 1734).

[20] Her role emerges from the Stuart Papers in the Royal Archives at Windsor Castle: her correspondence with James commences on 25 December 1730 (141/50), and its progress may be traced through the entries for Catherine Sheffield in the card index. Although her contribution to Cornbury's plot was dismissed by George Hilton Jones as 'a mare's nest', it is taken more seriously by Eveline Cruickshanks. See George Hilton Jones, *The Main Stream of Jacobitism* (Cambridge, Massachusetts, 1954), pp. 180–84; Eveline Cruickshanks, *Lord Cornbury, Bolingbroke and a Plan to Restore the Stuarts, 1731–1735*, Royal Stuart Papers, 27 (Huntingdon, 1986).

[21] Quai d'Orsay, Archives étrangères, correspondance politique, Angleterre 376, Londrès 3 mars 1732, ff. 252–53, 260; 377, Londrès 24 avril 1733, ff. 126–31; PRO State Papers Foreign (France), SP 78/198, ff. 130, 261; SP 78/200, ff. 182, 206, 219, 273; 78/201, ff. 22–23; SP 78/202, ff. 262, 272; SP 78/203, ff. 9, 19, 45, 94, 109, 127, 138, 142, 149, 154 (all dating from 1732). I am indebted to Eveline Cruickshanks and Andrew Hanham for bringing these references to my attention.

James in Rome, where she helped to draft the declarations of principle and grants of places with which they hoped to sway men of influence in James's favour. At the same time she was anxious to regain possession of her letters to Atterbury, but despite James's support she was unsuccessful. Although she remained on excellent terms with Atterbury's son-in-law Morice, Atterbury himself, now a thoroughly disillusioned exile, was, in James's words, 'uneasy, angry, jealous, & knows how to vent those passions' (Stuart Papers, 143/73; 148/94). She seems to have met him and passed to him a message from James, but he died without restoring to her the letters that caused her such anxiety.[22] Her concern in this respect was characteristic: according to Horace Walpole she was so afraid of the confiscation of her estates during her absence that she vested them in trustees. James had to reassure her that 'I cannot see how they can disturb you there, considering the precautions taken by us in all particulars', and to represent to her how unlikely it was that Atterbury was in league with Sir Robert Walpole.[23] Yet she was unusually bold, for a woman, in seeking the role of a statesman, as James's reservations about sending her to see Cardinal Fleury suggest:

I am affrayd your meeting with him will be of little use, by neither of you opening to one another, and it is the more necessary that you should make the greatest advances toward a mutual confidence on account of your being a woman, & so nearly related to a certain person, both which qualities will I fear be strong motives to the Cardinal to use reserve with you. (Stuart Papers, 147/88)

Although the embassy proved as fruitless as he had feared, his letters at this time do not give the impression that he is merely humouring a headstrong relation. On the other hand, he suffered some unease lest she should take their policy of recruiting men of influence to its logical but highly dangerous conclusion: in 1732 he writes, 'Pray put Walpoles being in my intrest out of your head, for I look upon it to be next to impossible.'[24] Unfortunately, she was to haunt James and his agents with this project for the rest of her life.

The Duchess seems to have returned to England in the autumn of 1731 in a mood of panic; for according to an observer at court, the young Duke, whom she had taken with her, was 'recalled from Rome by his Majesty's

---

[22] Stuart Papers, 148/167, seems to contradict the report cited by Bennett, pp. 302–3, that she had refused to see Atterbury and that he had burned her letters in contempt. Her later efforts to obtain them show that she at least believed otherwise.

[23] Walpole, *Reminiscences*, pp. 93–94; Stuart Papers, 145/80; 148/52.

[24] Stuart Papers, 154/190. Allegations in popular histories of Jacobitism that she had actually betrayed Jacobite plans to Walpole on her return to England in 1731 are apparently extrapolated from William King, *Political and Literary Anecdotes of his Own Times* (London, 1819), pp. 36–39. King, a friend of Pope, Swift and Orrery, wrote his recollections in old age: if his allegations are accurate, they would fit more naturally into the last years of the Duchess's life, when she was definitely in correspondence with Sir Robert (see below). While it is true that fears were expressed during Cornbury's initiative that she and her associate Colonel William Cecil were vulnerable to any pretence by Walpole to be secretly on their side, it does not appear that she was actually suspected of having betrayed the plot (Cruickshanks, *Cornbury*, p. 4; Stuart Papers, 249/30).

express letter, because of a report that the Duchess, his mother, had private meetings there with the Pretender, or his wife' (Egmont, I, 206). When he presented himself at court the king received him in silence; but James congratulated the Duchess in a letter on having been so far 'unmolested', and reminded her that no one could bring proof against her, since not even witnesses 'belonging to me, or in my Family ever saw you & I together' (Stuart Papers, 150/55, 157). The panic over, she was soon planning another trip, which commentators were not slow to connect with Atterbury's death on 3 March 1732. Within days of his death she had informed James of her intention to return and had charged Morice to burn her letters if he found them among his father-in-law's effects. By April she was back on the continent, consulting both with James and with his Paris agent Colonel O'Brien about the confusion surrounding Atterbury's papers, which had first been seized by his confidant Lord Sempill and were subsequently distributed under the supervision of the French government.[25] Despite her evident concern, however, James's expressed desire at the beginning of April to have her back in Paris may suggest that diplomatic as well as personal considerations had prompted her journey (Stuart Papers, 152/133).

Contemporary gossip also connected her with the scandal of the Charitable Corporation, a body set up to loan small sums on security, the pledges being held in warehouses under the supervision of one John Thomson.[26] When in October 1731 Thomson and his cashier concluded a career of systematic fraud by absconding, a committee of the House of Commons was set up to investigate. Up to this point, to judge by the surviving evidence, there was no particular reason to connect the Duchess with Thomson; but by early May he was confined in the Castle of St Angelo in Rome where he was apparently being used by James to demonstrate his care for the British people: in return for certain guarantees for Thomson and his associates, declared James's Roman banker Belloni, their Paris agent Robert Arbuthnot would hand over Thomson's papers so that justice might take its course.[27] It was presumably this proposal, received by the House of Commons on 10 May 1732, that fuelled the gossip about the absent Duchess's possible connection with a fraud which now began to take on the appearance of a Jacobite plot: both Houses

[25] Despite Sherburn's objection that Atterbury's papers were back in England by the end of April, the Duchess's activities in France do indeed show her concern about her letters to him (*Corr.*, III, 296; Stuart Papers, 152/35, 133; 153/24; 154/163, 164; *The Stuart Papers*, edited by John Hulbert Glover (London, 1847: only one volume published), I, xxvii, xxxix; Bennett, p. 305). For Lord (a Jacobite title), alias Robert Sempill, whose son Francis was to be James's chief English agent in the 1740s, see Melville Henry Massue, Marquis de Ruvigny and Raineval, *The Jacobite Peerage*, facsimile of 1904 edition edited by Roger Ararat (London, 1974).

[26] An example of such gossip is given in Egmont, I, 282. For a full account of the Charitable Corporation, see *Historical Register*, 17 (1732), pp. 108–26, 220–32, 255–81.

[27] Stuart Papers, 153/89; 154/159; 155/101, 179. Robert Arbuthnot, brother of Pope's friend John, was a Jacobite banker in Paris: see index to *Corr.*

of Parliament joined in declaring Belloni's letter to be 'an Artifice of the Enemies to the Government, calculated to insinuate a favourable Opinion of the Pretender's Party, under a Pretext of great Zeal for Justice and Affection for the *English* Nation'; and it was burnt by the common hangman. Arbuthnot gave in to threats of bankruptcy and forfeiture, and handed over Thomson's papers without guarantees, leaving their aggrieved owner to petition James for release and compensation (Stuart Papers, 154/132, 159). The case for the Duchess's complicity in his fraud would be stronger if Thomson could be shown to have been a Jacobite before his flight: although he begins his correspondence with James by protesting his loyalty, goes to Paris on some kind of mission after his release from prison, and finally receives James's grudging financial support (if only to prevent his being of use to the English government), he may have been simply a plausible liar with an eye to the main chance. For many contemporaries, however, even the slightest association between so notorious a fugitive and the cause espoused by the suspiciously absent Duchess would have been enough.

James himself suggests that there was some truth in both strands of gossip when on 16 July he promises her news 'of what relates to the affairs of the Bishops papers & of Thomson' and refers to the danger she had been in in England from 'the power of those who were certainly very intent on bringing you into trouble' (Stuart Papers, 154/180). Moreover, the Duchess herself had asserted her innocence in suspiciously specific terms when on 6 June she wrote to Sir Robert Walpole, apologising if she had given offence by not asking the Queen's permission to go abroad, and claiming that she had gone only to settle her accounts with Arbuthnot and to dispose of her Paris house.[28] She acknowledges in her letter that she does not know him personally; and her decision to make her excuses to him may reflect the unease about him that she had expressed, in typically disingenuous style, to Philip Yorke, later Lord Chancellor Hardwicke, during a dispute in 1727 apparently concerning the ground-rent of Buckingham House: 'I had on severall occasions before in great & small matters receiv'd many proufe's that I was (either by fals misrepresentation's or for some cause I could not guess at) not at all in Sr R. Walpoles favour'.[29] In her letter of excuse to Sir Robert in 1732 she is particularly keen to deny 'the silly reports . . . that I had receiv'd mony in the corporation affair, and I fear'd the discovery of it: that I had papers among some of the late bishop of Rochester's that I wanted to get again; and that I was affraid of being in England now'. In reply she received what amounted to a polite snub; for as Sir Robert wrote to his brother, enclosing her 'choice parcel' for the Queen's attention, 'I thought she deserv'd no regard at all'.

[28] William Coxe, *Memoirs of the Life and Administration of Sir Robert Walpole*, 3 vols. (London, 1798), III, 126–28.
[29] Hardwicke Correspondence, BL Add. MSS 35585, f.83.

While the Duchess was labouring to avert the dangers of a career in political subversion which she, seconded by James and Cornbury, took perfectly seriously, Pope, no doubt anxious to dissociate himself entirely from her dangerous schemes, was declaring to the Jacobite apostate Bathurst that she was scarcely sane.[30] On 9 July, having referred to Bathurst's notorious womanising, he turned to the subject of the Duchess's journey:

There is One Woman at least that I think you will never run after, of whom the Town rings with a hundred Stories, *why* she run, & *whither* she is run? Her sober Friends are sorry for her, & so truly am I, whom she cutt off from the number of them three years agoe. She has dealt as mysteriously with you, as with me formerly; both which are proofs that We are both less mad, than is requisite, for her to think quite well of us. I am told in town, she is sending her Son to Oxford, and that you, (whose Gallantry is to make her amends for your defects in Politicks) intend to see him there.

(Corr., III, 295–96)

This is the first statement of a theme which was to become standard in the Duchess's later years, typified by Horace Walpole's description of how in 1741, 'more mad with pride than any mercer's wife in Bedlam', she 'came t'other night to the opera *en princesse*, literally in robes red velvet and ermine'.[31] Whereas his libels of Lady Mary often fail to harmonise with other sources, his estimate of the Duchess's pride is vindicated by her own words, for example to Lady Huntingdon; and his sense that her later behaviour amounted to insanity was widely shared, not only by Pope, but also by Lord Orrery, Lord Hervey and William King.[32] Walpole's details may be exaggerated; but his accounts of her ritual humiliation of an insufficiently deferential creditor, her refusal to visit the court of Versailles unless accorded royal honours, and her insistence on occupying a box like the royal one at the opera in Paris all chime in harmony with the growing extravagance of words and actions recorded in other sources.[33] Observers no doubt recollected that her maternal grandmother, one of the notoriously unstable Savages, had been insane from the Restoration until her death in 1705, believing herself to be a queen and insisting on being addressed accordingly.[34] The Duchess herself, a passionate devotee of visionary schemes, conformed neatly to the assumptions of the age regarding her sex's predisposition to mental disorder. When Pope alluded to the 'Passions' that 'have overturn'd Mind & Body' just before her death in 1743, Orrery was able to reply by drawing the connection between the strength of her passions and the risk of madness implicit in the female constitution:

[30] For Bathurst's withdrawal from the Atterbury plot, see Bennett, p. 230.
[31] *HW Corr.*, XVII, 253–54.
[32] *Corr.*, IV, 440–42; *Lord Hervey and his Friends*, edited by the Earl of Ilchester (London, 1950), p. 99; King, *Political Anecdotes*, pp. 36–39.
[33] *HW Corr.*, XVII, 254; XVIII, 192–93.
[34] De Sola Pinto, pp. 120–25.

Death only can give relief to Passions of that soart. but I observe that People in her disposition of mind live generally to a great Age. 'The days of Women are threescore years and ten, and if they be so strong to attain to fourscore years, yet is their Strength then but Madness or Folly'.   (*Corr.*, IV, 440–42)

This is reminiscent of Nahum Tate's reflections on the tragedy of Dido, 'Great minds against themselves Conspire', a commonplace in relation to both sexes, but in particular harmony with assumptions of an emotional and imaginative imbalance in the female sex: the psalmist's original for Orrery's parody offers the strong man not madness and folly, but labour and sorrow.[35]

At the same time as Pope was expressing to Bathurst his doubts of the Duchess's sanity, the effects of her uneasy subjectivity were becoming ever more obvious in her relations with James. His letters of September and October 1732, for example, show that she is ridiculously apprehensive of his crediting gossip against her, and when he congratulates her on her improvement in health he hints at his suspicion that her troubles are largely psychosomatic: 'But let me beg of you not to let cross accidents & disappointments affect you so much' (Stuart Papers, 155/130; 156/27). She evidently harassed him with her need for approval and he responded as best he could: 'I doubt not but that the D^{ss} of B^m always acts & speaks to the best of her judgement on all accasions, It were to be wished every body else had her good sense and her good nature, For matters might then be managed both more smoothly & with more success' (179/17). Yet despite all annoyances, she retained his affection: in August 1735, after the Cornbury plot had finally collapsed, he wrote, 'I long to take a walk with you in your Garden', a poignant remark from an exile who had seen Britain only during the abortive rising of 1715.[36] In November, after her son's death from consumption, he wrote to her of his desire that confidential papers about Atterbury's trial should be entrusted to her, stating that 'I am very sure you will do all that is right and proper about them', a sign that, however she might doubt it, he still took her seriously (Stuart Papers, 183/159).

Her son Edmund's death on 30 October 1735 at the age of nineteen was the great watershed in her life: he was not only the last Duke of Buckingham of the Sheffield line, but also her last hope of founding a line ennobled by her Stuart blood.[37] Her inner life, in harmony with past Stuart splendours, found its characteristic expression in rituals which seemed exaggerated, even offensive, to observers attuned to the less sacramental style of public life under the Hanoverians; and like the zeal to see her late husband flattered in print that irritated Pope, or the ceremonial mourning on the anniversary of her

---

[35] Henry Purcell, *Dido and Aeneas*, facsimile of 1st edition of libretto, 1680 (London, no date), p. 8; Psalms 90:10. Compare Dryden's 'Great Wits are sure to Madness near ally'd', a generalisation based on his assessment of Shaftesbury (*Absolom and Achitophel*, line 163; *Poems of Dryden*, I, 221).

[36] Cruickshanks, *Cornbury*, p. 9; Stuart Papers, 181/165.

[37] G.E.C., *Peerage*, Edmund Sheffield, Duke of Buckingham and Normanby.

grandfather Charles I's execution that later surprised Lord Hervey, the com-
memorative arrangements for Duke Edmund were by the standards of the
time lavish to excess.[38] When he died in Rome a death-mask was taken; and
this was used to construct the wax effigy which was carried in procession,
dressed in his robes of state, when he was finally buried in Westminster Abbey
the following January.[39] This anachronistic pomp, which had already been
old-fashioned when in 1715 she and her husband had commissioned an effigy
on the death of their three-year-old son Robert, underlined her assumption
of quasi-royal status: when in 1743 the Duchess's own effigy – which she had
commissioned at the same time as Edmund's – was carried in state at her
own funeral it was almost certainly the last ever to be so carried in England
(see plate 2). To grace his funeral she also presided over a formal lying in state
at Buckingham House, and she reportedly exposed herself to a predictable
rebuff when she tried to borrow the Duke of Marlborough's hearse from his
widow.[40]

By early 1735 Pope had been reconciled to the Duchess, probably because
he no longer saw her as fully responsible for her actions. He would certainly
have been moved by her sufferings during Edmund's last illness, more particularly since he had a close connection with the invalid in Mrs Honoretta
Pratt, a Tory acquaintance of Swift, Bethel and Patty, who acted as the Duke's
nurse and the Duchess's companion.[41] After Edmund's death, Pope professed to read his papers with respect. He also composed an epitaph in which the
young man is characterised as, in worldly terms, altogether more modest in
achievement than his ancestors ('a Race, for Courage fam'd and Art, / Ends
in the milder Merit of the Heart'), an emphasis which, despite gestures in accordance with the opposition rhetoric of the time towards a lost career as
'Patriot' and parliamentarian in 'a sinking State', may not have harmonised
with the Duchess's vision, for in the event she decided not to inscribe Pope's
verses on the tomb.[42] The mother who had from his childhood sought for her
son a prestigious marriage through which he might perpetuate her royal

[38] Walpole, *Reminiscences*, p. 96.

[39] I am grateful to Canon Anthony Harvey of Westminster Abbey for his help with questions
about the effigies of the Sheffield family, and to Sheila Landi, Natalie Rothenstein and Julian
Litten of the Victoria and Albert Museum for detailed information. The effigies were restored
in 1987 and are now on show in the Abbey Museum. Descriptions and photographs are given
by L. E. Tanner and J. L. Nevinson, 'On Some Later Funeral Effigies in Westminster
Abbey', *Archaeologia*, 85 (1936), 169–202 (pp. 183–88).

[40] *Gentleman's Magazine*, 6 (1736), 54; Walpole, *Reminiscences*, pp. 95–96. At other times the
Duchesses were on terms of somewhat prickly civility. The Duchess of Marlborough had a
longstanding grudge against the Duchess of Buckingham's mother: in 1677, when John Churchill was engaged to his future wife, his parents almost succeeded in persuading him to marry
the far wealthier Catherine Sedley (BL Add. MSS 61476, ff. 76–77; de Sola Pinto, pp.
135–36).

[41] Mrs Pratt is described in *Gentleman's Magazine*, 39 (1769), 461–62. For her friendships see
Corr., IV, 21, 446; *Swift Corr.*, III, 53–55, 223–24; IV, 206–7, 312–13, 326; *HW Corr.*, XVIII,
65; Blount Letters, II, 215–17.

[42] *Corr.*, IV, 65; *TE*, VI, 326.

blood, and who had sent him to learn the art of war under his Stuart uncle
Lord Berwick, may well have had reservations about the concept of virtue implied in Pope's claim that in being 'a Saint' the last Duke had been something
greater than the 'Chiefs or Sages' among his ancestors.[43] In contrast, Orrery, whose diffuse poem on the occasion also praises Edmund as 'an Off'ring
fit for Heaven', makes a point of setting his soldierly virtue in the context of
his Stuart descent:

> Valiant in Arms, *France* saw his martial Fire
> Kindling where *Berwick*'s did in Blood expire.[44]

In comparison with Pope's approach it is interesting to consider a poem which
must have come even closer to the proud mother's expectations, a birthday
poem which Atterbury had composed for Edmund some years before his
death.[45] Atterbury presents the youth as both soldier and statesman, describing how his admirers

> Now see their Hero, dreadful in the Field,
> The slaughtering Weapon for his Country wield;
> Now with inspiring Eloquence restore
> Freedom to Senates, sunk or aw'd before.

He is to challenge his forebears on their own ground:

> Recal the Chiefs of your illustrious Race
> . . .
> Nor think their Toils have your Dismission won.

Moreover, providing that Edmund's health can be properly established,
Atterbury is prepared to endorse the Duchess's dynastic ambitions, foreseeing

> Heroes descending thro' the sacred Line
> Which shall in our remotest Annals shine.

Yet for the Duchess the poem's crowning glory was probably Atterbury's
ingenious parallel history in allusion to her Stuart blood:

> O may our Isle of her *Marcellus* tell,
> How long he liv'd, and how lamented fell,
> May no fam'd Bard th'untimely Youth bewail,
> Nor our *Oct*— sink to hear the Tale!

Since Marcellus was Augustus' heir elect, the son of his sister Octavia, the
implications are plain – and treasonable.[46] Ironically, the omen that Atter-

---

[43] *The Orrery Papers*, edited by the Countess of Cork and Orrery, 2 vols. (London, 1903), I,
38.

[44] John Boyle, Earl of Orrery, *A Poem Sacred to the Memory of Edmund Sheffield, Duke of Buckingham*
(London, 1736).

[45] F. Atterbury, *Antonius Musa's Character . . . to which is added, To the Duke of B**, on his Birth-
Day: A Poem* (London, 1740).

[46] The parallel is not to be taken too literally, as James had two healthy sons. For Marcellus,

bury here strives to avert was to be fulfilled in Edmund's early death; but
unlike Virgil and Atterbury, Pope could not offer a shared sense of dynastic
and political loss: refusing the role of Jacobite court poet, he writes principally
with compassion for a woman whose 'justest Pride' and 'many Hopes' were
buried with her son. Although Pope could not risk in a public inscription what
Atterbury could confide to a manuscript compliment, his refusal of even the
slightest gesture towards the military and dynastic strongly suggests that his
honest feelings fall well within the limits set by prudence, and Horace Walpole
may have been right to claim that Pope had Edmund in mind when he complained, with reference to the burden of inventing 'random Praise', that 'each
Mother asks it for her Booby Son'.[47]

The Duchess's brother James was deeply concerned for her: three days
after his nephew's death, ignorant of the bad news, he wrote to express hopes
for his recovery; a fortnight later he asked how she was bearing 'the mellan-
choly news of your Friend's loss'; and the following March he explained that
'I am noways surprized at your silence, considering your present situation'.[48] All the time, however, he had been discussing his political plans in
the same letters, and in August 1736 he brought her and her close associate
Colonel Cecil into his project of backing the new Journal Common Sense, conceived by James and by its editor Charles Molloy as an organ of opposition
to the government which would focus sentiment favourable to the Jacobite
cause.[49] It may be that the Duchess had spoken to Pope about Common Sense,
for according to O'Brien, 'mr pope, que jusqua present, a evité dentrer dans
aucune affaire de party, a offert a molloy tout les secours qui depondront de
luy'; but if Pope had in fact been as forthcoming as this, his words would have
represented not the Jacobite commitment that James and the Duchess were
eager to assume, but the growing disgust with Walpole's government expressed
in his Epilogue to the Satires and in his association with the opposition grouped
around the Prince of Wales. James and his court typically blinked at the
unpalatable truth that opposition need not mean Jacobitism; and in July
1737, having declared that 'her present uneasy situation made her look with
indifference on every thing but what related to the Kings intrest', the Duchess
claimed that 'the Tories are impatient for the Restoration, but The Whigs not
quite so fond of it, but that if there were a good number of Forreign Troups
it is not doubted but they would be also for it', and 'that Card[l] Fleury, The
King of Spain &c must be infatuated, if they do not now something for the
King' (199/146). Her analysis would not have met with universal approval.

The Duchess was the less likely to question the plausibility of her schemes

see The Aeneid of Virgil, edited by R. D. Williams, 2 vols. (London, 1972), I, 151–52 (Book
VI, lines 854–86), 514–16.

[47] Epilogue to the Satires, II.106–7; TE, IV, 319, note.
[48] Stuart Papers, 183/159; 184/47; 186/71.
[49] George Hilton Jones, 'The Jacobites, Charles Molloy, and Common Sense', Review of English
Studies, 4 (1953), 144–47.

because it was so obvious to her that her sex was an obstacle to her being taken
seriously: it was too easy to console herself with the illusion that this was the
only obstacle. In the same letter as the analysis of prospects quoted above she
reports indignantly that 'she has been too credibly informd That Col OBryan
being asked by Card¹ Fleury or Mr Chauvelin if he thought she was fit to be
trusted with a secret, answerd, she is but a Woman you know'. She returns
to the theme in a survey of affairs in 1741, in which her impulsive and scarcely
legible hand, punctuated by dashes and spilling into margins, sprawls
headlong over sheet after sheet (238/104). Referring sarcastically to herself as
'of a Sex not to understand these high matters', she makes no secret of her
contempt for the way business is being carried on in defiance of her advice:
'how the sublimer Sex will act a little time will now produce', she notes
scathingly. In view of her tone it is hardly surprising that correspondence with
her is so sparsely represented among James's papers after 1735. What does
survive suggests that when not absorbed in personal grievances she persisted
in schemes that could only have confirmed male prejudices about her sex's
unfitness for politics.

Her personal grievances hinged on her husband's will, which had left the
Sheffield estates to Edmund with the condition that if he died without issue
they should go to his illegitimate half-brother Charles Herbert, who was to
take the Sheffield name and continue the line.[50] The Duchess's devotion to
her husband's memory did not extend to welcoming his bastard into the place
she had hoped to reserve for an heir of her own Stuart blood (although she
was affable to his other illegitimate children as long as they behaved with
deference); and it was no doubt with her encouragement that Edmund made
a will which left his father's property to his mother. This was a futile gesture,
since the law held that by dying childless he had fulfilled his father's condition
for the transfer of the estates to Charles Herbert. The Duchess, who professed
to believe that her husband had not meant to limit her son's power in this
way, attempted repeatedly to have Herbert's claim set aside, until in 1739 he
obtained a perpetual injunction forbidding her to contest the issue further.
Pope's ambivalence on the case, which he did not hesitate to express to
Orrery, one of her closest associates, suggests that even they felt she was
incapable of seeing reason:

I am this very day wholly taken up in solliciting Lords to attend the Duchess of Buckingham's Cause, which comes on to morrow. I wish her Success, if it be as just as
undoubtedly she thinks it.   (*Corr.*, IV, 65)

In harsher moods he saw her litigation as a downright breach of piety towards
the husband she had professed to love:

---

[50] For her husband's will, see *Character of John Sheffield*, pp. 35–48. Her litigation is summarised
    in *HW Corr.*, XVII, 254. She expresses her dissatisfaction with the interpretation upheld by
    the courts in BL Add. MSS 9129, ff. 90–92.

Last night, her Lord was all that's good and great,
A Knave this morning, and his Will a Cheat.

(*Characters of Women*, line 141)

James too was made to feel the force of her resentment: in July 1737 she complained that 'it was publickly said she would carry it to Rome if she got it, so Mr Sheffield had better have it'; later the same month she again expressed herself at length on the subject and in January 1739 James acknowledged receipt of yet 'two packets' more, 'all relating to your private affairs' (Stuart Papers, 199/146). Furthermore, he can only have been dismayed to learn from her pen how Sir Robert Walpole was gaining in her estimation by an obviously devious appearance of sympathy with her 'injustices' at law. In 1737 she told James that Walpole had been commiserating with her, and that 'she thinks as she did in wishing what she expected about him & would wonder if he did not agree to treat reasonably', even though, knowing her brother's prejudice, she conceded that 'she expects no answer to this particular' (199/146). The late eighteenth-century historian William Coxe includes in his manuscript collections for his *Memoirs of the Life and Administration of Sir Robert Walpole* an account of 'a mysterious correspondence' between Sir Robert and the Duchess, 'under the style and character of quakers . . . mostly written in a jargon which it is impossible to decipher'.[51] Influenced by King's *Political Anecdotes* and by a similar account preserved by the eighteenth-century collector of political reminiscences Henry Etough, Coxe believed that 'she made him the depositary of her secrets'; but the letters which he preserves, according to him 'a few of the most intelligible' of a collection testifying to 'frequent interviews' during a correspondence 'of considerable duration', do not show her actually passing information, although they do show her attempting to negotiate in an archly insinuating style which made her and any secrets she may have possessed extremely vulnerable to Sir Robert, had he ever thought it worth his while to corner her. Having once charmed her into believing the implausible fiction of his secret Jacobite sympathies, Sir

---

[51] Add. MSS 9129, ff. 82–113. Coxe's account, though based in part on the original letters interleaved with his notes, is highly suspect in many of its details. King related many years later that the Duchess's associate Colonel Cecil 'suffered himself to be cajoled and duped by Sir ROBERT WALPOLE' and that she, being 'half-mad', was persuaded by Cecil to pass to Walpole 'all the letters and instructions which she received from Rome', and finally 'offered to marry him, which Sir ROBERT very civilly declined' (*Political Anecdotes*, pp. 36–39). None of these allegations against her can be substantiated from the surviving primary evidence. Etough preserves a broadly similar account, for which he does not cite sources (BL Add. MSS 9200, f. 212). Although he had several interviews with Sir Robert after he became Earl of Orford, he states that he did not know of the minister's dealings with the Duchess until 'a considerable time' after writing the memoirs based on these interviews. For the dangers to which she exposed herself, see Sir Robert's dealings with Cecil, whom he was allegedly annoyed to see arrested since he was more use to the government going transparently about his Jacobite business (Add. MSS 9129, ff. 105–6); and the trap set for the Jacobite historian Thomas Carte (Paul S. Fritz, *The English Ministers and Jacobitism between the Rebellions of 1715 and 1745* (Toronto, 1975), p. 124).

Robert no doubt gleaned more from her than she in her exuberant self-conceit ever realised. It was probably owing to her that he felt able to make his most direct attempt to penetrate the Jacobite system when in 1739 he apparently wrote to James with a pretended offer of service, to which James, more prudent than his sister, returned a cautiously non-committal reply.[52]

Although most of the letters which Coxe preserved are undated, it seems that the correspondence blossomed during the years of her litigation against Charles Sheffield. According to Etough she had been introduced to Sir Robert by Lord Hervey, then Vice-Chamberlain to the King, who had shrewdly backed her against William Pulteney when he, as trustee of her estates during one of her trips abroad, had made difficulties about giving the title back into her hands.[53] Thus Hervey acquired both a debt of gratitude to himself and a potential source of intelligence for Sir Robert, who proceeded to express his sympathy with the Duchess's complaints: because he has expressed contempt for Mrs Sheffield's 'paltry practices' she feels that she can 'take ye liberty of complaining of them with ye more freedom'.[54] He also helped her practically by procuring a crown lease for her; and in a letter of 1738 or 1739 which thanks him for this as well as making the usual complaints about her litigation, she shows how dangerous her confident, high-spirited response to the minister's overtures could have proved:

I can hardly hold . . . from laughing, nay laughing almost out with my little friend Pope (tho we have not met a good while to confer notes) to see what I have seen, to know what I now know, that this tremendous will of the poor Duke of Buckinghams that has been so cruelly metamorphosed of late into constructions he would infallibly have turnd any one out of Doors that would have propos'd to him to do as he is imagined to have done, by well intentioned Persons.   (Add. MSS 9129, f. 90)

She is in fact teasing Sir Robert about his appearance in the recently published first dialogue of Pope's *Epilogue to the Satires*:

> Seen him I have, but in his happier hour
> Of Social Pleasure, ill-exchang'd for Pow'r;
> Seen him, uncumber'd with the Venal tribe,
> Smile without Art, and win without a Bribe.
> Would he oblige me? let me only find,
> He does not think me what he thinks mankind.
> Come, come, at all I laugh He laughs, no doubt,
> The only diff'rence is, I dare laugh out.   (line 29; *TE*, IV, 300)

Her foolhardy twisting of the lion's tail takes little account of the precariously placed poet whom she so easily patronises.

---

[52] Add. MSS 9129, ff. 74–77.
[53] Add. MSS 9200, f. 212.
[54] This letter survives as a single item among the West Papers, BL Add. MSS 34728, f. 1.

It seems likely that an element of flirtation entered into her obsession with Sir Robert, although King's statement that she went so far as to propose marriage, and Etough's that her 'pleasure and satisfaction' in his company 'increased . . . into the passion of love' may simply be in a tradition of gossip which had already accused her of solacing her widowhood with the favours of Pope and Dr Chamberlain.[55] Sir Robert indeed teases her about their quasi-amorous correspondence in a postscript to one of the notes proposing a 'quakers' meeting' that they left for each other at various shops: 'The hand that writes this, knows not to whom it is address'd, but suspects it to be an affair of gallantry.'[56] One of the Duchess's letters suggests, however, that her main preoccupation was the hope of engaging him with hints of a parallel between himself and Lord Clarendon. She hints that if he were to lend his weight to a restoration his daughter could be married to the future King's younger brother and become Duchess of York. (Horace Walpole later confirmed that his father told him of such a proposal.)[57] Using cant names in a manner reminiscent of some of the less convincing contrivances among the Stuart Papers, she writes to him of 'the Quaker' (herself) and of her 'sort of relation', who 'has a bright genius and a handsome person and is said to have a good title to a great fortune' which has been 'sufferd for some reasons to sleep at present', and she claims that the difference of religion between him and 'a little niece which appertains to the Quakers correspondent' need not be an obstacle to their marriage. She pays this correspondent and his late wife Maria Skerret, for many years his mistress, the compliment of believing that 'this girl . . . must degenerate from both her parents not to give hopes, that if they should ever be marryd, no fools would ever be transmitted from them to posterity'; and she sends her a copy of complimentary verses and a 'little treatise', which together with the Bible and *The Whole Duty of Man* she pointedly recommends as a better foundation for the female character than the fashionable Methodism. It is even possible, as Coxe believed, that the bridegroom proposed was not, as Horace Walpole reported, the younger but the elder son, the Young Pretender himself; but in either case it is almost impossible that either of the families concerned would even have considered such a match.

This cultivation of Sir Robert was not the Duchess's only unsolicited effort on James's behalf in these years, for in 1741, having ostentatiously applied to the Duke of Newcastle for 'a safe conveyance' to France ('notwithstanding

---

[55] King, *Political Anecdotes*, pp. 36–39; Add. MSS 9200, f. 212; Sherburn, *Early Career*, pp. 294–95.

[56] Add. MSS 9129, f. 95.

[57] Add. MSS 9129, ff. 102–3. There is some evidence for placing this proposal in 1742, when on Sir Robert's fall from power he was created Earl of Orford and took steps to legitimise his daughter (his second wife's child, born before their marriage). In the Duchess's eyes her new status as an Earl's daughter would presumably have added to her attractions (*HW Corr.*, XVIII, 389–90).

I am ye Duke of Berwick's Sister I am much afraid of a privateer'), where she claimed to have business concerning an orphan entrusted to her care, she set off for Paris.[58] When James learned of her departure he wrote to her in terms that make it clear that her diplomatic mission was not of his devising: whilst he makes the best of the situation and thanks her for making a journey solely on his behalf, he adds significantly, 'I must earnestly recommend you not to importune the old Gentleman [Cardinal Fleury] too much', for 'teazing him can serve for nothing but to make him peevish' (Stuart Papers, 234/181). James evidently knew the dangers of her intemperate zeal; and when in September she wrote to him in the throes of her grief at the death of a friend he told her that 'you really should not have writ it in the condition you were then in', and suggested that she could more usefully put her weight behind the opposition in England (236/70). She, sensing that she was being trifled with, indignantly endorsed his letter, 'I really doe not understand by these barren instructions when I am to doe if I would succeed in what I am directed.' Later that year she demanded reassurance that he was not going behind her back to Bolingbroke, Pulteney or Walpole; she panicked over a letter she found on the floor of her lodgings which James dismissed as either of 'no relation to our private affairs' or as 'a piece of nonsense writ on purpose to puzzle'. At the end of the year, during her journey home from her fruitless and self-imposed task, she sent him the tirade in which she wrote mockingly of her inferiority in politics to 'the sublimer Sex' (238/41, 95, 104). Soon after her return, however, she was writing with her usual aplomb to the Duchess of Marlborough, accusing Her Grace of spreading lies about her journey, expressing the hope that she had not defamed the late Duke of Buckingham in her writings, disclaiming any understanding of a compromising letter from Orrery which had been delivered to the Duchess of Marlborough by mistake, and politely threatening her with a visit: 'Witt & humour I doubt not of meeting with, mixt with lighter subject above my levell to apprehend probably'.[59] The passionate inventiveness and dramatic self-projection that enabled her to respond so resiliently – if unconvincingly – to continual discoveries and disappointments effectively disqualified her from a service requiring a cool sense of political feasibility. In comparison with Lord Sempill, James's newly appointed chief agent in England, who was arguably almost as deficient in this respect as the Duchess, she was notably lacking in the restrained and plausible manner necessary to be taken seriously: it was easy for him to patronise a woman so obviously unbalanced, 'whose good heart really deserves all those attentions that are consistent with prudence'; but it was his spurious calm and control that proved the more dangerous.[60]

---

[58] Newcastle Correspondence, BL Add. MSS 32697, f. 156.
[59] Blenheim Papers, BL Add. MSS 61478, ff. 70–72.
[60] Francis Sempill's shortcomings are exposed by Jones, *Jacobitism*, pp. 212–19, 229–30.

James was not the only friend to experience the truth of Pope's irony at the Duchess's expense:

> Who breaks with her, provokes Revenge from Hell,
> But he's a bolder man who dares be well:
> Her ev'ry turn with Violence pursu'd,
> Nor more a storm her Hate than Gratitude.

(Characters of Women, line 129)

She bombarded her friends with excessively long letters in a hand they could hardly make out, harping endlessly on her grievances. Orrery for example, one of her most faithful supporters, wrote to warn his wife:

> By this Post goes a large Packett to you from the D^{ss} which will puzzle you as much as if it were Arabick: it is, I beleive, a Detail of her whole Affairs, an account of her base usage, and monstrous Affronts She has met with, and some kind civilities and tender expressions towards You, wishing much to see You here. You will answer it on these topicks accordingly.[61]

Her behaviour was noticeably odd. Pope, who was still receiving his annuity from her, described to Orrery an encounter with her in July 1742 which suggests that her moods swung wildly between the buoyant energy typical of her letters and fits of deep depression:

> She left me really concernd for her, & heartily wishing no man afflicted her peace of mind more than I would do, and that I could do her any good office; but in the nature of Things it seems impossible. She also payd me her small debt, but I could not persuade her to come into the House but sate with her in her Coach at my door. We mentiond you with honour, & I look upon whatever she may think in my favour, as wholly owing to your kind Conduct.   (Corr., IV, 406)

From this it seems likely that Orrery had played a part in effecting the reconciliation between Pope and the Duchess; but finally even he forfeited her good opinion, as Sempill reported to James after her death on 13 March 1743:

> The poor Duchess and Col Cecil had confounded, alarm'd, and distracted all the King's friends in England by displaying openly their jealousies against himself, Lord Orrery, and against Lord Barrymore and Lord Sempill and all that they could imagine might have an understanding with any of them. Lord Orrery found this jealousy growing to a degree of rage, and therefore judg'd it could only be cur'd by time and absence, wch is the cause of his remaining in the Country.

(Stuart Papers, 249/30)

Sempill, anxious not to be blamed for the rift, inveighed against 'the low insinuations' of one of the Duchess's associates, the 'spiteful, selfish . . . detestable, sordid' Colonel Brett, an opinion that James evidently did not share (248/157; 249/30, 43). What is clear is that the Duchess, blind to the danger of her cherished schemes, was furious with those whom she blamed for

---

[61] *Orrery Papers*, II. 161–62; compare Stuart Papers, 213/65; 240/37.

ousting her from her position at the heart of affairs. Even after her death, according to Sempill, Cecil was still indulging his 'reveries of a mad-man':

By the Duchess's last dispositions and some circumstances that Col Cecil boasted of to me, I suspect that he flatters himself to be in the way of gaining Robert Walpole.

(249/30)

James, despite his trust that 'she was cautious in such matters almost to an excess', had seen to it that for some time she had had no access to sensitive information; for after her death, although 'very sorry', he admitted that he 'would be much more so, if I thought that event would be a real Loss', adding that her papers could in any case 'do little or no prejudice to any particular person' (249/31, 40, 102).

Notwithstanding James's caution with her, the 'last dispositions' to which Sempill refers cannot have been other than frightening to the English Jacobites:

It is said she deliver'd all her papers to Lord Hervey two days before her death, Those who were well acquainted with her Grace are astonish'd at this disposition.

(248/182)

Sempill also confides that she 'had been thought delirious for some time', a belief consistent with the surprising report that she had appointed Hervey and Sir Robert Walpole to act as executors alongside her old friend Orrery. Although Hervey was not in fact named as an executor, Sempill conveys the tendency of her arrangements accurately enough.[62] Her will, made on 15 February 1743, a month before her death, continues her policy towards Sir Robert by naming him as the first of her executors, with a legacy of £240 if he accepted – which he did not.[63] Hervey, who as the King's Vice-Chamberlain and Queen Caroline's confidant, and more recently Lord Privy Seal, had been until his fall from power in July 1742 a pillar of the Whig establishment almost comparable to Sir Robert, received the Duchess's favour not through her will, but through a separate deed granting him Buckingham House for life, and through the marriage she arranged just before her death between her heir Constantine Phipps, her grandson by her first marriage, and Hervey's daughter, on terms exceptionally favourable to the bride's family.[64] This, if Etough is correct, represented a magnificent return on Hervey's earlier championship of the Duchess's rights against Pulteney, an action which with hindsight savours more of calculation than of knight-errantry. Thus came about the ironic spectacle of the Duchess's funeral, a

---

[62] The court copy of her will is PRO Prob 11/727/66.

[63] Sir Robert's refusal of the executorship is confirmed by the absence of his name from the list of accredited executors annexed to the court copy of the will.

[64] Halsband, *Hervey*, pp. 96–100, 255, 302–3. The arrangements are discussed by Dorothy Margaret Stuart, *Molly Lepell: Lady Hervey* (London, 1936), p. 118. The most detailed account, apparently based on family tradition but unfortunately without citation of sources, is D. A. Ponsonby, *Call a Dog Hervey* (London, no date), p. 78.

sumptuous coda to the Stuart ceremonial tradition, but with the daughter of
the Hanoverian courtier-in-chief as chief mourner.[65] Hervey, now fallen
from power, was thoroughly disillusioned with the administration; his wife,
perhaps surprisingly, had a reputation for sentimental Jacobitism; and
Horace Walpole was convinced that he must have sworn fealty to James in
order to gain the Duchess's favour: yet in view of her generosity to him it is
hardly necessary to posit such a conversion to account for the fact that, as
Sempill reported, he made 'no dishonourable use . . . of the Duchess's
papers'.[66] Yet, alarmed as the main body of the English Jacobites were,
there can be no doubt that she died in the hope that her bold wooing of the
King's minister and chief courtier would bring about a restoration where 'the
sublimer Sex' had failed. James's tribute to her a few days after her death
shows how well he understood and valued the sister who had, in her later
years, been such a danger to his hopes: 'She had many good qualities, & an
uncommon zeal & affection for me & my Cause' (249/43).

As she lay dying she was an object of compassion to Lady Huntingdon,
whom she firmly declined to see, presumably even less inclined than before
to hear the spiritual privileges of rank called into question. Horace Walpole
reported with delight how she had made her attendants promise not to slight
her rank by taking advantage of her unconsciousness to sit down before she
was dead; and how she had arranged the details of her funeral with the
Garter-King-at-Arms as she lay on her deathbed.[67] With more compassion,
Pope, who had so resolutely refused to be drawn into the role of Jacobite court
poet, alluded to her pretensions with a whimsical irony in a letter to Orrery:
'I fear her Poet will soon shed real Tears for her, as he will be of no use to
any other Princess or Potentate whatsoever' (*Corr.*, IV, 440–41). In the same
letter, however, he has described a 'King's poet or Historiographer' (in relation to a work that Lady Orrery wants him to subscribe to) as 'the two greatest
Lyers in Literature': in reality he has come to cherish his neglect by the great;
and it is only now that the Duchess's patronage is no longer a threat that he
can joke about it. Without sacrificing the perspective of 'Atossa', with its
almost awe-struck sense of a larger-than-life perversity, he now feels the
pathos of her character: 'her Fate has been hard upon her, but not so hard
as herself, for her Passions have overturn'd Mind & Body' (pp. 440–41).

Pity turned to anger and contempt when Pope learned of the Duchess's
disposal of her property. Writing to Bethel he perhaps expressed himself more
openly than he would have done to her executor and former confidant Orrery:

---

65 *Gentleman's Magazine*, 13 (1743), 191.
66 Walpole, *Reminiscences*, p. 96; Stuart, *Lady Hervey*, pp. 114–46; Stuart Papers, 249/30.
67 Although the story of the promise not to sit down until she was dead may be mere gossip, the
funeral directions dictated from her deathbed still survive. Some of Walpole's details of her
funeral, however, are definitely exaggerated (*HW Corr.*, XVIII, 193, 203; Tanner, p.
180).

I have no Vanity nor pleasure that does not stop short of the Grave. The Duchess of Buckingham has thought otherwise, who orderd all manner of Vanities for her own funeral, & a Sum of Money to be squanderd on it, which is but necessary to preserve from starving many poor people to whom she is indebted. I doubt not Mrs Pratt is as much astonishd as you or I, at her leaving Sir Robert Walpole her Trustee, & Lord Hervey her Executor, with a Marriage Settlement on his Daughter, that will take place of all the Prior debts she has in the world. All her private Papers & those of her Correspondents are left in the hands of Lord Hervey, so that it is not impossible another Vol. of my Letters may come out: I am sure thay make no part of her Treasonable Correspondence, (which they say she has Expressly left to him) but sure this is Infamous Conduct towards any common acquaintance. And yet this Woman seem'd once, a Woman of great honor & many generous Principles. I know you are one of those that will burn every Scrap I write to you, at my desire, or I really should be praecluded from performing the most common offices of Friendship, or even writing that I esteem & love any man.   (*Corr.*, IV, 446)

He was by no means alone in condemning the pride displayed in her final dispositions; but his fury at seeing his letters, however innocuous, put into the hands of his old enemy is particularly understandable, since if Hervey had chosen to hand them to Curll for publication, lack of evidence would have been no obstacle whatsoever to the insinuation that Pope had connived at the Duchess's treason.[68] Moreover, his moralising contempt for her funeral plans was widely shared, although it was his own sense of impending death (he had in fact little more than a year to live), with the realisation that the only worldly act that could survive him was to do good to those who would live after him, that sharpened his sense of the injustice done to people like Mrs Pratt, who despite years of bearing cheerfully with the Duchess's moods and illnesses was not even mentioned in her will. The great lady whom Pope had found most congenial as an unfortunate lady had signally failed to respond to the needs of others. Yet he had always known that the poor had no place in her heart; for in the version of 'Atossa' he gave to the Prince of Wales he had written, referring to her lack of an heir and the likelihood of the estate's going to the hated Charles Herbert:

> Cursed chance! this only could afflict her more
> If any part should wander to the poor.   (*TE*, III.ii, 162)

After her death, when the property had in fact gone to obscure relations, he amended the lines, no doubt with a certain satisfaction in the ways of Providence:

> To Heirs unknown descends th'unguarded store
> Or wanders, Heav'n-directed, to the Poor.
> (*Characters of Women*, line 149)

Like Sempill, Pope is misinformed about the exact provisions of the will;

[68] For comment on her pride, see *Gentleman's Magazine*, 13 (1743), 191–92, reprinting an essay from the *Champion* of 7 April. For Curll's previous exploitation of a single innocuous letter from Pope to the Duchess, see *Corr.*, III, 477, 481.

but although the Duchess may have distributed smaller gifts and remembrances from her deathbed, it remains a strikingly impersonal document. She is principally concerned to settle her estate on her grandson Constantine Phipps, and failing him his younger brother or her godson, Orrery's son. Another major interest is 'to make an ample amends' – a somewhat chilling emphasis – for the 'respectful behaviour' of one of her husband's illegitimate daughters. There are no bequests of purely sentimental value, and no money for the poor, although there are human touches in her annuity of £20 to her under-butler 'to help him better to support his large Family' and in an annuity of £12 and a lump sum of £50 for a foundling girl in her care. Yet what understandably caught Pope's attention was the vanity that put pomp before people, and the folly or malice of exposing her friends' letters to Hervey. It was in this mood that he took out the 'Atossa' lines that he had written during their estrangement and revised them for publication.

2

However vividly the poet's accumulated exasperation, pity and contempt fire the portrait, 'Atossa' represents more than an individual. Indeed, Pope indirectly testifies to the fact that he is drawing a type by absorbing into the character elements of his discarded attack on the Duchess of Marlborough – thus causing the acrimonious confusion over identification which bedevils eighteenth-century discussion of 'Atossa'.[69] Despite their opposite affiliations, the two widowed and therefore independent Duchesses shared a passion for politics and a vigour of feeling and expression which led contemporaries to bracket them together. Horace Walpole, for example, remarks that 'the Duchess of Buckingham was as much elated by her owing her birth to James 2^d, as the Marlborough was by the favour of his Daughter'; and he delighted in imagining the indecorous skirmish over Marlborough's hearse between the Duchess of Buckingham and 'Old Sarah, as mad and proud as herself'.[70] For Hervey too they figured as comparable highlights in the social scene: in the same letter as he gibes at the Duchess of Marlborough as 'Old Aetna' he begs his correspondent, 'Contez-moi quelque chose des extravagances de cette folle la Duchesse de Buckingham' (Ilchester, p. 99). The readiness of as careful a reader as Elizabeth Montagu to accept 'Atossa' as a just depiction of the Duchess of Marlborough is a striking indication of the tendency to respond more to the perceived type than to individual details: 'Mr Pope never met with a Woman whose Character had such strong marks & so various, so I think he has never succeeded so well in his Censures of any of our Sex'.[71]

[69] These complex matters are summarised in TE, III.ii, 166–70, and in Mack, Life, pp. 746–50.
[70] Walpole, Reminiscences, pp. 91, 95–96.
[71] Mrs Montagu's comments are quoted in full in Mack, Collected in Himself, p. 547.

Even the apocryphal allegation that Pope claimed to each that 'Atossa' was a portrait of the other emphasises their shared status as celebrated female eccentrics (*TE*, II.ii, 168–69). By stepping so decisively outside the quiet and private realm in which well-conducted ladies centred their lives they furnished contemporaries with strong defensive motives for derision; but they completed the ruin of their reputations by their failure to apply to their own behaviour the sense of the ridiculous that they were so ready to bring to bear on others.

Both in their trenchant self-expression and in their commitment to political enterprises, the Duchesses resembled Lady Mary, as Pope recognises in his linking of 'Atossa' to its companion portraits in *Characters of Women*. Having begun from the premise that the generic female character is lack of character ('Nothing so true as what you once let fall, / Most Women have no Character at all'), he dwells on fluidity, inconsistency and inner chaos as the marks of the sex, confronting in the first of the characters which illustrate his remarks a basic unease about a particular kind of inconsistency:

> *Rufa*, whose eye quick-glancing o'er the *Park*,
> Attracts each light gay meteor of a Spark,
> Agrees as ill with *Rufa* studying *Locke*
> As *Flavia*'s diamonds with her dirty smock,
> Or *Flavia*'s self in glue (her rising task)
> And issuing fragrant to an ev'ning Mask
> So morning Insects that in Muck begun,
> Shine, buzz, and fly-blow, in the setting-sun.[72]

This emphasis on filth and sensuality is part of a well-established male response to women perceived as stepping out of line; and Lady Mary, who focuses Pope's amorous hurt as well as his specific unease with intellectual women, is again crucial: 'Flavia' was her name for herself in her poem on the smallpox; and Pope later changed this first appearance of 'Flavia' to the more explicit 'Sappho' (*LM Essays*, pp. 201–4). The second appearance of the character Flavia (this time the name is not changed in later versions) as 'a Wit' with 'too much sense to Pray' also fits Lady Mary (witness the religious scepticism and thoughts of suicide expressed in her poem of 1736, 'With toilsome steps', pp. 290–91). More important than any personal allusion, however, is the implication that mental distinction in a woman is an anomaly that reduces the female soul to chaos, a theme which points forward to the colossal perversity of Atossa:

> Wise Wretch! with Pleasures too refin'd to please,
> With too much Spirit to be e'er at ease,
> With too much Quickness ever to be taught,
> With too much Thinking to have common Thought:

---

[72] Line 21 in *TE*, but here quoted in the first published text of 1735. I have followed *TE* in correcting 'fragrant' for 'flagrant' in line 26.

> Who purchase Pain with all that Joy can give,
> And die of nothing but a rage to live.   (line 95)

He is most explicit about his complicated response to this kind of woman
when he describes yet another pretender to wit, whom he cites in support of
his comparison of women to tulips (which owe their variegations to carefully
cultivated virus disease), 'Fine by defect, and delicately weak':

> 'Twas thus Calypso once each heart alarm'd,
> Aw'd without Virtue, without Beauty charm'd;
> Her Tongue bewitch'd as odly as her Eyes,
> Less Wit than Mimic, more a Wit than wise:
> Strange graces still, and stranger flights she had,
> Was just not ugly, and was just not mad;
> Yet ne'er so sure our passion to create,
> As when she touch'd the brink of all we hate.   (line 44)

In this last phrase he touches the heart of the matter: the brightness and
originality of such women was crucial to his most vivid pleasure in the sex;
but these qualities seemed always to verge on the abhorrent. Thus he is left
in life as in the poem with his soberer but stable feeling for the benign 'Contradiction' that is Patty, a contradiction in so far as she is a woman, but
atypical of her sex ('a softer Man') in so far as she has integrity (lines
269–72). To be a good woman by his rules is to be something eccentric in relation to the observed characteristics of the sex. In contrast, the pictures of the
gallery in which female wit is confronted point unmistakably forward to
Atossa, whom Pope is to present as the archetype of her sex.

He signals this by his rhetorical introduction to the portrait, 'But what are
these to great Atossa's mind?' Like a monarch in procession she occupies the
central position in the poem, and she has the longest portrait of any.[73] She
justifies this eminence by summing up her sex in a double sense. First, there
is no possible kind of female behaviour that she does not at some time display.
Second, because this variety means that she has no stable identity, she carries
her sex's distinguishing mark of having 'no Character at all' to the ultimate
extreme: 'Scarce once herself, by turns all Womankind!' (line 116). This
damaging implication is complicated, however, by the model that Pope
acknowledged in the version sent to the Prince of Wales in 1738, 'That wild
Epitome of Womankind!', which echoes Dryden's satire on a former Duke
of Buckingham, the Zimri of *Absolom and Achitophel*:

> A man so various, that he seem'd to be
> Not one, but all Mankinds Epitome.

---

[73] For the significance of this central position see Alastair Fowler, *Triumphal Forms: Structural Patterns in Elizabethan Poetry* (Cambridge, 1970), p. 87; Howard Erskine-Hill, 'Heirs of Vitruvius:
Pope and the Idea of Architecture', in *The Art of Alexander Pope*, edited by Howard Erskine-Hill
and Anne Smith (London, 1979), pp. 144–56 (p. 153).

> Stiff in Opinions, always in the wrong;
> Was every thing by starts, and nothing long.[74]

Zimri, in the context of the poem, epitomises mankind only in the first sense, that he displays by turns all the behaviour possible for men: there is no implication that in so doing he is typical of men. Indeed, Dryden presents him as an oddity, implying the desirability of the stable characters that Pope finds it very much harder to assert in *Characters of Women* than in *Characters of Men*. When the two poems are read together, his argument proves hopelessly tangled, for in the first he boasts that his theory of the ruling passion can find consistency even in women, and he includes a parsimonious old woman and a vain dying beauty among his six examples of the ruling passion's persistence in death. These female characters are no less distinct or consistent than the four men, nor do they represent either 'the Love of Pleasure' or 'the Love of Sway' which in *Characters of Women* he claims to be almost the only ruling passions found in the sex.[75] In *Characters of Women* he is preoccupied with his deep unease both at the moral flux in which he believed many women to live, and, more questionably, at what he saw as the destabilising effect of all the qualities implied by brightness for women. Suggestively, however, he was unable to reconcile this troubled perception with his calmer and more optimistic considered statements about the human race as a whole.

Like Dryden, moreover, Pope in other contexts admits that men too can be prey to inner disorders unfocused by any apparent ruling passion, a state of affairs far more disturbing than any he is prepared to contemplate at the close of *Characters of Men*. Only a few years later he writes of his own spiritual state – and in an intriguing reference touches yet again on the woman who is never far from his thinking on the destablising power of wit:

> You laugh, half Beau half Sloven if I stand,
> My Wig all powder, and all snuff my Band;
> You laugh, if Coat and Breeches strangely vary,
> White Gloves, and Linnen worthy Lady Mary!
> But when no Prelate's Lawn with Hair-shirt lin'd,
> Is half so incoherent as my Mind,
> When (each Opinion with the next at strife,
> One ebb and flow of follies all my Life)
> I plant, root up, I build, and then confound,
> Turn round to square, and square again to round;
> You never change one muscle of your face,
> You think this Madness but a common case.
>
> (*Imitations of Horace*, Epistles, I.i.161; *TE*, IV, 291)

The imagery of ebb and flow recalls a moment earlier in the poem when inconsistency has been put forward as the basis of his much-prized moderation:

---

[74] *Absolom and Achitophel*, line 545 (*Poems of Dryden*, I, 231).
[75] *Characters of Men*, lines 117, 238–47; *Characters of Women*, lines 207–10.

As drives the storm, at any door I knock,
And house with Montagne now, or now with Lock
. . .
Back to my native Moderation slide,
And win my way by yielding to the tyde.   (lines 25, 33)

Pope's identity too, for good or ill, is rooted in inconsistency; and his imagery of water in motion specifically recalls 'Atossa':

No Thought advances, but her Eddy Brain
Whisks it about, and down it goes again.
                              (*Characters of Women*, line 121)

Pope in effect admits that his own life has something in common with her chaos; indeed another irony that he directs against her seems apposite:

Who, with herself, or others, from her birth
Finds all her life one warfare upon earth:
Shines in exposing Knaves, and painting Fools,
Yet is, whate'er she hates and ridicules.   (line 117)

Just as Dustin Griffin has argued that Pope is stimulated to denounce the Sporus of *To Arbuthnot* (Lord Hervey) partly by recognising in him weaknesses he fears in himself, so it may be that in the towering rage and pride of Atossa he explores not simply the faults of a woman who had charmed, enraged and amused him by turns, but tendencies whose danger he sensed in his own inner life.[76] As early as 1717, for example, he had declared that 'the life of a Wit is a warfare upon earth'; and the phrase had proved an apt summing up of his ceaseless involvement in quarrels both literary and personal, in the course of which he had often been denigrated as more perverse than those he satirised (*Prose Works*, I, 292). There is an obvious defensive advantage in relocating dangers that are too close to home in a realm separate from oneself; and Pope alerts us to this possibility when in *Characters of Women* he adapts an aphorism from his earlier 'Stanzas: From the French of Malherbe', changing 'As children birds, so men their bliss pursue' to 'Pleasures the sex, as children Birds, pursue' (line 231). More specifically, several of the points used against women have clear applications to his own life. Women of the Atossa, Flavia/Sappho, Calypso type, for example, are easily censured for wit and display since these represent transgressions of the submissive privacy prescribed for their sex; but retirement is also the ideal that Pope acknowledges for himself in his 'Ode to Solitude' and in many of his letters.[77] He too could sometimes regard poetry and wit as meretricious distractions from the legitimate goals of his inner life.[78]

---

[76] Dustin Griffin, *Alexander Pope: The Poet in the Poems* (Princeton, 1978), pp. 182–88.
[77] See 'Observations on the Retired Life' in the index to *Corr.*
[78] *Imitations of Horace*, Epistles, I.i.17–22 (*TE*, IV, 279–81).

The Twickenham commentary shows how effectively Pope aimed his shafts at the Duchess of Buckingham's private life, a life which, although he presents it simply as the characteristic summit of female perversity, enabled him to confront from a safe vantage point the far wider and more disturbing paradox of the talented spirit that destroys its own happiness. In a final triumph for 'the sublimer Sex', Pope, ably seconded by Horace Walpole, has left 'Atossa' to posterity as the accepted history of the Duchess of Buckingham.

3

In comparison with the Duchess of Buckingham, Sarah Duchess of Marlborough provided only a late, brief and superficial episode in Pope's experience of women: indeed, had it been longer or less superficial, it could hardly have been the success it was. Quite apart from the vivacity, wit and quarrelsomeness which, to judge by his relations with Lady Mary and the Duchess of Buckingham, would have made the Duchess of Marlborough an unlikely candidate for his long-term friendship, it is surprising to find the woman who had been so aggressive a Whig making court so enthusiastically and so successfully to a poet whose natural alignment had always been with the Tories.[79]

The political gulf between the two had been very clearly shown in a correspondence which took place in 1723 between the widowed Duchess and her unsuccessful suitor, the widower Charles Seymour, Duke of Somerset.[80] The Duchess was anxious to procure a suitable inscription for the obelisk planned in memory of her husband at Blenheim, which her architect, Sir John Vanbrugh, wanted to place on the site of the house where Henry II had kept his mistress, 'because it would give an opportunity of mentioning that King whose Scenes of Love He was so much pleas'd with', although she objected that 'if there were obelisks to bee made of what all our kings have don of that sort the countrey would bee stuffed with very odd things'. Closer to her heart was the Duke's glory; and this was where Pope came into her schemes: 'I fancy Mr Pope could add something very right to this Inscription, but that His inclinations are so different from ours as to Liberty, and I don't know Him at all, but if You approve of this thought perhaps we may find out some Friend of His that will perswade Him to exert His Talent upon this occasion which I would acknowledge in the way that would be most agreeable to Him.' So just is the sense of the political division between them expressed here that it is surprising to find Somerset reporting a positive response:

Mr Pope is . . . mightyly well pleased with the Honour your Grace Designs him, &

---

79 The Duchess explains the politics of her younger days in *An Account of the Conduct of the Dowager Duchess of Marlborough* (London, 1742). The Tory case against her and the Duke is detailed by Mack, *Last and Greatest*, pp. 198–99.

80 Blenheim Papers, BL Add. MSS 61457, ff. 29, 33–35, 36, 38.

promises to doe his utmost to pleas you, tho, hee sayes, hee never did doe any thing
of this kind before; hee desires a copy of it, & of the inscriptions already done or intended to bee in & about the Place, & that if your Grace hasse any perticular or
Generall Directions he may know it, to bee his Guidance & assistance in his Performance. Hee alsoe hasse one condition to make, hee prays, that if hee should bee so
fortunatte to pleas your Grace it may not bee known hee is the author, this last condition supports your Grace's first aprehension of him, but yet, lett that bee my care, hee
shall very strongly Exert all your thoughts & Directions.

It is tempting to speculate as to whether Pope planned all along to find an
excuse which would give less offence than a direct refusal. It was certainly an
honour to be noticed by so great a lady, especially in the face of the bitter
enmity between their parties in the reign of Anne; and he may initially have
trusted to his rhetoric to subvert the more offensive of the Duchess's intentions for the 'venal song' required (*TE*, VI, 358). Whatever his reasoning,
he was soon trying to extricate himself gracefully. Although Somerset had
hoped 'to bring him to receive your Grace's instructions from your own selfe',
he soon had to announce a setback:

If I had had an opertunity last night, you should have known all that Mr Pope sayd
to mee yesterday morning, in excusing himselfe to bee the onely author of those inscriptions, intended, for Blenheim which hee thinks deserves the considerations and
abilitys of more Persons them one to doe them as they ought to bee done. When your
Grace will make mee so Happy to command my attendance I will then enter more into
the perticular reasons hee gives for it, which at present seemeth to mee not to bee
wrong, but of that you will then bee the best judge; hee offers to bee one of that number
and expresses himselfe very respectfully to bee at your Grace's Service in any thing
hee is master off.

After this no more is heard of the project, and in 1728 the Duchess accepted
an inscription by an even more surprising candidate, the former Tory
Secretary of State Bolingbroke.[81] This willingness on the Duchess's part not
to enquire too closely into the commitments of 'usefull knaves' shows a kind
of detachment which was to be crucial to her later friendship with Pope –
on his side, one suspects, as well as on hers.

His views on the Marlboroughs had apparently remained constant over the
years, for when in 1731 he came to compose Epistle IV of the *Essay on Man*
he included a type-figure of false happiness that clearly recalled the Duke (*TE*,
III.i, xiii–xiv):

> Now Europe's laurels on their brows behold,
> But stain'd with blood, or ill exchang'd for gold
> . . .

[81] David Green, *Sarah Duchess of Marlborough* (London, 1967), pp. 248–50. A new biography,
based on the Blenheim Papers as recently rearranged and catalogued by the British Library,
is being prepared by Frances Harris.

What greater bliss attends their close of life?
Some greedy minion, or imperious wife,
The trophy'd arches, story'd halls invade,
And haunt their slumbers in the pompous shade.   (IV.295, 301)

Originally there seems to have been more; for Mack argues that an expanded character of Marlborough which Pope wrote into this passage in a printed copy of 1734, as if for inclusion in the next edition, represents 'a return to the manuscript rather than a new *ad hoc* creation' (*Last and Greatest*, p. 200). This fuller version, never published (either because Pope realised that its specificity detracted from the effect of the type, or because the Duke's widow, now disillusioned with Walpole, was becoming increasingly acceptable to Pope's friends), shows that his negative feelings towards the Marlboroughs were still strong in 1734; and this conclusion is confirmed by a gibe at the Duchess's avarice in *Imitations of Horace*, Satires II.ii, published the same year.[82] Moreover, Anne Arbuthnot (daughter of Pope's friend John) told Spence that Pope had also written a full-scale attack on the Whig hero's 'imperious wife':

In the satire on women there was a character of the old Duchess of Marlborough, under the name of Orsini (wrote before Mr. Pope's being so familiar with her, and very severe).   (Spence, no. 375)

This has the ring of truth; for as Osborn notes in his commentary on the anec-dote, 'Orsini' was an unmistakable allusion to a Spanish court favourite who had, like the Duchess, fallen from favour with her Queen; but, although Spence tempts the reader to surmise that only Pope's friendship with the Duchess prevented its appearance in *Characters of Women*, he had in fact aban-doned it by the time that he came to work on 'Atossa', in the aftermath of his quarrel with the Duchess of Buckingham in 1729 (*TE*, III.ii, 40–43). It was apparently because Bolingbroke recognised lines and phrases of 'Orsini' in the manuscript of 'Atossa' discovered after Pope's death that he jumped to the erroneous conclusion that Atossa was the Duchess of Marlborough: one such clue may have been a couplet which had been printed in the Prince of Wales's copy of 'Atossa' but which was dropped from later editions as too obvious an allusion to the notorious acrimony surrounding the building of Blenheim:

Thus, while her Palace rises like a Town,
Atossa cheats the Lab'rer of a crown.   (III.ii, 166–70)

Another detail which seems to have originated in 'Orsini', but which survived into all editions of 'Atossa', is 'Full sixty years the World has been her Trade': when Pope was working on *Characters of Women* the Duchess of Marlborough was in her seventies, the Duchess of Buckingham only in her

[82] Satires, II.ii.121–22 (*TE*, IV, 63).

early fifties. Yet in the light of their contemporaries' tendency to see these extraordinary noblewomen as two of a kind it is tempting to speculate that more of 'Atossa' than a few details had pre-existed in 'Orsini':

> Who, with herself, or others, from her birth
> Finds all her life one warfare upon earth:
> Shines, in exposing Knaves, and painting Fools,
> Yet is, whate'er she hates and ridicules.
> No Thought advances, but her Eddy Brain
> Whisks it about, and down it goes again.
> Full sixty years the World has been her Trade,
> The wisest Fool much Time has ever made.
>
> (*Characters of Women*, line 117)

Presented with a type so close to contemporary perceptions of her own character, it is hardly surprising that the Duchess of Marlborough, as War-burton told Spence, was sceptical of Atossa's alleged identity; but there is no evidence to support the claims made after his death that she had paid him to suppress the character (Dearing, pp. 334–36). Whatever she knew, or thought she knew, she did not allow her knowledge to spoil their pleasure in each other's company.

With the Duchess of Marlborough Pope played out in reverse the typical drama of his attraction to witty and assertive women, for having started by disapproving of her he came in the end to enjoy a relationship of mock gallantry which enlivened the years when, as he told Bethel, 'most of those I love, are travelling out of the world, not into it' (*Corr.*, IV, 446). She was an undeniably great lady who flattered him by her approaches, one too old for him to fear courtship, and too disillusioned with her former political allies to try to recruit him for schemes he disapproved. Yet, more ominously in the light of his previous responses to women, she had acted a role at odds with the conventional estimate of her sex, an estimate that even she was prepared to endorse – at least on paper:

Women signify nothing unless they are the mistress of a Prince or a first Minister, which I would not be if I were young; and I think there are very few, if any women, that have understanding or impartiality enough to serve well those they really wish to serve.[83]

In her preface to her *Account* she admits that her desire for self-justification 'has sometimes carried me beyond the sphere, to which the Men have thought proper, and perhaps, generally speaking, with good Reason, to confine our Sex', adding, as if surprised at herself, 'I have been a kind of Author' (p. 5). To her face, Pope declares only his fascination with the qualities that make her exceptional, whimsically allowing her superiority to merely conventional people ('I don't wonder some say you are Mad, you act so contrary to the

---

[83] *The Opinions of Sarah Duchess-Dowager of Marlborough* (no place, 1788), p. 120.

rest of the World'); but behind her back he acknowledges that there is, potentially at least, a darker side (*Corr.*, IV, 359). The Duchess had after all much
in common with other assertive women whom he had met younger, known
longer and come to find intolerable.

She was, for example, directly comparable with the Duchess of Buckingham in that she too was looking for an author to polish her writings in her
own defence. When the Duchess of Marlborough lent him her materials for
the *Account* he evidently suspected that he was the chosen victim, for he claimed
to find in them 'so much Goodness, & so much Frankness of Nature, that I
should be sorry you ever thought of writing them better, or of suffering any
other to do so' (*Corr.*, IV, 258–59). Soon, however, he was able to provide
her with a suitable 'other' in the person of his impoverished friend the Roman
Catholic historian Nathaniel Hooke, who was to be made 'easy for Life' by
the proceeds of his work on the *Account*.[84] Thus Pope contemplated the
haughtiness of his friend's patroness with more detachment than he had
brought to the Duchess of Buckingham and her 'Character'; and he moralised
in relative ease on Hooke's impatience of 'the effects of a Court Life, the
Dependence upon the Great, who never do good, but with a View to make
Slaves' (*Corr.*, IV, 430). Having evaded both the question of the obelisk and
that of the political memoirs, Pope was well placed to enjoy a great lady who
would have infuriated him had he been obliged to perform the services for her
that he had attempted for the Duchess of Buckingham: the only writing he
actually did for the Duchess of Marlborough was an inscription for a bust of
a man they both admired, the Patriot hero Admiral Vernon (IV, 421). Even
as it was, his patience could be tried by 'the old Lady who has made my
Friend's Fortune', as he reveals to Ralph Allen, another new friend of his
later years, who also helped Hooke:

I have been so detain'd, where I could not without an Imputation of Ingratitude refuse
to pass some time, that it was past my power to avail myself of Lord Chesterfields offer
of carrying me halfway to you. The Lady flamed upon it, & would hear of no such
thing; her Coach should carry me any whither, but I must be left with her by that
Lord.   (IV, 420)

Quite apart from the obligation Pope felt towards the Duchess on Hooke's
account, she was an undeniably brilliant personality whose gossip of bygone
politics and flights of metaphysical speculation were rendered amusing rather
than threatening or offensive by the age, illness and disillusion that neutralised the threat of her assertiveness (IV, 405). Pope evokes her style as
raconteuse in a letter to their mutual friend Hugh Hume, Earl of Marchmont:

There are many hours I could be glad to talk to (or rather to hear) the Duchess of

---

[84] *Corr.*, IV, 383. *DNB*, Nathaniel Hooke, relates how he lost his money in the South Sea
Bubble (but compare this account of his relations with Pope and the Duchess with Dearing,
pp. 334–36). The *Account* as published contains no acknowledgement of Hooke's work.

Marlborough: so many Incidents happen, beside what Providence seems to have any regard to, in the Lives & Deaths of Great Men, that the world appears to me to be made for the Instruction of the Lesser only, & those great ones for our Laughter . . . I could listen to her with the same Veneration, & Belief in all her doctrines, as the Disciples of Socrates gave to the words of their Master, or he himself to his Daemon (for I think she too has a Devil, whom in civility we will call a Genius.)

(IV, 459)

Here again is the familiar problem of how a woman with a genius can possibly be respectable; yet Pope is now so little stirred by such scruples that it is tempting to wonder how he would have reacted to Lady Mary had they met only in old age. Although when Pope first told Swift in 1739 that 'the Duchess of Marlborow makes great Court to me, but I am too Old for her, Mind & body', he was just fifty and she in her late seventies, her strong constitution and his subjection to the lifelong and now increasingly severe symptoms of Potts' Disease effectively put them on a level (IV, 178). Her vitality gave him the genuine if superficial pleasure of re-entering the world of witty flirtation which had been his in the happy days before he had found fault with Teresa and Lady Mary, as he demonstrates when he teases his ancient beauty by pretending that her fickleness is the result of youthful diffidence:

Had you sent away Sir Timothy [Hooke?], only, to re-call another, it had been but a natural Change in a Lady (who knows her Power over her Slaves; & that how long soever she has rejected or banish'd any one, she is sure always to recover him) But to use me thus – to have won me with some difficulty, to have bow'd down all my Pride, & reduced me to take That at your hands which I never took at any other; and as soon as you had done this, to slight your conquest, & cast me away with the common Lumber of Friends in this Town – What a Girl you are? – I have a mind to be reveng'd of you, and will attribute it to your own finding yourself to want those Qualities, which are necessary to keep a Conquest, when you have made one, & are only the Effects of Years & Wisdome.   (IV, 381)

Perhaps the unprecedented submission to which Pope mysteriously refers is simply his acceptance of the overtures of one of 'the Great' whom he would never have thought of approaching for himself, and his subsequent submission, at least in part, to her autocratic manners.[85]

It is intriguing to speculate on the Duchess's motives for cultivating a poet so opposed to everything the Churchills had stood for. She was certainly lonely, sick and avid for witty conversation; but the major stimulus on her side was probably her disillusion with Walpole, which encouraged her, without much success, to look for signs of hope in the ranks of the disaffected. Like Pope, who had sneered in his 'One Thousand Seven Hundred and Forty' at the venality of 'the Patriot Race', she was far from convinced by their claim to present an alternative:

[85] The passage could also be incorporated into the allegations that Pope accepted money to suppress 'Atossa': see Sherburn's note.

Some of those people who call themselves *patriots*, are certainly very good men; – but I am very sure the whole party don't mean the same thing. They don't all go in a straight line to pursue steadily the right points; but they act coolly, sometimes one way and sometimes another, as they think it will turn most to what they secretly have in view, some to keep places they are in possession of, and others to get into them.

(*Opinions*, p. 67; compare *Corr.*, IV, 382)

Her basic views were still such as Pope could hardly have approved ('surely the Tories are the worst, and have always done the most mischief'); but despite her pervasive anxiety about the state of the nation Pope was happy to enjoy her company without pursuing such topics to the point at which they would have quarrelled over principles (*Opinions*, p. 60). Indeed, there is no more striking instance of his deliberate detachment than his failure to object to the charges of hypocrisy made in her *Account* against his revered friend the late Robert Harley, Earl of Oxford.[86] This was no doubt part of his strategic assertion that friendship, not the purging of the state, was the business of their old age:

I wish your Grace were younger, and I stronger, by twenty years; and if we could not drive out Boars, we might at least plant Vines, under which we & our Posterity might sit, & enjoy Liberty a few years longer. As it is, we can enjoy nothing but Friendship, (the next great blessing to Liberty) if any will last even so long as Our Lives.

(*Corr.*, IV, 412)

In personal as well as political matters he avoided controversy, no doubt aware how easy it was to quarrel with her: he had cleared the initial hurdle in their relationship when in 1740 he returned the infamous 'Green Book', in which she recorded the wrongs allegedly done her by her children, with the soothingly evasive sentiment that 'I wish Every Body you love, may love you, & am sorry for every one that does not' (IV, 258). Age and illness finally enabled him to disengage his feeling for a combative woman from the irritable core of his beliefs, whether about morality, politics, gender or his own self-esteem; and the pleasure that remained, though dismissed by David Green as 'a playing-at-friendship, a tongue-in-cheek diversion to enliven old age', was both genuine and durable within its shrewdly drawn limits (Green, p. 304). Pope touched her impulsive generosity: she wanted to leave him a legacy, to buy his Twickenham home for him, to give him a coach and horses, and, not least in his eyes, to help him buy a house in town which she surely understood was to be for Patty's use after his death (*Corr.*, IV, 382, 457–58). Indeed, Pope's declaration to the Duchess that 'Your New Lady, if once fixed, is unalterable, as I have experiencd for above twenty years tho' I never once did her any real Service, only for meaning it' suggests that his pleasure in seeing Patty appreciated was a crucial factor in the friendship; although Patty later told Spence that she had thought Pope over-impressed by the Duchess (Spence, no. 284). Anne Arbuthnot too, whom Pope described to

---

[86] See the Duchess's *Account*, pp. 6, 208–10; *Corr.*, IV, 389.

Swift as 'like Gay, very idle, very ingenious, and inflexibly honest', was a welcome guest to the Duchess; and the correspondence evokes a happy inter-change of visits that brightened these last years not only for the Duchess and for Pope, but also for Patty and Anne (*Corr.*, IV, 419, 432). In addition, the old lady and the prematurely aged poet brought an experienced tenderness to each other's complaints of ill health: not only did her conversation restore to him something of the brilliance of former days, but she also took it in good part if he fell asleep (IV, 465). His last letter to her, describing his sufferings in detail, concludes poignantly, 'The first 2 or 3 days, that I feel any Life return, I will pass a part of it at your Bedside; in the meantime I beg God to make Our Condition supportable to us both' (IV, 498). '

Perhaps Lady Huntingdon alone was permitted to speak to the Duchess of ultimate truth, although it is hard to conceive that even she dared to hint that the Duchess might have herself to blame for her isolation. Unfortunately, the Duchess's letters to her seem to have been heavily revised for publication; but in letters dating from the years of the Duchess's friendship with Pope, she apparently admitted to the Countess her preoccupation with the fact that 'we must die – we must converse with earth and worms', and she confessed that 'I always feel more happy and more contented after an hour's conversation with you, than I do after a whole week's round of amusement'.[87] Moreover, in words that hint at the desperation which made her seek diversion with, among others, the poet she playfully (one hopes) refers to in the same letter as 'that crooked, perverse little wretch at Twickenham', she confides, 'When alone, my reflections and recollections almost kill me, and I am forced to fly to the society of those I detest and abhor.' Although it is extremely unlikely that Pope really came into that category by the time she got to know him, the contrast between her relatively frivolous relationship with him and the more honest and comforting friendship she enjoyed with Lady Huntingdon is telling.[88]

Although the heart-to-heart honesty of the Duchess's confidences to Lady Huntingdon is closer to the usual understanding of friendship, indeed closer to Pope's own in relation to those he most deeply loved, it would be wrong to assume that his feeling for the Duchess and hers for him was a pretence. It was a cruel irony that Bolingbroke's assumption, after the poet's death, that 'Atossa' represented a betrayal of her generosity should have provided so

[87] *Countess of Huntingdon*, I, 25–26. I am grateful to Frances Harris for pointing out the discrepancy between these letters and the Duchess's usual style.
[88] The Duchess's reference in this letter to an attack to be made on Pope by Lady Huntingdon's aunt and his friend Lady Fanny Shirley probably links her remarks with his dispute with his neighbours the Shirleys over the lopping of some trees in 1740, about which he wrote the 'Epigram: On Lopping Trees in his Garden'. The quarrel cannot have been very bitter, since in 1739 Lady Fanny had presented him with a standish and pens as an exhortation to pursue his attacks on the government, for which she received his thanks in verse; and in 1743 she offered to take him and Patty to visit the Duchess in her coach (*TE*, VI, 378–80, 385–86; *Corr.*, IV, 457).

bitter an epilogue to the relationship (Mack, *Life*, pp. 746–49). She, with a realistic sense of Pope's delight in satire, had apparently asked after his death that any attacks on her or the Duke found among his papers should be destroyed; but she had not allowed her suspicions to interfere with the mutual pleasure that brightened their declining years. Ironically, this most satisfactory of Pope's relationships with women of her type was possible only when both were worn out by age and sickness, and when both had made a deliberate commitment to superficiality.

8

Victims of state

1

Less dazzling than Lady Mary or the Duchesses of Buckingham and Marlborough, yet equally bound up in politics, were two women whom Pope found more readily assimilable to the model of the unfortunate lady. One, Henrietta Howard (1688–1767), was mistress to a reigning monarch with whom she had no influence: the other, Mary Caesar (1677–1741), enjoyed high standing among the courtiers of a monarch who was never to reign. They were very different characters: Mrs Howard was so discreet, perhaps so uninterested, that she left no evidence of her political convictions beyond her personal commitment to a circle of Tory friends; while Mrs Caesar was a committed Jacobite who strove constantly to mould her friends into a community of Stuart loyalists. Both had careers interesting in themselves, and left written accounts of experiences which seemed to them particularly crucial, and both evoked Pope's deepest concern when they responded with courage to adversity. In both relationships he was able to deal to his own satisfaction with women whose lives had a marked political dimension by focusing on the personal; for, as his dealings with his two Duchesses show, he was happiest when he could pity or relieve a woman's pains and injustices, less happy when forced to respond directly to a female politician.

2

Pope met Henrietta Howard, née Hobart, later Countess of Suffolk, in about 1717, when she was a woman of the bedchamber to Caroline, Princess of Wales, and he, with Swift and Gay, was still in the habit of frequenting the court. Although Pope acted for many years on the assumption that his friends might well benefit by her influence – which was generally presumed to have increased when, in about 1718, she became the Prince's mistress – for himself he had no aspiration to the preferment traditionally dispensed by royal mistresses, since his whole attitude to the poetic vocation was formed by the knowledge that his religion debarred him from convenient sinecures. Yet he would obviously have liked the Prince and Princess to appreciate his work as well as to provide for his friends, since both actions would have

confirmed the sympathy to the Tories that many hopefully but mistakenly
deduced from the Prince's enmity to his father. In this sense, Pope's friendship with Mrs Howard had the element of calculation unavoidable in dealing
with those who are assumed to have power; yet it was also a genuine response
to a woman who revealed the nobility in suffering that was the mark of an
unfortunate lady, who welcomed his enthusiastic help with the landscaping of
her estate at Marble Hill, and who soon entered on a friendship with Patty
that he was delighted to encourage. Moreover, his personal indignation at her
sufferings was intensified by the fact that her persecutors were invariably his
political opponents: at first a husband in the pay of George I, who used his
power over her to distress the Prince and Princess of Wales at the time when
the Tories still hoped that the new reign would end their effective proscription; and later, when this hope had proved unfounded, the new King and
Queen themselves. Yet this reinforcement of his sympathy for Mrs Howard
by his own political antipathies, a response strikingly different from the frank
acceptance of female power traditionally exacted by royal mistresses, was only
one element in his concern. Indeed, it was conducive to their friendship that
owing to her paradoxical status at court she was never in a position to exert
such power; for although she was to retain her position for almost twenty
years, by the usual criteria of royal mistresses she was a failure from the first.
For her contemporaries, her most striking quality was the detached reticence
which made her friends call her 'the Swiss', a quality without which she could
not have survived; but her studied coolness had unfortunate effects, for she
seemed unable to relax into spontaneity even with her friends (*Suffolk Corr.*,
I, 64). One Margaret Bradshaw, for example, hints affectionately at frustration with Mrs Howard's reserved nature, describing her graphically as 'as
close as a stopped bottle'; and despite Pope's long and loyal attachment to her
it was at least in part from her that he drew the type of empty good breeding
that he called Cloe, 'Content to dwell in Decencies for ever'.[1] Indeed, it
seems that in the last years of his life he and Patty had nothing more to do
with her, a breach which has an obvious relevance to his decision in the year
of his death to include 'Cloe' in *Characters of Women*.

Like Lady Mary, whom Pope also met at court at about the same time, Mrs
Howard was already embroiled in marital difficulties when he met her.[2] She
had been born in 1688, the third daughter of Sir Henry Hobart, fourth
baronet, of Blickling Hall in Norfolk, who was killed in a duel in 1698.[3]
After her mother's death in 1701 she seems to have lived with Henry Howard,
fifth Earl of Suffolk, whose wife had previously been married to Henrietta's
great-grandfather. It was through this connection that in 1706 she married

[1] *Suffolk Corr.*, I, 69; *Characters of Women*, lines 157–80 (*TE*, III.ii, 63–64).
[2] This account draws on Marie P. G. Draper, *Marble Hill House and its Owners* (London, 1970),
pp. 7–10.
[3] G.E.C., *Complete Baronetage*, 5 vols. and index (Exeter, 1900–1909), I, 13.

Plate 3 Henrietta Howard, later Countess of Suffolk, by Charles Jervas, *c.* 1724.

Charles Howard, the Earl's youngest son, later to succeed as ninth Earl – although this would have seemed a remote possibility at the time of her marriage.[4] Lord Chesterfield, who was later her close friend, believed that they had married for love; and, given her orphan state, it is easy to understand the appeal of an early marriage within the circle of her adopted family.[5] However, Charles Howard seems to have had little else to recommend him: he was more than ten years her senior, by all accounts a surly and unpleasant character; and he seems to have had no income apart from his earnings as an army officer (although later, as if blaming her for his difficulties, he claimed that he 'was not a beggar when he first knew you'); so it did not bode well for the marriage when a few months afterwards he sold his troop for £700.[6] He later claimed that it was at his suggestion that his wife's capital had been placed in trust for her; but whatever his initial good intentions, he soon brought a suit in Chancery against her trustees, who included his own stepmother, in order to gain control of her entire £6,000 fortune (Add. MSS 22627, f. 40v). This action, which consumed the capital whose dividends she claimed she was only too happy to pay into his hands, suggests that his need to dominate already eclipsed any consideration of financial prudence. Not only his wife but also their landladies testified to their poverty, her lack of clothes, food and servants, and his gambling, drunkenness and violence (ff. 40–46). Their only son, Henry, later tenth Earl of Suffolk, was born in 1707; and far from providing him with a secure home they continued to live precariously, with friends or in cheap lodgings, often apart, and frequently in debt, going by false names to avoid their creditors.

It was Mrs Howard who enabled them to break out of this hopeless situation, for nothing constructive was to be looked for from her husband. She decided, apparently at the cost of separation from their son, that they should go to Hanover and ingratiate themselves with the Electress Sophia and her son George, so that they would be in a good position to solicit court employment as soon as Queen Anne should die and the Hanoverian succession take effect. The plan should perhaps call into question the later tendency to see her as a dyed-in-the-wool Tory: her father had after all been an enthusiastic supporter of the Revolution, and her marriage had connected her with an equally Whiggish family; so it was appropriate for her and her husband to seek preferment befitting their aristocratic connections at the Hanoverian

---

[4] G.E.C., *Peerage*, Charles Howard, ninth Earl of Suffolk; *Report on the Manuscripts of the Marquess of Lothian, Preserved at Blickling Hall, Norfolk*, Historical Manuscripts Commission (London, 1905), pp. 143–44 (hereafter *Lothian MSS*).

[5] *The Letters of Philip Dormer Stanhope, Earl of Chesterfield*, edited by Lord Mahon, 5 vols. (London, 1845–53), II, 440.

[6] Chesterfield, II, 440; Hervey, p. 40; G.E.C., *Peerage*; BL Add. MSS 22627, f.39. (Add. MSS 22626–27 comprise the Howard papers from which J. W. Croker compiled the heavily censored *Suffolk Corr.* Further extracts relating to the Howards' marital problems are conveniently but inaccurately transcribed in Lewis Melville, *Lady Suffolk and her Circle* (London, 1924), pp. 156–72).

court.[7] Yet Howard's malice and fecklessness were now so ingrained that, far from helping the plan forward, he took and spent the money his wife had saved for the journey; and when in a second attempt to raise the sum she refused an offer of eighteen guineas for her hair – described by Chesterfield as 'extremely fair, and remarkably fine' – he sneered at her for turning down more than it was worth.[8] It is a tribute to her persistence that they finally arrived in Hanover a few months before the Electress Sophia's death in 1714, in time for Mrs Howard to prove herself, as Horace Walpole recorded, 'extremely acceptable to the intelligent Princess Sophia', who promised her that if she lived to succeed to the throne – which she did not – she would make Mrs Howard a woman of the bedchamber.[9] It was in fact Sophia's granddaughter-in-law Caroline who, on becoming Princess of Wales later the same year, gave Mrs Howard the post. Charles Howard, although in his wife's view occupied principally in devising new means to torment her, had found time to ingratiate himself with the future George I; and in 1714 he was appointed groom of the bedchamber to the new King (Add. MSS 22627, f. 42). Because the households of the King and the Prince of Wales were initially under the same roof at St James's Palace, the Howards were able to continue to live together as man and wife; but material security did not alter their mutual antagonism.[10]

The years from about 1717 when Pope first knew Mrs Howard were for him a gregarious time, as he joined in lighthearted diversions with the Maids of Honour, with Lady Mary, with Gay, and was on friendly terms even with the Prince and Princess themselves.[11] Indeed his first reference to Mrs Howard in verse, written around the beginning of 1717, speaks more of the witty frivolity of this circle than of understanding of her character; for it is unlikely that at this time there were any grounds for the slur on her marital fidelity that he hints at in inviting three of the Princess's Maids of Honour to meet him:

> But shou'd you catch the Prudish itch,
>   And each become a coward,
> Bring sometimes with you Lady R—
>   And sometimes Mistress H—d,
> For Virgins, to keep chaste, must go
> Abroad with such as are not so.
>
> ('The Court Ballad', line 43; *TE*, VI, 182)

If the ambiguous 'so' relates to 'Virgins', this is a perfectly decorous allusion

---

[7] G.E.C., *Baronetage*, I, 13; G.E.C., *Peerage*, Earls of Suffolk.

[8] Add. MSS 22627, f. 41; Chesterfield, II, 440.

[9] *Diary of Mary, Countess Cowper, 1714–1720*, edited by Spencer Cowper, 2nd edition (London, 1865), p. 26.

[10] According to Howard, they lived together for twelve years, i.e. until 1718, although they were in fact separated by the end of 1717 (Add. MSS 22627, f. 39, and see below).

[11] *Corr.*, I, 426–29; Martin, pp. 146–48.

to two women whose married status satisfies the prime requirement in a chaperone; but if it relates to 'chaste' the implications for Mrs Howard are damaging, especially since Lady Rich was known for her marital infidelity (*LM Letters*, I, 269; II, 23). It is hard to imagine that Mrs Howard, who even after she had become the Prince of Wales's mistress, 'from the propriety and decency of her behaviour was always treated as if her virtue had never been questioned' was pleased with such wit, especially when on the brink of the crisis which was to lead to her separation from her husband and capitulation to the Prince.[12]

Tensions between the King and the Prince were already building up; and when the two households separated in December 1717 the split provided a larger frame for the breaking up of the Howard's marriage, which had previously straddled the uneasy alliance between father and son (Hatton, pp. 201–10). As early as August, Mrs Howard was struggling on paper with the nature of her obligations to a husband whom she found intolerable:

What is ye Marriage Vow? A Solemn Contract where two engage. The Woman promises Duty, affection and Obedience to the mans commands; to Guard that Share of his Honour reposed in her keeping. what is his part? to guide, to protect, to Support and Govern with mildness. have I perform'd my part? in word and deed. how has CH answer'd his? in no one Article. how guided? to Evil; how protected or suported me? left destitute wanting ye common necessarys of life; not always from misfortunes, but from Choice. what (from justice as well as from humanity nay even from his vows) ought to have been mine; employ'd to gratifie his passion's. how Govern'd? with Tyranny; with Cruelty, my life in Danger. then am not I free? all other Engagements cease to bind, if either contracting party's fail in their parts. Self preservation is ye first law of Nature, are Married Women then, ye only part of human nature y^t must not follow it? are they expected to act upon higher Principles of Relegion and honour than any other part of the Creation. if they have Superiour Sense, Superiour fortitude and reason, then why a Slave to what's inferiour to them? how vain, how trifling, is my reasoning! look round and see how few of my Sex are intyttled to govern, look on mySelf, consider myself, and I shall soon perceive it is not I that am Superiour, but as I reflect on one who is indeed, inferiour to all Mankind. how dangerous is Power in womens hands? do I know so many Miserable Wives from mans Tyranick Power as I know unhappy and rediculous Husbands only made so by too much indulgence; nay, do I know one Single instance where great tenderness if attended with submission to a woman's will is not unfortunate to the Husband either in his honour his quiet, or his fortune. then own the power justly placed however I am ye sufferer but still I must believe I am free. what do I propose from this freedom? [illegible] to hate the man I did before dispise. wou'd I proclaim my missery my shame? wou'd I revenge my wrongs? the first gives pitty or Contempt but no redress. the second not in my power without involving mySelf his honour now is mine: had I none before I married? can I devide them? how loose his, and keep my own?   (Add. MSS 22627, f. 13)

This is a unique example of Mrs Howard's private voice, freed from the restraints she imposed on herself in writing and speaking to others; and it

---

[12] Walpole, *Reminiscences*, p. 66.

shows the depth of the scruples that made it impossible for her either to share her intimate distresses with her friends during her marriage or later to glory in the prestige of being a royal mistress. She deeply distrusts her own sex and believes the authority of a husband necessary to form wifely virtue; and she is convinced, despite her grasping at the notion of her pre-marital integrity, that her moral character would be destroyed by making her husband's wrong-doing public. Thus the main thrust of her argument, that marriage is a con-tract that can be dissolved by default, is stifled by her reverence for the authority of the sex that oppresses her.

These reflections offer an insight into Mrs Howard's real situation when, in September 1717, Pope described to Patty and Teresa how he had met her on a visit to Hampton Court:

I met the Prince with all his Ladies (tho few or none of his Lords) on horseback coming from Hunting. Mrs Bellendine & Mrs Lepell took me into protection (contrary to the Laws against harbouring Papists), & gave me a Dinner, with something I liked better, an opportunity of conversation with Mrs Howard. We all agreed that the life of a Maid of Honor was of all things the most miserable; & wished that every Woman who envyd it had a Specimen of it.   (*Corr.*, I, 427)

Mrs Howard's carefully sustained composure at this time is in painful con-trast to the acrimonious disintegration of her marriage, which reached its crisis when in December the King ordered his son's household out of St James's Palace. On this occasion she proposed to leave with the Princess, but her husband was outraged at the implied slur on his marital authority; and as tempers flared she said things for which she later felt the need to apologise: 'I am sensible those words I spoke the last time I saw you, was very wrong, and impertinent; and I shall not pretend to justifie that Conversation' (Add. MSS 22627, f. 16). Her persistent sense of the respect due to him is in this context particularly striking; but his violent temper was soon to give her just the excuse she needed to evade her conviction of a husband's authority, for she records that he sent her a message 'that you wou'd have nothing more to say to me nor consider me as your Wife nor wou'd not concern y^{r}Self with what I did' (f. 18). This was a weak move on his part, since it fortified her against his repeated threats to repossess her by force (ff. 17, 39).

Mrs Howard always stressed that her loyalty to the Princess to whom she owed her employment had been a major factor in her decision to accept his dismissal, but it is unlikely that she had even envisaged at this stage that she might become the Prince's mistress, for both Hervey and Horace Walpole imply that he remained preoccupied with Miss Bellenden until she formed the attachment which led to her marriage in 1720.[13] Once Mrs Howard had grasped her chance 'to preserve my life wch from y^r former behavior when I was in y^r power I have often thought in danger and to have some little quiet

[13] Add. MSS 22626, ff. 37, 40; Hervey, pp. 40–41; Walpole, *Reminiscences*, pp. 60–62; *Suffolk Corr.*, I, 57.

during the remainder of it', she was determined not to go back; and if
Howard, for his part, really wanted her back, it can only have been for the
pleasure of tormenting her. She was probably correct in thinking that he
would not have bothered had he not been bribed with 'the poor precarious
expectation of Court favours' (Add. MSS 22627, ff. 24, 31). In effect Howard
was being used as an instrument in the King's campaign to force the wives
of gentlemen of his household to leave the Princess's service, as did four ladies
of the bedchamber in 1718; and in pursuit of his aim of making life difficult
for his daughter-in-law, he went as far as involving the Archbishop of Canter-
bury on Howard's behalf; but Mrs Howard stood firm in the declaration that
she was not a wife as the other wives were, since she had 'been directly
dismissed by you and absolutely discharged your Company, after y^r passions
having led you to say more of me than I can wth decency repeat'.[14]

Mrs Howard's success in remaining calm and resolute under a persecution
that was to last ten years owes much to friends who not only gave practical
help but also sustained her belief in the justice of her cause. The brothers
Lords Argyll and Islay, her guardian Lord Trevor and her trustee Dr
Welwood proved invaluable, and her brother-in-law the eighth Earl of Suffolk
made no secret of the fact that he preferred her to his dissolute brother.[15] Yet
as the years passed her claims to have acted blamelessly were undermined by
the fact that at some point, probably in 1718, she had entered on an
adulterous liaison with the Prince of Wales, and after her lover's accession to
the throne her husband was able to taunt her with her 'unwarrantable
Motives' for leaving him, 'and what the World will interpret the occasion of
it' (Add. MSS 22626, ff. 21, 30). Her reply that 'I know of no unwarantable
Motive that induced me to abandon you' is probably not the prevarication
it seems; for the liaison with the Prince was almost certainly the result and
not the cause of her leaving her husband (f. 22). She continued to believe that
her son would have taken her part if he had been old enough to understand;
but she was powerless to prevent her husband, with his affectation of moral
superiority, from denying her access to him and teaching him to despise her,
a lesson in which, despite the carelessness towards him which worried his
wife, he was unreservedly successful (ff. 30, 31; *Corr.*, II, 446).

Horace Walpole took a realistic view of Mrs Howard's capitulation to the
Prince:

Nor do I suppose that Love had any share in the Sacrifice She made of her virtue. She
had felt poverty, and was far from disliking power. Mr Howard was probably as little
agreeable to her as he proved worthless.   (Walpole, *Reminiscences*, p. 62)

By becoming the Prince's mistress she gained a protector who could defend
her from her husband, while to have refused would have been to risk dismissal

---

[14] Halsband, *Hervey*, p. 34; Add. MSS 22627, ff. 15, 25, 27–29, 31.
[15] *Suffolk Corr.*, I, 42; Hervey, p. 136; Draper, p. 10.

into his power. Moreover, as Walpole suggests, the idea of being in a position of power cannot have been unattractive to a woman used to being threatened and abused; and Chesterfield notes that she did not reject flattering solicitations for royal favours, despite her avowed inability to procure them (Chesterfield, II, 441). Yet it is clear that to a woman who took her duty as a wife as seriously as she had done even after years of misery, the sacrifice of her chastity was a real one, which she strove to palliate by the correctness of demeanour which allowed a friend like Chesterfield to deny that the relationship was more than platonic, and led even an unsympathetic observer like Hervey to note the strength of the appearances against her being the Prince's mistress.[16]

Yet if, as Walpole surmises, Mrs Howard thought the role of mistress would confer any kind of power, she had misread the Princess, who, in Hervey's words, 'wisely suffered one to remain in the situation whom she despised and had got the better of, for fear of making room for a successor whom he might really love, and that might get the better of her' (Hervey, p. 43). Walpole, whose father had collaborated with Caroline in the systematic manipulation of a King whom neither was willing to trust with policy, saw how formidable a figure she had been:

Her understanding was uncommonly strong; and so was her resolution; from their earliest connection She had determined to govern the King, and deserved to do so; for her submission to his will was unbounded, her sense much superior.

(Walpole, *Reminiscences*, pp. 70–71)

This was the woman who spent 'seven or eight hours tête-à-tête with the King every day', schooling herself into 'saying what she did not think, assenting to what she did not believe, and praising what she did not approve' so that she could insinuate her opinions 'as jugglers do a card, by changing it imperceptibly, and making him believe he held the same with that he first pitched upon' (Hervey, pp. 72–73). In contrast, Mrs Howard was doubly disqualified from intrigue: she was so deaf that she heard only what was directly and loudly addressed to her; and although her letters to friends show that she was by no means lacking in wit of a gentle and affectionate kind, Horace Walpole found her 'mental qualifications' to be 'by no means shining'.[17] Nor could she aim at power through beauty, for though 'well-made', 'remarkably genteel' and 'well drest with taste and simplicity', 'her face was regular and agreeable rather than beautifull'. Indeed, her very expression betrayed the unlikeliness of her becoming a powerful mistress: 'her eyes and countenance showed her character, which was grave and mild'. Hervey, always quick to note such ironies, believed that 'she had a good head and a good heart, but had to do with a man who was incapable of tasting the one or valuing the other'.

[16] Chesterfield, II, 441; Hervey, p. 41; Walpole, *Reminiscences*, 66–67.
[17] Hervey, pp. 41–42; Walpole, *Reminiscences*, p. 65.

Thus Mrs Howard found herself less exalted than trapped in an emotional tyranny which, as Hervey remarks, 'would have been insupportable to anyone whose pride was less supple, whose passions less governable, and whose sufferance less inexhaustible' (Hervey, p. 43). For Caroline, bound by duty and ambition to listen respectfully to a bore who delighted in snubbing her, to respond complaisantly to his desires for other women, and on occasion to help procure them for him, Mrs Howard took on as the years passed the vital role of being a rival whom she could torment to her heart's content; for Mrs Howard's financial and marital situation, given added piquancy by the impossibility between well-bred women of referring directly to the services to the Prince on which everything hinged, made her as safe a plaything for her tormentor as a cat with its claws drawn (Hervey, pp. 44, 72–75, 131–33). Indeed, to judge by what Lady Suffolk later told Horace Walpole, the pleasure of seeing her squirm was not the least of the bonds between Caroline and her husband:

Till she became Countess of Suffolk, she constantly dressed the Queen's head, who delighted in subjecting her to such servile offices, tho always apologizing to *her good Howard*. Often her Majesty had more compleat triumph. It happened more than once, that the King coming into the room while the Queen was dressing, has snatched off her handkerchief, and turning rudely to Mrs Howard, has cried, 'because you have an ugly neck yourself, you hide the Queen's!'   (Walpole, *Reminiscences*, p. 68)

Ironically in view of Pope's later dislike of Caroline, she lived well up to the ideal of a wife presented in *Characters of Women*, a correspondence that complicates any desire on the reader's part to accept uncritically Pope's recommendation to the powerless on how to gain power without appearing to challenge its source:

> She, who ne'er answers till a Husband cools,
> Or, if she rules him, never shows she rules;
> Charms by accepting, by submitting sways,
> Yet has her humour most, when she obeys.[18]

Pope presents this as an amiable deception; but both for Caroline herself and for the others who became pawns in her game of controlling her husband by stealth it had consequences which were far from benign. Her dogged manipulation of his sexual caprice was in effect the direct cause of her death; for knowing 'that her power over the King was not preserved independent . . . of the charms of her person', she refused to admit that she had what she angrily called 'a nasty distemper', pathetically attempting even on her deathbed to conceal her ruptured intestine from her physicians.[19] In a sense she was more a royal mistress than Mrs Howard: she used his desire for her

---

[18] *Characters of Women*, line 261 (*TE*, III.ii, 64–65). Compare the ironic account of Caroline, lines 181–98, and, among other comments, the lines on her death (*TE*, VI, 390–93).
[19] Hervey, pp. 318, 325–28; Walpole, *Reminiscences*, pp. 73–74.

for political ends; she laid aside her own real interests in reading and discussion to feign enthusiasm for his ignorant and self-satisfied talk; she pretended
not to be offended by his rudeness even when he brought tears to her eyes;
and she took pleasure in humiliating the less attractive woman who was bound
to him by duty and necessity. For her part, Mrs Howard could be seen as
more like 'some virtuous, obedient, and dutiful wife' – which according to
Hervey was how the King's enemies represented her when he finally tired of her
– than a royal mistress: far from being able to sell herself at a high price, she was
obliged to provide services which were not particularly appreciated, largely
because she needed the King's protection (Hervey, p. 118).

In this context her studiedly undemonstrative manner is more readily com-
prehensible. Although the company of friends like Caroline's Maids of
Honour and of amusing visitors like Pope, Gay and Swift seems to have provided a major compensation for the difficulties of her situation, these friends,
who either denied outright or preferred to ignore the fact that she lived at
court as a kept mistress, could not be invited to share the distresses of a role
which was never directly acknowledged. If some of them ultimately found her
disagreeably undemonstrative, it was perhaps a natural consequence of the
habitual discretion learned by having much to be discreet about. Hervey
recognised that her calmness had nothing to do with apathy, remarking that
'few people who felt so sensibly could have suffered so patiently'; and when
in old age she told Horace Walpole how Swift had come to dislike her, he was
evidently struck by the contrast between the pain she must have felt and 'her
calm dispassionate manner'.[20]

Direct evidence for Mrs Howard's early relationship with Pope is sparse,
although he certainly visited her in company with Lord Peterborough, who
was at this time addressing her in so highly wrought a style of gallantry that
she called on Gay to help her answer his letters (*Suffolk Corr.*, I, 122–74).
Indeed, Peterborough's enthusiasm apparently extended to reworking a verse
compliment that Pope had written for Lady Mary into one to Mrs Howard,
the poem usually attributed to Peterborough under the title, 'I said to my
heart' (see chapter 6.4). By about 1724, however, Mrs Howard was evidently
important enough to Pope for him to commission her portrait from Jervas.[21]
Clearly designed to form a pair with Kneller's 1720 portrait of Lady Mary
in Turkish dress, the picture shows Mrs Howard in undress style with loose
hair, leaning pensively on her arm against the background of an indeter-
minate sunset landscape (see plate 3). By choosing to complement his image
of the now less congenial Lady Mary with an image of Mrs Howard which
so clearly echoes the conventional representation of the poet musing at sunset,

---

[20] Hervey, p. 115; Walpole, *Reminiscences*, p. 52.
[21] Julius Bryant, *Mrs Howard: A Woman of Reason, 1688–1767, Catalogue of an Exhibition held
at Marble Hill House in 1988* (London, 1988), pp. 22–23, plate p. 34. The picture passed to
Patty on Pope's death, and when she died Lady Suffolk bought it at her sale and gave it to
Horace Walpole.

he prefigures the appreciation of her melancholy sensibility that was soon to
become an explicit theme in his writing about her.

Pope never repeated the kind of levity towards Mrs Howard that he had shown
in the 'Court Ballad'; for he soon found in her the integrity in adversity that was
the hallmark of his unfortunate ladies; and her project for a house and gardens at
Marble Hill, near his Twickenham home, offered a context for friendly service
and shared interests that helped to turn esteem into friendship. The land was part
of a settlement on her by the Prince in the early 1720s, intended to guarantee her
'some Provision . . . with which . . . Charles Howard shall not have any thing
to doe or intermedle', and Pope's eagerness to help was no doubt heightened by
the symbolic value of the house to a woman who had never since childhood had
a home she could call her own (Draper, p. 12). For her Pope made an exception
to the assumption of courtly corruption that was already an integral part of his
moral rhetoric. Writing to Gay in 1723 he comments:

> Mrs. *Howard* has writ you something or other in a letter which she says she repents.
> She has as much Good nature as if she had never seen any Ill nature, and had been
> bred among lambs and Turtle-doves, instead of Princes and Court-Ladies.
>
> (*Corr.*, II, 182)

Behind the moral commonplace is an obvious, and delusory, political calculation on Mrs Howard's presumed influence with a Prince who seemed likely to
reverse his father's policies. Many of the difficulties of her later career at court
arose directly from this kind of calculation; for at bottom the Prince and Princess
liked the Tories no better than George I had done; and although George II's first
choice of minister, Lord Wilmington, was a friend of Mrs Howard's, he
demonstrated his incompetence so conclusively that Caroline was soon able to
re-establish Sir Robert Walpole at the head of a system in which she, not Mrs
Howard, would exercise a woman's traditional power.[22] Henceforth Tory wits
like Swift were no longer encouraged, Pope and Gay gradually moved into open
opposition, and Mrs Howard was trapped in a position where she could do no
good to her friends and was constantly accused of forcing Tory policies on the
King.[23] Yet Pope proved his friendship to have been far more than a political
expedient by continuing to insist on her integrity when Swift, disillusioned by
her failure to procure solid favours for him, angrily denied that she had ever
meant to help him. Moreover, Pope strove constantly to promote her friendship
with Patty, even giving her the honoured place of the 'friend' he had wished for
Patty in his birthday poem of 1723 (*Corr.*, II, 235).

In verses written in about 1725 which are closely related to the letters in which
he introduced Mrs Howard to Swift, Pope sets her personality in the paradoxical context of her commitment to a way of life usually associated with
shallowness and hypocrisy:

[22] Hervey, pp. 29–39, 44; Walpole, *Reminiscences*, pp. 48–51.
[23] For Swift's relations with Mrs Howard and the court, see Irvin Ehrenpreis, *Swift: The Man, His
Works, and the Age*, 3 vols. (London, 1962–83), III, 523–25, 587–93.

I know the thing that's most uncommon;
    (Envy be silent and attend!)
I know a Reasonable Woman,
    Handsome and witty, yet a Friend.

Not warp'd by Passion, aw'd by Rumour,
    Not grave thro' Pride, or gay thro' Folly,
An equal Mixture of good Humour,
    And sensible soft Melancholy.

'Has she no Faults then (Envy says) Sir?'
    Yes she has one, I must aver:
When all the World conspires to praise her,
    The Woman's deaf, and does not hear.

                    ('On a Certain Lady at Court'; *TE*, VI, 250)

Rather like Swift in the birthday poems to Stella that pointedly discount the physical effects of age, Pope confronts Mrs Howard's embarrassing and painful disability in order to reach behind conventional praise to what he considers more important.[24] Like Patty at the close of *Characters of Women*, Mrs Howard is ideal because she is atypical. Good humour holds its expected place in the hierarchy of female virtues; and here it is balanced by the 'sensible soft Melancholy' which suggests not only that Pope finds in her the contemplative sombreness of mood that drew him to Judith Cowper and, in more complex ways, to Patty, but also that he recognised something of the darker pressures which made her good humour a feat worthy of respect. 'Melancholy' is also a key term in the sensibility to landscape that Pope shared with Patty; and pleasure in designing landscape, including the grottoes that were for Pope so symbolically fertile a feature of garden design, is central to the record of his friendship with Mrs Howard in the early 1720s.[25]

The years 1726–27, when Pope, Gay and their friends were cheered by two visits from Swift, who was at this stage charmed with his new friend Mrs Howard, seem, at least on the surface, years when she shared to the full in the Scriblerian high spirits: Pope wrote his 'Lines on Swift's Ancestors' on a sketch of Swift's memorial to his grandfather that he had sent to her; she was one of the party that sent him the versified 'Receipt to Make Soup'; Pope and Swift collaborated in 'Bounce to Fop', a satirical familiar epistle from Pope's dog to hers; and she joined in the general homage to *Gulliver's Travels* with tongue-in-cheek solemnity.[26] Yet at the same time she was suffering acute pain, probably connected with her deafness; and in June 1727 the accession of her lover as George II brought with it distressing complications.[27]

Those who mistakenly credited her with power over her lover deluged her with congratulations and solicitations; and her old social set was broken up

24 Swift, *Poems*, II, 720–22, 734–36; *Suffolk Corr.*, I, 309–12, 319–23; Hervey, pp. 41–42.
25 Martin, pp. 147–66; Mack, *Garden*, pp. 41–76.
26 *TE*, VII, 251–54, 366–71; *Swift Corr.*, III, 185–86.
27 *Corr.*, II, 446, note; Add. MSS 22627, f. 19.

by her removal to court, as Patty notes in a letter of congratulation which has remarkably little of joy about it:

Till I received a message from dear Mrs. Howard by Mr. Schutz I thought the kindest thing I could do was not to trouble you with any visits or letters, and I wish others had been as considerate of you; for the contrary (I hear) has had the effect I apprehended it would, of making you ill, which I am heartily sorry for. I have rejoiced, and shall always, at every thing that happens to your advantage, and yet I have been in the spleen ever since you left Richmond; but as I know you love to do good, I shall tell you, you have it almost as much in your power to please me now as when I was your neighbour; for every time you let me hear from you, or let me know when I may wait upon you conveniently, as I am quite out of your way, I shall look upon it as a greater mark of your kindness.

I wish you would employ me at Marble Hill, I cannot but fancy I might do you some service there. I am so very dull and I might say (which would be some excuse) not very well, and very low spirited, that I will make no apology for saying no more.

(Add. MSS 22626, f. 6)

Amidst these troublesome changes, Mrs Howard's husband, now bereft of his place at court, intensified his persecution, giving rise to a situation whose ironies were not lost on Hervey: 'She was to persuade a man who had power to torment her not to exert it, though it was his greatest pleasure; and to prevail with another who loved money and cared but little for her to part with what he did like in order to keep what he did not' (Hervey, p. 49). Part of Howard's campaign was to threaten to drag his wife bodily from the Queen's carriage; and the Queen later confessed to Hervey, standing in the upstairs room where she had granted Howard an audience, that 'as I knew him to be so brutal, as well as a little mad, and seldom quite sober', she 'did not think it impossible that he might throw me out of that window' (p. 136). It is hardly surprising that a man who could raise such apprehensions in the Queen was an object of terror to his wife.

In the midst of Mrs Howard's anxieties she received a playful letter from Swift which began, kindly – if tactlessly – enough, 'I wish I were a young Lord, and you were unmaryd' (Swift Corr., III, 230). Her reply is a moving testimony to her deliberate cultivation of good humour:

I did desire you to write me a love letter but I never did desire You to talk of marrying me. I had rather you and I were dumb as well as deaf for ever then that shou'd happen; I wou'd take your giddyness, your head-ake or any other complaint you have, to resemble you in one circumstance of life. so that I insist upon your thinking your self a very happy man, at least whenever comparasion between you and I. I likewise insist upon your taking no resolution to leave England till I see you which must be here for the most disagreeable reason in the world and the most shocking. I dare not come to you. believe nobody that talks to you of the Queen, without you are sure the Person likes both the Queen, and You. I have been a Slave twenty years without ever receiving a reason for any one thing I ever was oblig'd to do. and I have now a mind to take the pleasure once in my life of absolute power which I expect you to give me in obeying all my orders without one question why I have given them.   (III, 231)

Pope, who a few days after the accession had written lightheartedly to report
on events at Marble Hill, where he, Swift and other friends were celebrating
the birth of a calf, changed his tone completely when he learned of the state
of siege in which she was living (*Corr.*, II, 435–36, 445). This letter, with its
typical response to a deserving but unfortunate lady, shows more than any
other in this sparsely preserved correspondence the intensity of his appreciation of the 'sensible soft Melancholy' which less 'sensible' friends sometimes
failed to recognise:

Madam, – Your Letter unfeignedly gives me great disquiet. I do not only *Say* that
I have a True Concern for you: Indeed I feel it, many times, very many, when I say
it not. I wish to God any method were *soon* taken to put you out of this uneasy, tormenting, situation. You, that I know feel even to Delicacy, upon several triffling occasions,
must (I am sensible) do it to a deep degree, upon one so near & so tender to you. And
yet, as to the Last thing that troubles you, (the odd usage of Mr H. to his Son) I would
fain hope some Good may be derived from it. It may turn him to a Reflexion, that
possibly his Mother may be yet worse used than himself; & make him think of some
means to comfort himself in comforting her. If any Reasonable creature, (any creature
more reasonable than his Horses, or his Hounds, or his Country Gentlemen) were but
about him, sure some Good might arise from it?
    It is a trouble to me not to be able to see & talk to you while you stay at Kensington.
I will not fail to wait on you at London the next week, And yet God knows, when I
reflect how little use or Good I can be to you, but meerly in Wishes, it is a sort of
Vexation to me to come near you.
    As for Mrs Blount, I verily believe she thinks you would take little satisfaction, much
less comfort, in seeing her; I am otherwise very confident she would have been with
you. (tho I also remember she has talkd of getting to see you by any method she could
modestly propose, for a week past) In earnest she is so much your sincere Servant to
my certain knowledge, that she would Prefer it to all she can do here.

(II, 445)

The rhetoric of sympathy is backed up not only by the shared joke about
Patty's infuriating indecisiveness, but also by Pope's eager prosecution of Mrs
Howard's business regarding Marble Hill, which is alluded to later in the letter; yet it says something of the limits of his empathy that he goes on to allude
both to Swift and to Gay in ways that imply they are still looking to her to
make their fortunes, a train of thought uncomfortably close to the complica-
tion of distresses for which he professes such concern.

    All that saved Mrs Howard from falling into her husband's power was the
Queen's determination not to have her system of domination upset; yet to be
protected on these terms was at best the lesser of two considerable evils.
Although Howard was in a weaker position now that his royal patron was
dead, and although his wife's advisers were confident that his misbehaviour
had been so flagrant that even random accusations in a divorce suit would
have scared him into making terms, he was now looking to gain in money
what he had previously hoped in preferment (Add. MSS 22627, f. 20). It was
only when the King added £1,200 a year to Mrs Howard's allowance, which

she passed on to her husband, that he agreed to sign an undertaking to molest her no further (Hervey, pp. 49–50, 136–37). Another factor may have been an act of Parliament enabling his brother, the eighth Earl of Suffolk, to dispose of part of his estate; but whatever the details of the settlement, Gay was able to report to Swift in March 1728 that 'she is happier than I have seen her ever since you left us', an opinion that Patty shared.[28] Yet despite Mrs Howard's initial relief, the crisis had underlined her dependence on the Queen and her realisation of this led to an irritability that the Queen did not fail to improve to her own advantage. Years later, infuriated by Hervey's respect for Mrs Howard's wisdom and self-control, the Queen told him:

But, after all this matter was settled, the first thing this wise, prudent Lady Suffolk did was to pick a quarrel with me about holding a basin in the ceremony of my dressing, and to tell me, with her little fierce eyes, and cheeks as red as your coat, that positively she would not do it; to which I made her no answer then in anger, but calmly, as I would have said to a naughty child: 'Yes, my dear Howard, I am sure you will; indeed you will. Go, go! fie for shame! Go, my good Howard.; we will talk of this another time.'

About a week after, when upon maturer deliberation she had done everything about the basin that I would have her, I told her I knew we should be good friends again; but could not help adding, in a little more serious voice, that I owned of all my servants I had least expected, as I had least deserved it, such treatment from her, when she knew I had held her up at a time when it was in my power, if I had pleased, any hour of the day, to let her drop through my fingers – thus – (Hervey, p. 137)

Even now, Mrs Howard could only keep her side of the bargain with her husband as long as she was in the King's pay; so, on the rare occasions when she did lose her temper, she was easily brought back into line. The insulting offer to Gay in 1727 of the post of gentleman usher to the two-year-old Princess Louisa had already demonstrated the contempt with which her protégés were regarded; and Swift, though still superficially friendly to her, had even before George II's accession composed a character of her that impugned both her power and her sincerity, as if challenging her to do the impossible for him (Ehrenpreis, III, 590).

Pope and Patty maintained their friendship with Mrs Howard for at least ten years after the resolution of her marital problems in 1728. These were the years during which events gradually enabled her, not without pain, to extricate herself from a confinement which had become almost as irksome as her marriage had been. As early as 1729 she and Lady Hervey discussed the king's coolness towards her and her inclination to retire from court (*Suffolk Corr.*, I, 335). In addition to the King's oddly detached attitude to his chosen mistress, she had also to contend with Sir Robert Walpole, who had from the beginning shrewdly chosen to support the wife against the mistress.[29]

[28] *The Letters of John Gay*, edited by C. F. Burgess (Oxford, 1966), pp. 133–34; *Corr.*, II, 478, 491.
[29] Walpole, *Reminiscences*, pp. 50–52.

An improvement in her situation came about when in 1731 her husband became ninth Earl of Suffolk, for as Countess of Suffolk she could no longer be required to carry out the demanding and relatively menial duties of a woman of the bedchamber; and the Queen, obviously concerned not to lose the woman who had proved so convenient a mistress for her husband, offered her the choice of becoming lady of the bedchamber or mistress of the robes. She chose the latter, which gave her more time to herself and relieved her of the uncomfortable duty of performing intimate services for the Queen; and for a time she was sure that she would be happier (*Suffolk Corr.*, II, 1–2). She had the additional satisfaction of finding that her late brother-in-law, the eighth Earl of Suffolk, had expressed his approval of her by leaving his personal property not to his brother, who inherited his title, but to 'his welbeloved sister in law Henrietta Howard' (Draper, p. 38). Typically, the insulted husband threatened to contest the will (Add. MSS 22626, f. 53).

Finally, however, all such annoyances came to an end with her husband's death in September 1733 (Draper, p. 38). Caroline could no longer rely on Lady Suffolk's residual fear of her husband to keep her at court; nor, apparently, could she use the King's attachment to his mistress to the same end, for, as Hervey noted, 'they were so ill together that, when he did not neglect her, the notice he took of her was still a stronger mark of his dislike than his taking none' (Hervey, pp. 114–15). The prospect of the termination of this liaison, the focus of her life for twenty years, brought a deep sense of personal rejection as well as the hope of freedom, as her farewell letter to the King was to demonstrate; and, supported by Patty, she left in the late summer of 1734 for six weeks in Bath, as if to test, by a longer absence from court than she had ever risked before, whether the King really could do without her (Add. MSS 22626, f. 6). Yet in the letter Pope wrote to Patty as he travelled to join them there is no hint that this is anything but a simple pleasure trip:

Lady Suffolk has a strange power over me: She would not stir a days Journey either East or West for me, tho she had dying or languishing Friends on each Quarter who wanted & wishd to see her. But I am following her chariot wheels 3 days thro' Rocks & Waters, & shall be at her feet on Sunday night. I suppose she'l be at Cards, & receive me as coldly as if I were Archdeacon of the place. I hope I shall be better with you, who will doubtless have been at Mass, (whither Mr Nash at my request shall carry you constantly when I come) and in a meek & christian-like way.

(*Corr.*, III, 434–35)

Pope seems to have noticed already that Lady Suffolk could find his company less than fascinating, especially when he was too ill to be lively; and, although the letter is a piece of teasing that Patty is obviously meant to pass on to her friend, it is easy to discern in this caricature the emerging traits of a Cloe, 'So very reasonable, so unmov'd / As never yet to love, or to be lov'd.'[30] Yet

---

[30] *Suffolk Corr.*, I, 384–85; *Characters of Women*, line 165.

in view of her circumstances it is hardly surprising that the self-discipline required to maintain her discretion and good humour resulted in a composure that could strike her friends as distinctly cool.

On her return to court she found herself entirely neglected and even insulted by the King, and a fortnight later she went to the Queen and attempted to tender her resignation (Hervey, pp. 117–18). Hervey, fascinated, noted that they were together for more than an hour and a half, and some time later he took advantage of the Queen's anger at Lady Suffolk's subsequent remarriage to learn what had been said:

Upon the Queen's mentioning Lady Suffolk's behaviour to her upon her leaving the Court, I said that was a thing that had excited my curiosity more than any incident that had ever happened since my being in it; for that I could not possibly imagine that Lady Suffolk could come to Her Majesty and say: 'Madam, your husband being weary of me, I cannot possibly stay in your house or your service any longer'; and yet, if she did not say that, I could not comprehend what it was she did say. The Queen told me Lady Suffolk had not spoken her sense in those words, but that they differed little in their purport from what I imagined was impossible for her to suggest. 'Then, pray, Madam', said I, 'may I beg to know what was Your Majesty's answer?' 'I told her', said the Queen, 'that she and I were not of an age to think of these sort of things in such a romantic way, and said; "My good Lady Suffolk, you are the best servant in the world, and, as I should be most extremely sorry to lose you, pray take a week to consider of this business, and give me your word not to read any romances in that time, and then I dare say you will lay aside all thought of doing what, believe me, you will repent, and what I am very sorry for" '.   (Hervey, p. 135)

Lady Suffolk herself kept a memorandum of this conversation, and in old age she dictated from it to her nephew John Hobart, sharing with him her confession to the Queen – inconceivable to Hervey – that the King 'has been dearer to me than my own brother'.[31] She too remembered how the Queen had taunted her with adhering to 'a principle out of "Clelia" or of some other Romance' and had hypocritically assured her that if she was patient 'the King will treat you as he do's the other Lady's', adding maliciously, 'and I suppose that would satisfy you'. However, a factor which emerges only from Lady Suffolk's account is her conviction that the King's particular unpleasantness to her was the result of slander spread at court during her absence in Bath: both in her final letter to the King and in this interview with the Queen she pressed to be told what the accusations were; and although both women must have known what was at issue, neither would give the other the satisfaction of declaring what Lady Suffolk much later confided to Horace Walpole:

George 2d parted with Lady Suffolk on Princess Amelie informing Queen Caroline from Bath that the Mistress had interviews there with Ld Bolingbroke. Lady Suffolk above twenty years after protested to me that she had not once seen his Lordship there,

---

[31] *Lothian MSS*, pp. 166–70; Add. MSS 22626, ff. 8–9.

& I shoud beleive She did not, for She was a woman of truth: but her great intimacy
& connection with Pope & Swift, the intimate friends of Bolingbroke, even before the
death of George 1st, & her being the channel thro' whom that Faction had flattered
themselves they shoud gain the ear of the new King, can leave no doubt of Lady
Suffolk's support of that party. Her dearest friend to her death was Lord Chetwynd,
the known & most trusted confident of Lord Bolingbroke.

(Walpole, *Reminiscences*, p. 19)

Lady Suffolk stayed the week that the Queen demanded of her, but by
November 1734 she had composed her final letter to the King – which she
may never have sent – and had gone for good, leaving Caroline, in Hervey's
words, 'both glad and sorry' (Hervey, p. 116). As he remarked on a different
occasion, Caroline 'would not permit herself to see that the wife in her breast
was perpetually combating the Queen, and the woman revolting against the
politician' (p. 192). She had mocked Lady Suffolk for basing her conduct on
the romances which she too loved to read; and from her position of ruthless
pragmatism she had good grounds for jealousy of a woman who could afford
to act idealistically (pp. 74–75). Ironically, the only thanks she had from her
husband for the sacrifices she had made in order to try to keep him under her
safe governance was that the King – who was far from suspecting how far
his political credit depended on her surreptitious control – 'snubbed her for
it, and said: "What the devil did you mean by trying to make an old, dull,
deaf, peevish beast stay and plague me when I had so good an opportunity
of getting rid of her" '.[32]

Other observers agreed that politics was at the heart of the problem between Lady Suffolk and the King; and even if the specific allegations about her
and Bolingbroke were false, they served to focus the obvious truth that her
best friends were Tories, which could only be an irritant in a Whig court.[33]
It is ironic that no evidence whatsoever survives to show that she had any
ideological commitment to Toryism: connected by birth and marriage with
Whig families, and looking for advancement to the Hanoverian succession,
the sole political policy she can be shown to have urged on the King was that
of advancing the Tory friends who had clustered around her during the years
when their proscription had seemed likely to end with her lover's accession,
and when friends were what she needed above all. It may be that her silence
on political issues is simply another aspect of her discretion, but it seems
equally likely that what has gone down in history as her political commitment
was rather a personal commitment to her friends.

Lady Suffolk's retirement from court, though painful, inaugurated the happiest period of her life, for in 1735, in her late forties, she married George
Berkeley, brother of her old friend Lady Betty Germaine, and enjoyed for the
first time the experience of living with a man who appreciated her (*Suffolk*

---

[32] Hervey, p. 191; compare Walpole, *Reminiscences*, p. 131.
[33] Hervey, p. 117; *The Manuscripts of the Marquess Townshend*, Historical Manuscripts Commission, eleventh report, Appendix IV (London, 1887), p. 242.

Corr., II, 125). Yet, poignantly, she was never able to put the King entirely
behind her: Horace Walpole once saw her 'ready to sink' at the prospect of
playing cards at the same table as his new mistress; and she confided to him
that she was deeply moved by the King's death, the more so since he and his
mistress had passed her without recognising her only a few days previously.[34] As if she felt his scornful gaze upon her, she delayed her marriage until
he was safely out of the country, courting her new rival in Hanover. His
response to the news, in a letter to the Queen which she showed to Hervey,
was typically brutal:

'J'étois extrèmement surpris de la disposition que vous m'avez mandé que ma vieille
maîtresse a fait de son corps en mariage a ce vieux goutteux George Berkeley, et je
m'en rejouis fort. Je ne voudrois pas faire de tels présens à mes amis; et quand mes
ennemis me volent, plut à Dieu que ce soit toujours de cette facon.'

(Hervey, p. 134)

Patty was still at this point a close friend, frequently staying with the newly
married couple; and Lady Suffolk still saw and corresponded with Pope, who
was helping her with legal problems over Marble Hill as late as 1739, in which
year she gave him a much-appreciated eiderdown. Although the scarcity of
direct evidence makes judgement difficult, there are hints that she was on occasion less than rapturous about Patty and Pope, and that her friends felt no
inhibitions about criticising them to her.[35] As early as 1731 she had complained to Gay that 'I never see Mr Pope nor Mrs Blount, though I never go
to Marble Hill without sending to them: she has been ill, but was well the last
time I sent; but you know she has a peculiar pleasure in refusing her friends'
(*Suffolk Corr.*, II, 20). Pope too was to be exasperated by Patty's inability to
act decisively to fulfil her own wishes, and her perverse doubts as to whether
her friends really wanted to see her must indeed have been irritating, but this
is a particularly interesting comment insofar as it comes from a committed
friend, but one who, unlike Pope, had no vested interest in idealising Patty.

Lady Hervey, who as the celebrated Maid of Honour Molly Lepell had
been friendly both with Pope and with Lady Suffolk, had no compunction in
describing Patty to her in 1734 as 'some *proud flesh* that is grown to his *side*'
and 'will prove a *mortification*', a hostile comment which sits uneasily with the
apparent intimacy between Patty and her correspondent at that time (*Suffolk
Corr.*, II, 105–6). The Duchess of Queensberry too, though in a friendlier
manner, refers to Patty's reluctance to visit when invited: 'Nobody here is
acquainted with Mrs Blount, except myself, whom she will not be acquainted
with' (II, 112). A few months after Lady Suffolk's remarriage she herself felt
the force of Patty's awkwardness when on a visit to Stowe with her and Pope
Patty welcomed visitors who were not on visiting terms with their host (II,
143). Lady Suffolk was so embarrassed that she left the room 'under the

[34] *HW Corr.*, IX, 318; XXXIII, 313.   [35] *Corr.*, III, 474; IV, 212; Draper, p. 42.

pretence of writing'. Pope himself may have felt he deserved more consideration from her, as he apparently expressed annoyance when she failed to fetch
him for a visit so that he had to make his own way to Marble Hill. Yet these
were minor frictions at most, and in her own mind she was quite sure what
had caused the decisive breach between them. She told Horace Walpole that
Pope had asked her to return his letters – a request which complicated
several of his relationships as he began to gather his epistolary works for
publication – and she had responded by reminding him that years ago he had
confessed that he kept copies of all the letters he sent.[36] Finally she put an
end to the subject by telling him, falsely, that she had burned them, and she
believed that he never forgave her.

The way in which Horace Walpole records this seems to take for granted
that Pope and Lady Suffolk had fallen out, and the exchange raises the question of whether she herself believed that 'Cloe', first published as a fragment
in 1738 and incorporated into *Characters of Women* in 1744, was an attack on
her. If so, it is remarkable that in 1739 she still gave Pope his eiderdown; and
on the basis of such evidence Ault strongly denied that 'Cloe' related to her
(*New Light*, pp. 266–75). Yet the traits described, the plausible story of her
asking her footman to remind her to ask after Patty (whose illnesses were
usually more tedious than serious), the use of the name by which Lord Peterborough had praised her, and its introduction, in its final context in *Characters
of Women*, by Patty (who would naturally want to exempt her best friend from
Pope's denigration of the sex) make it hard to deny that the germ of the
character has to do with Lady Suffolk. Indeed, the passage could easily be
read as a warning to Patty, a revocation of Pope's earlier wish that Lady Suffolk might prove to be the 'friend' of his birthday lines (*Corr.*, II, 235):

> 'Yet Cloe sure was form'd without a spot – '
> Nature in her then err'd not, but forgot.
> 'With ev'ry pleasing, ev'ry prudent part,
> 'Say, what can Cloe want?' – she wants a Heart.
> She speaks, behaves, and acts just as she ought;
> But never, never, reach'd one gen'rous Thought.
> Virtue she finds too painful an endeavour,
> Content to dwell in Decencies for ever.
> So very reasonable, so unmov'd,
> As never yet to love, or to be lov'd.
> She, while her Lover pants upon her breast,
> Can mark the figures on an Indian chest;
> And when she sees her Friend in deep despair,
> Observes how much a Chintz exceeds Mohair.
> Forbid it Heav'n, a Favour or a Debt
> She e'er should cancel – but she may forget.
> Safe is your Secret still in Cloe's ear;

[36] Walpole, *Reminiscences*, p. 141.

> But none of Cloe's shall you ever hear.
> Of all her Dears she never slander'd one,
> But cares not if a thousand are undone.
> Would Cloe know if you're alive or dead?
> She bids her Footman put it in her head.
> Cloe is prudent – would you too be wise?
> Then never break your heart when Cloe dies.
>
> (*Characters of Women*, line 157)

Bearing in mind that Cloe became more firmly associated with Lady Suffolk when in 1744 she was presented in *Characters of Women* as someone personally known to Patty (which is true of none of the other characters), it seems likely that by then a cooling of his friendship which he had not been prepared to admit in 1739 had become irreversible. In support of this interpretation it should be remembered that Lady Suffolk and her friends were not uncritical of Pope and Patty, and that she believed he never forgave her over his letters. After 1739 neither she nor her husband is mentioned in his extant correspondence, and her place in the letters as Patty's constant companion is taken increasingly by the Catholic widow Lady Gerard.[37] Despite Lady Suffolk's proximity to Twickenham there is no record of her having joined Pope's other friends around his deathbed; and there is no evidence in Patty's papers of communication between them after Pope's death in 1744: indeed Lady Suffolk is not even mentioned in Patty's will of 1762.[38] Only a few days before Pope's death Lady Suffolk's nephew, John Hobart, had written casually to her that 'Pope and Swift for you laid by satire, and joined for once in panegyric', as if to suggest that both friendships were equally in the past (*Suffolk Corr.*, II, 205). Had she still been close to Pope it would have been inconceivable that her nephew, who with his sister had lived with her at Marble Hill since soon after her second marriage, would have alluded so lightly to a man who was well known to be dying only a few miles away (Draper, pp. 40, 42).

Yet the history of the decline in her friendship with Pope and Patty remains conjectural: in an age addicted to secret history 'the Swiss' remains decorously silent on what we would most like to know. When she turned to writing about her experiences, as she did in her reflections on marriage and her recreation of her final confrontation with the Queen, it was to clarify and justify her actions to herself, and perhaps to those close to her, not to gratify the curiosity about the secret lives of the great to which Hervey so skilfully appeals. Even in old age she exasperated her nephew by her habitual discretion: avid for news of a scandalous marriage he complains that 'You are always so properly upon the reserve that it will be difficult for me to draw any of the most interesting particulars from you' (*Lothian MSS*, p. 178). Since the most painful areas of her own life had been the stuff of scandal, it is understandable that she recoiled from discussion of such topics. She had surely

---

[37] References to Lady Gerard occur in Pope's letters from 1734 onwards: see *Corr.*, index.
[38] Spence, nos. 621–59; Blount Papers, c.65.

not become as cold and shallow as 'Cloe' seems to suggest — she certainly
belied it in her devotion to her second husband, her niece and nephew and
a great-niece who also came to live with her — but excessive reserve was both
a natural and an unfortunate limitation in a woman for whom intimacy had
meant above all becoming trapped in alien systems of power (Draper, p. 42).
Whatever Pope believed, the sensitivity she habitually cloaked in reserve remained keen; and on one occasion, when invited by Lady Huntingdon to hear
Whitefield preach, she apparently revealed just how fiery her temper was:

Mr. Whitefield's lectures to the 'brilliant circle' at Lady Huntingdon's were evidently
as faithful as they were eloquent. The well-known Countess of Suffolk found them so.
Lady Rockingham prevailed on Lady Huntingdon to admit this beauty to hear her
chaplain; he, however, knew nothing of her presence: he drew his bow at a venture,
but every arrow seemed aimed at her. She just managed to sit out the service in silence,
and when Mr. Whitefield retired she flew into a violent passion, abused Lady Huntingdon to her face, and denounced the sermon as a deliberate attack on herself. In
vain her sister-in-law, Lady Betty Germaine, tried to appease the beautiful fury, or
to explain her mistake — in vain old Lady Eleanor Bertie and the Duchess Dowager
of Ancaster, both relatives of Lady Suffolk, commanded her silence: she maintained
that she had been insulted. She was compelled, however, by her relatives who were
present, to apologize to Lady Huntingdon: having done this with a bad grace, the
mortified beauty left the place, to return no more.   (*Countess of Huntingdon*, I, 98)

Some exaggeration may be suspected; but the account seems too circumstantial and too accurately dated (soon after the deaths of Lady Suffolk's son and
second husband, which occurred in 1745 and 1746 respectively) to be entirely
without foundation, even if the author's imagination runs away with him over
the 'beauty' of a woman in her late fifties. As a precedent for such passion
there is the incident with the Queen's basin; and it would be in character for
the woman who had taken such a serious view of her duty to a delinquent
husband to be morbidly sensitive about her past. If the author of Lady
Huntingdon's life is to be believed, her resentment of this kind of religious
intrusion on her private griefs continued so strong that during her last illness
she refused to see Lady Huntingdon, thus achieving a kinship with the
Duchess of Buckingham which might have surprised those who knew only the
passive, decorous and good-humoured demeanour of her years at court.

    If, as seems almost certain, Pope had Lady Suffolk at least partly in mind
in composing 'Cloe', it is tempting to believe that he was indignant at some
failure of warmth towards Patty and himself: in particular, he had worked
hard to promote her intimacy with Patty; and there is no knowing what
advances in independence and self-confidence he had vainly hoped to see
Patty make under her tutelage. Perhaps it was true that Lady Suffolk was very
highly selective about those in whom she was prepared to take a close interest;
but it was certainly not the case that, like Cloe, she concealed mere vacancy
under her genteel charm. Rather than concealing too little, her facade

concealed too much, and much of that was bound to be centred on the painful experiences of her own life. Yet when she turned on the Queen or Lady Huntingdon she showed a passionate self-assertion which, though foreign to the unfortunate ladies whose causes Pope embraced in life, is characteristic of the Unfortunate Lady of his poem, a perception which takes us back to the problem of Lady Mary. If Lady Suffolk had regularly denounced her persecutors and asserted her belief in herself she could hardly have been characterised as a 'Cloe'; but Pope's distaste for female fire was far stronger than whatever reservations about empty politeness he had evolved from his experience of 'the Swiss'.

3

In Mary Caesar, née Freeman, with whom Pope corresponded from at least 1723, he encountered a Jacobite as idealistic as her patroness the Duchess of Buckingham and as eager to recruit him as poet to the movement, but one who nevertheless proved a durable if not an intimate friend.[39] With her husband Charles, formerly Queen Anne's treasurer of the Navy and coordinator with Count Gyllenborg of the Jacobite plot of 1716–17, she was a close associate of the Harleys and of Prior, Jervas and Swift; and Pope had in all probability known of her for a long time before their extant correspondence began in the early 1720s, when his need to recruit subscribers for his *Odyssey* gave her a unique opportunity to earn his gratitude.[40] Her efforts on his behalf were quite out of the ordinary; and in recognition of the fact he placed an asterisk by her name in the list of subscribers and expressed his gratitude in an august pun:

I took another liberty with Your own Name, which you knew nothing of, nor I dare say could have Suspected; & have made a Star of Mrs Caesar, as well as of Mrs Fermor. If any body asks you the reason of this, quote to 'em this verse of Virgil,

– Processit Caesaris astrum.[41]

Another service she performed was to introduce him to Judith Cowper, with whom he proved to have far more in common, and the richness of this correspondence highlights the relative lack of imaginative sympathy in his

[39] Robert Clutterbuck, *The History and Antiquities of the County of Hertford*, 3 vols. (London, 1815–27), III, 384; Howard Erskine-Hill, 'Under which Caesar? Pope in the Journal of Mrs Charles Caesar, 1724–1741', *Review of English Studies*, 33 (1982), 436–44. For an anonymous painting of Mary Caesar, see plate 4.
[40] Sedgwick, Charles Caesar (article by Eveline Cruickshanks); *Corr.*, II, 164.
[41] *Corr.*, II, 293. Pope quotes Virgil, *Eclogues*, IX.47 ('Caesar's star has risen') in a punning allusion to the comet taken by the Romans to be the soul of Julius Caesar ascending into the heavens, a motif which also recalls the apotheosis of Belinda's lock at the end of the *Rape*.

Plate 4   Mary Caesar (date and artist unknown)

sincere but relatively dutiful letters to Mrs Caesar (see chapter 6.4). He frequently has to apologise for not having written, and he obviously failed to visit her home at Benington in Hertfordshire as often as she would have liked: it is clear that their friendship was not one deeply based in shared sensibility.[42]

Mrs Caesar appears to far greater advantage in her own writings and in letters to her from her husband and her closest friends than in the somewhat dry memorials of what Orrery called 'a Friendship with the finest Genius of our Age'.[43] Her correspondence, which if her Jacobitism were not attested elsewhere would only occasionally raise the suspicion, shows her assiduity in cultivating acquaintances: like Pope, who collected and published his correspondence at least in part because, as he told Swift in 1730, 'the Fame I most covet indeed, is that, which must be deriv'd to me from my Friendships', she preserved correspondence as testimony to her friends' probity and the lustre which their approval reflected on her and her husband (*Corr.*, III, 101). Thomas Hay, Viscount Dupplin, wrote to him that 'It is a bold & presumptuous undertaking for any person to write to you who has seen those terrible repositories which adorn your Lady's closet'; and she evidently expected others to show similar respect to the letters she wrote them, for Pope teased her that she found anything easier to forgive than his having sketched his garden on the back of one.[44] The object of her documentary temple of memory was not simply friendship, but the solidarity of a circle devoted to the support of legitimate monarchy – which for the Caesars, after the death of Queen Anne in 1714, meant the exiled Stuart line. Jacobitism represented for them a continuation of the Tory values celebrated, for example, in a poem addressed to Mrs Caesar on a wedding anniversary by one Philogamus, perhaps before the Queen's death had brought such values into question. The poem opens with a comparison of Mrs Caesar to Venus, mother of Aeneas, an allusion steeped in implications of divinely sanctioned hereditary rule:

> With heavenly Charms thus Cytherea glow'd,
> Alike from her a Julian Issue flow'd.
>
> (Rousham Letters, A, no date)

The imperial pun was never far from the invention of those who wrote about the Caesars, especially since they prided themselves on their descent from an Elizabethan ancestor actually called Sir Julius Caesar.[45] By serving Elizabeth I as personal physician he had set a precedent to which Mrs Caesar

[42] *Corr.*, II, 262, 490; III, 39, 118, 331.

[43] Mrs Caesar's manuscript book is preserved with other family papers as BL Add. MSS 62558–59. Personal letters to her and her husband are at Rousham Park in Oxfordshire, in unpaginated volumes lettered A–H; and I am grateful to Mr and Mrs Charles Cottrell-Dormer for their kindness and hospitality in making it possible for me to study the collection. For Orrery's remark, see G, 24 February 1733.

[44] Rousham Letters, C, 26 September 1731; *Corr.*, III, 39.

[45] For this line of descent see Edmund Lodge, *The Life of Sir Julius Caesar* (London, 1827); but note that Lodge confuses Mrs Caesar's husband with his cousin of the same name (p. 71).

clung with fervour; and Philogamus was sure to please when he went on to predict her children's destinies:

> Leaders in War and Counsellours of State,
> Form'd to Support a Sinking Nations Fate:
> Resolv'd to hand, with Zeal undaunted, down
> The Public Rights with hazard of their Own,
> And guard unhurt the Mitre and the Crown.

Royal portraits played an important part in her cult of royalist virtue, with pride of place given to a group of royal portraits presented by their subjects, Elizabeth (given to Sir Julius), Anne (given to Charles Caesar) and the Old Pretender (given to Mrs Caesar), the message being reinforced by a set of hangings representing the Restoration of 1660, a silent admonition to anyone sceptical of the feasibility of James's return.[46] James's agent Anne Oglethorpe, who delivered James's picture to her in 1717, reports that 'she shows it to everybody and cannot be a moment without looking at it'; and Mrs Caesar herself describes how she led Lord Cowper through the gallery of these royal images, eliciting from him suitably loyal comments along the way (*Calendar of Stuart Papers*, IV, 554). Lord Dupplin's comments suggest that she may have used her documentary archives in a similar way; and when examined from this point of view her letter-books do reveal, if not the Jacobite commitment that it would have been dangerous to commit to writing, at least a rhetoric of virtue harmonious with a Tory and a Jacobite outlook. A letter from the Count and Countess Gyllenborg, involved with Charles Caesar in 1716 in a plot for a Jacobite restoration, is typical: Mrs Caesar sends them the Duke of Buckingham's *Works*, and they ask for pictures of the Caesars to adorn their country house in Sweden, where 'wee daily endeavour to imitate your good order neatness and pretty contrivances' (Rousham Letters, F, no date). Now although Mrs Caesar was accustomed to such praise – in another anniversary poem she is commended as 'discreet / To judge where Plenty & Profuseness meet', and she designed herself a table which so impressed Orrery that he sent a carpenter to copy it for him – the primary purpose of the letter is to express political solidarity: the cult of good housekeeping and loyalty to old ties pays implicit homage to Jacobite ideology, prizing a traditional virtue opposed to the sophistication of the usurping court and its moneyed backers.[47]

Frequently, however, Mrs Caesar did not receive the willing response to her hints that she would have liked; for, reluctant herself to admit any distinction between Tory and Jacobite, she often courted the friendship of men who, like Swift and Pope, were determined to ignore or to resist her ideological pressure. Sometimes she even tried her arts on convinced Whigs: Dupplin, for example,

---

[46] *Calendar of Stuart Papers*, IV, 301, 414–15, 547, 554; Add. MSS 62558, ff. 3, 6, 15.

[47] Rousham Letters, F, undated; G, 22 October 1733. In Mrs Caesar's scrapbook is preserved a loose sheet on which the poem is attributed to Mr Parnham (Wren Library, Trinity College, Cambridge).

though the son and grandson of Jacobites, actively supported Walpole and Newcastle; and William Capell, third Earl of Essex, returned a distinctly contrary response to the effusion of Jacobite precedents and double meanings that she sent him on the birth of his son:

I hope as you do, (in Part) that he will serve His King and His Family with the same zeal His Great Grand Father did his King. & that he will always remmember the Gratefull returns was made after the Restoration by that House for the loss of live, & Fortune. & that He is a Russel as Well as a Capell, whos Ancestor was Companion to His Grandfather Murther'd in the Tower. which I, nor I hope none of mine will ever forgett.[48]

It seems that in her letter of congratulation, probably encouraged by the fact that the Whig Earl's first wife had been Jane Hyde, Lord Cornbury's sister, Mrs Caesar had dwelt on the creation of the Earldom of Essex at the Restoration for the baby's great-grandfather, in recognition of his father's service to the royal cause, which had led to his execution and the sequestration of the family estates. Essex, on the other hand, intimates that he reads the story not in the context of a family loyalty to the House of Stuart as such, but rather to a more broadly conceived national good; for he goes on to remind Mrs Caesar of the Whig precedents in his son's genealogy: the great-grandfather thus honoured by Charles II was a Whig who died in suspicious circumstances in the Tower, where he was confined along with the child's maternal great-grandfather William Lord Russell, who was subsequently executed as a plotter against the King.[49] This is a polite but uncompromising rejoinder to a style of insinuating compliment that Mrs Caesar's correspondents had to resist or evade if they were not to be swept along with her equation of virtue with Jacobitism.

Such persistent single-mindedness could no doubt be tedious, but despite some evidence that she could be an object of affectionate fun when her back was turned, she was essentially an attractive woman, both in appearance and in personality (*Corr.*, II, 496; III, 88). To judge by a portrait apparently painted soon after her marriage, she was almost pretty enough to justify the compliment (in yet another of the anniversary tributes that mark the couple's popularity) of being addressed as 'so beautifull an Epitome of ye Creation', and being exhorted 'to multiply such glorious Abridgements of ye Universe'.[50] She preserved the affection of her husband and children to a

[48] For Dupplin, see G.E.C., *Peerage*, Thomas Hay, ninth Earl of Kinnoull. Essex's letter is preserved in Rousham Letters, G, 7 February 1733. For his connections, see G.E.C., *Peerage*, William Capell, third Earl of Essex.
[49] G.E.C., *Peerage*, Arthur Capell, first Earl of Essex; *DNB*, William Russell, styled Lord Russell. When Essex refers to the baby's 'grandfather' as 'Murther'd in the Tower' he means his great-grandfather, the first Earl, whose death was officially described as suicide.
[50] Her portrait, at Rousham, shows her in an unusual costume of red, white and blue, equipped for archery (see plate 4). For the poem, by Edward Cobden of nearby Sandon, writing on the opening of the Caesars' chapel on their wedding anniversary, 1720, see Rousham Letters, A.

touching degree; for when after nearly thirty years of married life she had to
go to Bath for her health, her husband, who even when confined in the Tower
had complained that 'yᵉ want of your company is much yᵉ worst part of my
confinement', declared that he would 'think myself as happy on the day that
restores you to me in health as I thought myself on that day that first made
you mine', while her daughter-in-law lamented the change in their home: 'I
hardly could take it for the Same place now you are from it whose Obligeing
good Temper makes everybody love you.'[51] Her husband responded to news
of her increase in spirits with a pleasure which in an age so suspicious of
female vivacity shows how successfully her vitality had been taught to run in
acceptable channels: he is glad to hear 'that you begin to get up your Spirits,
(news that perhaps would not please all Husbands) but you who know so well
how to govern them can't have too much'.[52]

In this respect it suited her very well to have married into an atmosphere
of political intrigue: during the Gyllenborg plot she had acted the part of an
innocent with such verve that one of the government searchers, impressed but
not convinced, paid her the treasured compliment that 'there are Women that
have as much Resolution as Men'; and while her husband was imprisoned
in the Tower, where their patron Lord Oxford had been confined since 1715,
she was zealous in visiting and carrying messages for the Tory prisoners, comforting her children meanwhile for their father's absence.[53] Although these
were years of great danger, they were evidently the high point of Mrs Caesar's
career, when the absence of the men – whose prerogatives she was far from
resenting – thrust her into the front line of the secret campaign. As if reluctant to relinquish the exaltation of those formative experiences, in the quieter,
less inspiring years that followed she imposed upon herself a mission almost
certainly of her own devising: as well as making her home a centre of politically edifying hospitality, she cultivated individual Tories with an almost professional thoroughness, and whenever she could she confronted them with the
texts, pictures and historical parallels which in her view made Jacobitism the
necessary consequence of political integrity.[54] She was unfailingly pleasant
and obliging, always happy to run errands for the Duchess of Buckingham,
or to retrieve from her lovingly ordered archives copies of poems that the
Duchess had lost, to chaperone Lady Masham's daughter to a party, or to 'set
round the Fire & talk Politicks' with Anne Onslow.[55] She worked hard to

[51] Rousham Letters, D, 1 February 1717; F, 13 September–1 November 1730.
[52] Rousham Letters, F, 15 April 1731.
[53] Add. MSS 62558, ff. 4, 6–7; Rousham Letters, D, 1 February 1717–11 October 1718; DNB,
  Robert Harley, first Earl of Oxford.
[54] She records in her book that she did not begin to save papers until after she had helped Prior
  by securing subscriptions to his edition of his poetry, i.e. after 1718, which coincides with the
  end of the dramatic period of her husband's career (Add. MSS 62558, f. 61).
[55] Rousham Letters, E, undated; F, undated; H, 28 September 1739. Anne Onslow was
  probably related to the Caesars' acquaintance Arthur Onslow, Speaker of the House of Commons (Add. MSS 62558, ff. 57, 67).

raise subscriptions for Mary Barber, Swift's protégé from Ireland; and Pope, who had benefited by a similar zeal, told Lord Oxford that she 'never wrote a letter but to a good purpose'.[56]

Pope's compliment was, however, less simple than might appear, for it was also a gallant excuse for a trait that many of Mrs Caesar's friends teased her about: that is, her extreme and surprising reluctance to write letters. Surrounded as she was by some of the best writers in the land, she felt herself to be so incompetent that she shrank from letting them see her efforts:

As Righting was Never my tallent, so allways avoid'd it. if possible, which made the then Lord Harly say, at Wimple to Lady Harriat and Mr Prior. we must go to meet her at Royston Races, for she is in earnest haveing rote.

But how terrifid'd when my Lady told me, they had shewn it to Mr Prior, tho she at the same time said he lik'd it. laughing told me He would not say how well, but bid me right on and never mind spelling.

Pope says sometimes too many letters in my words. Never too many words in my letters.   (Add. MS 62558, f. 55)

Orrery went so far as to complain that she was so busy apologising for her spelling that there was hardly anything else in her letters; so Prior's advice, though perhaps patronising, was also salutary.[57]

It was only two years after the beginning of her correspondence with Pope that she started work on the manuscript book from which this confession is taken. Over and above the considerable interest of the events and opinions recorded, the work, carried on intermittently over twenty years, offers the fascinating paradox of a substantial piece of writing persevered in by a woman who doubted her ability to write at all. Her book, which is divided into five sections, has its origin in the grief she felt when on 30 May 1724 she heard in a letter from her husband of the death of Robert Harley, first Earl of Oxford: 'The Loss Lord Oxford is to Mr Caesar, maks me reflect on the many changes of His Fortune, since I had the Honor and Happines of being His Wife' (Add. MSS 62558, f. 1). Ten years later she returns to her motives for beginning a task in some ways so uncongenial:

My Begining to wright was for amusement. when maloncarly on the Death of Our Great Friend Treasurr Oxford, and the Absence of Mr Caesar, to whom I had not the least thought of showing it to, Not Thinking it could haue stood the Test of His Good Understanding.   (f. 55)

Yet her author's pride soon overcame her diffidence, for the first section, completed about the end of 1724, ends with her husband's seal of approval: 'Mr Caesar was att London when I wrot this. but so Parssial when att Home. to say it should be Lay'd Upon the Table in my Picture' (f. 17). This was a compliment peculiarly apt to a woman to whom pictures meant so much: she

---

[56] Ehrenpreis, III, 635–36, 733, 759; Rousham Letters, F, 4 October 1729, undated; G, undated.

[57] Rousham Letters, G, 1 January, 20 January 1736.

took it to heart and wrote on, fortunate in a husband who, though an
accomplished writer (if a less than wholly consistent speller) himself,
appreciated her too well to be superior about the misspellings, grammatical
oddities and obscurities of narration that cloud the surface of her writing.[58]

Mrs Caesar's book reveals a complete and spontaneous absorption in her
husband's career and interests. This is most strikingly demonstrated at the
end of the third section of her book, where she writes as proudly of his
ancestors as if they had indeed been her own, listing their services to the royal
line, from James I's grandmother the Countess of Lennox, through Mary I,
Elizabeth, James I, Charles I and Charles II, down to Anne (ff. 51–54). Even
the gaps in this list suggest a pious attachment to hereditary right; so it is
disconcerting to read in other accounts of the Caesars that the family's more
recent representatives had expressed quite other views. Mrs Caesar, probably
in all sincerity, dwells exclusively on those aspects of the family she has married into which give a precedent for the ideology she shares with her husband.
For example, she commemorates his grandfather in highly selective terms:

He was Chose for the County of Heartford to serve in the Bless'd and Healing Parlia-
ment [i.e. at the Restoration]. and Mea'd Sr Henry by the King in Lord Clarendons
Lodgings in White-hall. and the same King Made His son Sr Charls at Cambridg
Who serv'd for the same County. and Was Father to Mr Caesar Treasure of the
Navy to Queen Ann of Bless'd Memory.   (f. 54)

Yet Sir Henry seems to have inclined to the Presbyterians; and of his son
Charles it is recorded that he 'declined all public employments during the
reigns of King Charles the Second and King James his brother, and affected
not the Roman party nor their proselytes'.[59] Moreover, he 'abhorred those
who would purchase the favour of their Prince with the price of the rights of
the people', a sentiment which hardly fits the Tory mould into which his
daughter-in-law seeks to recast the family history.

In fact it was her own family that could claim an impeccable Tory lineage:
her grandfather, Ralph Freeman of Aspenden, also in Hertfordshire, had
made a point of abstaining from public life under the Commonwealth and had
taken in, ostensibly as tutor to his children, the local royalist clergyman Seth
Ward, a founder member of the Royal Society, and later Bishop successively
of Exeter and of Salisbury.[60] Of her father, presumably reared under Ward's
influence, Mrs Caesar wholeheartedly approved, praising him long after his
death as 'my Good Father Who was Perfect in Every Virtue'; but his heir,
her brother Ralph Freeman, was to become her open enemy.[61] Fraternal

[58] For examples of his verse, see Add. MSS 62558 (quoted by Erskine-Hill, 'Caesar', pp. 437, 442).
[59] Sir Henry Chauncy, *The Historical Antiquities of Hertfordshire*, 2 vols. (London, 1700–1826;
reprinted Dorking, 1975), II, 346.
[60] For further details, including a contemporary drawing of her childhood home at Aspenden
Hall, see Chauncy, I, 240–51.
[61] Add. MSS 62558, f. 60; Rousham Letters, C, 17 October 1729; D, 8 May 1723; F,
23 October 1730.

feeling can hardly have been enhanced by her marriage in 1702, which united her with her family's traditional political opponents: in 1690, for example, her future father-in-law Sir Charles Caesar had been voted in for Hertford, but on appeal had lost the seat to her brother on the grounds that the Quakers who constituted Caesar's majority were not entitled to vote.[62] In 1714 the rivalry between the two families took a new turn when on the death of Queen Anne Mrs Caesar's husband was excluded from office along with his patron Lord Oxford, and decided to commit himself to the restoration of Anne's half-brother James. In contrast, despite the royalist tradition of his family, Ralph Freeman threw in his lot with the Hanoverian regime and, though a Tory, became the government candidate at elections (Sedgwick: Charles Caesar, Ralph Freeman). The death of Mrs Caesar's father in 1714 made it even easier for her to detach herself from her own family, leaving the way clear for her idealisation of her husband's (Clutterbuck, III, 384). In effect she compensated herself for her brother's betrayal of the Freemans' royalist tradition by insinuating that the family into which she had married had been similarly committed. This was the easier for her since her husband, whatever the limitations and fluctuations of his commitment to James (he seems, for example, to have stood out resolutely against schemes that he believed dangerous or impracticable; and he was suspected later in life of having been bought off by Walpole), was firmly embedded in a circle whose present ideology effectively masked other such family evolutions, notably in the case of the Harleys.[63] In this context, Jacobitism could be seen as the natural home of the old country party: Mrs Caesar's brother, a candidate kept in place by the government, still represented a kind of corruption that the last two generations of Caesars would have recognised, although it was now being practised by a Whig administration. Indeed, a century later, when Charles Caesar's Jacobite connections had been forgotten, Clutterbuck was able to classify him simply as a supporter of 'the party called the Country Party', while the democratic propagandist Thomas Oldfield admired him as a heroic opponent of 'the despotic measures of Sir Robert Walpole'.[64]

By her handling of her husband's family history Mrs Caesar demonstrates a power of shaping the past to serve a vision of the present which suggests that her book is far more than a naive transcript of experience. Despite its mixture of memoir, journal and commonplace book, it is in fact generated by a coherent vision of a group of friends formed in the golden age of Queen Anne, and the values which they embody for her. She restricts herself entirely to this theme: we would never know from her book that she was the busy mother of a family or that the Mr Freeman who figures in her pages was her brother;

[62] Thomas Hinton Burley Oldfield, *The Representative History of Great Britain and Ireland*, 6 vols. (London, 1816), IV, 25.
[63] For the Puritan alignment of earlier generations of Harleys, see *DNB*, Sir Robert, Lady Brilliana and Sir Edward Harley.
[64] Clutterbuck, II, 285; Oldfield, IV, 26.

and she has nothing to say about her life before 1705, when her husband's political career entered its first dramatic phase. She is also unconcerned to set her recollections in a clear narrative framework, for her motive in writing is evidently not so much to record or interpret events as to compose a work of devotional, even rhapsodic commemoration. She told Mary Barber that she had thoughts of writing a history of her own times; but this would necessarily have been a work in a very different style, in which incidents would have had to be ordered not by thematic and symbolic association but by chronology and causality; and if her exaggerated consciousness of her technical shortcomings and her cherishing of men's appreciation of her writing is any indication, she was probably too inhibited by the authority and implicit masculinity of historical writing even to experiment with such an ambitious undertaking.[65]

Although ostensibly a prose narrative, Mary Caesar's book is in many respects closer to the panegyrical poetry of the Renaissance, and among contemporary writers her favourites are poets whom she is able to idealise as servants of the royal cause. First among them stands Prior: according to one John Lockman, 'Prior, sweet Bard, in Anna's golden Days, / Was proud to hail Thee in his deathless Lays'; but she loved him less for his gallantry to her or for his skill in verse than for his loyalty, as she saw it, to the house of Stuart.[66] On his death she wrote:

The World Knew M[r] Prior to be a Fine Poet but M[r] Caesar who had the Pleasure of his Friendship Esteem'd that As the least Qualification he was Master of, being Superiour to all Temptation, True to His Trust. and to His Friend. His Conversation was Not more Plesant then Instructing but with Such an Air of Politness and Good Breeding, that a Stranger Entering the Roome would Not a thought Him a Poet, As Naver being Full of Him Self nor Satirocl on others. See Him a Young Man Riseing in King Williams Court. and yet even then with what Decency did He Treat His Unhappy Sovereign in His Carmon Seculare for the year 1700

> Janus, Mighty Deity
> Be Kind; and as thy Searching Eye
> Does Our Modern Story Trace
> Finding Some of Stuart's Race
> Unhappy, Pass ther Annals By:
> No Harsh Reflection Let Rememberance Raise
> Forbear to Mention what thou Canst Not Praise.
> (Add. MSS 62558, f. 8)

She was especially impressed by Prior's refusal to benefit himself by incriminating Lord Oxford in the years after 1714: she writes, 'But Alas they knew Little of that Great Man who After being the Queens Minister and Plenipotentiary in France . . . Rather Chose to Support Him Self by

[65] Rousham Letters, G, undated.
[66] John Lockman, 'To M[rs] Caesar, after seeing that Lady at Buckingham House', Add. MSS 62559, ff. 15–16. No poems by Prior to Mrs Caesar have been identified.

Publishing His Works by Subscription' (f. 3). In fact, as she later mentions
in passing, she had been a principal promotor of this subscription (f. 61).

There was some justification for her idealisation of Prior as a Jacobite poet,
for during his embassy to France he had indeed negotiated, under Oxford's
direction, with the exiled court; but in her dealings with Pope she tried to
stretch the implications of his association with the wits of the age of Anne
further than they would go. A key text for her was *Windsor Forest*, which she
read in the light of her own emotions at the time of the Peace of Utrecht:

O the Delight I Felt in hearing Her Magisty from the Thrown Deliver That Speech
Which Gave Her So Much joy.

> At Length Great Anna said – Let Discord Ceace
> She Said, the World Obey'd, and all Was Peace.   (f. 51)

She loved to recollect how 'in the Happy Day's of Queen Ann' Pope had written, also in *Windsor Forest*, that 'Rich Industry Sits Smiling on the Pleine/
And Peace and Plenty Tell a Stuart Reigns'; and it is likely that she supported
the *Odyssey* subscription at least partly because she saw Pope's translation as
asserting the centrality of her political grouping to the national culture, an
interpretation suggestively close to Oldmixon's hostile, 'This Papish Dog . . .
has translated HOMER for the use of the PRETENDER' (f. 45; Guerinot, p. 40).
Her favourable view of Pope had already been confirmed by his 'Epistle to
Robert Earl of Oxford', prefaced to the memorial edition of Parnell's *Poems on
Several Occasions* that he brought out in 1721, for she was impressed by the 'Great
Truth and Beauty' of Pope's characterisation of the man who had first raised her
husband to high office. Her conviction that the poet was of her party had been
further strengthened by his editing of the Duke of Buckingham's posthumous
Works in 1723, and especially by the danger that had briefly hovered over him
when, as she so excitedly records in her book, the government condemned them
as seditious.[67] Because of the damaging suspicion of implication in the plot,
Pope delayed publishing his proposal for the *Odyssey*, and Mrs Caesar no doubt
found in the project of recruiting subscribers privately the whiff of clandestine
politics that she loved.[68]

She marked her adoption of Pope into her inner circle by asking, in typical
fashion, for his picture; and he, conscious of her pride in having promoted
Prior's subscription, sent her the first of the flattering notes whose unusually
formal layout struck Sherburn as a deliberate concession to her 'noble
Roman' pretensions:

Madam, – It is no new thing for us Poets, to be oblig'd to Mrs Caesar: I therefore
do as you order me. I beg you to accept a vile Print which I promis'd you at Lord
Harley's. I will soon have the honour of sending you a better.

                                                                    (*Corr.*, II, 126)

---

[67] Sherburn, *Early Career*, pp. 219–28; Add. MSS 62558, ff. 11, 17; see chapter 7.2.
[68] Sherburn, *Early Career*, pp. 250–51.

At about the same time he was further integrated into her circle by her introduction of Judith Cowper, niece of her valued convert to Jacobitism, Lord
Cowper, formerly Whig Lord Chancellor.[69] A more jealous woman might
have resented the lively friendship that resulted, but Mrs Caesar, unfailingly
generous to her friends, was genuinely pleased. Meanwhile, she continued to
receive elegant and flattering notes from Pope, condoling with her on the loss
of Lord Oxford, announcing her stellification in the *Odyssey* subscribers' list
and asking her to reimburse a lady subscriber who had fallen on hard times,
but on several occasions he had to apologise for not keeping in touch more
regularly.[70]

A year of particular triumph for Mrs Caesar was 1729, when her son eloped
with an heiress worth £30,000, a welcome reversal of the tendency of money
to pass out of rather than into the family: generous payments to Jacobite
agents, losses in the South Sea Company and the expenses of Charles
Caesar's re-election in 1727 had all taken their toll.[71] Even better, Mrs
Caesar's new daughter-in-law had been Ralph Freeman's ward and the
destined bride of his son; and Lord Strafford for one had no doubt that the
elopement represented a sister's revenge: 'I dear swear she had no smale hand
in the match tho it was against the inclinations of her own Brother but such
a Brother, no one can blame her for taking care of her own son before his.'[72]
Or, to express Mrs Caesar's emotions in the cruder words of the ballad *Upon
the Royston Bargain, or Alehouse Wedding*, 'We have now sav'd our bacon.'[73] A
less cynical account comes from Grace Cole, a friend of the Caesars whose
father acted the part of best man:

Young Mr Caesar married a pretty agreeable Girl last fryday with thirty thousand
pounds Twas quite a Love story She rose from Her Guardian's Table (who was M^r
Freeman,) the moment she had dined and with Coll^l Creamers Daughter who was the
Companion of Her flight Walked near a Mile where Charles was waiting for Her with
a Coach and My Pappa (who he beg'd in friendship to go with Him) and away they
wheel'd and was married.   (Hughes, p. 197)

Lord Oxford told Pope almost immediately after the wedding that 'young mr
caesar is married to a very great Fortune & much to the satisfaction of his
Father & mother, I write this because I belive you will take notice of it to
them', and a few days later Miss Cole, having visited the Caesars in town,
was able to report that 'Mr. Pope dined with us was in quite a Gay Humour
and consequently most Charming Company'.[74] His high spirits were evidently

---

[69] *Corr.*, II, 197; *DNB*, William first Earl Cowper; Add. MSS 62588, ff. 10–12.

[70] *Corr.*, II, 235, 293, 391, 490; III, 39.

[71] For young Caesar's marriage, see *Corr.*, III, 56; Helen Sard Hughes, 'A Romantic Correspondence of the Year 1729', *Modern Philology*, 37 (1939), 187–200 (pp. 197–98). For his
parents' difficulties, see Sedgwick.

[72] Rousham Letters, C, 17 October 1729.

[73] The ballad is cited in EC, VIII, 260 and is given in full in [Steevens], *Additions*, I, 131–34.

[74] *Corr.*, III, 56; Hughes, p. 198.

expressed in a playful flattery of Miss Cole to which she confessed herself
highly susceptible.

It is clear from this episode that far from being bound to Mrs Caesar merely
by her persistence and his gratitude he was genuinely fond of her, yet it is
equally clear that when nothing occurred to bring her to his attention – such
as meeting Lord and Lady Oxford – he could let long periods elapse without
getting in touch (*Corr.*, III, 118). In 1728, for example, he twice apologised
for his silence; and in 1730 he was shocked to learn that she had 'been long
very ill' (II, 490; III, 39, 118). To judge by a note of 1729 which, rarely in
this correspondence, approaches the kind of teasing characteristic of his
letters to Teresa and Patty, he was charmed rather than irritated by her
perseverance in a friendship that might otherwise have lapsed – as his correspondence with Judith Cowper seems to have done:

Your Behavior toward me is charming, & equal to any Virtue in the most heroic
Romance. Your forgiveness extends to every point but one; you still remember the
Drawing on the back of a Certain Letter; which after all was but joyning together the
two things my heart was most full of, my Friend & my Garden.   (III, 39)

Her illness sent her in 1730 to Bath, where she received cheering news
about her married son, who had been involved in a chancery suit against
Ralph Freeman and a son of her sister Elizabeth Elwes over his wife's fortune:
'My Brother Freman & Nephew Elwes Councell insisted that ye receiver
should be continued in & that my son should be allowed but 400 pounds a
year till is wife came of age.'[75] This family discord seems to have been matter for triumph rather than grief to Mrs Caesar, whose husband concludes his
report by describing with satisfaction how her brother and nephew had
attracted 'very sever reflections from every body in Court'.

Although Mrs Caesar's book continues to pass over disasters and dwell on
small triumphs, her family's fortunes were in fact to decline from this point
onwards. Her son's new wealth, for whatever reasons, did not prove the
answer to his parents' problems; and in 1732 their property was seized for
debt (Sedgwick: Charles Caesar). Lord Egmont commented with some
perplexity that 'Mr. Caesar was always looked on as a man of sense and fortune, and had a very great employment under Queen Anne; his estate was
3,500l. a year, and he was not noted for extravagance' (Egmont, I, 213). It
was only because he was an MP that he escaped imprisonment; and when he
lost his seat in 1734 he was immediately arrested. During the increasingly difficult years after 1730 Pope sympathised with Mrs Caesar the more because
of the native good humour that not only supported her amid her troubles but
also left her as much energy for her friends as ever. In 1735, for instance, he
wrote a complimentary note about some wine he was sending which seems to
go far deeper than mere politeness:

[75] For Elizabeth Elwes, see Clutterbuck, III, 348; Rousham Letters, F, 23 October 1730.

Notwithstanding you expect I should write to you about nothing but Mum, I must disappoint you, by telling you I wish you better things than any I can send you. Your Temper is too good to need any thing to Compose your Spirits; & I only sincerely wish your Fortune and Happiness were equal to your Merit & Patience. I shall never forget your Zeal for your friends; & I am sure They owe you the same Warmth & Services, which it was always in your inclination to render them.   (*Corr.*, III, 509)

In the previous year she had urged Pope and Mrs Barber to write congratulatory poems on Lady Margaret Harley's marriage to the Duke of Portland; and although both declined, Mrs Barber's verse apology testifies to Mrs Caesar's lively participation in the family's joy.[76] A more surprising instance of her resilience had come to Swift's disillusioned ears: 'I have been told that you are a great Courtier, at least of the Queen's, for which I envy you much because I am wholly out of her favour' (*Swift Corr.*, IV, 81). In view of her unflinching loyalty to the Stuart cause, this can only have been a brave – and typically ambitious – attempt to deploy her charm in aid of her family.

Her faith that good must ultimately triumph was sustained throughout her life by meditation on her favourite poets; and at this difficult juncture she was consoled by lines from Lord Lansdowne:

A Passage thear so reliv'd my mind, I rote it in my Pockit Book. Dineing that day at Mr Gors I Show'd it Him and Mr Comptton, saying as the carecter Tallid so I hop'd Would the Event

> 'Vertue Like yours; Such Patience in Adversity
> 'And in Prosperity Such Goodnes
> 'Is Still the Care of Providence   (Add. MSS 62558, f. 39)

She remembered this when in 1736 her husband's supporters secured his re-election at their own expense, news which even she admitted 'Could Carsly gane belefe' (f. 40). To her London home came visitors to report rejoicings 'beyond Imaganation' in the Hertfordshire constituency, where the absent Charles Caesar had been chaired by proxy, the streets had been illuminated even where his opponent's interest was strongest, and 'there Ceas'd not the Cry of Caesar For Ever Even from Children that Lispted it' (ff. 40–41). Released from prison, he went to meet his constituents amid renewed celebrations: his old eminence seemed restored; and, with his wife watching intently from the sidelines, he flung himself into the campaign for war against Spain.

Of particular interest with regard to the Caesars' friendship with Pope is an anecdote in the book about the debate on the Spanish Convention in the Lords in March 1739.[77] The story, told her by Lord Shaftesbury, concerned

---

[76] *Corr.*, III, 411; Mary Barber, *Poems on Several Occasions* (London, 1734), 'To Mrs Mary Caesar, upon seeing her just after the Marriage of her friend, the Lady Margaret Harley', pp. 236–37.

[77] Mrs Caesar's account, in Add. MSS 62558, f. 78, is far from explicit and should be compared with *The Parliamentary History of England from the Earliest Period to the Year 1803*, edited by T. C. Hansard, 36 vols. (London, 1806–20), IX, 1091–1264.

Bathurst, whose waverings had already earned him her disdain, and who was pursuing a strategy of backing the Prince of Wales against the King, despite the fact that exactly these tactics had proved futile when on the accession of George II he had failed to win favour from the King whom he had so assiduously courted as Prince.[78] On that occasion, according to Mrs Caesar, Pope had written an epigram, which is preserved only in her book:

> Bathurst Lements the truth the Psalmist sings
> And finds that Princes are the Sons of Kings.   (f. 78)

Now she heard that Bathurst, having spoken against the address of thanks to the King on the Spanish Convention, and knowing that the Prince of Wales, who had never voted before, intended to divide with the opposition against his father at the end of the debate, had taken it into his head to delay this long-awaited triumph by moving for an adjournment, and had had to be dissuaded by his colleagues. She seems to have interpreted this as panic at the realisation that his association with this filial rebellion would finally put him beyond the pale with the present court, without assuring him of any more recompense in the new reign than he had previously found in a parallel situation. She remembered with glee that when his association with the Prince had first been reported, her husband had predicted its futility by capping Pope's couplet:

> Bathurst forgetts that what the Psalmist Writ
> Is strictly True, and he'll Again be Bitt.

The Caesars had been out of active Jacobite correspondence for almost ten years; but to judge from this gibe and from Mrs Caesar's enmity to Bolingbroke, the idea of an opposition really, as distinct from nominally, focused on Prince Frederick rather than James Stuart remained laughable to them.

Later that year Pope's political judgements again coincided with hers, and he sent her his *One Thousand Seven Hundred and Thirty Eight* specifically because he knew she would like what he had said about Spain. His disgust was not specifically Jacobite; but she had never been one to admit such distinctions, and he was astute enough in handling this potentially difficult friendship to play on the fact:

Mr Pope sent His Poem of 1738 beleveing as he say'd I should find sumthing to like. Soon hit On it

> – the Spaniard did a Waggish Thing
> Who Cropt Our Ears and sent them to the K—[79]

Stirred to indignation, she wrote her own comment:

---

[78] For Shaftesbury, an anti-Walpole Whig, see G.E.C., *Peerage*, Anthony Ashley Cooper, fourth Earl of Shaftesbury.

[79] *One Thousand Seven Hundred and Thirty Eight* (*Epilogue to the Satires*), I.17–18 (*TE*, IV, 298); Add. MSS 62558, f. 59.

Not so in Great Eliza's Days

Meaning it for prose, looking at it thought of Butler (one for sence the Other for rime)

(Venter'd)

The Dread of Spain, Her Subjects Prais

This day told it Pope, He Laffing say'd, Butler ment that for the Poets but you wrote Vers Without knowing it, and then make a good One for rime.

In 1739, in the midst of his renewed career as parliamentarian, Charles Caesar suffered a stroke – although his wife, dwelling in typical style on the positive side of events, mentions the fact only when celebrating his recovery:

May the 4 O happy Day, through the Permission of Providence and care of Dr Mead, Mr Caesars helth is so Restord as to venter Out which he had Not done from March the 12 when early to the House he went to show he was Not an Absente which Comfortted him, as he exprest in his Illnes, a polsy on One side of his boddy.

(Add. MSS 62558, f. 80)

He had in fact only two years to live; and his decline was further darkened later that year by the death of his close friend Thomas Wentworth, third Earl of Strafford (G.E.C., *Peerage*). Others found Strafford stupid, proud and tedious; but to the Caesars he was ever dear as negotiator of the Peace of Utrecht, loyal promoter of the Stuart cause, and last survivor of the group of Queen Anne's servants on whom the book is centred. Charles Caesar's grief was intense:

Mine alass Seems Nothing when Recollecting what I saw Mr Caesar felt when he told me he had Lost a True Friend, I soon guest the rest, that Death had now Seiz'd the Last Minister of Queen Ann his Great and Dear Friend the Earl of Strafford who had Abided with him On the Rock, no Storms nor Beatings of the waters Could Tearify them, They Stood Firm and Unshaken Seaing Some Come from, Others go to the Crown. But the most Wonderfull was a set of Men, Not haveing Strength of Mind Longer there to Abide Looking Out. Saw a Bunch of White Feathars sproting On the surface of the Glittering Water that Gentlely Play'd att the foot of the Rock, thather they Flew, They Pursu'd (What) Rebellion in Every Light. Lord Strafford when take-ing His Last leave of us, speaking of them with contempt smiling say'd to Mr Caesar, Our case is Very hard being forc'd to help support them against Sr Robert Walpole, who has not ill Nature annufe to Use Us so ill, as they would do if in Power. The Dut-chis of Buckingham still when we meet Morn the Lose of the Agreabill Polite and No-ble Earl of Strafford Ever Ready to Serve, with Head, Hand, and Heart.

(Add. MSS 62558, f. 81)

The white feathers presumably refer to the insignia of the Prince of Wales, and those who pursue them are rebels 'in Every Light' because they oppose not only 'James III' but also the King they have set up in his place. In con-trast, the steadfast Jacobites are to Mrs Caesar like the man in the parable who built his house on the rock: as so often it is death that sets her ideals in the clearest perspective, as her eulogy brings to the surface the fusion of political and personal values from which her life and writing derive their energy.

One of those on whom the Caesars looked down from their rock was Pope's beloved Bolingbroke; whereas they regarded the Duke of Wharton, whom Pope had accused of lacking 'an honest heart', as an occupant with them of the high moral ground.[80] Mrs Caesar was therefore as irritated by Pope's praise of 'All-accomplished St. JOHN' in the second dialogue of *One Thousand Seven Hundred and Thirty Eight* as she had been pleased by his irony at the expense of those who attempted to palliate Spanish piracy in the first.[81] It was apparently while she was reproaching him for his signal failure to detect Bolingbroke's falsity that they fell to discussing the text in detail and, resorting to her collection of his poetry, Pope found it incomplete:

Mising a line I had cotted. Pope looking mist the Poim. sent it with These (I saying how shall I contrive room for all your Works)

> O all-Accomplish'd Caesar! on thy Shelf
> Is room for all Popes Works – and Pope him self.

                                        (Add. MSS 62558, f. 83)

Having atoned by transferring the resented epithet to the objector, Pope was rewarded by a verse of her own composition:

> 'Tis true Great Bard Thow on my Shelf Shall Lye
> With Oxford, Cowper, Noble Strafford by.
> But for Thy Windsor a New Fabrick Raise
> And There Triumphant Sing Thy Soverain's Praise.

This rejoinder, which links Pope with the statesmen closest to her heart, marks the climax of her campaign to recruit him as laureate to 'James III' and, significantly, what she wants is another poem on the lines of her favourite *Windsor Forest*, showing that for her there is a simple continuity between the loyal Toryism of that vanished age and the Jacobitism of the present.[82] Pope can have been in no doubt of her meaning, but the necessary equivocation of her challenge gave him the opportunity yet again to be polite, grateful, but not committed. 'Mr Pope Came in Person with thanks', she records, but there was to be no Jacobite *Windsor Forest*.

This is the last reference to Pope in the book, but there is no reason to doubt that he continued to see her during the remaining eighteen months of her life, which, despite the political enthusiasm which still enlivened her writing, were to prove a time of increasing sadness leading to final collapse. Although 1740

---

[80] *Characters of Men*, line 193 (*TE*, III.ii, 31). Mrs Caesar compares Bolingbroke and Wharton in Add. MSS 62558, f. 69. See Erskine-Hill, 'Caesar', pp. 441–42.

[81] *Epilogue to the Satires*, I.17–18; II.139 (*TE*, IV, 298, 321).

[82] These lines were first satisfactorily explained by Erskine-Hill, 'Caesar', pp. 442–44. Mrs Caesar proclaims her authorship in her scrapbook, where she preserves Pope's couplet in his own hand (Wren Library, Trinity College, Cambridge, f. 4).

began well, with Charles Caesar fit enough in June to stand successfully for re-election, the year ended with the shock of their elder son's death: young Charles Caesar, a cavalry officer, was killed in action.[83] Perhaps he had decided that his father, whom in letters to his sister he calls 'ye old Emperor', was too old, sick and impoverished to care for his children, for in his will he appointed his cousin William Freeman to be his daughter's guardian (Add. MSS 62559, f. 12v). This increased his parents' grief; and an anguished letter from Charles Caesar senior to William Freeman begs to know if it is really true, and where he can see his son's will.[84] In reply, William confirms his guardianship, which he emphasises was forced on him by young Charles's 'earnest importunity', and he states that 'not knowing at this Juncture where to place the Ladys I took them for the present to my own home'.[85] The situation is perplexing: far from despising his former rival for his wife's hand, young Charles had begged him to care for her children, and the home to which they were taken was still presided over by their grandmother's now aged enemy, her brother Ralph.

Despite this family sorrow, the New Year of 1741, the last that either of the Caesars was to see, found Mrs Caesar politically buoyant as ever:

The Dutchess of Buckingham Sending to Mr Caesar and I to Pass the First day of this Year 1741 at Buckingham House it gave me Pleasure and Pain for what is so Pleasing as to be distinguisht by Those One Highly Honners. and it floung my Mind Back On the Dismall 1641 which I thus Exprest

> Sad Forty One, Britton Still feels Her Crime,
> May This, Showr Blessings On Our Suffring Isle.

Lord Quarendon thus Wrot Under.

> In Beter Times may matchless Caesar Sing
> Still live, to Love her Country – and her King   (f. 84)

Finally, however, on 2 April 1741, Charles himself died, leaving his property in trust for his creditors, and to his wife nothing but arrears of rent and 'such plate, jewels and other personal property as may be free from debt' (Clutterbuck, II, 285). She had maintained her faith in the ultimate vindication of her cause amidst political and domestic adversities to an extent that had impressed Pope and which must still impress the reader of her book, but now she found herself overwhelmed by a grief in proportion to her love, and during the few months she survived him her friends found it impossible to comfort her. The Duchess of Buckingham invited her to Buckingham House, where she met John Lockman, who, comparing the widowed state in which he found her to the early radiance celebrated by Prior, urged her to imitate the courage shown by the Duchess in the same predicament. He conveniently forgets how much younger and richer the Duchess had been, and he does not confront the fact that while the Duchess, confident in her Stuart blood, had

---

[83] Add. MSS 62558, f. 82; Lodge, p. ii.   [84] Rousham Letters, C, 16 December 1740.
[85] Rousham Letters, C, 18 December 1740.

found a reason for living in a personal political crusade, Mrs Caesar had
always experienced this consuming passion of her life vicariously, through her
husband's role as conspirator and parliamentarian. With the love of her life
she had also lost her primary relation to the world. Yet Lockman suggests that
her grief was perverse in its excess:

> But I first saw Thee, sadly sunk with Fears;
> To healing Comfort deaf, & wild in Tears;
> With Sights reflecting on the Turns of Fate;
> Comparing this; with thy once blissful State.
>
> (Add. MSS 62559, f. 15)

Orrery wrote to her in June to urge on her the reflection that such misery
could only grieve her husband:

> How can he deem his State compleatly blest
> While Sorrow reigns unconquer'd in your Breast?
> Nor is your Heart of ev'ry joy bereft,
> Your Daughters live, and still one Caesar's left.
>
> (Mrs Caesar's Scrapbook, f. 8)

It was true that she still had three children: although Julius's suitability to
represent the family may be doubted (he never married and was the constant
companion of the actress Peg Woffington), her daughters were both affectionate, although their dowerless condition (neither ever married) can only
have afflicted their mother.[86] There is something less than wholly sympathetic in Orrery's response to her loss, and it emerges still less pleasantly
in his remark to Swift in July that 'Mrs *Caesar* is still all tears and lamenta-
tions, although she may certainly be numered *inter felices, sua si bona norint*'
(*Swift Corr.*, V, 206).

Nothing remains of Pope's response to this final disaster in the life of his
faithful if fussy friend and benefactor, but it is inconceivable that he was
anything but a genuine sharer in her distress. Her collection of letters lapses
at the end of 1740, the narrative of her book ends in February 1741, and after
her husband's death almost the only sign of her old activities is the gluing of
Orrery's consolatory poem into her scrapbook; so it is not surprising that no
record of condolences from Pope has come down to us. His importance to her,
however, was as clear to Lockman, who met her for the first time as a widow,
as her pride in her friendship with the long-dead Prior. Whatever her importance to Pope – and it is unlikely ever to have been less than that of a
courageous, resilient and altruistic, if politically misguided woman – he was
an essential part of her public image, and if he had not actually written a
poem on her bereavement, Lockman suggests that she could profit by
rereading the *Essay on Man*:

---

[86] Lodge, pp. 63–64; Janet Dunbar, *Peg Woffington and her World* (London, 1968): for references
to Colonel Julius Caesar, see index.

Read thy lov'd Pope, his heavenly Numbers show,
What We to God, Our Selves, & Country owe:
Show that the Mind, in Glory shines Confest,
If most it Struggles, when tis most opprest.
Weigh well this Truth: thy Will to Heaven resign,
Then Prior's Fair Heroine must yield to Mine.
(Add. MSS 62559, f. 16)

Mrs Caesar died in July 1741 and her book ensures that when she is remembered at all she is remembered as she would have wished, as the friend of politicians and poets. Yet it is clear that Prior was supreme in her affection, partly for political reasons and partly because for her a poet had above all to be a gentleman. Complimentary as he had always been, Pope had seldom gratified her with the Jacobite equivocations she yearned for, and she could not share his views on the relative merits of Wharton and Bolingbroke. Moreover, there may be more than passing amusement at the vanity of authors, typified by Pope, in her allusion to the format of his *Works* of 1717: 'Now take sanction with Pope, who Introduces his Works with the Complements made him, therefore it Aught by me to be done, to Palliate my perceverence' (f. 56). In contrast with her beloved Prior, who was 'Naver . . . Full of Him Self or Satirocl on others', and who published his works only to save himself from being forced to incriminate Lord Oxford, Pope was perhaps too much the career poet, as he was certainly too little the potential laureate of James III, to touch the deeper springs of her devotion (ff. 3, 8–9).

The very last entry in her book confirms the narrowly Tory fervour with which she clung to the sententiae of her favourite authors. Under the newspaper cutting of Charles Caesar's death she has written with a shaking hand:

Alas, there's no Expression
To tell my Dismal Woe   (Add. MSS 62558, f. 86)

At the bottom of the page she has added, 'DB page 189'; and if, following her hint, we turn to this page in Volume I of *The Works of John Sheffield Duke of Buckingham*, we find the conclusion of his lament 'On the Loss of an only Son, Robert Marquis of Normanby', the four-year-old grandson of James II whose effigy still stands in Westminster Abbey (see plate 2). The Duke had written, 'Alas, there's no Expression / Can tell a Parent's Woe!', and Mrs Caesar, by echoing this cry, gives a final and telling testimony to the union of politics, poetry and friendship that gave meaning to her life. Although her political interests had often made her path intersect with Pope's, her partisan intensity left her at cross purposes with a poet of far wider sympathies: for his part he had taken the measure of her preoccupations and had learned to deal with her safely and to a large extent sincerely within the limits they entailed.

9

'I love you upon unalterable Principles'

1

However much Pope valued other female friends, once his mother was dead and Lady Mary had become his enemy it was unquestionably Patty who meant most to him. In his last extant letter to her, written a few weeks before his death, he declares, 'I love you upon unalterable Principles', yet, in the words of a pioneer of women's intellectual history, she seems 'a very commonplace personage to rank as a poet's friend'.[1] For Pope, however, this was a crucial part of her enduring appeal. Tenderness and sensibility, even when they made her infuriatingly helpless, were conventional female traits, her favourite romances were accepted if not approved as satisfying a distinctively feminine taste; her writing, more deferential than her sister's to the conventions of spelling and punctuation, entirely lacks her flair; and her most striking deviations from fashionable feminity were in the direction of economy, rural retirement and healthy exercise, the kind of nonconformity that grave men invariably commended.

Pope's letters reveal a great deal of his feeling for Patty, but of her feeling for him we have very little direct evidence. Only one substantial exchange of letters survives: it is impossible to be sure whether she was his friend or his mistress, and some, influenced by Warburton, a late arrival in Pope's circle who saw older intimates as rivals, have accepted his portrayal of her as a cold-hearted parasite.[2] She may herself have been responsible for the evident destruction of the bulk of her letters to him: after 1725 nothing survives to match the spontaneous delight that had made her write in 1714 to her 'Dear Creature', 'my charming Mr Pope', and even this is recorded only because Pope quoted it in his reply (*Corr.*, I, 268). What is beyond doubt is his

[1] *Corr.*, IV, 511; Myra Reynolds, *The Learned Lady in England, 1650–1760* (Gloucester, Mass., 1960; reprint of edition of 1920), p. 350.

[2] For their exchange of letters, see *Corr.*, IV, 462–63. For Warburton, see chapter 9.5; Mack, *Life*, pp. 736–45, 765–68; Ruffhead, pp. 405, 548; *TE*, III.ii, 46–47; VI, 65, 126–27; S. G. Wright, 'Ruffhead's Life of Pope', *Bodleian Quarterly Record*, VII (1932–34), 12. For subsequent elaborations of Warburton's insinuations, see Johnson, III, 190; William Lisle Bowles, *The Works of Alexander Pope Esq.*, 10 vols. (London, 1806), I, lxix–lxxi, cxvii–cxviii, cxxviii–cxxxi; II, 340; *Lessons in Criticism to William Roscoe . . . with Further Lessons in Criticism to a Quarterly Reviewer* (London, 1826), pp. 136–46; *A Final Appeal to the Literary Public relative to Pope* (London, 1825), pp. ix–x; *The Works of Lord Byron*, 17 vols. (London 1832–33), VI, 388–89.

Plate 5   Martha Blount in later life (pastel drawing, artist unknown)

commitment to her, nurtured by her congenial sensibility, which provided a permanent context for the fantastic, descriptive aspect of his creativity that he had earlier shared with Lady Mary and Judith Cowper. Patty was an avid reader of romances, and in her patient sufferings at the hands of her family could almost be seen as a romantic heroine herself. Moreover, she possessed a sensibility to landscape that Mrs Radcliffe's heroines would have respected: as early as 1717 she had apparently given him the 'romantic description' of Stonor which he repaid by his sombre and meditative description of his moonlight ride to Oxford, and for the rest of his life he sent her descriptions of landscape – notably of the Gothic ruins of Netley Abbey, which he visited in 1734 – strikingly different from the mainstream of his correspondence, conceived for her 'Romantic Taste' but by no means peripheral to his creativity.[3] In a letter from Stowe in 1739 he shows the deep association between his love for her and the contemplation of landscape when he speaks of 'Envying myself the delight of it, because not partaken by You, who would *See* it better, & consequently enjoy it more', and he takes his leave to go back into the garden with the words, 'I'm going into the Elyzian Fields, where I shall meet your Idaea' (IV, 185–86).

2

Patty's home life presented a painful contrast with her aspirations to rural peace, for by trying to be loyal both to Pope and to her sister she exposed herself to constant harassment. It was in 1725 that Pope first confided to Caryll his belief that Teresa was spreading scandal about his relation to Patty (see chapter 5.4). A few weeks later he lamented Patty's inability to treat the gossip with the contempt it deserved: 'your injured kinswoman is made too uneasy by these sinister practices, which especially from one's own family are terrible' (*Corr.*, II, 361). In June 1729 he further accused Teresa of unkindness to her mother ('I found her all in tears, and the family in an uproar'); in July he hinted that the scandal of her behaviour would soon break out openly, although 'I know too much to imagine my discovery wou'd do any good, or operate upon her shame'; and later the same month he spoke out more plainly:

In a word the faults are two. That lady has an intrigue of half a year's standing (as the servants of the family, who were turn'd away once a month last winter, loudly declared, and as both the town and country begin to talk very largely of) with a married man. The circumstances of this I care not to tell, but (if those nearest her say true) they are very flagrant.

   The other fault is outrage to the mother beyond all imagination, – striking, pinching, pulling about the house, and abusing to the utmost shamefulness. This also is so public that the streets in London and villages in the country have frequently rung

[3] *Corr.*, I, 429–30; Martin, pp. 190–93; and see chapter 5.4.

of it. – those of the family declaring it everywhere, and some of them parting immediately upon these violences, which are frequent on all trifles, and repeated.

(III, 36, 38, 40–41)

The Carylls, to whom Teresa 'had behaved so admirably' – perhaps by making no secret of her boredom with life at Ladyholt – that Patty did not expect her to be invited again, took the news very seriously; and Mrs Caryll, Patty's godmother, proposed sounding her mother by letter, to give her the chance to confide her ill usage at Teresa's hands (III, 45). Pope considered success unlikely, for reasons which give a sinister impression of Teresa's hold over her mother and sister; and his fears were borne out by the event, for when Mrs Blount received the letter, 'she carried it to the eldest daughter, whom I saw in the afternoon looking very much out of humour' (III, 47). Teresa appears as a tyrant whom no one dares resist; and Pope's belief that she would go so far as to gatecrash a family council from which her insulted kinsman had purposely excluded her begins to sound plausible:

As I before told you when you pressed me concerning the daughter's wicked usage of the mother, so I tell you concerning the other article, that what I said was extorted merely for force of what I knew was due to so long a friendship as yours (when you so strongly desired it), and little from any hope I could entertain of amendment on their parts. Therefore it is my sentiment rather to conceal what one cannot remedy, if you find upon tryal made by Mrs C—'s letter to the poor mother (which I perfectly approve) she should not open herself fairly or dare to show that she feels and would redress her grievance. It is much my opinion that she will not, from several instances I've heard and some I've seen. Nay, I've known her, when she could not exclude one daughter from the censure, speak of both as unkind to her, &c., tho' the fact was wholly transacted when the younger was absent.

I think it not impossible if the mother should consent to visit you (with whatever intent) that the elder uninvited would go with her. It is exactly what I've known her do to many people. At least if both the mother and younger daughter comply with your invitation (which I dare say the first will not without leave from or concert with the elder) I durst lay a wager she would not stay behind, so that I really think there's little hope on that side.

On the other I find your — takes your letter as only a kind civility, which you have been some years hindered from offering because *the whole family might* (indeed very well) *be too much for any civil society*; and that since her sister had behaved so admirably to you, it gave you a handle to ask them separately, which she concludes you would always willingly have done to herself. If, therefore, you took occasion just to tell her you had a particular reason for inviting her, from some reports (in general) that touched the credit of her family, and someway endangered her own by being linked with them and censured with them, it might have more effect. Otherwise she knows what a weary life she must lead if she does it by herself, when she returns to them. And as I told you, she has so much weak tenderness for them, in thinking her residence with them conceals and softens many things, that she is in danger of sacrificing every regard of her self, – health, character, interest, &c., to that alone.

The trial is all you can make: there is no serving any people without their co-operation. Your part is good and generous; but in truth that's all. I expect little success, but from some accident which by ruining one may save the other.

(III, 44)

Patty never gave in to Pope's pressure to leave her family; and he resisted with equal firmness Caryll's hints that he might best help her by marrying her. In November 1729 he denied '*tendresse* or any partiality', adding:

I know myself too well at this age to indulge any, and her too well, to expect as much folly in my favour as she shows for her relations. For truly that would be more than one poor woman could supply.   (III, 70)

Despite the genuine doubt of his attractiveness to Patty that seems to underlie Pope's joking self-deprecation, Caryll persisted, and later the same month Pope wrote him a long declaration. It seems that there had been gossip to the effect that he wanted to separate Patty from her family so that he could set her up as his mistress, but if this had been the case, it is hard to see, in the light of their lifelong commitment to each other, why he would have persisted in refusing the financial help that would have enabled them to marry:

I receive a secret contentment in knowing I have no tie to your God-daughter but a good opinion, which has grown into a friendship with experience that she deserved it. Upon my word, were it otherwise I would not conceal it from you, especially after the proofs you have given how generously you would act in her favour; and I farther hope, if it were more than I tell you that actuated me in that regard, that it would be only a spur to you, to animate, not a let to retard your design. But truth is truth. you will never see me change my condition any more than my religion, because I think them both best for me.

This day I went to see her, and she shewed me your letter . . . I find her weakness (from the good principle that the junction of her fortune or income with theirs prevents the approach of the ruin of their affairs) operates too unreasonably in her own pre-judice. I have often represented to her of late since this conduct of her sister's, that even in that View she had better lend them the equivalent and live out of the danger and discredit.

It is not possible to tell you too much of the sense she seems to have, and certainly has, of your kindness, and how right she takes it of you. But it is one thing to take it right *of you*, and an other, to take it right *to herself*. I fear she will not do the latter, unless you join with me in a strong representation of the matter. Above, all, conceal that you had the hint from me; she'll think, very naturally, it is from a servant maid whom Lady B. sent them, and who left 'em partly on account of this scandalous affair last winter. She will be willing I dare say to soften the thing to you, as she did to me till I had a too strong conviction of it from others, and even then I'm satisfied she con-cealed all she could from me; but you are sensible her tenderness here must ruin her own character, while she hopes to cover her sister's, which made me want a coadjutor in so important an advice. It is certain moreover she'll be the last woman, whom anybody will speak to, on what so nearly concerns her family, therefore liable most to suffer, and know of the scandal least, even when it becomes public. Of course she must be thought privy or consenting to it.   (III, 74–75)

Meanwhile, Pope tried to help Patty with two pressing problems, her health and her finances. In the latter respect she was theoretically no worse off than her mother and sister, whose allowances were also often in arrears; but Patty was not extravagant, and Swift for one felt that her economies simply went to swell Teresa's wardrobe (*Swift Corr.*, IV, 79, 172). Patty's excuse that her mother needed her financial support exasperated Pope, who was similarly convinced that Mrs Blount 'lives much more upon her, if she live in common' (*Corr.*, III, 47). His favoured solution would have been to force Michael to pay Patty regularly, and to persuade her to live alone on the whole of her income; and although the latter proved beyond his powers, he did succeed in applying some useful pressure to Michael through the legal efforts of his friend Fortescue (III, 455). It may also have been through Pope that Patty came to bank with Slingsby Bethel, and it was certainly through her friendship with Pope that she came to rely on George Arbuthnot as her legal advisor.[4]

Pope found himself less able to help Patty in respect of her health, as he told Caryll in 1729:

My mother and I have both been ill and your god-daughter, I think, is never well two days together. There is no wonder in all three: old age in the first, a crazy constitution in the second and uneasiness and ill-usage in the third, may equally induce and continue diseases.   (*Corr.*, III, 61)

Patty, as Pope had already made clear to Caryll, was far from being a woman to make light of her sister's flirtations. Moreover, she was a constant witness to Teresa's unkindness to their mother, perhaps the object of similar unkindness herself, and certainly the butt of her mother's undiscriminating criticism. Mrs Martha Blount senior, ironically called 'Pax', was the only person Pope ever sincerely wished to see confined in a convent: chronically unable to assert herself, she had in effect ceded authority to Teresa; and, like typical victims of domestic violence, mother and younger daughter strove to conceal their sufferings, unable even fully to desire separation from Teresa's dominating personality (III, 41). To judge by Pope's account of Patty's illness following the death of their mutual friend Gay in 1732, her ill health, which Pope frequently associates with the family conflict that she refused to confront openly, was a characteristic outlet for emotional distress, and thus, perhaps, a condition of the ostensible cheerfulness under strain that he praised in her:

Your god-daughter has been very ill. I no sooner saw the death of my old friend Mr Gay, whom I attended in his last sickness (it was but three days), but she fell very ill, partly occasioned by the shóck his death gave her. Dr Arbuthnot who attended the one was constantly with the other, and has had better success with her. During her whole

---

4 For Slingsby Bethel see *Corr.*, IV, 87, 365; Blount Letters, I, 163. For correspondence with George Arbuthnot and William Murray, see Blount Letters, I, 123–56. It seems significant that while Patty's nephew Michael dealt principally with Catholic professionals (the banker Anthony Wright; the physician Dr Jernegan; the lawyer Mannock Strickland, Michael's father-in-law), Patty's equivalent dealings were with Protestant friends of Pope (F. G. Hilton Price, *A Handbook of London Bankers* (London, 1876), pp. 140–41; J. C. H. Aveling, *The Handle and the Axe* (London, 1976), p. 272; Blount Papers, c. 65).

illness, the worthy family set open all their windows and doors, and washed the house and stairs to her very door twice in the week in which her recovery depended upon being kept warm; and had a constant clatter of doors, and removal of chairs, and all the noise that could possibly be made, while she was ordered to be composed to rest by the Doctor. This I saw and heard, and so did Dr. Arbuthnot, who very humorously asked, as he went up and down their stairs, why they did not sell and make money of their sashes, and leave the windows quite open?   (III, 337)

Apart from seeing that she was attended by Dr Arbuthnot, Pope could do little except encourage her to spend as much time as possible away from home. His promotion of her friendship with Mrs Howard was only one of his efforts in this direction; yet, as he confided to their mutual friend Hugh Bethel in 1737, 'it seems to little purpose, that she parts for the Summer months with what is the Bane of her Quiet, (which is the Health of the Soul, & upon which the health of the Body so much depends,) when she constantly returns in the Winter, to the same House, the same Company, and the same Uneasiness' (IV, 85).

3

As might be expected, letters between the Blount women in London and Michael in Winchester, where he had moved in order to economise by letting Mapledurham, give a different picture. Teresa certainly shows the bent of her character in her long and gossipy letters to her brother; yet despite the special affinity that seems to have bound her to Michael, the purpose of her letters is almost invariably to demand money. She and Patty, far from living in declared enmity, are shown in her letters conferring on the details of Michael's various proposals, and one letter begins with Patty acting as amanuensis, continues with Teresa taking up the pen, and concludes in Patty's hand (Blount Papers, c. 63). Their mother also harps on the financial theme, upbraiding Michael in 1737 with a poignant 'I cannot waite, as you young ons may; I have no time to loose'; and in 1739 she calls him 'unkind', reproaching him that 'you must know that I want itt before due'.

Despite such irritations they seem from their letters an affectionate family. Both sisters visit Michael; and, whilst he retails in his letters to Teresa the kind of social chat that she demanded, he is also on good terms with Lady Gerard, who was gradually to replace Lady Suffolk as Patty's constant companion. It is unfortunate that nothing is preserved of any but the briefest and most formal correspondence between Patty and Michael, but it seems likely that he had less in common with her than with Teresa. Like Teresa, he was apparently addicted to town pleasures, for in 1726 one of his companions was killed in a brawl after an all-night party which began at the theatre and ended in a tavern (Dilke, I, 166). It is true that he came into his inheritance to find his house stripped of furniture, his woods cut down, his outbuildings ready

to collapse, and his finances in a state which no exertion of prudence could
have righted, but he shows how close his priorities amidst the wreck were to
Teresa's when he qualifies his expense of £600 for 'plate & jewells, Coach,
Chariot Horses &c to begin Housekeeping' with the note that 'my Dr Wife
was so prudent not to accept of Diament Earings'.[5] When he died in 1739,
in his mid forties, a grief-stricken Teresa expressed to his son sentiments
which make a striking contrast with Pope's conception of her: 'I lov'd non
so wel on Earth; unless my dear old mother, on her; I hope; to double my
care; happy if I can any ways suply; the loss of her son' (Blount Letters, II,
33). Although Pope had not invented the troubles in the Blount family, their
letters offer a balancing perspective on his compulsive polarisation.

Pope's idealisation of Patty is however in harmony with the perceptions of
other correspondents. One such was Louis Schrader, a Hanoverian diplomat
in London, who was piqued to find himself posted back to Hanover (Blount
Letters, I, 11–55). There he attended Frederick Prince of Wales, and read
'Mr Pope's Preface to Shakespear with him; that he might see how Men of
Great Sense do Judge of Books and Learning' (f. 27). He wrote to Patty from
1725 to 1729, and as late as 1754 she bought a lottery ticket for him (Blount
Papers, Accounts of Martha Blount). His letters cannot be judged entirely
free of calculation, since, sharing the general illusion as to Mrs Howard's
influence on the king, he several times asked Patty to speak to her on his
behalf; but Patty was sceptical of the courtly arts which led him, for example,
to dismiss the charge of backing the Prince against his father with an airy 'As
if a man could love one, without loving t'other' (f. 47). Soon after Schrader
was separated from his charge by the Prince's recall to England in 1728, his
reply to her letter of commiseration shows that she has challenged his idealisation of the Prince:

I remember often to have commended the Prince to you. You, that are sincere,
suspected my veracity, and told me then: You had heard another Description of him.
You are so kind to make amends to me now.   (f. 45)

Whilst Schrader makes gallant acknowledgement of Patty's physical
charms, he prefers to stress her mental and spiritual qualities: 'For my part
I have allmost forgott Your blue Eyes, Your white Skin, your Silver Colourd
hair, and all those Shining things; but I remember very wel, to have seen a
Person that for Complacency, has not her Fellow, that with the best and
strongest Judgment, has the Softest Temper' (f. 15). Moreover, he shows that
he really does trust her good nature by his teasing, hardly the demeanour of
a courtier simply flattering his way to the royal mistress's ear. When she
writes of her favourite reading he replies:

As to Romances, which you brag so much of, I am sure you read em very seldom.
They are odious things.   (f. 51)

[5] Blount Papers, Accounts of Michael Blount I.

On one topic, however, he went too far:

I am sorry you thought me capable of such Jokes, as you suspected I had, when I spoke of Swaddling Cloathes. I can assure you Madam, that I did not hear a word of a Match between You and Mr. P. You once told me, that no such thing would ever happen; how then should I believe it could? But this Country abounding in good linnen, and it being natural to think, that you will not allways escape the Trap, I would offer my humble services for providing you with fine Linnen.   (f. 18)

Such insistence on the peculiarity of her relation to Pope can only have been galling. Schrader for one was not long in recurring to the subject: he soon reminded her that Hanover produced excellent linen for 'wedding shifts', adding, 'And who knows how soon you may have occasion for it?' (f. 25)

A more acceptable gift was a parcel of paper cutouts for the fashionable craft of decorating screens and boxes, together with a method for preventing them from peeling off, communicated in confidence by no less an authority than the King's japanner (ff. 32–34). Patty went swiftly to work, for she was soon asking for more, confirming her preference for the solid forms of nature over its transient ornaments by specifying trees, whereas the popular taste, according to Schrader, was for flowers. It is salutary to be reminded that Patty, who made no pretence of being an intellectual, spent much of her time happily absorbed in such occupations; and that her discussions with Anne Arbuthnot on the technicalities of making up printed cottons represented a world as closed to most men as their discussions of the classics to her (Blount Letters, II, 6). Yet Schrader also pays tribute to her less conventional taste for exercise and the open air: 'I don't doubt but you are in the Country, and walk about 12 hours in the 24 according to your Laudable Custom' (I, 32).

Schrader frequently sends his regards to Teresa and her mother, which shows that Pope's partisanship was by no means universal. On his first arrival in Hanover he refers to having answered a letter from Teresa, but it seems that in the long term she was happy to leave the commitment of writing to Patty. Schrader may, however, have sensed more than he stated:

You love your Friends too much, you can refuse em nothing, Your complaisance fatigues you too much . . . I am sorry your health is so fickle. I wish it was as steaddy as your Temper, and your Mind.   (ff. 23a, 48)

So close is Schrader's response to Pope's that it may suggest the possibility that other members of his circle were simply echoing his idealisation, but the letters she received do not bear out any suspicion that she had become the object of a purely formal cult. The prime example of a friend under Pope's close influence is Swift, who seems to echo Pope's reports of Teresa's ill-treatment of Patty, but had also had the opportunity to witness its effects for himself during his visits to England in 1726 and 1727. His portrait of Patty, while recognisably that of the same personality as Pope's and Schrader's, stresses the traits which most appealed to him personally: a thrift almost equal

to his own, a readiness to share his long walks, and the unembarrassed
economy of wearing worn-out clothes for the purpose – even if he does tease
her that she has no decent clothes because of Teresa's extravagance.[6] He
also praised Patty as 'one of the best Letter-writers I know; very good sense,
civility and friendship, without any stiffness or constraint'. All these signs of
her detachment from the extravagance and artifice of fashionable feminity
were powerful attractions to the man who declared that every conceivable
'vice or folly' was 'equally detestable' in either sex (*Irish Tracts*, p. 93). Like
the recently dead Stella and his other female favourites, Patty was a fatherless
child of a pliable disposition, weak in health and deferential to his lofty and
didactic teasing, as an extant letter of hers to him amply demonstrates (Ehrenpreis, III, 405–6). Although she has spirit enough to rise to his teasing about
old clothes and chair-hire, and to tease him in return for his ungallant
frankness in attributing his writing to her solely to Pope's having said that she
wanted him to, what most clearly ranks her with the other favourites for
whom he combined the roles of father and schoolmaster is her diffidence in
exposing her writing to his criticism: 'I can't say I have a great inclination
to write to you, for I have no great vanity that way, at least not enough to
support me above the fear of writing ill' (*Corr.*, II, 475, 490–91). She also set
herself in the best light for this systematic despiser of sexual allure by a joke
against advancing age that placed her hopes of happiness firmly in moral exertion: 'I begin to fear I have no great prospect of getting any new danglers;
and therefore, in order to make a tolerable figure, I shall endeavour to behave
myself mighty well, that I may keep my old ones.' Almost a decade later, in
1736, Pope was able to gratify their long-absent friend with her perseverance
in his doctrines:

> Mrs B. sighs more for you, than for the loss of youth. She says she will be agreeable
> many years hence, for she has learn'd that secret from some receipts of your writing.
> (IV, 51)

Like Pope, Swift wanted Patty to throw off the burden of her family, but the
way in which he expresses that wish in 1728 also reflects his desire, perhaps
scarcely recognised, to recreate his lost happiness with Stella: 'my greatest
happyness would be to have you and Mr Pope condemned during my life to
live in Ireland, he at the Deanery, and you for reputation Sake just at next
door' (II, 477). This might seem like simple teasing of Patty for her
prudishness; but it is poignantly close to the arrangements he had made for
his decorous contacts with Stella (Ehrenpreis, II, 72–73).

Patty also corresponded with three women friends who gave her cause to
reflect that however awkward her position with regard to Pope, a good marriage, so called, could have been infinitely worse. These friends' marriages
had committed them to colonial exile, and only one of them seems to have

[6] *Corr.*, III, 475–77: *Swift Corr.*, IV, 56, 79, 172.

known anything like happiness. Even the cheerful Mrs Gumley, who enjoys
India despite a shipwreck and other difficulties, values her contact with Patty
as a link with a past life which is still dear to her: she dwells on the privilege
of having known Pope, reads his works eagerly as they reach her, and asks
if he has any commissions for her (Blount Letters, II, 77–86). Like Schrader,
the Gumleys began by writing to Teresa, but addressed themselves to Patty
when Teresa failed to reply. Teresa might impress at close quarters, but it was
Patty who took the trouble to keep in touch.

Also in India was Mrs C. Sadleir, who, though happy in her marriage, was
as unimpressed by the idleness of the natives as by the vulgarity of the col-
onists in 'this Dirty Corner of the World', where public entertainments were
forbidden and 'genteel flower'd Silk' was not to be had (III, 100–5). As she
ruefully comments: 'there is not in the World a better Place to tame a young
Girl'. Like both of Patty's other colonial correspondents, she remembers Pope
with respectful affection: 'I wou'd write to him to beg a Continuance of what
I am with so much justice proud of but that I am aprehensive of being
troublesome.' She sheds additional light on Patty both by her concern for her
health, sending a shawl because 'I remember when I was at home you was
very subject to Colds', and by a most striking testimonial to Patty's respectability: Mrs Sadleir's husband, whom she had married against her brother's
wishes while under his protection, was in her view 'a Man suitable to me in
Years and temper with good future expectations', whereas her outraged
brother had preferred suitors with more ready money who 'wou'd be sooner
taken for my Father'. In this family disagreement it is Patty whom she asks
to vindicate her to her parents against her brother's accusations, since 'I am
very sure from the just esteem they both have for you that 'tis in no body's
power so much as Yours'.

Mrs Sadleir's difficulty with her parents was a reminder of the prudential
approach to marriage that had denied the Blounts a serious chance in the marriage market; yet in the light of Patty's correspondences with these exiles who
clung so devotedly to their memories of Pope, it probably no longer seemed
so clear that they had won and she had lost. Indeed, in the confidences of
Hyde Beckford, exiled in what she called the 'Prison at Large' of Jamaica,
Patty had an object lesson in the dangers of 'the Pelf / That buys your sex
a Tyrant o'er itself'.[7] Mrs Beckford, whose father was George Clarke,
Lieutenant Governor of New York, and whose mother was Anne Hyde,
daughter of Edward Hyde, Governor of North Carolina, had married into the
enormously wealthy Beckford family of Jamaica, but her husband's kin had an
unenviable reputation for violence and immorality.[8] At first Mrs Beckford

[7] Blount Letters, II, 11–22; *Characters of Women*, lines 287–88.
[8] John W. Raimo, *Biographical Directory of American Colonial and Revolutionary Governors 1607–1789*
(Westport, Connecticut, 1980), pp. 262, 294; Boyd Alexander, *England's Wealthiest Son: A Study of
William Beckford* (London, 1962), pp. 30–31, 201; Frank Cundall, *The Governors of Jamaica in the
First Half of the Eighteenth Century* (London, 1937), p. 175.

writes cheerfully, commenting on Jamaican gossip as well as the London
society news that presumably reached her in print, but she also confides that
'I find Pope Gliding thro all my thoughts as surely he has the arte to please',
and she envies Patty her enjoyment of his garden as she remembers 'the Dear
Grotto & mount'. Perhaps at home she had been more intimate with Teresa,
as at first she writes to her as well as to Patty, addressing the elder sister as
'Dear Tere', the younger as 'Dear Mrs Blount'; but like Schrader and the
Gumleys she apparently found Patty the more responsive and was soon
addressing herself exclusively to her. Her hints of personal distress increased,
until in 1737, after seven years in Jamaica, she confided to Patty:

> Mr Beckford surtainly keeps a gentleman's wife here but this for gods sake to your self
> least it should be wrote him from home . . . you may easily believe if Mr B: kept a
> million it would not give me any Consern I only wish he had more that I might be
> quite alone tho god be thanked I am very little troubled I have followed your advice
> to a tittle & never will make him any answers when he would provoke me.

Here as in the earlier correspondence with Bridget Floyd is evidence of Patty's
role as confidante, and evidence moreover that she reacted to Beckford's
attempts to put his wife in the wrong exactly in accordance with Pope's·
idealising 'She who ne'er answers till a Husband cools'.[9] Moreover, Mrs
Beckford's experience of exile and rejection made it clear that, whatever the
vexations of life with Teresa, there were worse fates than to be a spinster in
the metropolis, surrounded by friends and beloved by Pope.

4

Patty's problems with her family persisted up to Pope's death in 1744, for
even when her mother died in 1743 she refused to be detached from her sister.
In Pope's correspondence with Caryll this is a perpetual grief to both men,
yet for Pope it was also the crux of the relationship which after his mother's
death was his most vital contact with the opposite sex. Unfortunate ladies
always compelled his attention; and by persisting in living with her sister,
Patty – no doubt innocently – ensured her permanent membership of this
select band. Moreover, by urging this highly conventional woman to set
herself up as an independent person, Pope was actually inviting her to behave
like a very different kind of woman, the kind he invariably fell out with. In
a letter to Patty from Bath in 1714, in the happy days of his flirtation with
both sisters, he had described Lady Sandwich, daughter of the notorious Earl
of Rochester, as having 'all the Spirit of the last Age, & all the gay Experience
of a pleasureable life', and as being 'that easie, lively, & independent
Creature that a sensible woman always will be' (*Corr.*, I, 261). Here, before
his quarrels with Teresa and with Lady Mary, he recommends, no doubt

[9] *Characters of Women*, line 261.

partly in fun, a counterbalance to Patty's primness, yet it is one thing to be briefly charmed by an eccentric at a watering place, quite another to incorporate such an acquaintance into the sober texture of everyday life.

Thus, as Pope in later life reiterates his frustration at Patty's refusal to help herself, he reaffirms the limitations which make her permanently dear to him. In 1730, for example, he writes to Caryll: 'I expect little good to her, thro' her own indolence and goodness (not to say weakness) of nature' (III, 110). The paradox is fully intelligible in the light of current prescriptions for female excellence. As he remarked on an occasion when his emotions were less deeply involved, 'A very good woman would make but a paltry man' (*Prose Works*, II, 161). In effect, because Patty is the kind of woman he approves, she is not going to do the only thing that would set his mind at rest. It is therefore only superficially surprising that Pope's crowning tribute to Patty, *Epistle to a Lady: On the Characters of Women*, arose out of these years of frustration. He told Swift in 1733: 'Your lady friend is *semper eadem*, and I have written an epistle to her on that qualification in a female character' (*Corr.*, III, 349). The motto, 'the same forever', associated with the emblem of the reborn phoenix, had been used by Elizabeth I and Anne to assert both constancy and continuity, despite their childless condition.[10] Swift, however, would have recognised the sigh of resignation in Pope's use of the phrase: Patty will never make the radical change that she most needs. In the poem, nonetheless, Patty's quality of being 'semper eadem' is presented only in its positive aspect, associated with the resilient good humour that Pope had earlier recommended to women in 'With the Works of Voiture' and the *Rape*. This interpretation of the theme echoes words he had used to Caryll in 1732: 'I see your god-daughter as constantly as I go to London, and I think nobody should be changed towards her, as she is always the same' (*Corr.*, III, 274). Ironically, the poems in which Pope had first praised the constant charm of good humour had been enlivened by his pleasure in Teresa, but now he proclaims it as the distinctive triumph of the younger, quieter sister.

Characters of Women has a complicated and obscure textual history, owing partly to its incorporation of pre-existing fragments, and partly to Pope's omission from the published texts of some recognisable attacks on living individuals, a precaution which created gaps that Warburton seems to have been only partially successful in restoring after the poet's death.[11] Further complications arise from the rewriting the poem seems to have undergone prior to its first publication in 1735 to make it into a companion piece for the newly composed *Characters of Men*, and from the apparent addition of new material shortly before Pope's death in 1744 (Leranbaum, pp. 64–81). The disappearance of all the manuscripts adds to the difficulty of regarding any

[10] Frances Yates, *Astraea: The Imperial Theme in the Sixteenth Century* (London, 1975), p. 65; Marie Axton, *The Queen's Two Bodies: Drama and the Elizabethan Succession* (London, 1977), pp. 116–30.
[11] See Brady for objections to the restored text as given in *TE*.

version now available as a full representation of Pope's intentions at any given time: ironically, the poem which accuses women of living in a state of flux has itself no reliable and self-evidently coherent form.

In 'Sylvia', one of the many short poems which Pope quarried for materials for *Characters of Women*, he had already indicated what was to be one of the controversial elements in his definition of the sex:

> *Men*, some to Business, some to Pleasure take,
> But ev'ry Woman's in her Soul a Rake.[12]

It is to his expansion of these lines in *Characters of Women* that he entrusts the task of relating his gallery of female portraits to the ambitious claims made in *Characters of Men* and the *Essay on Man* for the ruling passion as universal key to human behaviour:

> In Men, we various Ruling Passions find,
> In Women, two almost divide the kind;
> Those, only fix'd, they first or last obey,
> The Love of Pleasure, and the Love of Sway.
>   That, Nature gives; and where the lesson taught
> Is still to please, can Pleasure seem a fault?
> Experience, this; by Man's oppression curst,
> They seek the second not to lose the first.
>   Men, some to Bus'ness, some to Pleasure take;
> But ev'ry Woman is at heart a Rake:
> Men, some to Quiet, some to public Strife;
> But ev'ry Lady would be Queen for life.   (line 207)

These, the most dogmatic lines in the poem and the least enlivened by its complex energy of action and metaphor, provided a predictable focus for adverse reaction by eighteenth-century women readers. One respectable woman is said to have objected simply that she was not 'at heart a Rake' (Ayre, II, 53). Pope replied that she was of course not a woman but a saint, a piece of gallantry which presumably gave him the satisfaction of undercutting her claim to exemption, since she proved herself 'Woman enough to be pleas'd with the Compliment'. Unfortunately, the source for this exchange is notoriously unreliable, but even if it is pure invention it shows at least that contemporaries were aware of the affront to virtuous women implicit in Pope's dogmatic theorising.

Another response, which takes issue with these lines in the context of a wider deference to Pope as the poet who penetrates 'th'arcana of the soul, / The secret springs wch move and guide the whole', was printed in the *Gentleman's Magazine* in 1736.[13] Whilst tacitly admitting that Pope has fairly depicted the

---

[12] 'Sylvia', lines 15–16 (*TE*, VI, 287).

[13] Anne Viscountess Irwin, 'An Epistle to Mr Pope by a Lady, Occasioned by his *Characters of Women*', *Gentleman's Magazine*, VI (1736), 745. For Lady Irwin, see G.E.C., *Peerage*, Rich, fifth Viscount Irvine (*sic*).

degraded state of her sex, the author, Lady Irwin, denies that ruling passions are sexually specific:

> Women must in a narrow orbit move,
> But power alike both males and females love.

This 'narrow orbit', she asserts, is ordained by an education which proposes sexuality as sole source of power and advancement, since women are

> Told that their charms a monarch may enslave,
> That beauty like the gods can kill or save.

For models of truly respectable women she looks to antiquity, when she believes that the sex was 'taught by philosophy all moral good', and she urges Pope to address modern women in poetry which will lift them above the sensual frivolities of fashionable life: 'New passions raise, their minds anew create'. In effect, she blames society for corrupting women, much as Pope had done in 'With the Works of Voiture', and like him she presents as her ideal a perpetual because spiritualised flowering of female charm:

> Then wou'd the *British* fair perpetual bloom,
> And vie in fame with ancient *Greece* and *Rome*.[14]

As these lines demonstrate, women are still for Lady Irwin definitively the fair sex. Moreover, she still accepts the nurturing of men as their highest distinction:

> No more can we expect our modern wives
> Heroes shou'd breed, who lead such useless lives.

Nevertheless, despite this implicit acceptance of contemporary prescriptions, her poem effectively challenges Pope's dismissal of female imperfection as determined by sexually specific ruling passions, and suggests that he should pursue the more constructive path of instilling a nobler philosophy than the prevailing glorification of erotic allure.

Although Mary Wollstonecraft does not consider *Characters of Women* at length in her *Vindication of the Rights of Woman*, she too seizes in passing on the lines on the ruling passion, making much the same point as Lady Irwin, but without a trace of her deference to the great poet:

It would almost provoke a smile of contempt, if the vain absurdities of man did not strike us on all sides, to observe, how eager men are to degrade the sex from whom they pretend to receive the chief pleasure of life; and I have frequently with full conviction retorted Pope's sarcasm on them; or, to speak explicitly, it has appeared to me applicable to the whole human race. A love of pleasure or sway seems to divide mankind, and the husband who lords it in his little haram thinks only of his pleasure or his convenience.[15]

[14] Compare 'With the Works of Voiture', lines 31–48, 57–80 (*TE*, VI, 63–64).
[15] Mary Wollstonecraft, *A Vindication of the Rights of Woman*, edited by Carol H. Poston, Norton Critical Editions (London, 1975), pp. 72–73.

For her, the conventional rhetoric of female softness which she finds in *Characters of Women* is a degrading glorification of inadequacy: 'nor should girls ever be allowed to imbibe the pernicious notion that a defect can, by any chemical process of reasoning, become an excellence' (p. 40). As an example of such reasoning the poem springs readily to her mind:

It would be an endless task to trace the variety of meannesses, cares, and sorrows, into which women are plunged by the prevailing opinion, that they were created rather to feel than reason, and that all the power they obtain, must be obtained by their charms and weakness:

> Fine by defect, and amiably weak!

And, made by this amiable weakness entirely dependent, excepting what they gain by illicit sway, on man, not only for protection, but advice, is it surprising that, neglecting the duties that reason alone points out, and shrinking from trials calculated to strengthen their minds, they only exert themselves to give their defects a graceful covering, which may serve to heighten their charms in the eye of the voluptuary, though it sink them below the scale of moral excellence?[16]

This is only one of the many contexts in which she forcefully suggests that the arts of weakness are the arts of a whore, and she hints further at the perversion that needs to despise where it desires in a scornful allusion to Pope's confession of his paradoxical attraction to Calypso:

It follows then that cunning should not be opposed to wisdom, little cares to great exertions, or insipid softness, varnished over with the name of gentleness, to that fortitude which grand views alone can inspire.

I shall be told that woman would then lose many of her peculiar graces, and the opinion of a well known poet might be quoted to refute my unqualified assertion. For Pope has said, in the name of the whole male sex,

> Yet ne'er so sure our passion to create,
> As when she touch'd the brink of all we hate.   (p. 26)

Pope and she are momentarily at one in identifying male oppression as the cause of women's grasping at power: just as he asserts that they look for power in order to escape being denied pleasure, so she argues that 'the cunning, which I allow makes at present a part of their character . . . is produced by oppression' (p. 193: compare lines 211–14). Yet from this point of contact their reasonings diverge radically, for whereas Pope can idealise an artful management of the strong by the weak, she is incensed by men's advocacy of such degrading insincerity:

> She, who ne'er answers till a Husband cools,
> Or, if she rules him, never shows she rules;

---

[16] Wollstonecraft, p. 62, quoting *Characters of Women*, line 44: she misquotes 'amiably weak' for 'delicately weak'.

Charms by accepting, by submitting sways,
Yet has her humour most, when she obeys.   (line 261)

How grossly do they insult us who thus advise us only to render ourselves gentle, domestic brutes! For instance, the winning softness so warmly, and frequently, recommended, that governs by obeying. What childish expressions, and how insignificant is the being – can it be an immortal one? who will condescend to govern by such sinister methods!   (p. 20)

In her final allusion to *Characters of Women* Wollstonecraft uses Pope to enforce a fundamental point, and one which Pope himself would have rejected with indignation: there is, she asserts, a cynical and self-serving circularity in the idealisation of female frailty, since it is used to justify women's subjection to arbitrary male authority:

If women are to be made virtuous by authority, which is a contradiction in terms, let them be immured in seraglios and watched with a jealous eye. – Fear not that the iron will enter into their souls – for the souls that can bear such treatment are made of yielding materials, just animated enough to give life to the body.

Matter too soft a lasting mark to bear,
And best distinguish'd by black, brown, or fair.

The most cruel wounds will of course soon heal, and they may still people the world, and dress to please man – all the purposes which certain celebrated writers have allowed that they were created to fulfil.   (p. 188)

Such objections as these were of course rare, for in Pope's lifetime the notion of female softness and the normative status of the male in human society seemed part of the natural order. It did not apparently strike his readers as odd that a poem dedicated to a woman should present such a spirited claim to have weighed the female character and found it wanting, even when the consequence is that its addressee cannot be simply the best of her sex, but has to be a kind of hermaphrodite, 'a softer Man' (lines 269–80). Even the gallantry of the prose Advertisement, which to modern eyes so clearly denies that the sex deserves the respect so ostentatiously tendered, was simply what Pope's female readers were conditioned to accept:

The Author being very sensible how particular a Tenderness is due to the FEMALE SEX, and at the same time how little they generally show to each other; declares, upon his Honour, that *no one Character* is drawn from the Life, in this Epistle. It would otherwise be most improperly inscribed to a *Lady*, who, of all the Women he knows, is the last that would be entertain'd at the Expence of Another.

Such women were equally unlikely to question the credentials of a man who took upon himself the authoritative role of artist and connoisseur, interpreting Patty's sex to her on the basis of portraits which he himself draws and selects.[17]

---

[17] For a wide-ranging critique of this authority and its implications, see Carole Fabricant, 'Pope's Portraits of Women: The Tyranny of the Pictorial Eye', in *Women and Men: The Consequences of Power*, edited by Dana V. Hiller and Robin Ann Sheets (Cincinnati, 1976), pp. 74–91.

Only recently has it become usual to recognise the arbitrary assumption of
male authority which determines many of the basic procedures of *Characters
of Women*. As Mary Wollstonecraft's adversarial and necessarily reductive
reading of the poem shows, ideological analysis which tacitly accepts Pope as
the normative voice of his age can work powerfully to warn the reader of the
unpalatable doctrines implied by an art whose foundation in structures of
social power has frequently been ignored, and a variety of feminist critics have
recently begun to explore this aspect of *Characters of Women*.[18] Yet as we
compare Pope's text with others from the period it becomes clear that far from
fitting easily into a scheme of gender assumptions, *Characters of Women* causes
its author distinct unease. In this respect, as we might expect of a poet who
was not only an unusually sensitive explorer of multiple points of view, but
also in many respects a disadvantaged member of his sex, he is revealed as
a less than fully typical spokesman for the age. In effect, his attempts to evade
and extenuate the consequences of contemporary prejudices are more
interesting – and more characteristic – than the predictable fact that he is
unable to approach the subject without them.

This conclusion emerges with particular clarity from a comparison of
Characters of Women with the two satires on women included in Edward
Young's *Love of Fame: The Universal Passion*, a collection which inspired Pope
to improve on the formal model evolved by his predecessor, while appropriating it to his own, very different, political alignment.[19] In presenting the
various characters who figure in his satires on women, Young frequently and
explicitly condemns various kinds of behaviour simply because he holds them
to be inappropriate to the sex: but Pope, reluctant to admit (even to himself?)
that arbitrary gender prescriptions play a part in his perception of women,
chooses instead to stress that the behaviour he satirises is unworthy of a
human being. Young declares bluntly that women are 'by nature born to
soothe and entertain', and assumes his readers' agreement that certain
activities and ambitions are self-evidently ridiculous in women:

> They drive, row, run, with love of glory smit,
> Leap, swim, shoot flying, and pronounce on wit.   (Satire V.131)

For Young the only activities that befit women are those calculated to 'sooth
and entertain' judicious men like himself. Secure in this belief, he is unabashed

---

[18] For recent feminist readings which imply Pope's typicality, see Pollak, pp. 108–27;
Fabricant, 'Pope's Portraits'; Laura Brown, *Alexander Pope*, Rereading Literature (Oxford,
1985), pp. 101–7. For differences between Pope and other writers, see Nussbaum, pp. 143–58;
and, in particular, Hammond, pp. 184–94.

[19] *Love of Fame*, Satires V and VI, in *The Complete Works of the Rev. Edward Young*, edited by John
Doran, 2 vols. (London, 1854); Charlotte Crawford, 'What was Pope's Debt to Edward
Young?', *ELH*, 13 (1946), 157–67.

about issuing positive instructions, tellingly assimilating even the art of conversation to the essentially erotic ideal of 'sweet reluctant amorous delay' so delightful to Milton's Adam:

> Naked in nothing should a woman be,
> But veil her very wit with modesty.
> Let man discover, let not her display,
> But yield her charms of mind with sweet delay.

> (*Paradise Lost*, IV. 311; Satire VI.107)

It is a good indication of the general acceptance of such thinking as both morally edifying and genuinely altruistic in its concern for women that the reliably pedestrian Ruffhead goes into raptures over this passage. 'How exquisitely chaste is Young's idea of female modesty!' he exclaims, and in comparison finds *Characters of Women* lacking not only in the positive precepts offered by Young ('How moral, how tender, and persuasive is the conclusion of the fifth satire, where he directs the fair *whom*, and *how*, they should study to charm') but also in 'that urbanity and tenderness, which so soft a subject seems peculiarly to demand' (pp. 289–91). Significantly, Pope has erred not only in failing to spell out approvingly the limits arbitrarily placed on women by men, but also in affronting the alluring softness of the female with the forthrightness of a satirist of the human condition. In his refusal to fulfil the expectations of this highly conventional reader, Pope reveals his unease with such complacent endorsement of repressive prescriptions.

In poems stimulated by women who evoked his admiration and approval, Pope typically expressed a consciously liberal attitude to the predicament of women in his society; and he clearly intends his celebration of his beloved Patty to take its place in this context of deliberate sympathy. Yet, in effect, this commitment gives rise to various tensions and discontinuities in *Characters of Women*, as it comes into conflict both with personal assumptions and with unavoidable elements in the culture in which he has to work. The choice of genre, for example, is problematic, for he addresses Patty not in any conventional kind of love poetry but in a familiar epistle, a genre which insists on the addressee's status as a friend worth talking to; but whereas his epistles to Cobham the Patriot, Burlington the patron of architecture, and Bathurst the easy-going representative of the Tory landed interest invite readings in terms of the addressees' well-known public roles and responsibilities, there is no equivalent way of individualising a good and therefore private woman. While the public life of men offered a range of different careers, the private life that was the good woman's primary context was relatively stereotyped, offering no convenient shorthand for indicating individual identity. For those who knew Patty, the epistle was not without the personal allusions associated with the genre; but for most readers the compliment intended by the choice of genre has been thwarted by the impossibility of constructing a public face that is both individual and respectable, a difficulty which, combined with Patty's decorous refusal to let Pope address the epistle to her by name and Warburton's hostile desire to deprive her of the honour of the dedication, has produced a tradition of reading in which the existence of an individual addressee hardly figures.[20]

Tension between public and private, between woman as speaker and woman as good listener, emerges also in Pope's initial decision to distinguish Patty by quoting the aphorism she 'once let fall', a phrase which achieves an artful ambiguity as to whether this was a sally of effortless wit or simply an involuntary lapse into unflattering truth. The remark is in fact so hostile to her own sex that it ironically reinforces the subordination that the rhetorical strategy seems designed to challenge. Although it is understandable, in an age when female ignorance, idleness and consumerism were felt to be on the increase, that women impatient with such frivolity should be likely to protest, with Lady Mary, that 'my only Consolation for being of that Gender has been the assurance it gave me of never being marry'd to any one amongst them', such exasperation itself served a wider male strategy of divide and rule. Swift for example rejoices in the fact that Stella 'rather chose men for her companions', and declares in his 'Letter to a Young Lady on her Marriage' that he 'never yet knew a tolerable Woman to be fond of her own Sex'.[21] By citing Patty in this vein Pope commits himself to presenting her as an anomaly: at the end of the poem he praises in her qualities which he labels as belonging to his sex as well as those he feels to be proper to her own. Up to this point, faced with the problem of protecting her from the damaging implications of his generalisations, he makes the touchingly inadequate concession, when he has something potentially detrimental to her to say of her sex, of changing the 'you' that implicates her to the 'they' that seems to put her to one side (compare lines 202–6, 209–14, 219–42).

Such a strategy, however, does nothing to protect her from the poem's most brutally anti-feminist couplet:

> Woman and Fool are two hard things to hit,
> For true No-meaning puzzles more than Wit.   (line 113)

This echoes an aphorism that clearly relates Pope to the libertine tradition of his youth: 'Women, as they are like riddles in being unintelligible, so generally resemble them in this, that they please us no longer when once we know them' (*Prose Works*, II, 159). The couplet suggests in addition a major source of Pope's interest in the sex: they are, with Mac Flecknoe and the dunces, denizens of the poetically fertile and alluring realm of 'true No-meaning'.[22] Yet however significant in creative terms, this remains an insult quite at odds with his conception of the woman to whom the poem is dedicated, although

[20] *Corr.*, III, 451; *TE*, III.ii, 46–47.
[21] *LM Letters*, II, 33; Jonathan Swift, *Miscellaneous and Autobiographical Pieces, Fragments and Marginalia*, edited by Herbert Davis (Oxford, 1969), p. 235; *Irish Tracts*, p. 88.
[22] *Mac Flecknoe*, lines 5–6, 15–24 (*Poems of Dryden*, I, 265).

it is by no means an unwarranted deduction from the doctrine that she 'once let fall' and from the wider belief in female softness in which her disillusion takes its place. The irruption into the poem of what Ruffhead castigates as 'downright rudeness' is in terms of his politely patronising attitude to women principally a lapse of taste, but it is more significantly a sign of conflict between the personal esteem that Pope has come to feel for a particular woman and the libertine smartness which is part of his inheritance as a wit (Ruffhead, p. 283).

The manner in which Pope comments on the portraits which he brings in evidence can also be read as suggesting underlying unease. Repeatedly he implies dismissively, perhaps defensively, that a subject defined by its incoherence does not warrant scrupulous craftsmanship:

> Pictures like these, dear Madam, to design,
> Asks no firm hand, and no unerring line.
>
> (line 151; compare lines 17–20, 113–14)

Such an attitude may be related to the fact that although the most striking of the portraits evolve more or less organically from individuals who genuinely engage his curiosity – Atossa being the prime example – others are synthetically produced from the division and recombination of pre-existing fragments.[23] Perhaps the defensive tone also has something to do with the artificiality of such 'proofs' for a theory which performs the vital service of relocating in the other sex the instability that he had to grapple with in his own consciousness (see chapter 7.2). This was not, moreover, a simple negative in his life: it is crucial to the simultaneous sympathy with hunter and hunted in *Windsor Forest*, to the Ovidian ebb and flow of Eloisa's contrary passions, and to the celebrated doubleness of vision of the *Rape* and the *Dunciad*. If opposites could really be accommodated only within a hopelessly fluid female identity, he as a man could hardly have achieved such effects. Indeed, as Felicity Rosslyn argues, *Characters of Women* owes the distinction of being 'the only one of the four "Moral Essays" which reverberates in the mind long after reading, and gives the impression of meaning more than it says' to precisely that creative delight in variousness, in the shifting colours of sylphs and rainbows, that it is the poem's ostensible purpose to control and subordinate.[24]

Further signs of tension in Pope's approach to his subject emerge specifically from his attempt to bring his reflections into the structure of his projected Opus Magnum. One of the inconsistencies highlighted by his exposition of the doctrine of the ruling passion is that instability, which in *Characters of Men* is a crucial problem for humanity as a whole, becomes in *Characters of Women*

23 *Characters of Women*, lines 45–68 and notes; Schmitz, 'Peterborough's and Pope's Nymphs'; Grundy, 'Pope, Peterborough, and the Characters of Women'.
24 Felicity Rosslyn, ' "Dipt in the Rainbow": Pope on Women', *Parnassus*, 12–13 (1985), 179–93.

the distinguishing characteristic of women. Similarly, it is difficult in
Characters of Women to win acceptance for the claim that the sex is almost
entirely divided between the ruling passions of 'the love of Pleasure' and
'the love of Sway' when the only two women in *Characters of Men* have been
analysed in terms of the ruling passions of avarice and vanity. When Pope
thinks of women as 'Men', i.e. people, they take their place, though a limited
one, as part of a richly perplexing world; but when he thinks of their sex 'only
as contradistinguished from the other' he feels the compulsion to narrow and
define, even at the expense of consistency.[25] The difficulty of setting men/
people over against women is further underlined when Pope applies to women
an aphorism of Malherbe which he had formerly translated in its original
application to humanity in general: 'Pleasures the sex, as children Birds, pursue'.[26] Likewise, when he praises his ideal as 'Mistress of herself, tho' China
fall', behind the commonplace of reproof to frivolous women lies Horace's
more general criterion of sanity, 'posset qui . . . signo laeso non insanire
lagenae', paraphrased by Pope as 'Not quite a Mad-man, tho' a Pasty
fell'.[27]

Yet most poignant of all the signs of strain in *Characters of Women* is its inability to sustain the buoyant, apparently disengaged wit with which he had
negotiated the minefields of sexual politics in the *Rape*. From this point of view
Characters of Women opens well, with a deliberate pleasure in preposterous teasing. From the double-edged quotation of Patty's aphorism Pope leaps at once
via the image of minting metal ('too soft a lasting mark to bear') to the conclusion – no doubt far from Patty's intention – that, lacking the characters by
which people are properly known one from another, women, like animals, are
'best distinguish'd by black, brown, or fair'; and while his addressee is
presumably still dazed by what she has innocently unleashed, he leaps again
into a ludicrously exaggerated review of what he calls in his note 'attitudes
in which several ladies affected to be drawn, and sometimes one lady in them
all':

> How many pictures of one Nymph we view,
> All how unlike each other, all how true!
> Arcadia's Countess, here, in ermin'd pride,
> Is there, Pastora by a fountain side:
> Here Fannia, leering on her own good man,
> Is there, a naked Leda with a Swan.
> Let then the Fair one beautifully cry,
> In Magdalen's loose hair and lifted eye,
> Or drest in smiles of sweet Cecilia shine,
> With simp'ring Angels, Palms, and Harps divine;

[25] *Characters of Men*, lines 238–47; *Characters of Women*, lines 207–10; Pope's note on the title of
Characters of Women.
[26] *Characters of Women*, line 231; *TE*, VI, 7.
[27] *Characters of Women*, line 268 and note; *Imitations of Horace*, Epistles II.ii.190 (*TE*, IV, 179).

Whether the Charmer sinner it, or saint it,
If Folly grows romantic, I must paint it.   (line 5)

As he proceeds he wilfully confuses elements of a recognisable seventeenth-
and eighteenth-century mode of portraiture with the distinct tradition in
which the sitter is simply a vehicle for a religious or mythological subject.[28]
He begins plausibly enough with the pastoral poses of the great which were
in effect simply a variation on the conventional undress portrait: whether such
a sitter is 'Arcadia's Countess' (the Countess of Pembroke), whose portrait
with a lamb dates from the 1680s, or Pope's and Patty's friend the Duchess
of Queensberry, painted as a milkmaid in the 1720s, she is still every inch the
aristocrat, gracefully poised in flatteringly simple dress amidst purely
decorative animals and implements.[29] To change the image to 'ermin'd
pride' requires only a change of clothes and setting: the sitter's identity is by
no means as dependent on the 'character' as Pope claims. He becomes more
obviously preposterous when he contrasts the covert sensuality of Fannia in
a double portrait with her husband, with the open lewdness of her portrait as
'a naked Leda with a Swan', for the latter invokes a genre quite distinct from
portraiture: appropriate as it might have been for a real-life Fannia to have
her portrait painted in this celebrated erotic character, no one in fact did so.
In the next couplet Pope's evocation of Magdalen portraits is almost equally
exaggerated: if anything, it suggests Titian's dramatic characterisation of the
penitent sinner, in which luxuriant hair is her only covering, rather than the
decorous nominal Magdalens produced as portraits. Kneller, for example,
painted even the royal mistress the Countess of Orkney as a relatively
restrained and adequately draped Magdalen, and when in 1715 he painted
Patty herself in this character he limited himself to well-groomed 'loose hair'
and a pot of ointment: there is no hint that this Magdalen is about to do
anything so undignified as to 'beautifully cry'.[30] St Cecilia too, though a
popular portrait character, produces no transformation in the sitter: indeed,
Pope would have a stronger case arguing from the other side of his proposi-
tion, that women are more like each other than men, for whether in Kneller's
'Hampton Court Beauties' or in Lely's earlier 'Windsor Beauties', described
by Pepys as 'good, but not like', the similarity between the different women
is far more striking, at least to modern eyes, than the difference between different seventeenth- and eighteenth-century portrayals of the same woman.[31]

[28] For an account which accepts Pope's conflation of the two traditions, see Jean H. Hagstrum,
The Sister Arts: The Tradition of Literary Pictorialism and English Poetry from Dryden to Gray (Chicago,
1958), pp. 236–37.
[29] For reproductions of these portraits, see *TE*, III.ii, following p. 48, and Ribeiro, plate 30.
[30] For Titian, see Hagstrum, plate XXI. For Kneller's Magdalens, see J. Douglas Stewart, *Sir
Godfrey Kneller and the English Baroque Portrait* (Oxford, 1983), no. 545 (plates 40a, 40c); nos.
695–701, a series of one sitter which includes a Magdalen, a Diana and a St Cecilia; and no.
98, of Patty, which is reproduced in Mack, *Life*, p. 633.
[31] Oliver Millar, *The Tudor, Stuart and Early Georgian Pictures in the Collection of Her Majesty the
Queen*, 2 vols. (London, 1963), nos. 257–66 (plates 107–116); nos. 351–58 (plates 152–59); *The*

Moreover, Pope himself was represented in different characters by Jonathan Richardson, and there is no suggestion that this brought his individuality into question, since the point of drawing him as Chaucer and as Milton was precisely to stress his triumph in the character of poet (Wimsatt, nos. 19, 37). Although the lack of such firmly established public characters perhaps made the convention more of a risk to female individuality, actual paintings do not bear out Pope's claim that women seem completely different people when painted in different characters, and to Patty his exaggerated and wantonly confused review of familiar genres presumably signalled that laughter rather than lamentation was the appropriate response.

Another example of unacceptable argument introduced with deliberate aplomb is the comparison of women to tulips, where Pope again undercuts his footing as he goes:

> Ladies, like variegated Tulips, show,
> 'Tis to their Changes that their Charms they owe;
> Their happy Spots the nice admirer take,
> Fine by defect, and delicately weak.   (line 41)

There are two signs that this is not simply the crude reductionism that it seems. The first is that there is a satirical edge to the phrase 'nice admirer' in this context, the deliberate infection of the strain to damage the uniform colour of the petals. Pope's contempt for such narrow study and manipulation of nature, anticipated by Young in his character of Florio the tulip-fancier, was later to be expressed in the *Dunciad*, in which a carnation-fancier disputes with a butterfly collector, little to the credit of either.[32] The perceptions of the 'nice admirer' provide Pope with the basis of a surprising and impressively technical conceit, but the dubious moral status of the horticulturalist's taste undercuts any suggestion that this is a proper way to judge women. This leads to the second hint that more, or less, is going on than meets the eye, for the comparison is illustrated without even a typographical break by 'Calypso', adapted from a fragment which had originally begun 'Sylvia *my* heart in wond'rous wise alarmed' (my italics); and it is now capped by a couplet that confirms to followers of Pope's relations with women the allusion to his own excitement about women whose energy and confidence he cannot approve:

> Yet ne'er so sure our passion to create,
> As when she touch'd the brink of all we hate.
>   (line 51; compare *TE*, VI, 286–88)

The reworking of this fragment, apparently meant originally as a sketch of the lively and uninhibited Duchess of Hamilton, has led Pope into defining the

---

Diary of Samuel Pepys, edited by Robert Latham and William Matthews, 11 vols. (London, 1970–83), IX, 284.

[32] *Love of Fame*, II.21–56; *Dunciad B*, IV.397–458 (*TE*, V, 381–85).

crucial mechanism of his doomed but irresistible attraction to women like Teresa and Lady Mary – a mechanism which, for all we know, Patty need not have understood at all (note on lines 45–52). Yet here he recognises the crux, whether or not he ever realised its significance for those particular relationships; and the fact that he presents this taste, which his judgement condemns as perverse (*'our* passion' and 'all *we* hate' suggest moreover that it is a characteristic male perversity), as an illustration of the tulip theory implies that such a decadent response is comparable to the obsessive fantasies of the tulip-fancier, and is certainly not compatible with the proper interest in his fellow creatures that the would-be philosopher of the Opus Magnum should be seen to aspire to.

Yet however artful these instances of ironic disengagement from the commonplaces of female subordination, in the poem as a whole, which includes the levelling of women with fools and their confinement within a system which allocates them only two of the myriad ruling passions of humankind, Pope achieves nothing like the elusiveness of the *Rape*. That had been a commission at one remove from his personal concerns, dating from the brighter days when the world seemed relatively full of possibilities and when he could still enjoy flirting with a Teresa or a Lady Mary; but now he had set his face firmly against such women; his mother and other beloved friends were dead; the narrowing prospect of premature old age stretched before him; and Patty, now the unique object of his deepest devotion, persisted in denying him what he most wanted. Ironically, in her contrasting roles as Teresa's sister and his friend, she exemplified the paradox 'no Ass so meek, no Ass so obstinate', presented in *Characters of Women* as a contrast with his well-tempered ideal (line 102). In the face of this impasse with the woman he idealised, and of the loss and bitterness that had closed off other intimacies, it is hardly surprising that the virtuoso evasions of uncommitted gallantry are harder to sustain.

What is perhaps more surprising in a poem dedicated to Patty is the absence of Teresa, long established in his letters as the natural foil for Patty. To have identified Teresa in the poem would have mortified the loyal Patty, but nonetheless Pope sees to it that the shade of Teresa's chosen lifestyle hovers unmistakably: over Rufa's search for the 'light gay meteor of a Spark'; over the persistent obsession with appearance; over the various talkative would-be wits; but most of all over the desolate but ever-eager old age of the pleasure-seekers, part of which, with the obvious contrast evidently in mind, he had already incorporated into a revision of his lines 'To Mrs M.B on her Birthday'.[33] Indeed, the two ruling passions he attributes to the sex, 'the Love of Pleasure, and the Love of Sway', together sum up his conception of the elder sister.

Such an allusion is available only to intimates, and this is true also of the host of potential contrasts between Patty and the satiric portraits which

---

[33] *Characters of Women*, line 22, note on lines 243–48; *TE*, VI, 244–47.

occupy the first part of the poem. Unlike Silia, for instance, Patty is resigned
to the effects of her smallpox and to the constant rashes with which her extremely fair skin responded to sun or stress: as she tells Swift, the charms of
the spirit are what matter.[34] Unlike the shallow, acquisitive Papillia, Patty
deeply loves trees and landscape, although she was never to own or control
land herself (lines 37–40). Her good-humoured acquiescence in a conventional role contrasts with Calypso's eccentric charms; and Narcissa's moral
caprice is a foil to her consistent and moderate piety (lines 45–68). Philomedé,
in whom Patty probably recognised elements of Congreve's mistress Henrietta Churchill, provides an instructive comparison with Patty's resignation to
being the chaste friend of a poet and a purely theoretical connoisseur of the
niceties of her favourite romances (lines 69–86). Her pious constancy of mood
amid her difficulties contrasts with Flavia's atheistic oscillations between
bravado and despair, and Pope's stress on the perversity that turns Flavia's
exceptional gifts to torments underlines his respect for Patty's better use of
her modest talents (lines 87–100). Among the brief vignettes that bridge the
passage from Flavia to Atossa several provide similar contrasts: and once past
the climax of Atossa, Pope explicitly turns to Patty as the amiable if deluded
would-be defender of her friend Cloe, before he brings the tour to a close with
an ironic allusion to *semper eadem*, the motto of Queen Elizabeth and Queen
Anne that he had privately applied to Patty. In a satirical glance at the hymn
of praise to Queen Caroline with which Young concludes one of his satires
on women, Pope stresses the vacuity of the one public character that society
sanctions for the sex:

> The same for ever! and described by all
> With Truth and Goodness, as with Crown and Ball.
>   (line 183; compare *Love of Fame*, VI.569–86)

Yet before he can manoeuvre the poem to his final celebration of Patty as
truly 'the same for ever', his systematising ambition obliges him to produce
the much-resented lines that establish the poem's place in the Opus Magnum
– and again we are reminded of Teresa:

> In Men, we various Ruling Passions find,
> In Women, two almost divide the kind;
> Those, only fix'd, they first or last obey,
> The Love of Pleasure, and the Love of Sway.
>   That, Nature gives; and where the lesson taught
> Is still to please, can Pleasure seem a fault?
> Experience, this; by Man's oppression curst,
> They seek the second not to lose the first.   (line 207)

Ironically, this would have been a very plausible extenuation of Teresa's

---

[34] *Characters of Women*, lines 35–36; *Corr.*, II, 491.

behaviour, although we can hardly imagine Pope making it: there remains a vast distance between his conscious and sympathetic questioning of society's impositions on women and his fury against those whose autonomy hurt him personally. Yet the description of the ageing beauties who 'haunt the places where their Honour dy'd' is wistful rather than vengeful, a belated valediction to the social world he had once shared with Teresa, and which she, rejecting private life and the prescribed female virtues, persists in inhabiting. Severe as he was in prose, with his sarcastic references to her 'eternal youth', his verse cannot resist the pathos of a predicament which, as he writes, he is perhaps not fully conscious of as hers (*Corr.*, III, 370).

It is with evident relief that he turns to Patty with the apostrophe 'Ah Friend', which, as Mack points out, is 'the one word in the language that denotes relationships of equality and permanence'.[35] So begins the happiest part of the poem, in which, as Mack again notes, the moon is transformed from 'the Cynthia of this minute' into a calm dispenser of 'more sober light'.[36] The lines are familiar: evolving from Pope's early comparison of Judith Cowper as mildly reflective moon to Lady Mary as glaringly assertive sun, they traverse the whole span of his reaction to the women who touched 'the brink of all we hate' (line 52):

> Ah Friend! to dazzle let the Vain design,
> To raise the Thought and touch the Heart, be thine!
> That Charm shall grow, while what fatigues the Ring
> Flaunts and goes down, an unregarded thing.
> So when the Sun's broad beam has tir'd the sight,
> All mild ascends the Moon's more sober light,
> Serene in Virgin Modesty she shines,
> And unobserv'd the glaring Orb declines.   (line 249)

Teresa and all her glittering kind are conclusively denounced in the idealistic and no doubt unnoticed falsehood that the rising moon distracts attention from the setting sun. In Pope's quixotic defence of the self-effacing female ideal we sense the depth of his desire to respond as vividly to what he conceived of as goodness as to the brilliance which in the end would only disgust him. It is a moving moment, as much for the impasse indicated by the implausible conceit as for its declaration of quietly sustaining love.

From this climax of commitment the poem descends to a graceful close, via a portrait of the ideal woman in, as it were, the generic subjunctive: this is Patty as she would have been, had she fulfilled the prescribed destiny of her sex by acquiring and managing a husband with the discretion that she had recommended to Hyde Beckford.[37] Yet the 'Sister' she did have; and it was

---

[35] *Characters of Women*, line 249; Mack; *Life*, p. 632.
[36] *Characters of Women*, lines 20, 254.
[37] *Characters of Women*, line 262. Pollak, pp. 126–27, sees the portrait as a direct falsification of the historical Patty.

apparently because the reference, in the first editions, to the ideal woman's
hearing 'Sighs for a Sister with unwounded ear' pointed too clearly to his
early attachment to Teresa, that he changed 'Sister' to 'Daughter', thus
displacing attention from the 'Sister's charms' (previously 'younger charm')
that had played such a large part in his early friendship with Patty:

> Oh! blest with Temper, whose unclouded ray
> Can make to morrow chearful as to day;
> She, who can love a Sister's charms, or hear
> Sighs for a Daughter with unwounded ear;
> She who ne'er answers till a Husband cools,
> Or, if she rules him, never shows she rules;
> Charms by accepting, by submitting sways,
> Yet has her humour most, when she obeys;
> Lets Fops or Fortune fly which way they will;
> Disdains all loss of Tickets, or Codille;
> Spleen, Vapours, or Small-pox, above them all,
> And Mistress of herself, tho' China fall.   (line 257)

Yet the awkward fact remains that Patty is one of the sex whose claims to
integrity he has dismissed; so he must resort to a stratagem to maintain the
appearance of consistency:

> And yet, believe me, good as well as ill,
> Woman's at best a Contradiction still.
> Heav'n, when it strives to polish all it can
> Its last best work, but forms a softer Man;
> Picks from each sex, to make its Fav'rite blest,
> Your love of Pleasure, our desire of Rest,
> Blends, in exception to all gen'ral rules,
> Your Taste of Follies, with our Scorn of Fools,
> Reserve with Frankness, Art with Truth ally'd,
> Courage with Softness, Modesty with Pride,
> Fix'd Principles, with Fancy ever new;
> Shakes all together, and produces – You.   (line 269)

To judge by these antitheses, although woman is God's 'last best work', she
can become an adequate person only by appropriating qualities defined as
masculine. The theme of virtue as balance, and the moderation that entails
'yielding to the tyde' are crucial to Pope's moral poetry, yet their exemplifica-
tion in terms of gender is complicated by the insistence of the culture on maintaining arbitrary boundaries: the pattern here, with its alternating 'your' and
'our' uneasily suggests that some parts of Patty's character are more properly
hers than others.[38] Although Pope's combination of legal and physical handi-
caps had ruled out for him certain conventionally male roles, and although
he had come to value and to exploit creatively tendencies in himself that were
closer to female stereotypes, it is hardly surprising that his criticism of limiting

[38] *Imitations of Horace*, Epistles, I.i.34 (*TE*, IV, 281).

gender prescriptions operates only at the most self-conscious levels of his dealings with women, without transforming the underlying structures of his judgement. Only this level of assumptions can account for the irony that while he deliberately reaches for 'masculine' qualities to dignify the woman he loves, he loves her precisely because, unlike the other women who had most strongly attracted him, her 'masculine' traits did not include the delight in public display crucial to his life as a professional poet.

The most intimate part of the poem is its close, in which the awkward scaffolding of the Opus Magnum is recalled only by the pathos of the twin representatives of women's alleged ruling passions:

> Be this a Woman's Fame: with this unblest,
> Toasts live a scorn, and Queens may die a jest.
> This Phoebus promis'd (I forget the year)
> When those blue eyes first open'd on the sphere;
> Ascendant Phoebus watch'd that hour with care,
> Averted half your Parents simple Pray'r,
> And gave you Beauty, but deny'd the Pelf
> Which buys your sex a Tyrant o'er itself.   (line 281)

His teasing gallantry, as he draws attention to the colour of her eyes and pretends to have forgotten her age, confirms that despite her quasi-male qualities she is still for him one of the sex defined as fair, but there is far more to his peroration than such obvious flatteries. He represents her parents praying that she might be rich and beautiful – Lister who had willed her an inheritance he did not have, and Pax who lived to find that an attractive but dowerless daughter could put paid to any prospect of peace or respectability. Yet here for once Pope lays aside his hostility to Patty's family, and calls her parents no worse than 'simple', and that for assuming that wealth would have brought her happiness. In spirited contrast, echoing feelings he had first expressed, probably to Teresa, twenty years previously in 'With the Works of Voiture', he claims that what Patty's society saw as failure was actually a triumphant escape from a 'Tyrant' husband – a reflection which could only have gained plausibility from some of her married friends' experiences in the intervening years (*TE*, VI, 63). At the same time, he is clearing the ground for a discreet but forceful assertion of his own importance, an echo of the age-old poets' claim to confer immortality. By working out the conceit of Phoebus as 'the gen'rous God, who Wit and Gold refines' he can at last associate her with the sun and with the glitter of wit, so central – and ominous – in his most vivid experiences of attraction to women; but now the threat is neutralised because the 'Wit', or mental endowment, is shown in her under the relatively unthreatening forms of 'Sense' and 'Good-humour', while for wit in its specific sense of verbal virtuosity she has her poet, who devotes his wit to her. The ungranted part of the prayer, the 'Gold', is a blessing in disguise for him as much as for her, as it assures him of the vacant place at her side on which he had come to depend. With great delicacy, however, he avoids any gesture of self-assertion out of keeping with the intimacy of the tribute. There is nothing, for instance, like the proclamation that closes the *Rape*:

> *This Lock*, the Muse shall consecrate to Fame,
> And mid'st the Stars inscribe *Belinda*'s Name!
>
> (*Rape*, V.149)

Instead he drops himself with contrived casualness into the tally of her riches, almost as unexpected as the Bibles on Belinda's dressing-table:

> The gen'rous God, who Wit and Gold refines,
> And ripens Spirits as he ripens Mines,
> Kept Dross for Duchesses, the world shall know it,
> To you gave Sense, Good-humour, and a Poet.   (line 289)

These closing lines, with their use of the art that he offers her to argue away her material disadvantages, form a moving parallel with the good humour that he praises in her: both friends in their different ways make the best of a situation that for him as cripple as for her as old maid falls so far short of the ideal.

5

The 1730s saw a succession of deaths and disruptions which focused Pope's desire to see Patty comfortably settled before he died. Soon after his mother's death in 1733 he pleaded with her in the light of his resignation to dying before her:

It is a real truth, that to the last of my moments, the thought of you, and the best of my wishes for you, will attend you, told or untold: I could wish you had once the constancy and resolution to act for your self, whether before or after I leave you (the only way I ever shall leave you) you must determine: but reflect, that the first wou'd make me, as well as your self, happier; the latter could make you only so. Adieu.

(*Corr.*, III, 386)

But on this subject she remained immovable.

The appearance of *Characters of Women* early in 1735 prompted Caryll to renewed hopes that Pope meant to solve Patty's problems by marrying her, a suggestion that Pope jestingly brushed aside. However, it was a difficult year in which to avoid the topic, since it saw both the second marriage of Lady Suffolk, now happy at last and consequently relying less and less on Patty, and the public re-marriage of the dying Lord Peterborough to Anastasia Robinson, which enabled the former singer not only to face the world as his widow, but also to inherit the house he was so anxious to complete for her before he died (pp. 474, 487–88). Both marriages provided public vindication and a measure of consolation after long difficulties, and Pope's commission from Peterborough to help his widow lay out her gardens involved him in long and poetically fertile visits to this congenial Catholic friend in the setting created for her as a final testament of marital love. Although the train of Pope's thought is far from clear, it seems to be at about this time that he starts to think of doing something similar for Patty.[39]

The atmosphere from which he wanted to rescue Patty is well illustrated by Teresa's contemptuous response to Lady Suffolk's marriage:

> my Person has been, almost, in town, only some days in Richmond, I doe not dislike my Pass-time; Y^e Summer has been Wet, & I have several I know in London but as my Sister lives, at Lady Suffolks, more a happyness; Company al day; to behold ye happy Pair; & at night, to see her deaf-Ear, & his Lame-leg: put into a Bed on Purpose baught, for ye unexpectid Nuptialls; ye queens Consent I dare say was not wanting.[40]

Marble Hill, which was gradually to fade out of Patty's life in the following years, had in fact provided exactly the kind of refuge she needed; and in an attempt to interest her in another alternative to home, Pope in 1736 persuaded her to spend a fortnight on her own in a small country house belonging to Fortescue: as he told the owner, 'I fancy, if she once felt the Sweets of Independency, & Peace, she could not return to noise and oppression' (*Corr.*, IV, 26). Predictably, although Patty enjoyed her stay, she was not inspired to leave home (pp. 183–84).

With Caryll's death in 1736 Patty lost the principal sharer in Pope's concern for her, yet despite his dwelling on her problems in his correspondence with others of their mutual friends he was by no means constantly with her. As early as 1730 he had written to Gay with rueful exaggeration that she had 'advised me to pass more time in my studies', going on to reflect that 'she wou'd compleat all her kindnesses to me by returning me to the Employment I am fittest for; Conversation with the dead, the old, and the worm-eaten' (*Corr.*, III, 135). This may simply reflect his characteristic self-belittlement with regard to women; but as his desire to see Patty separated from her family increased, it seems that, as he confessed to Bethel in 1738, his pique at what he saw as her obstinacy had become an effective barrier to intimacy:

> Mrs Blount is at Kew & so is her Sister in the neighborhood: They have left their house in town, & taken another, into which our friend has the Resolution to goe with them, the only Resolution she has being to go counter to her Friends advices – I remonstrated to her in vain, early enough – I see her less than usual, as she hath been constantly with Lady Gerard, in Town & at Kew, & as the distance from me thither exceeds my walking, & takes up 4 or 5 hours going & coming: But the main reason is, that I see there's no good to be done her, & she fretts me too much, who am too seriously concern'd for it.   (IV,113)

In similar vein, he closes a letter to her in 1739 in which he has proposed

---

[39] For Lady Peterborough, see Martin, pp. 185–86, 189, 193–96. Pope starts to think of his home's passing into other hands in *Corr.*, IV, 34, 40–41.

[40] Margaret Blum, 'Two Letters from Teresa Blount to the Countess of Coningsby', *Notes and Queries*, 221 (1976), 348–52 (p. 350).

that she should visit some mutual friends with the confession, 'But this, I know, is a Dream: and almost Every thing I wish, in relation to You, is so always!' (p. 188) Moreover, if the unauthorised printing of 'The First Ode of the Fourth Book of Horace' in 1737 is correct in using Patty's name, as the prominence of the moon and its associated flux of waters may perhaps suggest, this sense of grasping at shadows also had its dimension of erotic frustration:

> – But why? ah PATTY, still too dear!
> Steals down my cheek th'involuntary Tear?
>   Why words so flowing, thoughts so free,
> Stop, or turn nonsense at one glance from Thee?
>   Thee, drest in Fancy's Airy Beam,
> Absent I follow thro' th'extended Dream,
>   Now, now I seize, I clasp thy charms,
> And now you burst, (ah cruel!) from my arms,
>   And swiftly shoot along the Mall,
>   Or softly glide by the Canal,
>   Now shown by Cynthia's silver Ray,
> And now, by rolling Waters wash'd away.
>
> (*TE*, IV, 148–53; line 37)

Yet her intransigence, whatever its precise nature, did not mean indifference: in the autumn of 1740, when he was too ill to cross the river to visit her at Richmond as often as he would have liked, she was 'as kind as she can in coming to me', and in 1742 it was she who remonstrated with the tiresomely adoring correspondent of his last years who called herself Amica.[41] Moreover, although Ruffhead's allegation that she neglected Pope in his last illness seems to have come from Warburton, Warburton himself had spent all of the last three weeks of Pope's life with the Allens at Prior Park, not returning until the funeral; and in 1755 he tacitly agreed with Spence that 'Mrs. Blount's coming in gave a new turn of spirits or a temporary strength to him, very agreeable to what we saw of him in his last month.'[42] We know she was there on at least one occasion, from the anecdote that when she arrived to find him sitting outside she said to Marchmont, 'What, is he not dead yet?', and it is by no means necessary to accept Johnson's assumption that her words were unkindly meant.[43] When Spence interviewed her in 1749, five years after Pope's death, she spoke of him soberly but tenderly, remembering the vivacity that had charmed her when she first knew him, his piety to his father's memory, his resemblance in charity to his mother, his pleasure in helping his friends, and his tendency to 'be duped into too high or too good an opinion of people, from the goodness of his own heart, and his general humanity' (Spence, nos. 12, 101, 284, 358). Most evocative of all, she offered

---

[41] *Corr.*, IV, 269; Mack, *Life*, pp. 796–801; Martin, pp. xxi–xxii.
[42] Ruffhead, p. 548; *Corr.*, IV, 522; Spence, no. 641.
[43] Johnson, III, 190; Mack, *Life*, p. 811.

a rare glimpse of the sensibility that united them: 'I have often seen him weep in reading very tender and melancholy passages' (no. 409). Whatever her intimate response to his love, it is clear that she had relished his conversation from an early age, had shared with him romantic tastes that other men might have disdained, had sincerely esteemed his good qualities, and had proved over many years a loyal though by no means a constant companion.

Warburton's hostility to Patty, the prime cause of the derogatory treatment of her character that later became standard, was brought into relief by a quarrel which darkened the last year that she and Pope were to share. In the mid 1730s Pope had begun a late but intense friendship with Ralph Allen of Prior Park near Bath, and by 1742 he had introduced Patty to Mrs Allen and had begun to mention her in his letters.[44] It is hard not to feel that he was forcing the pace, for he was soon confiding her intimate family troubles to the Allens and trying to arrange for her to rent a house from them, hoping that she would 'come at last to her Senses & fix in your neighbourhood', and looking forward to a time when 'she will become as Sure and constant Friend, as well as Tenant, for years to come' (*Corr.*, IV, 430). But tactics which had once worked with Mrs Howard were to prove less effective with Mrs Allen. Patty too may have had reservations: although in April 1743 Pope told the Allens of her mother's death and her sister's aggravations of her distress, and went so far as to arrange for the Allens to invite her for a therapeutic visit, she did not in the end go (IV, 452–53).

When, at the end of July, Patty finally took up their invitation, she arrived to find tension already in the air, for Allen had refused Pope's request to borrow a house on his estate as a lodging for Warburton, himself and the imminently expected George Arbuthnot (IV, 461). Further strain apparently resulted from Patty's expectation of being driven to the Catholic chapel in Bath in Allen's coach, for Allen, who was Mayor that year, is said to have agreed only 'on condition she would go the back way, & leave it at some little Distance' (Spence, no. 361, note). The principal offence, however, seems to have arisen from Mrs Allen's outrage at secret visits made by Patty to Pope's bedroom before the family was stirring. Allen's niece and heiress Gertrude Tucker, who was in 1745 to become Mrs Warburton, later recounted that 'she lay at that time in the next room to Pope, & that every Mor^g between 6 & 7 o'clock, Mrs Blount used to come into his Chamber, when she heard them talk earnestly together for a long time. & that when they came down to breakfast, M^{rs} B: usd alys to ask him how he had rested that night.'[45] Although Mrs Warburton later claimed that Patty had called her 'the only Person in the House, that had been civil to her', and had given her 'a little bawble, that hung to her watch' on parting, it seems not unlikely that she had been responsible for passing on the intelligence to her aunt; for after the

<hr/>

[44] Erskine-Hill, *Social Milieu*, p. 227; *Corr.*, IV, 387.
[45] Duncan C. Tovey, *Gray and his Friends: Letters and Relics* (Cambridge, 1890), p. 281.

quarrel Pope pointedly referred to 'Listeners at doors'.[46] The 'earnest conversation' was in all probability simply Patty venting her dissatisfaction with
the family Pope was so intent on idealising; for she had a shrewd understanding of his constitutional weakness for thinking too well of people
(Spence, no. 284).

In 1749 Patty gave Spence her account of what had happened:

> I soon observed a strangeness of behaviour in them. They used Mr. Pope very rudely,
> and Mr. Warburton with double complaisance (to make their ill-usage of the other the
> more apparent). Me they used oddly, in a very stiff, and over-civil manner. I asked
> Mr. Pope, after I had been there three or four days, whether he had observed their
> usage of him. He said he had taken no notice of it, but a day or two after, he said that
> 'the people had got some odd thing or another in their heads'. This oddness continued,
> or rather increased, as long as they stayed.   (no. 361)

Warburton's stance was evidently part of his campaign to ingratiate himself
with Allen, who only a year after Pope's death 'gave him his niece and his
estate, and by consequence a bishoprick' (Johnson, III, 169). Much as Pope
laboured to idealise Warburton, he was for once jolted into telling Patty, 'W.
is a sneaking Parson, & I told him he flatterd' (*Corr.*, IV, 464). He also let
slip the elaborate mask of his politeness to Mrs Allen: 'however well I might
wish the Man, the Woman is a Minx, & an impertinent one, & he will do
what She would have him'.

This was the worst of times for Patty to face a crisis, with her mother only
three months dead, increased pressure from Pope to leave Teresa, and cor-
responding pressure from Teresa to stay. Even allowing for Pope's desire to
rouse the Allens' sympathy, the account he had given them in April suggests
a person on the verge of breakdown:

> An unaccountable Tenderness she has for her Sister who is practising upon her every
> way, and a Dejection of Spirits, have thrown her into so weak a condition, that I dread
> the Consequence, if she be left but a few days longer here; and this weakness is made
> an Argument against her Journy: She is in Terrors at every thing.   (IV, 452)

After Pope's departure from Prior Park with Arbuthnot she stayed on for
several days, and wrote to him of her anger and disgust:

> I hope you are well. I am not. My spirits are quite down, tho they should not. for
> these people deserve so much to be dispised, one should do nothing but Laugh. I pack-
> ed up all my things yesterday, the servants knew it, Mr & Mrs Allen, never said a
> word, nor so much as asked me how I went or where, or when. in short from every
> one of them much greater inhumanity than I could conceive any body could shew. Mr
> Warburton takes no notice of me. tis most wonderfull. they have not one of 'em named
> your name, nor drank your health since you went. they talk to one another without
> putting me at all in the conversation.   (IV, 426)

---

[46] For a variety of unpleasant contemporary allegations about Gertrude Tucker, see Erskine-
Hill, pp. 234–35; Dilke, II, 273; *Corr.*, IV, 464.

Here, with a vengeance, is the plain style praised by Swift. In contrast, Pope's celebration of her sufferings, in which he gallantly stresses the altruism of her outrage, is almost rhapsodic:

So strange a disappointment as I met with, the extreme Sensibility which I know is in your nature of such monstrous Treatment, & the bitter Reflection that I was wholly the unhappy cause of it, did really so distract me while with you, that I could neither speak, nor move, nor act, nor think. I was like a Man stunn'd, or stabbd, where he expected an Embrace. And I was dejected to death, seeing I could do or say nothing to comfort, but ev'ry thing rather to hurt you. But for Gods sake know, that I understand it was Goodness & Generosity you showed me under the appearance of Anger itself; When you bid me first go to Lord B.'s from them, & then hasten hither, I was sensible it was in resentment of their Conduct to me, & to remove me from such Treatment, tho You stayed alone to suffer it yourself. But I depended you would not have been a *Day* longer in the House, after I left you last; and of all I have endur'd, nothing gave me so much pain of heart, as to find by your Letters you were still under their roof. I dread their provoking you to Any Expression unworthy of you. Even *Laughter* would be taking too much notice. but I more dread your Spirits, & falling under such a dejection as renders you incapable of resolving on the Means of getting out of all this. You frighten yourself more, than were you in any other house, you would be sensible you need do. If you would go directly to London, you may without the least danger, go in a Coach, & Six of Kings Horses, (with a servant on horseback, as far as Marlborow, writing to John to meet you there) for 6 or 7 ll as safe no doubt as in any Nobleman or Gentlemans Coach.   (IV, 463)

Just as at home, she is more inclined to complain about her problems than to solve them, and he fears that the longer she delays the less able she will be to act at all. In her letter she had expressed her intention of leaving, but in explaining that her plan to travel in the coach of a friendly lord had come to nothing she had given the impression of an extreme and worrying fastidiousness about her means of transport, so that Pope here feels he has to apply persuasion before she will even consider the obvious course of hiring a coach (IV, 462). He then proposes a whole series of alternative arrangements, begging her to leave the house where he fears she will 'intimidate your poor Soul to death'. His whole attitude in the letter underlines his perception in her of a helplessness arising from 'extreme Sensibility' which casts on him the responsibility for her welfare. It is the story of the later phase of their relationship in miniature, revealing the ironic role of frustration in heightening his devotion.

This is in fact the only substantial exchange of letters between Pope and Patty now extant; and it shows poignantly how in daily life as well as in *Characters of Women* he idealised this touchy and indecisive woman along the lines of his archetypal unfortunate lady. What he calls 'extreme Sensibility', thereby aligning it with the 'romantic taste' for fantasy and landscape that he revelled in gratifying, is in this context a sensitivity to insult which has resulted, apparently, in her using words to him that he is anxious to palliate as 'Goodness & Generosity . . . under the appearance of Anger itself'; and it is suggestive of his experience of her temper that he warns her against being roused to 'Any Expression unworthy of you' and stresses his own resolution to 'show my Resentment without lessning myself'. Perhaps owing to her formative experiences of dependence on unreliable men and domination by Teresa, Patty was chronically indecisive. Lacking the ability to assert herself constructively, or to express her dissatisfaction to those responsible, she seems to have found an outlet for her distress not only in her frequent illnesses but also in bitter complaints to Pope, and perhaps to other close friends. If, as seems likely, he was used to bearing the brunt of her anger with third parties, this must have been a powerful incentive to his efforts to help her out of her situation of chronic distress.

A further glimpse of the way Patty dealt with anger is provided by her quarrel with their old friend and fellow Catholic Nathaniel Hooke, an impoverished scholar to whom Allen's patronage was especially valuable. She later told Spence that when she had urged Pope to seek 'satisfaction' from Allen, Hooke, who was with them at the time, had taken it 'in the genteel sense of the word, and imagined she would have Mr. Pope fight him' (Spence, no. 361). There must have been considerable bitterness in her tone to give rise to such a fear: the incident powerfully suggests a strain in Patty's character that Pope's stress on good humour sought to minimise. Moreover the almost comic idea that anyone could have expected a man as feeble and deformed as Pope to issue a challenge underlines the pathos of his limited power to satisfy the expectations women had of his sex. It would be surprising if Patty had never felt irritation at the fate that had offered her only a man who in so many ways hardly counted.

Another sign of Patty's difficulty in dealing openly with her distress over her treatment by the Allens – which was of course particularly hard to share with friends since it amounted to a slur on her chastity – comes from her strangely whimsical correspondence at the very height of the trouble with the Duchess of Queensberry, who wanted her to come on a visit. The Duchess, former patron of their beloved Gay, was an old friend, but Patty was not prepared to take her into her confidence. Although only a few years previously Patty had been complaining to Pope (not, of course, to the Duchess) that she had failed to invite her, at this painful juncture Patty is determined not to see her, and at the same time not to admit that anything is wrong (Corr., IV, 212). On 3 August 1743 the Duchess acknowledged a letter in which Patty had confessed, with apparent playfulness, to being 'the most touchy wrong headed woman in all England' in refusing her invitation; and on 22 August the Duchess responded to what she obviously took as playful self-mockery with a dismissive 'why should one waist time by talking to the incorragable' (Blount Letters, II, 90; III, 163). Patty's exasperating diffidence and indecisiveness were all too familiar, but in this case they concealed misery that the Duchess, who actually reproaches her with failing to pass on Bath gossip, is far from guessing. We are left wondering how often Patty's celebrated good humour functioned as an unhealthy avoidance of difficult emotions, and how often Pope found himself burdened with problems that she could neither cure nor share with others.

It must have been well before the quarrel with the Allens that Pope had begun negotiations to buy a house in town, since on 5 August George Arbuthnot, acting as his agent in a matter in which no Catholic was legally allowed to act at all, agreed to buy a twenty-six-year lease on the last house in Berkeley Street at the Berkeley Square end, undertaking to complete by the end of the month (Blount Letters, III, 132–34). Meanwhile the owner of the house he leased at Twickenham had died, and he was also negotiating to buy that: he refers to it as 'a wise bargain for me, & my heirs', and seems to be considering offering it to one of his male friends (*Corr.*, IV, 446, 467). In September he showed that he envisaged Patty's taking over the town house when he recorded in a memorandum that 'The House in Berkley Street for 26 years to come is mine also and I give the same to Mrs M Blount' (Blount Papers, c. 65). This was one aspect of his desire to dispose of his estate in good works that would live after him, rather than in the kind of vain pomp for which he criticised the Duchess of Buckingham, and a house was less liable than some of his efforts on Patty's behalf to be 'renderd impracticable or disagreable to her, by malicious Insinuations', as he had complained to Bethel (*Corr.*, IV, 446, 476). In December he provided further for her in his will, by which she was to have £1,000 outright, all his goods and chattels, and the income from his estate for life (*Prose Works*, II, 508). In March 1744, however, he explained to Bethel that he had given up the idea of buying his Twickenham home:

I've determind not to purchase this, which will cost me 1200 ll & instead of it to lay out 3 upon a cheap one in London, seated in an airy high place. If I live but 5 months I shall never be able to live about, as I us'd, in other peoples houses, but quite at Ease, to keep my own hours, & with my own Servants: and if I don't live there, it will do for a Friend, which Twitnam would not suit at all.   (*Corr.*, IV, 508)

Patty's needs were constantly present to him in these last months, although the demands she made on his loyalty over her anger with his new friend Allen were painful to him, as he moved towards a reconciliation that cannot have been welcome to her. This is the subject of his last extant letter to her, in which he admits that he has been reconciled to Allen despite Allen's refusal to confess even that there had been a quarrel, still less to assign a cause; and he tells Patty that he has told Allen, 'I could answer for it, Mrs Blount was never likely to take any notice of the whole so far from misrepresenting any particular', in effect giving a guarantee of good behaviour on her behalf (IV, 510–11). Patty cannot have been pleased with this fresh instance of his compulsion to think well even of those she despised, but she would surely have been furious had she seen a letter he had written to Allen a few days previously, in which, with an unpleasant and no doubt unconscious irony, he says of Mrs Allen's health what he was so accustomed to say of Patty: 'I don't know a more Vexatious and painful Anxiety, than when those we love are obstinate against their own Good' (IV, 509).

Whatever implied disloyalty Patty may have sensed in his last letter, it ended with confirmation that his frustrated desire to see her happy was strong as ever: indeed it may be that he is already encouraging her to move into the town house that is to be hers:

I assure you I don't think half so much what will become of me, as of You; and when I grow worst, I find the anxiety for you doubled. Would to God you would Quicken your haste to settle, by reflecting what a pleasure it would be to me, just to see it, and to see you at ease; & then I could contentedly leave you to the Providence of God, in this Life, & resign my Self to it in the other! I have little to say to you when we meet. but I love you upon unalterable Principles, which makes me feel my heart the same to you as if I saw you every hour. adieu

This seems a fitting final scene in a relationship which, despite its many fruits in both their lives, had come to centre on an endless circling between his frustration and her obstinacy. We do not know whether she was at his deathbed, although her frequent companion Anne Arbuthnot was certainly at Twickenham ten days before he died (Spence, no. 649). We know this only because she made a remark striking enough for Spence to record it, but, apart from the aphorism that opens *Characters of Women*, Patty had never been noted for striking remarks.

6

Although Pope had already taken possession of the Berkeley Street house and spent £90 on repairs, he had been unable to complete the purchase before he died, owing to the death of the vendor and the inability of his widow to produce the deeds.[47] When Pope died on 30 May 1744 his sister was enraged to find that Patty, not she, was the principal beneficiary of his will; and not content with blocking the purchase of the Berkeley Street house (on the grounds that as heirs to the residue of Pope's estate after Patty's death she and her sons stood to gain nothing from a lease which might have expired by then), she threatened to go to court to have the will set aside (Blount Letters, I, 123).

The complicated difficulties of this sale, represented in the Blount archives by a mass of legal documents, carry Patty's story over the crisis of Pope's death – which is hardly reflected in her papers – into a period in which, with the brilliant if partial light of his commentary extinguished, her inner life, never particularly open to investigation, recedes almost entirely into the shade. The trivia can, however, be suggestive. In the summer after Pope's

47 Papers relating to this complicated negotiation are: Blount Letters, I, 124–52; III, 131–34; Blount Papers, c. 65; Accounts of Martha Blount.

death she had apparently written to her aunt Mrs C. Webbe to say that she had changed her mind about accepting her invitation to go into the country with her; but Mrs Webbe explained that since 'you told me if Mr Pope dy'd you shou'd not go into the contry' she had invited someone else; and she added, 'therefore pray blame none but your self for the disapointment' (Blount Papers, c. 63). This seems a brusque way of dealing with a bereaved person; perhaps the impatience springs from long experience. Not everyone was as ironically accepting of Patty's indecisiveness as the Duchess of Queensberry, and at Patty's age no one else was likely to find in her inability to confront her life with assurance the exasperating fascination that had for so long intensified Pope's preoccupation with her.

Meanwhile, annoyances multiplied upon her. Although Mrs Rackett dropped her challenge to Pope's will, she persisted in her refusal to allow the Berkeley Street house, where Patty was now living, to be paid for out of his estate. Patty was finally forced to buy it out of her own income: she paid the agreed price of £315 on 12 April 1746, together with a much-resented £63 in interest. George Arbuthnot and William Murray went to considerable trouble to look after her interests, and their correspondence suggests that she was a somewhat querulous client. She naturally resented Mrs Rackett's success in making her pay for the house that Pope had meant to give her; and when it came to selling the fittings of the Twickenham house she seems to have held out for a higher price than her advisers thought she could hope for.

At the same time she was involved in quarrels which brought old friendships into question. In June 1744 her horizon was darkened by the 'vile scandalous and barbarous treatment . . . receiv'd from Spence', to quote the sympathetic words of Lord Delawarr, to whom, among others, she turned for help (Blount Letters, II, 60, 163). It seems hardly conceivable that the mild-mannered Joseph Spence is the villain, and there is a hint that this Spence may be attached to the royal household, but it may be that Patty had heard of Spence's promise to let her enemy Warburton use his anecdotes in his projected biography of Pope; and if so, she would have been under no illusions as to how the material affecting her would be slanted.[48] A correspondence with Mrs Pratt soon after Pope's death shows that the story later enshrined in Ruffhead's *Life*, that she had forced Pope to mention Allen unfavourably in his will, was already being used against her: she concludes her angry protestation of innocence with the lament that 'the only person that could justify me is gone'.[49] If she had in fact fallen out with Spence, she was on good terms with him again by 1749, when she told him, just as she had told Mrs Pratt, 'I had never read his will, but he mentioned to me the part relating to Mr. Allen, and I desired him to omit it, but could not prevail on him'

[48] Spence, pp. xxviii–xxix. It is also conceivable that Patty feared that she or others would be politically compromised by Warburton.
[49] Blount Letters, II, 216–17; Ruffhead, pp. 547, 576; Johnson, III, 195–96.

(Spence, no. 360). In view of the fact that Pope had recently borrowed exactly the sum returned to Allen by the will, recent commentators have doubted that this provision was meant as a rebuke, so it is perplexing to find Patty tacitly suggesting that it was (Spence, no. 360, note). Perhaps she is rebutting a charge that is emotionally true although factually misconceived: certainly the pacific image she here presents is a long way from the anger that frightened Hooke. A chilly letter from him, which may relate either to the earlier affair of the duel or to the later question of the will, shows that he was unimpressed with a letter she had shown him to prove her innocence:

I am far, very far, from desiring you should be in the wrong, in any part of conduct. On the contrary, I shoud have an extreme pleasure in thinking, that your anger has never got the better of your Reason.[50]

Grieved as Pope would have been to see his family and friends in conflict with Patty, it remained true that he had succeeded in his prime objective of making her an offer of independence that she could not refuse. She was now established in a home of her own; and from 1745, when she began her household accounts, she became financially autonomous for the first time.[51] Yet Pope must have realised that he could not leave money to Patty without at least some of it finding its way into Teresa's pocket: over the fifteen remaining years of Teresa's life Patty lent her more than £150, mostly in very small amounts, and there is no indication that any of this was repaid. From 1756 she also paid Teresa's rent, perhaps a small price to pay for not having her under the same roof. For her part Teresa continued to press her nephew for money and to correspond with Mrs Nelson, whose strikingly frivolous response to the danger of their friends after the Jacobite invasion of 1745 harks back to an attitude that Patty and Pope had long outgrown.[52] Yet Patty remained faithful to her sister, to the extent of asking the Duchess of Queensberry in 1752 whether she could bring Teresa on a visit (Blount Letters, III, 4–5). In reply the Duchess stressed that 'our nut shell' was far too small, 'tho the King himself were to borrow our little habitation of Peter-sham'. It is hard to avoid the suspicion that the Duchess simply could not bear the prospect of Teresa's company.

Teresa died on 7 October 1759 after a long illness and her burial at St Pancras Church was organised by Michael, who also administered her estate (Blount Papers, c. 65). When in 1758 she had mentioned in a letter to Michael that she had received a visit from Mr Cox, the Englefields' chaplain, the pious

---

[50] Blount Letters, II, 104. The letter, dated January 1744, would relate most obviously to the affair of the duel; but if the date is Old Style it could relate to Pope's will, as its opening reference to the return of an enclosure from Patty suggests; for she told Spence that she had sent Hooke a letter from Pope that showed her innocence (Spence, no. 360). She seems also to have shown this letter to Mrs Pratt (Blount Letters, II, 216).

[51] Blount Papers, Accounts of Martha Blount.

[52] Blount Letters, III, 171. Compare Pope's letter to both sisters in 1715, *Corr.*, I, 308–9.

Mary Eugenia had written to her husband, 'I hope he will go to her often.'
In a letter of condolence to Patty the Catholic chaplain Thomas Phillips
admitted that although he had known Patty for twenty years, his acquaintance with Teresa had been only 'very slender' (Blount Letters, II, 185–205).
He knew, however, how much Patty would miss her: 'Tho' your Sister's long
infirmities rendered her death, in some sense, not untimely, yet your great
tenderness for her must, I am persuaded, make it very sensible to you.' These
hints that Teresa had had little time for the clergy who played such an important part in her sister's life hardly come as a surprise. As well as Mr Phillips,
Patty corresponded with Mr Chapman, the priest of the chapel at Bath which
had figured in her quarrel with the Allens: he praised her for 'a remarkable
Instance of the *true Catholick* Spirit', probably referring to her behaviour on
that occasion (Blount Papers, c. 63). She also kept in touch with Francis
Southcote, a Benedictine of about her own age who to their mutual sorrow
had been forced to retire to the continent on account of ill health.[53] Her
association with Pope obviously enhanced her standing with at least some of
her clergy friends: Bethel's Yorkshire friend the Anglican clergyman William
Key was grateful to receive from her some pictures of the poet; and Mr
Phillips, who called her 'Clarissa', remarked that wherever her name was
mentioned in Pope's letters 'some circumstance which entertains & improves'
was sure to follow.[54]

Literary associations probably made little difference, however, to the
esteem felt for her by her nephew Michael and his wife Mary Eugenia. Their
pious domesticity would hardly have been congenial to Teresa; and it may be
significant that Patty (but not apparently Teresa) was godmother to one of
their children, Mary Martha, known as 'little Patty', who was still a baby
when her godmother died. Patty was also a valued correspondent of her
cousin, Matthew Swinburne, who later described her as 'a little, neat, fair,
prim, old woman, easy and gay in her manner and conversation'.[55]
Although he added that in comparison with Teresa's 'uncommon wit and
abilities' she 'seemed not to possess any extraordinary talents', he, like Pope,
valued her for her fidelity, and he declared that amidst his difficulties, which
centred on his relationship with his older brothers, there was 'no body I can
open my heart too but you' (Blount Letters, III, 67–87). Living abroad, he
became uneasy if he did not hear from her regularly: in June 1763, only a
month before she died, he complained that he had not had a letter for nearly

[53] Blount Letters, III, 110. For Francis Southcote, presumably a relation of Pope's early friend
Thomas (see index to Spence, Philip Southcote, Thomas Southcote), see *English and Welsh
Priests 1558–1800*, edited by Dominic Aidan Bellenger (Bath, 1984), p. 110.
[54] Blount Letters, II, 113, 205. William Key is presumably a relation of Bethel's physician Dr
Key: see under 'Kay' in index to *Corr.*
[55] *Pope*, edited by Warton, I, lxv. Warton's statement that she promised to leave Swinburne her
manuscript collections, but that he was deprived of them by her failure to make a will, is
incorrect: she did make a will, in which Swinburne is remembered, but as there was no specific
mention of her papers, they went to Michael Blount as part of the residue of her estate.

a year, and he mentioned that he had heard that she had hurt her arm in a fall. He concludes, 'you are the last of my friends Dear Cosen, that I can imagine would abandon me', a verdict well supported by the evidence of her loyalty to various unhappy friends. Horace Walpole gives additional testimony to her loyalty when he describes how he saw her after Pope's death 'with nothing remaining of her immortal charms but her *blue eyes*, trudging on foot with her petticoats pinned up, for it rained, to visit *blameless Bethel*, who was sick at the end of the street' (*HW Corr.*, XXXIII, 511). In another version of the anecdote he further stressed the loss of her beauty:

Patty Blount was red-faced, fat, and by no means pretty. Mr Walpole remembered her walking to Mr. Bethell's, in Arlington Street, after Pope's death, with her petticoats tucked up like a sempstress.[56]

To judge by the only picture of Patty in later life (see plate 5), this was accurate if unkind; but for Pope, 'those blue eyes', the sole link between the plump Patty of middle age and the graceful young woman captured by Jervas, had long since been eclipsed by more fundamental qualities. 'She is as constant to old friendship as any man', he had told Swift; and both men, whatever their indignation at Walpole's implied sneer, would have respected the image of her unabashed simplicity, which presents so telling a contrast to 'the Ghosts of Beauty' who represented for Pope the worst and characteristic destiny of her sex.[57]

At the beginning of December 1762 Patty's accounts were taken over by an amanuensis, and on the thirteenth she made her will, naming various relations, servants and Catholic friends (Blount Papers, c. 65). Just before she died in July 1763 she received a letter from Frances Browne, the remarried widow of one of the Fermors, giving news of their mutual friend Lady Shrewsbury, née Dormer, and inviting Patty to visit the old Fermor house at Tusmore: the familiar names, like those mentioned in her will, recall the inbred Catholic world from which *The Rape of the Lock* had sprung.[58] Perhaps in retrospect the years she had spent amongst the Scriblerians seemed a brief cosmopolitan excursion from the world into which she had been born and in which she was to die.

Patty died suddenly on 12 July 1763, a month after her seventy-third birthday.[59] On the seventeenth, Mary Eugenia wrote to her husband from Mapledurham, commenting on his 'Surprise, Hurry and expeditious Journey', and expressing concern that 'my poor Dear Aunt, coud only receive the Sacrament of Extream Unction' (Blount Papers, c. 65). She went on to express the hope that 'she has been preparing in a periticular manner for

[56] Sir James Prior, *Life of Edmond Malone* (London, 1860), p. 437.
[57] *Corr.*, IV, 135; *Characters of Women*, line 241.
[58] Blount Letters, II, 35; G.E.C., *Peerage*, George Talbot, seventeenth Earl of Shrewsbury.
[59] Blount Papers, Mortuary Book.

Death on account of her advanced Age, and very infirm state of health'. Fortunately, Mr Cox was able to reassure Michael that his aunt had indeed made
a good end. Moreover, apart from a few small legacies, Patty had left everything
to Michael; and Mary Eugenia, herself very pleased with her keepsake of a
diamond cross, commented that 'as to my Aunt's not Leaveing any thing to
Patty, she might think that leaveing to so good a Father woud be as well for
her Dear little God-Daughter'. Yet busy and affectionate as Mary Eugenia
is over the arrangement of mourning and settling of the estate, her overriding
preoccupation with her children unwittingly underlines the fact that the
Blounts' world will go on very well without their old aunt. She is in reality
far less concerned with Patty's death than with the birthday of their dead son
Charles ('he is Celebrating a truly Happy Feast in Heaven'); and as she
checks consignments of Patty's belongings against Michael's meticulous in-
ventories she is delighted by the appearance of little Patty's first teeth, and
happily reports, 'When I ask her where is Papa? she looks up at Your Picture
in the great Parlour.'

Michael arranged for Patty to be buried next to her sister in St Pancras church-
yard, and, with his wife's earnest approval, he paid several priests to say
mass for her. She lies in an unmarked grave, an obscurely private person in
death as in life, winning her place in literary history, such as it is, precisely by
refusing to be the kind of woman who makes a name for herself.[60] On hearing of
Pope's death the little-known poet Francis Hawling had sent to her a substantial
appreciation of Pope's career, in which, although he had never met her, he combined his reading of *Characters of Women* with his idea of her and of Pope's love for
her.[61] Following Pope's hints, Hawling outlined the generalised image, largely
defined by negatives, that was all that he could properly know of a good woman
familiar to him only through the publicity of art:

> Opos'd to Thee, He Drew ye Formal Prude,
> The Fickle, Vain, ye Foolish, and ye Leud.
> Taught Women, Sense and Virtue to Prefer,
> And what They Ought to be, by what you are;
> Pure as Ethereal Minds which Reignn above,
> As Seraphs Languish, and as Angels Love,
> With Truth's Calm Eye yor Beauties He Aprov^d,
> And made Immortal what so Dear He Lov'd.

[60] She was buried next to her sister, on the south side of the monument to 'Mr Eyres of Hasop'
(Blount Papers, c. 65). St Pancras was a customary burial place for London Catholics: Pope's
aunt Christiana Cooper had also been buried there.

[61] Blount Letters, I, 117–18. The poem is not included in Hawling's *A Miscellany of Original Poems
on Various Subjects*, Part 1 (London, 1752: the date on the title page is confused, and the promised
second volume seems never to have appeared). Some separately published poems are listed in
D. F. Foxon, *English Verse 1701–1750*, 2 vols. (Cambridge, 1975), pp. 335–36. Four plays by
Hawling are listed in David Erskine Baker and Stephen Jones, *Biographica Dramatica*, 3 vols.
(London, 1812), I, 318, but none was then extant and the authors were unable to discover
anything of Hawling's biography. A sample of his work is included in Lonsdale, pp. 200–1.

It is an ironic immortality, which has made her a familiar name but hardly a familiar person to readers of poetry: in literature as in life she stands 'in the shade' of her more brilliant, more ambitious contemporaries. Only in the documents of private life do her individual traits appear, complicating the age's icon of the good woman and pointing the ironies imposed by such stereotypes; but even these private sources illuminate her inner life only fitfully. The bright light of literary immortality shines instead on Belinda, Sappho, Atossa, creatures of the fascination with which female brilliance compelled Pope's divided imagination.

Bibliography

Manuscripts

Blount Archives
Accounts of Martha (Patty) Blount
Accounts of Michael Blount I
Accounts of Michael Blount II
Blount Letters
Blount Papers
Mortuary Book
Catalogue of the Blount Library by Richard Williams
Transcription by Richard Williams of the record of her children kept by Martha (Pax) Blount

British Library
Add. MSS 9129 (Coxe Papers)
Add. MSS 9200 (Etough Papers)
Add. MSS 22626–27 (Suffolk Papers)
Add. MSS 28101 (Cowper Anthology)
Add. MSS 32697 (Newcastle Correspondence)
Add. MSS 34728 (West Papers)
Add. MSS 35585 (Hardwicke Correspondence)
Add. MSS 61457–78 (Blenheim Papers)
Add. MSS 62558–59 (Caesar Papers)

Public Record Office
State Papers Foreign (France), SP 78/198–203
Probate 11/727/66 (will of Catherine Duchess of Buckingham)

Quai d'Orsay
Archives étrangères, correspondance politique, Angleterre 376–77

Rousham Park
Correspondence of Charles and Mary Caesar

Royal Archives at Windsor Castle
Stuart Papers

Wren Library, Trinity College Cambridge
Scrapbook of Mary Caesar

Printed Books

Abelard and Heloise, *Letters of Abelard and Heloise*, translated by John Hughes, 4th
    edition (London, 1722)
    The Letters of Abelard and Heloise, translated by Betty Radice (Harmondsworth, 1974)
Aden, John M., *Pope's Once and Future Kings: Satire and Politics in the Early Career* (Knox-
    ville, 1978)
Alexander, Boyd, *England's Wealthiest Son: A Study of William Beckford* (London, 1962)
Aquinas, St Thomas, *Summa Theologiae*, Latin text and English translation, 61 vols.
    (Blackfriars, Cambridge, 1963–76)
Aristotle, *Historia Animalium*, translated by D'Arcy Wentworth Thompson (*The Works
    of Aristotle*, edited by J. A. Smith and W. D. Ross, IV; Oxford, 1910)
    Generation of Animals, with an English translation by A. L. Peck, Loeb Classical
    Library (London, 1963)
Astell, Mary, *Some Reflections upon Marriage*, 5th edition (Dublin, 1730)
Atterbury, Francis, *Antonius Musa's Character . . . to which is added, To the Duke of B***,
    on his Birth-Day: A Poem (London, 1740)
    The Epistolary Correspondence of Francis Atterbury, 4 vols. (London, 1783–87)
Audra, E., *L'Influence francais dans l'oeuvre de Pope* (Paris, 1931)
Ault, Norman, *New Light on Pope, with some Additions to his Poetry hitherto Unknown*
    (London, 1949)
Austen, Jane, *Pride and Prejudice*, edited by Frank W. Bradbrook and James Kinsley
    (Oxford, 1970)
Aveling, J. C. H., *The Handle and the Axe* (London, 1976)
Axton, Marie, *The Queen's Two Bodies: Drama and the Elizabethan Succession* (London, 1977)
Ayre, William, *Memoirs of the Life and Writings of Alexander Pope, Esq*, 2 vols. (London,
    1745)
Aeschylus, with an English translation by Herbert Weir Smyth, Loeb Classical Library,
    2 vols. (London, 1957)
Babb, Lawrence, 'The Cave of Spleen', *Review of English Studies*, 12 (1936), 165–76
Baker, David Erskine, and Stephen Jones, *Biographica Dramatica*, 2 vols. (London,
    1812)
Barber, Mary, *Poems on Several Occasions* (London, 1734)
Beer, Gillian, ' "Our Unnatural No-voice": The Heroic Epistle, Pope, and Women's
    Gothic', *Yearbook of English Studies*, 12 (1982), 125–51
Bellenger, Dominic Aidan, ed., *English and Welsh Priests 1558–1800* (Bath, 1984)
Bennett, G. V., *The Tory Crisis in Church and State, 1688–1730: The Career of Francis Atter-
    bury, Bishop of Rochester* (Oxford, 1975)
Berry, William, *Pedigrees of the Families in the County of Hants*, County Genealogies
    (London, 1833)
Blum, Margaret, 'Two Letters from Teresa Blount to the Countess of Coningsby',
    Notes and Queries, 221 (1976), 348–52
Boileau, *Le Lutrin*, VI (*Oeuvres*, edited by Jérôme Vercruysse, 2 vols. (Paris, 1969))
Bond, Donald F., ' "Distrust" of Imagination in English Neo-classicism', *PQ*, 14
    (1935), 54–69

Boswell, James, *Boswell's Life of Johnson*, edited by George Birkbeck Hill and revised by L. F. Powell, 6 vols. (Oxford, 1934–50)
Boswell's Journal of a Tour to the Hebrides with Samuel Johnson, LL.D., edited by Frederick A. Pottle and Charles H. Bennett (London, 1936)
Boswell in Search of a Wife 1766–1769, edited by Frank Brady and Frederick A. Pottle (London, 1957)
Boureau-Deslandes, André François, *Réflexions sur les grands hommes qui sont morts en plaisantant* (Rochefort, 1714)
Bowles, William Lisle, *A Final Appeal to the Literary Public relative to Pope* (London, 1825)
Lessons in Criticism to William Roscoe . . . with Further Lessons in Criticism to a Quarterly Reviewer (London, 1826)
Bowyer, John Wilson, *The Celebrated Mrs Centlivre* (Durham, NC, 1952)
Boyle, John, Earl of Orrery, *A Poem Sacred to the Memory of Edmund Sheffield, Duke of Buckingham* (London, 1736)
Brady, Frank, 'The History and Structure of Pope's *To a Lady*', *SEL*, 9 (1969), 439–62
Brown, Laura, *English Dramatic Form, 1660–1760: An Essay in Generic Form* (London, 1981)
'The Defenceless Woman and the Development of English Tragedy', *Studies in English Literature*, 22 (1982), 429–43
Alexander Pope, Rereading Literature (Oxford, 1985)
Brownell, Morris R., *Alexander Pope and the Arts of Georgian England* (Oxford, 1978)
Bryant, Julius, *Mrs Howard: A Woman of Reason, 1688–1767*, Catalogue of an Exhibition at Marble Hill House in 1988 (London, 1988)
Buckingham, John Duke of: *see* Sheffield, John
Byrd, Max, *Visits to Bedlam: Madness and Literature in the Eighteenth Century* (Columbia, 1974)
Byron, Lord, *The Works of Lord Byron*, 17 vols. (London, 1832–33)
Cavendish, Margaret, Duchess of Newcastle, *The World's Olio* (London, 1655)
Chapin, Chester, 'Alexander Pope: Erasmian Catholic', *Eighteenth-Century Studies*, 6 (1972–73), 411–30
Chauncy, Sir Henry, *The Historical Antiquities of Hertfordshire*, 2 vols. (London, 1700–1826; reprinted Dorking, 1975)
Chesterfield, Philip Earl of, *The Letters of Philip Dormer Stanhope, Earl of Chesterfield*, edited by Lord Mahon, 5 vols. (London, 1845–53)
Churchill, Sarah: *see* Marlborough, Sarah Duchess of
Clutterbuck, Robert, *The History and Antiquities of the County of Hertford*, 3 vols. (London, 1815–27)
Conant, Martha Pike, *The Oriental Tale in England in the Eighteenth Century*, Columbia University Studies in Comparative Literature (New York, 1908)
Cowper, Mary Countess, *Diary of Mary, Countess Cowper, 1714–1720*, edited by Spencer Cowper, 2nd edition (London, 1865)
Coxe, William, *Memoirs of the Life and Administration of Sir Robert Walpole*, 3 vols. (London, 1798)
Crawford, Charlotte, 'What was Pope's Debt to Edward Young?', *ELH*, 13 (1946), 157–67
Croke, Sir Alexander, *The Genealogical History of the Croke Family, Originally Named Le Blount*, 2 vols. (Oxford, 1823)
Cruickshanks, Eveline, *Lord Cornbury, Bolingbroke and a Plan to Restore the Stuarts, 1731–1735*, Royal Stuart Papers, 27 (Huntingdon, 1986)

Cundall, Frank, *The Governors of Jamaica in the First Half of the Eighteenth Century* (London, 1937)

Dearing, Vinton A., 'The Prince of Wales's Set of Pope's Works', *Harvard Library Bulletin*, 4 (1950), 320–38

Delany, Sheila, 'Sex and Politics in Pope's *Rape of the Lock*', *English Studies in Canada*, 1 (1975), 46–61

Dennis, John, *Remarks on Mr. Pope's Rape of the Lock* (London, 1728)

DePorte, Michael V., *Nightmares and Hobbyhorses: Swift, Sterne, and Augustan Ideas of Madness* (San Marino, 1974)

Dilke, Charles Wentworth, *The Papers of a Critic*, 2 vols. (London, 1875)

Dorset, Charles Earl of, *The Poems of Charles Sackville, Sixth Earl of Dorset*, edited by Brice Harris (London, 1979)

Draper, Marie P. G., *Marble Hill House and its Owners* (London, 1970)

Dryden, John, *The Critical and Miscellaneous Prose Works of John Dryden*, edited by Edmond Malone, 3 vols. (London, 1800)

  The Letters of John Dryden, edited by Charles E. Ward (New York, 1942; reprinted 1965)

  The Poems of John Dryden, edited by James Kinsley, 4 vols. (Oxford, 1958)

Duffy, Eamon, ' "Englishmen in Vaine": Roman Catholic Allegiance to George I', *Studies in Church History*, 18 (1982), 345–65

Dunbar, Janet, *Peg Woffington and her World* (London, 1968)

Edelman, Nathan, *Attitudes of Seventeenth-Century France toward the Middle Ages* (New York, 1946)

Egmont, Earl of: *see* Historical Manuscripts Commission

Ehrenpreis, Irvin, *Swift: The Man, His Works, and the Age*, 3 vols. (London, 1962–83)

Erskine-Hill, Howard, 'A New Pope Letter', *Notes and Queries*, 218 (1973), 207–9

  The Social Milieu of Alexander Pope: Lives, Example and the Poetic Response (London, 1975)

  'Heirs of Vitruvius: Pope and the Idea of Architecture', in *The Art of Alexander Pope*, edited by Howard Erskine-Hill and Anne Smith (London, 1979), pp. 114–56

  'Alexander Pope: The Political Poet in his Time', *Eighteenth Century Studies*, 15 (1981–82), 123–48

  'Literature and the Jacobite Cause: Was there a Rhetoric of Jacobitism?', in *Ideology and Conspiracy: Aspects of Jacobitism 1689–1759*, edited by Eveline Cruickshanks (Edinburgh, 1982), pp. 48–69

  'Under which Caesar? Pope in the Journal of Mrs Charles Caesar, 1724–1741', *Review of English Studies*, 33 (1982), 436–44

  'Life into Letters, Death into Art: Pope's Epitaph on Francis Atterbury', *Yearbook of English Studies*, 18 (1988), 200–20

Fabricant, Carole, 'Pope's Portraits of Women: The Tyranny of the Pictorial Eye', in *Women and Men: The Consequences of Power*, edited by Dana V. Hiller and Robin Ann Sheets (Cincinnati, 1976)

  'Binding and Dressing Nature's Loose Tresses: The Ideology of Augustan Landscape Design', *Studies in Eighteenth-Century Culture*, 8 (1979), 109–35

Fairer, David, *Pope's Imagination* (Manchester, 1984)

Ferguson, Rebecca, *The Unbalanced Mind: Pope and the Rule of Passion* (Brighton, 1986)

Filmer, Sir Robert, *Patriarcha and Other Political Works*, edited by Peter Laslett (Oxford, 1949)

Finch, Anne: *see* Winchilsea, Anne Countess of

Foskett, Daphne, *Samuel Cooper and his Contemporaries* (London, 1974)
Fowler, Alastair, *Triumphal Forms: Structural Patterns in Elizabethan Poetry* (Cambridge, 1970)
Foxon, D. F., *English Verse 1701–1750*, 2 vols. (Cambridge, 1975)
Frankl, Paul, *The Gothic: Literary Sources and Interpretations through Eight Centuries* (Princeton, 1960)
Fraser, Antonia, *The Weaker Vessel: Woman's Lot in Seventeenth-Century England* (London, 1984)
Fritz, Paul S., *The English Ministers and Jacobitism between the Rebellions of 1715 and 1745* (Toronto, 1975)
G.E.C., *Complete Baronetage*, 5 vols. and index (Exeter, 1900–1909)
The Complete Peerage, revised by Vicary Gibbs *et al.*, 13 vols. (London, 1910–40)
Gagen, Jean Elizabeth, *The New Woman: Her Emergence in English Drama 1600–1730* (New York, 1954)
Garth, Samuel, *The Dispensary*, 9th edition (Dublin, 1725)
Gay, John, *The Letters of John Gay*, edited by C. F. Burgess (Oxford, 1966)
Poetry and Prose, edited by Vinton A. Dearing and Charles E. Beckwith, 2 vols. (Oxford, 1974)
Dramatic Works, edited by John Fuller, 2 vols. (Oxford, 1983)
Gentleman's Magazine
Glover, John Hulbert, ed., *The Stuart Papers* (London, 1847: only one volume published)
Goreau, Angeline, *Reconstructing Aphra: A Social Biography of Aphra Behn* (Oxford, 1980)
Gosselink, Robert N., 'Pope's Belinda: The Very Name of Coquette', *Papers on Language and Literature*, 14 (1978), 218–23
Green, David, *Sarah Duchess of Marlborough* (London, 1967)
Griffin, Dustin, *Alexander Pope: The Poet in the Poems* (Princeton, 1978)
Grundy, Isobel, 'Pope, Peterborough, and the Characters of Women', *Review of English Studies*, 20 (1969), 461–68
Gubar, Susan, 'The Female Monster in Augustan Satire', *Signs*, 3 (1977), 380–94
Guerinot, J. V., *Pamphlet Attacks on Alexander Pope 1711–1744: A Descriptive Bibliography* (New York, 1969)
Hagstrum, Jean H., *The Sister Arts: The Tradition of Literary Pictorialism and English Poetry from Dryden to Gray* (Chicago, 1958)
Halsband, Robert, 'Pope, Lady Mary, and the *Court Poems* (1716)', *PMLA*, 68 (1953), 237–50
The Life of Lady Mary Wortley Montagu, corrected edition (Oxford, 1961)
'Walpole versus Lady Mary', in *Horace Walpole: Writer, Politician, and Connoisseur*, edited by W. H. Smith (New Haven, 1967), pp. 215–226
' "The Lady's Dressing Room" Explicated by a Contemporary', in *The Augustan Milieu: Essays Presented to Louis A. Landa*, edited by Henry K. Miller *et al.* (Oxford, 1970), pp. 225–31
'New Anecdotes of Lady Mary Wortley Montagu', in *Evidence in Literary Scholarship: Essays in Memory of James Marshall Osborn*, edited by René Wellek and Alvaro Ribeiro (Oxford, 1979), pp. 241–46
The Rape of the Lock and its Illustrations, 1714–1896 (Oxford, 1980)
Hammond, Brean, *Pope*, Harvester New Readings (Brighton, 1986)
Hansard, T. C., ed., *The Parliamentary History of England from the Earliest Period to the Year 1803*, 36 vols. (London, 1806–1820)

Hanson, Ann Ellis, 'Hippocrates: Diseases of Women', *Signs*, 1 (Winter 1975), 567–84

Hatton, Ragnhild, *George I: Elector and King* (London, 1978)

Hawling, Francis, *A Miscellany of Original Poems on Various Subjects*, Part 1 (London, 1752: the date on the title page is confused, and the promised second volume seems never to have appeared)

Hervey, John Lord, *Some Materials towards Memoirs of the Reign of King George II*, edited by Romney Sedgwick, 3 vols. (London, 1931)

   Lord Hervey's Memoirs, edited by Romney Sedgwick (London, 1952)

Hillhouse, James T., 'Teresa Blount and "Alexis" ', *MLN*, 40 (1925), 88–91

Historical Manuscripts Commission, *The Manuscripts of the Marquess Townshend*, Eleventh Report, appendix IV (London, 1887)

   Calendar of the Stuart Papers, 7 vols. (London, 1902–23)

   Report on the Manuscripts of the Marquess of Lothian, Preserved at Blickling Hall, Norfolk (London, 1905)

   Diary of Viscount Percival, Afterwards First Earl of Egmont, 3 vols., Manuscripts of the Earl of Egmont (London, 1920–23)

   Tenth Report of the Royal Commission on Historical Manscripts, appendix, vol. IV (London, 1885)

Historical Register

Hobbes, Thomas, *Leviathan, or the Matter, Forme and Power of a Commonwealth Ecclesiasticall and Civil*, edited by Michael Oakeshott (Oxford, 1960)

Hopkins, Charles, *Epistolary Poems* (London, 1694)

Hopkins, John, *Amasia; or, The Works of the Muses* (London, 1700)

Horace, *Satires, Epistles, Ars Poetica*, with an English translation by H. Rushton Fairclough, Loeb Classical Library (London, 1929)

Howard, Henrietta: *see* Suffolk, Henrietta Countess of

Hughes, Helen Sard, 'A Romantic Correspondence of the Year 1729', *Modern Philology*, 37 (1939), 187–200

The Life and Times of Selina, Countess of Huntingdon, 2 vols. (London, 1844)

Hyde, Mary, *The Thrales of Streatham Park* (Cambridge, Mass., 1977)

Ilchester, Earl of, ed., *Lord Hervey and his Friends* (London, 1950)

Irwin, Anne Viscountess, 'An Epistle to Mr Pope by a Lady, Occasioned by his Characters of Women', *Gentleman's Magazine*, VI (1736), 745

Jack, Ian, 'The Elegy as Exorcism: Pope's "Verses to the Memory of an Unfortunate Lady" ', in *Augustan Worlds: Essays in Honour of A. R. Humphreys*, edited by J. C. Hilson *et al.*, (Leicester, 1978), pp. 69–83

The Jerningham Letters, edited by Egerton Castle, 2 vols. (London, 1896)

Johnson, Samuel, *Lives of the English Poets*, edited by George Birkbeck Hill, 3 vols. (Oxford, 1905)

Johnston, Arthur, *Enchanted Ground: The Study of Medieval Romance in the Eighteenth Century* (London, 1964)

Jones, Emrys, 'Pope and Dulness', Chatterton Lecture on an English Poet, 1968, *Proceedings of the British Academy*, 54 (1968), 231–63

Jones, George Hilton, *The Main Stream of Jacobitism* (Cambridge, Massachusetts, 1954)

   'The Jacobites, Charles Molloy, and *Common Sense*', *Review of English Studies*, 4 (1953), 144–47

Ben Jonson, edited by C. H. Herford, Percy and Evelyn Simpson, 11 vols. (Oxford, 1925–52)

   The Alchemist, edited by F. H. Mares, The Revels Plays (London, 1967)

King, William, *Political and Literary Anecdotes of his Own Times* (London, 1819)

Kirk, John, *Biographies of English Catholics in the Eighteenth Century*, edited by John Hungerford Pollen and Edwin Burton (London, 1909)

Kliger, Samuel, *The Goths in England: A Study in Seventeenth and Eighteenth Century Thought* (Harvard, 1952; reprinted New York, 1972)

[La Fayette, Marie-Madeleine Comtesse de], *Zaide: Histoire espagnol* (Paris, 1705)

Landa, Louis A., 'The Shandean Homunculus: The Background of Sterne's "Little Gentleman" ', in *Restoration and Eighteenth-Century Essays in Honour of Alan Dugald McKillop*, edited by Carrol Camden (Chicago, 1963)

Leranbaum, Miriam, *Alexander Pope's 'Opus Magnum' 1729-1744* (Oxford, 1977)

Locke, John, *Two Treatises of Government*, edited by Peter Laslett, 2nd edition (Cambridge, 1970)

Lodge, Edmund, *The Life of Sir Julius Caesar* (London, 1827)

Lonsdale, Roger, ed., *The New Oxford Book of Eighteenth Century Verse* (Oxford, 1984)

Lothian, Marquess of: *see* Historical Manuscripts Commission

Mack, Maynard, *The Garden and the City: Retirement and Politics in the Later Poetry of Pope* (London, 1969)

' "My Ordinary Occasions": A Letter from Pope', *Scriblerian*, 9 (1976-77), 1-7

'The Happy Houyhnhnm: A Letter from John Gay to the Blount Sisters', *Scriblerian*, 11 (1978), 1-3

'Pope's Copy of Chaucer', in *Evidence in Literary Scholarship: Essays in Memory of James Marshall Osborn*, edited by René Wellek and Alvaro Ribeiro (Oxford, 1979), pp. 105-21

Collected in Himself: Essays Critical, Biographical, and Bibliographical on Pope and Some of his Contemporaries (London, 1982)

ed., *The Last and Greatest Art: Some Unpublished Poetical Manuscripts of Alexander Pope* (London, 1984)

Alexander Pope: A Life (London, 1985)

Madan, Falconer, *The Madan Family* (Oxford, 1933)

Mahaffey, Kathleen, 'Pope's "Artimesia" and "Phryne" as Personal Satire', *Review of English Studies*, 21 (1970), 466-71

Marlborough, Sarah, Duchess of, *An Account of the Conduct of the Dowager Duchess of Marlborough* (London, 1742)

The Opinions of Sarah Duchess-Dowager of Marlborough (no place, 1788)

Marlowe, Christopher, *The Plays of Christopher Marlowe*, edited by Roma Gill (Oxford, 1971)

Martin, Peter, *Pursuing Innocent Pleasures: The Gardening World of Alexander Pope* (Hamden, Connecticut, 1984)

Massue, Melville Henry, Marquis de Ruvigny and Raineval, *The Jacobite Peerage*, facsimile of 1904 edition edited by Roger Ararat (London, 1974)

Maud, Ralph N., 'Some Lines from Pope', *Review of English Studies*, 9 (1958), 146-51

Melville, Lewis, *Lady Suffolk and her Circle* (London, 1924)

Messenger, Ann, *His and Hers: Essays in Restoration and Eighteenth-Century Literature* (Lexington, 1986)

Millar, Oliver, *The Tudor, Stuart and Early Georgian Pictures in the Collection of Her Majesty the Queen*, 2 vols. (London, 1963)

Milton, John, *The Poems of John Milton*, edited by John Carey and Alastair Fowler (London, 1968)

Montagu, Lady Mary Wortley, *The Letters and Works of Lady Mary Wortley Montagu*, edited by Lord Wharncliffe and revised by W. Moy Thomas, 2 vols. (London, 1861)

The Complete Letters of Lady Mary Wortley Montagu, edited by Robert Halsband, 3 vols. (Oxford, 1965)

Court Eclogs Written in the Year, 1716, edited by Robert Halsband (New York, 1977)

Essays and Poems and Simplicity, a Comedy, edited by R. Halsband and I. Grundy (Oxford, 1977)

[Montfaucon, Nicolas de, Abbé de Villars], *The Count of Gabalis; or, The Extravagant Mysteries of the Cabalists, Exposed in Five Pleasant Discourses on the Secret Sciences*, translated by P. A[yres] (London, 1680)

Morley, Richard, *The Life of the Late Celebrated Mrs. Elizabeth Wisebourne, Vulgarly Call'd Mother Wybourn* (London, 1721)

Morris, David B., *Alexander Pope: The Genius of Sense* (London, 1984)

Needham, Joseph, *A History of Embryology*, 2nd edition, revised with the assistance of Arthur Hughes (Cambridge, 1959)

Newcastle, Margaret Duchess of: *see* Cavendish, Margaret

Nicolson, Marjorie, and G. S. Rousseau, *This Long Disease, my Life: Alexander Pope and the Sciences* (Princeton, 1968)

Nussbaum, Felicity A., *The Brink of All We Hate: English Satires on Women, 1660–1750* (Lexington, 1984)

Oldfield, Thomas Hinton Burley, *The Representative History of Great Britain and Ireland*, 6 vols. (London, 1816)

Orrery, John Earl of: *see* Boyle, John

The Orrery Papers, edited by the Countess of Cork and Orrery, 2 vols. (London, 1903)

Pattison, William, *The Poetical Works of Mr. William Pattison* (London, 1728)

Pepys, Samuel, *The Diary of Samuel Pepys*, edited by Robert Latham and William Matthews, 11 vols. (London, 1970–83)

Perry, Ruth, *The Celebrated Mary Astell: An Early English Feminist* (Chicago, 1986)

Pilkington, Laetitia, *Memoirs of Mrs Pilkington, 1712–1750, Written by Herself* (London, 1748–1754; reprinted 1928)

Pollak, Ellen, *The Poetics of Sexual Myth: Gender and Ideology in the Verse of Swift and Pope* (Chicago, 1985)

Ponsonby, D. A., *Call A Dog Hervey* (London, no date)

Pope, Alexander, *The Works of Alexander Pope Esq.*, edited by William Warburton, 9 vols. (London, 1751)

The Works of Alexander Pope, Esq., edited by Joseph Warton, 9 vols. (London, 1797)

The Works of Alexander Pope Esq., edited by William Lisle Bowles, 10 vols. (London, 1806)

The Works of Alexander Pope, edited by Whitwell Elwin and William John Courthope, 10 vols. (London, 1871–86)

Pope's Own Miscellany: Being a Reprint of 'Poems on Several Occasions' 1717, edited by Norman Ault (London, 1935)

The Prose Works of Alexander Pope, edited by Norman Ault and Rosemary Cowler, 2 vols. (Oxford, 1936–86)

The Twickenham Edition of the Works of Alexander Pope, 11 vols. (London, 1939–69)

The Correspondence of Alexander Pope, edited by George Sherburn, 5 vols. (Oxford, 1956)

The Poems of Alexander Pope: A One-volume Edition of the Twickenham Text, edited by John Butt, corrected edition (London, 1968)

Price, F. G. Hilton, *A Handbook of London Bankers* (London, 1876)

Prior, Sir James, *Life of Edmond Malone* (London, 1860)

Purcell, Henry, *Dido and Aeneas*, facsimile of 1st edition of libretto, 1680 (London, no date)

Raimo, John W., *Biographical Directory of American Colonial and Revolutionary Governors 1607–1789* (Westport, Connecticut, 1980)

Reynolds, Myra, *The Learned Lady in England, 1650–1760* (Gloucester, Massachusetts, 1960; reprint of edition of 1920)

Ribeiro, Aileen, *A Visual History of Costume: The Eighteenth Century* (London, 1983)

Richardson, Samuel, *Clarissa; or, the History of a Young Lady*, edited by Angus Ross (Harmondsworth, 1985)

Riely, John, and W. K. Wimsatt, 'A Supplement to *The Portraits of Alexander Pope*', in *Evidence in Literary Scholarship: Essays in Memory of James Marshall Osborn*, edited by René Wellek and Alvaro Ribeiro (Oxford, 1779)

Rogers, Katharine, *The Toublesome Helpmate: A History of Misogyny in Literature* (London, 1966)

Rogers, Pat, 'Faery Lore and *The Rape of the Lock*', *Review of English Studies*, 25 (1974), 25–38

Eighteenth Century Encounters: Studies in Literature and Society in the Age of Walpole (Brighton, 1985)

Rosslyn, Felicity, ' "Dipt in the Rainbow": Pope on Women', *Parnassus*, 12–13 (1985), 179–93

Røstvig, Maren-Sofie, *The Happy Man: Studies in the Metamorphoses of a Classical Ideal, 1600–1760*, 2 vols. (Oslo, 1954–58)

Rousseau, George S., 'A New Pope Letter', *PQ*, 54 (1966), 409–18

Royal Commission on Historical Manuscripts: *see* Historical Manuscripts Commission

Ruffhead, Owen, *The Life of Alexander Pope, Esq., Compiled from Original Manuscripts, with a Critical Essay on his Writings and Genius* (London, 1769)

Rumbold, Valerie, 'Alexander Pope and the Religious Tradition of the Turners', *Recusant History*, 17 (1984), 17–37

Rymer, Thomas, *A Short View of Tragedy* (London, 1693)

Said, Suzanne, *Women and Female in the Biological Treatises of Aristotle* (Odense, 1982)

Schmitz, R. M., 'Two New Holographs of Pope's Birthday Lines to Martha Blount', *Review of English Studies*, 8 (1957), 234–48

'Peterborough's and Pope's Nymphs: Pope at Work', *PQ*, 48 (1969), 192–201

Schochet, Gordon J., *Patriarchalism in Political Thought: The Authoritarian Family and Political Speculation and Attitudes Especially in Seventeenth-Century England* (Oxford, 1975)

Sedgwick, Romney, *The House of Commons 1715–1754*, 2 vols., The History of Parliament (London, 1970)

Shakespeare, William, *The Works of Shakespear*, edited by Alexander Pope, 6 vols. (London, 1725, vols. II–VI misdated 1723)

Sharp, A. Mary, *The History of Ufton Court* (London, 1892)

Sheffield, John, *The Works of John Sheffield . . . Duke of Buckingham*, 2 vols. (London, 1723)

A Character of John Sheffield, Late Duke of Buckinghamshire (London, 1729)

Sherburn, George, 'The Fortunes and Misfortunes of *Three Hours after Marriage*', *Modern Philology*, 24 (1926–27), 91–109

The Early Career of Alexander Pope (Oxford, 1934)

'New Anecdotes about Alexander Pope', *Notes and Queries*, 203 (1958), 343–49

Sola Pinto, V. de, *Sir Charles Sedley, 1639–1701: A Study in the Life and Literature of the Restoration* (London, 1927)

Spacks, Patricia Meyer, *An Argument of Images: The Poetry of Alexander Pope* (Cambridge, Massachusetts, 1971)

The Spectator, edited by Donald F. Bond, 5 vols. (Oxford, 1965)

Spence, Joseph, *Observations, Anecdotes and Characters of Books and Men*, edited by James M. Osborn, 2 vols. (Oxford, 1966)

Letters from the Grand Tour, edited by Slava Klima (London, 1975)

Steele, Richard, *The Plays of Richard Steele*, edited by Shirley Strum Kenny (Oxford, 1971)

[Steevens, George], ed., *Additions to the Works of Alexander Pope*, 2 vols. (Dublin, 1776)

Sterne, Laurence, *The Life and Opinions of Tristram Shandy, Gentleman*, edited by Ian Campbell Ross (Oxford, 1983)

Stewart, J. Douglas, *Sir Godfrey Kneller and the English Baroque Portrait* (Oxford, 1983)

Stone, Lawrence, *The Family, Sex and Marriage in England 1500–1800* (London, 1977)

Stuart, Dorothy Margaret, *Molly Lepell: Lady Hervey* (London, 1936)

Stuart Papers, Calendar of the: see Historical Manuscripts Commission

Suffolk, Henrietta Countess of, *Letters to and from Henrietta, Countess of Suffolk and her Second Husband the Hon. George Berkeley*, edited by J. W. Croker, 2 vols. (London, 1824)

Swift, Jonathan, *The Poems of Jonathan Swift*, edited by Harold Williams, 2nd edition, 3 vols. (Oxford, 1958)

The Correspondence of Jonathan Swift, edited by Harold Williams, 5 vols. (revised edition, Oxford, 1965)

Irish Tracts and Sermons, edited by Herbert Davis and Louis Landa (Oxford, 1968)

Miscellaneous and Autobiographical Pieces, Fragments and Marginalia, edited by Herbert Davis (Oxford, 1969)

Tanner, L. E., and J. L. Nevinson, 'On Some Later Funeral Effigies in Westminster Abbey', *Archaeologia*, 85 (1936), 169–202

The Tatler, edited by Donald F. Bond, 3 vols. (Oxford, 1987)

Thomas, Elizabeth, *Pylades and Corinna; or, Memoirs of the Lives, Amours, and Writings of Richard Gwinnett Esq. . . . and Mrs Elizabeth Thomas Jun. . . .*, 2 vols. (London, 1731–32)

Thornton, Alice, *The Autobiography of Mrs. Alice Thornton*, edited by Charles Jackson, Surtees Society, 62 (Durham, 1873)

Thrale, Hester Lynch, *Thraliana: The Diary of Mrs. Hester Lynch Thrale (later Mrs. Piozzi) 1776–1809*, edited by Katharine C. Balderston, 2nd edition, 2 vols. (Oxford, 1951)

Tillotson, Geoffrey, 'Lady Mary Wortley Montagu and Pope's *Elegy to the Memory of an Unfortunate Lady*', *Review of English Studies*, 12 (1936), 401–12

Todd, Janet, ed., *A Dictionary of British and American Women Writers, 1660–1800* (London, 1984)

Tovey, Duncan C., *Gray and his Friends: Letters and Relics* (Cambridge, 1890)

Townshend, Marquess: see Historical Manuscripts Commission

Trimble, John, 'Clarissa's Role in *The Rape of the Lock*', *Texas Studies in English*, 15 (1974), 673–91

Trowbridge, Hoyt, 'Pope's *Eloisa* and the *Heroides* of Ovid', *Studies in Eighteenth-Century Culture*, 3 (1973), 11–34

Veith, Ilza, *Hysteria: The History of a Disease* (Chicago, 1965)

Verville, François Béroalde de, *Le Moyen de parvenir* (Chinon, no date)

Virgil, with an English translation by H. Rushton Fairclough, 2 vols., Loeb Classical Library (London, 1935)

The Aeneid of Virgil, edited by R. D. Williams, 2 vols. (London, 1972)

Voiture, Vincent de, *Poésies*, edited by Henri Lafay, 2 vols., Société des textes français modernes (Paris, 1971)

Walpole, Horace, *Reminiscences*, edited by P. Toynbee (Oxford, 1924)

The Yale Edition of Horace Walpole's Correspondence, edited by W. S. Lewis, 48 vols. (London, 1937–83)

Weinbrot, Howard D., 'Pope's *Elegy to the Memory of an Unfortunate Lady*', *Modern Languages Quarterly*, 32 (1971), 255–67

Williams, Aubrey, 'The "Angel, Goddess, Montague" of Pope's *Sober Advice from Horace*', *Modern Philology*, 71 (1973–74), 56–58

Wimsatt, William Kurtz, *The Portraits of Alexander Pope* (London, 1965)

Winchilsea, Anne Countess of, *The Poems of Anne Countess of Winchilsea*, edited by Myra Reynolds (Chicago, 1903)

Winn, James A., 'Pope Plays the Rake: His Letters to Ladies and the Making of the *Eloisa*', in *The Art of Alexander Pope*, edited by Howard Erskine-Hill and Anne Smith (London, 1979), pp. 89–118.

Winstanley, Gerrard, *The Law of Freedom and Other Writings*, edited by Christopher Hill (Harmondsworth, 1973)

Wollstonecraft, Mary, *A Vindication of the Rights of Woman*, edited by Carol H. Poston, Norton Critical Editions (London, 1975)

Woolf, Virginia, *A Room of One's Own*, 2nd edition (London, 1931)

Wright, Lawrence S., 'Eighteenth-Century Replies to Pope's Eloisa', *Studies in Philology*, 31 (1934), 519–33

Wright, S. G., 'Ruffhead's Life of Pope', *Bodleian Quarterly Record*, VII (1932–34), 12

Yates, Frances, *Astraea: The Imperial Theme in the Sixteenth Century* (London, 1975)

Young, Edward, *The Complete Works of the Rev. Edward Young*, edited by John Doran, 2 vols. (London, 1854)

Index

This is a selective index, principally of proper names, although some themes are arranged under the headings *gender*, *Jacobitism* and *women*. Pope's works are arranged under his name, under the subheading *Works*; but his relationships are entered only under the names of others concerned. Main headings for individuals are placed under title rather than family name, and married name rather than maiden name, except in the cases of individuals who figure in the text only under a previous name.